FRENCH CRIM

Drawing on the author's own unique observ   ~ich pre-trial
process, this path-breaking work combines en   ~red insights into the
daily working practices of police, *gendarmes*, p   ~ators and *juges d'instruction*
with a nuanced account of the complex political, legal, social and occupational
contexts in which the French system has developed. The book thus breaks new
ground in the field of comparative criminology, offering a much enhanced understanding of how an inquisitorially rooted criminal justice process operates
in practice and the factors that influence and constrain its development and
functioning. From the French Republican tradition of state-centred models of
authority, across the growing influence of the ECHR, to the local conditions
which determine the ways in which individual discretion is exercised, the French
model of investigative supervision and accountability is contrasted with more
adversarially based systems, and the way it protects the need for reliability of evidence and the interests of the accused are evaluated. The book also compares the
judicial and defence functions and the extent to which ECHR 'fair trial' guarantees are able to produce legal and ideological change within a process which
depends upon a central and judicially supervised investigating authority. This
book will be essential reading for teachers, researchers and students working in
the area of criminal justice, comparative criminal justice/criminology, as well as
French and European studies.

**La justice pénale française: un récit comparatif sur l'enquête et les poursuites
du crime en France**

En fondant son analyse principalement sur la première étude empirique systématique de la procédure préalable au procès, cette monographie ouvre de nouvelles
perspectives dans le domaine de la justice pénale comparée. En s'éloignant de réc-
its idéalisés d'enquêtes supervisées par le judiciaire, elle permet de mieux com-
prendre la façon dont une procédure pénale de type inquisitoire opère dans la
pratique et les facteurs qui influencent et restreignent son développement et son
fonctionnement. La justice pénale française s'inscrit dans un large éventail de
contextes : tradition républicaine française où l'autorité est centrée sur l'Etat,
influence grandissante de la Cour européenne des droits de l'homme, situations
locales hétérogènes qui déterminent la façon dont le pouvoir s'exerce au cas par
cas. Le modèle français d'enquête pénale est mis en contraste avec les procédures
de type plus accusatoire, et en particulier les différentes façons dont la fiabilité des
preuves peut être garantie, et les intérêts de l'accusé protégés.

  L'observation systématique des habitudes de travail quotidiennes de la police,
des gendarmes, des procureurs et des juges d'instruction sur différents sites et à
différentes périodes fournit un récit unique et détaillé de la façon dont le système

pénal français opère dans la pratique. La compréhension et la perspicacité acquises à partir de ces données ont ensuite fait l'objet d'une analyse légale et politique plus approfondie, qui aborde des questions telles que l'influence et l'interférence de l'Etat dans le cours de la justice, les rôles comparés des magistrats et des auxiliaires de justice, et l'impact des garanties europénnes du procès équitable sur le modèle inquisitorial français.

Une connaissance approfondie d'autres procédures pénales européennes est de plus en plus importante pour ceux qui travaillent dans le domaine de la justice pénale au Royaume-Uni (aussi bien que dans le domaine de la justice pénale comparée). Elle favorise l'application et l'évaluation des mesures telles que la décision-cadre du Conseil relative à certains droits procéduraux accordés dans le cadre des procédures pénale dans l'Union européenne, ou la récente réforme legislative en Angleterre et au Pays de Galles du rôle de la police et du procureur.

Ce livre est essentiel pour les enseignants, chercheurs, étudiants et décideurs dans les domaines de la justice pénale au Royaume-Uni et en Europe, de la justice/criminologie comparées et des études françaises et européennes.

Jacqueline Hodgson est professeur en droit à l'université de Warwick. Elle a conduit une série de recherches empiriques en France et au Royaume-Uni et est l'auteur de nombreuses publications sur la justice pénale et la justice pénale comparée.

French Criminal Justice

A Comparative Account of the Investigation and Prosecution of Crime in France

Jacqueline Hodgson
University of Warwick

·HART·
PUBLISHING

OXFORD AND PORTLAND, OREGON
2005

Published in North America (US and Canada) by
Hart Publishing
c/o International Specialized Book Services
920 NE 58th Avenue, Suite 300
Portland, OR 97213-3786
USA
Tel: +1 503 287 3093 or toll-free: (1) 800 944 6190
Fax: +1 503 280 8832
E-mail: orders@isbs.com
Website: www.isbs.com

Hart Publishing, Salter's Boatyard, Folly Bridge, Abingdon Rd,
Oxford, OX1 4LB
Telephone: +44 (0)1865 245533 Fax: +44 (0) 1865 794882
E-mail: mail@hartpub.co.uk
Website: http//:www.hartpub.co.uk

British Library Cataloguing in Publication Data
Data Available

ISBN 1-84113-429-5 (paperback)

Typeset by Compuscript, Shannon, Eire in Minion 10/12 pt
Printed and bound in Great Britain by
Biddles Ltd, Kings Lynn, England

Preface

This book is based primarily on data collected across six research sites in France, spanning two major periods of fieldwork and comprising direct observation, interviews and questionnaires. In providing an empirically-based account of the French pre-trial criminal process, the study aims to develop our knowledge and understanding of a procedure that has its roots in the inquisitorial tradition. But it is hoped that it will also provide the reader with more than this. Presented through the eyes of a common lawyer and contrasted with the more adversarial procedure in England and Wales, chapters 3 and 4 also interrogate the nature of some of the key legal functions within criminal justice – the prosecutor, the judge, the police and the defence. The influence of the European Convention on Human Rights is also considered, most notably in the discussion of the provision of defence guarantees in adversarial and inquisitorial-type procedures in chapters two and four. Broader contextual information to inform the reader's understanding is also set out: chapter one provides an overview of some key themes and features of French criminal justice and chapter two outlines the nature of recent legislative change. Extensive footnotes are provided for readers wishing to research further the french literature in particular and there is frequent cross-referencing between chapters.

In the period between the completion and publication of this book, France has seen the appointment of a new prime minister, Dominique de Villepin, as a result of France's vote of 'Non' to the proposed EU constitution. This change occurred too late to be incorporated into the main text of the book which was completed in March 2005, when the Raffarin administration was still at the helm.

June 2005

Acknowledgements

This book arises out of two periods of empirical research conducted across different sites around France. The first was funded by the Nuffield Foundation and the British Academy; the second, more substantial period, by the Leverhulme Trust. I am grateful to these funding bodies whose generous financial support provided travel and subsistence expenses during the initial project and enabled me to employ a full time research associate, Brigitte Perroud, during the second period of data collection. Brigitte was an excellent and resourceful researcher and I am indebted to her, as well as to Geneviève Rich, who was of enormous help to me in negotiating initial access to the field. In the writing of the book, I was also greatly assisted by a period of research leave funded by the Arts and Humanities Research Board, together with matching study leave granted by the University of Warwick.

The research itself would not have been possible without the co-operation and assistance of judges, prosecutors, police and *gendarmes* in France. These people gave generously of their time in answering our questions during periods of observation, in interviews and through the completion of questionnaires. They also made us feel welcome and demonstrated genuine support for the enterprise in which we were engaged. Although they remain anonymous throughout the pages of this book, we are nonetheless extremely grateful to them for sharing their knowledge and experience with us.

I would also like to express my thanks to John Bell, Emmanuel Breen, Stewart Field and René Lévy, all of whom read and commented on earlier drafts of the manuscript and were a real source of encouragement. Clive Emsley also read and commented on part of chapter 3 and Thérèse Lepicard and Chris Turner provided occasional translation advice. Warm thanks also to Richard Hart at Hart Publishing for his support and enthusiasm for the project throughout.

Finally, I must thank the friends (especially Mark Erickson) who have encouraged and supported me and who have tolerated my immersion in French criminal justice (even when on holiday) and my family, Mark, Ella and Lotte, who I suspect were as pleased as I when the book was finally completed.

March 2005

Contents

Table of Cases

TABLE OF STATUTES, TREATIES AND CONVENTIONS

Abbreviations

APJ	—	*agent de police judiciaire*
CDA 1998	—	Crime and Disorder Act 1998
CJPOA 1994	—	Criminal Justice and Public Order Act 1994
CNCDH	—	*Commission nationale consultative des droits de l'homme*
COPJ	—	*comparution par officier de police judiciaire*
CRS	—	*compagnies républicaines de sécurité*
CSM	—	*Conseil supérieur de la magistrature*
CPIA 1996	—	Criminal Procedure and Investigations Act 1996
CPP	—	*Code de procedure pénale*
DPP	—	Director of Public Prosecutions
ECHR	—	European Convention on Human Rights
ECtHR	—	European Court of Human Rights
EU	—	European Union
GAV	—	*garde à vue*
JAP	—	*juge de l'application des peines*
JI	—	*juge d'instruction*
JLD	—	*juge des libertés et de la détention*
MEE	—	*mis en examen*
OPJ	—	*officier de police judiciaire*
PACE 1984	—	Police and Criminal Evidence Act 1984
RCCJ	—	Royal Commission on Criminal Justice (1993)
RCCP	—	Royal Commission on Criminal Procedure (1981)
RPR	—	*Rassemblement pour la République*
SCHFPN	—	*Syndicat des commissaires et haut fontionnaires de la police nationale*
SM	—	*Syndicat de la magistrature*
TEU	—	Treaty of the European Union
TGI	—	*Tribunal de Grande Instance*
TTR	—	*traitement en temps réel*
USM	—	*Union syndicale des magistrats*

1

Introduction

This study seeks to provide a better understanding of the ways in which the French criminal justice process operates in practice. Much of the analysis draws upon empirical data collected across five sites in France, where the daily working practices of key legal personnel were observed. The study examines the legal structures of French criminal procedure and some of the factors which influence and constrain its development and functioning. These include the different status, training and organisation of legal personnel; the wider legal and political structures within which criminal justice is located and constructed—from the legacy of the 1789 Revolution to the growing influence of international norms such as those contained in the European Convention on Human Rights (ECHR); the working practices and ideologies of key legal actors charged with the investigation and prosecution of crime; and the impact of wider criminal justice policy and resources. The focus of the study is upon the process of criminal justice in France and, in particular, the ways in which it is able to protect the interests of the accused whilst at the same time ensuring the effectiveness of the criminal investigation. The analysis is, however, presented through the lens of a 'common law' observer and comparison is made at points with the criminal process in England and Wales in order to draw out contrasting features, as well as similarities, between the two procedures.[1] Rooted as they are in two different procedural traditions, with different organising features, each system acts as something of a foil against which to understand the other. Adversarial and inquisitorial models of criminal procedure operate, for example, quite different structures of police accountability and investigative supervision; delineate the police–prosecutor relationship differently; have different notions of what constitutes prosecutorial independence; allocate responsibility for the safeguarding of suspects' rights in very different ways; place different emphases on the investigative and trial phases; and afford different roles to the defence lawyer, prosecutor and judge.

---

[1] In this way, comparison acts more as a tool of analysis.

Background to the Study

Whilst there are a number of texts on 'French Law'[2] and some which take a pan-European or comparative approach,[3] until recently there have been remarkably few accounts of French criminal justice which are based upon systematic empirical research, despite the appeal of inquisitorial-based systems of justice to reform-driven commentators from other jurisdictions such as the UK, the USA and recently, India.[4] Of those studies which adopt an empirical approach, interviews rather than direct observation have been preferred in most instances.[5] In their study of 'the myth of judicial supervision,' Goldstein and Marcus (1977), for example, carried out a limited number of interviews[6] and observed several trials and requests for warrants in each of the three jurisdictions studied.[7] Leigh and Zedner's (1992) study of France and Germany for the Royal Commission on Criminal Justice (RCCJ) was also based upon interviews rather than observation, but in the absence of information indicating to whom they spoke (police, *procureurs, juges d'instruction*) or how many interviews were conducted, it is difficult to assess the proper weight to attach to their findings.[8] The last decade has seen an increasing number of studies which, rather than being driven by an interest in reform, are concerned to understand aspects of French criminal procedure on their own terms and from a comparative perspective. Horton (1995) carried out an unspecified number of extensive interviews across three sites in her study of policing policy in France. More recently, Bell (2001) employed an unspecified number of interviews in his work on French legal cultures, but using interviewees as informants on the process rather than providers of quantifiable data. Crawford (2000) conducted 50 interviews with key practitioners giving his work a strong empirical basis, but this was in a much narrower project restricted to the study of mediation in France. Field and West's (2003) study of defence lawyers in France is a welcome addition, employing both direct observation and semi-structured interviews, providing a broader qualitative empirical foundation for their work.

---

[2] Eg Bell *et al* (1998); West *et al* (1998); Elliot and Vernon (2000).

[3] Eg Markesinis (1994); Fennell *et al* (1995); Gessner *et al* (1996); Hatchard *et al* (1996); Delmas-Marty and Spencer (2002).

[4] Some of which are discussed below. In India, French criminal procedure was recently considered by the Committee on Reforms of the Criminal Justice System (2003), chaired by Justice VS Malimath (former Chief Justice of Kerala and Karnataka and former member of the National Human Rights Commission).

[5] Observation tends to be of public court hearings rather than the daily workings of key legal actors. See eg the accounts provided by McKillop (1997; 1998).

[6] In France, three public prosecutors, two defence counsel, two *juges d'instruction*, and two trial judges, all in Paris.

[7] Their research examined France, Germany and Italy and is perhaps the most empirically grounded account of that time.

[8] They themselves describe their study as 'inevitably impressionistic' (p 2).

In France too, there have been few systematic empirical accounts of the criminal justice process. The work of French scholars has tended to be at a broad theoretical level or, less frequently, a narrow empirical one[9] and Noreau and Arnaud (1998:282) note 'the importance accorded to theoretical work in France— empirical work is largely swept away both in volume and legitimacy'.[10] The empirical work that is carried out tends to be concentrated in state-funded research centres[11] (rather than in universities with privately funded projects) and so the focus is invariably upon law reform and policy and the results are not always well disseminated.[12] Much of the relevant research is carried out by those from disciplines outside law. For example, authored primarily by political scientists, there is an important body of work examining the role of the judiciary and its evolving relationship with the executive.[13] There is also a strong tradition of historical, and increasingly sociological, work in the areas of policing and criminal procedure.[14] Although this has tended to centre upon criminal and judicial statistics,[15] there are now a growing number of studies addressing the professional culture and ideology of policing,[16] the daily working practices of officers,[17] as well as their relationships with other legal actors in the criminal process.[18] Moreover, a number of these studies employ qualitative as well as quantitative methodologies.[19] Lévy's (1987) study of the Paris police, for example, is based upon an extensive period of

---

[9] Renouard (1994); Verrest (2000:218–21). See also the accounts of research in the 1980s in Faugeron (1993) and the 1990s in Faget and Wyvekens (1999).

[10] See Garapon's (1995) discussion of the symbolism and the potential of the power of the *juge* or *magistrat* and the need to move towards more nuanced accounts based upon practice.

[11] The Ministries of Justice and of the Interior are the principal donors. Historically, Paris has been the centre of such research activity, but criminological research is now also being conducted in a number of CNRS centres across France. See Faugeron (1993); Faget and Wyvekens (1999); de Maillard and Roché (2004:116).

[12] Noreau and Arnaud (1998).

[13] Eg Roussel (1998, 2000, 2003). Lawyers are also taking an interest in this area eg Breen (2003); Garapon (2003).

[14] See Robert (1991:32), as well as the studies described in Faugeron (1993:116) and Faget and Wyvekens (1999). The phenomenon of incarceration also continues to inspire the French research imagination, and fear of crime (eg the work of Roché from 1993 onwards), security (eg Dieu, 1999), social exclusion and victimisation studies have now also appeared on the socio-legal horizon. Interestingly, Pin (2002:248) describes French criminal justice policy as being increasingly inspired by victimology.

[15] Faugeron (1993:123). The development of a database of judicial statistics from the early 19th century (known as the Davido database, after André Davidovitch who began the work drawing on the figures from the *Compte général*, the predecessor to the *Annuaire statistique de la justice*) has provided useful historical information relating to, eg trends in prosecution. See Aubusson de Cavarlay *et al* (1991); Lévy (1993).

[16] See especially the work of Monjardet (1994).

[17] These studies focus upon a central locus of activity such as the police station or the underground. See the studies noted in Faget and Wyvekens (1999:156).

[18] For example police–*magistrat* relationships in Mouhanna (2001a); the practice of police detention and questioning in Lyon (Lemaître, 1994); and the interaction of policing, politics and justice in Gatto and Thoenig (1993).

[19] See also Fabien Jobard's (2002) investigation into police malpractice.

direct observation and a small number of formal interviews.[20] Lemaître's (1994) research into the practice of police detention in Lyon is also based upon observations and some 48 interviews, primarily with police and *magistrats*.[21] Renée Zauberman's (1997) in-depth study of the *Gendarmerie* is the result of some 900 hours of observation and 20 interviews.[22] And most recently, Mouhanna's (2001a) study of the relationship between the police and *magistrats* was conducted over a two year period, during which over 200 interviews were carried out and a period of observation undertaken. The findings of these studies (discussed in later chapters) support those of my own research, including observations on police techniques of interrogation, the police construction of written evidence and the importance of trust as a crucial component in the police–*magistrat* relationship. In addition, the current study seeks to build on the sociological accounts that emerge from the French research, and to locate these within a more specifically legal and comparative analysis. For example, the work of Lévy (1985) and Zauberman (1997) demonstrates the way in which the statements contained in the case file do not represent the simple transcription of interviews with witnesses and suspects, but are the result of a process of police construction. The current study goes on to explore the wider legal consequences of this process of construction: the extent to which evidence in the file can be said to be the product of a judicially supervised enquiry and therefore the reasonableness of placing such heavy reliance upon written evidence produced by the police in this way; or whether or not additional safeguards such as tape recording or the presence of a defence lawyer might be desirable, notwithstanding the more inquisitorial nature of French criminal procedure. The study takes a more socio-legal approach offering a comparative legal analysis of the roles and responsibilities of police (including *gendarmes*), prosecutors, defence lawyers and judges, an analysis that is also grounded strongly in extensive observational and interview data concerning the daily working practices of these legal personnel.[23]

---

[20] He spent 7.5 months with one section of the Paris *parquet* and 6.5 months with the police, producing over 1,000 pages of fieldnotes. He conducted around 10 interviews with *magistrats*, including 2 with senior police officers.

[21] This study shows a keen awareness of the importance of anchoring research within the social realities of practice. Conducted under the auspices of the IHESI (the *Institut des Hautes Etudes de la Sécurité Intérieure*, associated with the Interior Ministry) the study comprises some observation, but rests primarily on semi-structured interviews with 30 police officers of varying ranks, 14 *magistrats* (prosecutors, judges and *juges d'instruction*) as well as 3 lawyers and a forensic surgeon.

[22] Zauberman's extensive observations have enabled her to go beyond quantitative measures of clear-up rates and to examine the impact of a changing working culture where, in line with population shifts, many *gendarmes* are increasingly working in suburban settings as well as the tightly-knit rural communities of which they have traditionally been a part. See also the earlier work of Dieu (1993).

[23] It is hoped that this will go some way to filling the gap in this type of research, identified by French scholars. See Faugeron (1993:143); Garapon (1995); Faget and Wyvekens (1999:158).

Much of the interest in French criminal procedure shown by those outside France has tended to focus upon the possible solutions it might offer to the domestic ills of other jurisdictions.[24] In the 1970s and 80s, for example, disillusioned with the failure of the US justice system to measure up to its own adversarial rhetoric, American scholars sought an alternative to the practice of plea bargaining and the potentially arbitrary law enforcement produced by prosecutorial discretion.[25] In the 1990s, commentators in the UK saw the model of judicially supervised investigations as a possible means of avoiding the miscarriages of justice which continued to blight the criminal justice process in Britain in the last two decades of the 20th century.[26] However, in the absence of comparable empirical material describing the ways in which French criminal justice functions on a daily basis, many commentators have been misled into drawing false comparisons between critical empirical accounts of Anglo-American criminal justice and ideal-type models of French criminal procedure.[27] The *juge d'instruction* has been fetishised in this and held up as the solution to the failures of adversarialism—whether it be plea bargaining, or the police tendency to ignore exculpatory evidence in constructing a case against a suspect.[28] Yet, in practice, as discussed in subsequent chapters, the police also dominate the pre-trial process in France and the *juge d'instruction* is involved in less than 5 per cent of cases, the remainder being supervised by the public prosecutor, the *procureur*.[29] More recently, in the Criminal Procedure and Investigations Act (CPIA) 1996, the UK Government has introduced changes which purport to be drawn from the inquisitorial, rather than adversarial, tradition adopting a more co-operative 'cards on the table' approach. This is something of a misnomer, as the prosecution reveal only a selection of their material; it is only through the defence disclosing an outline of their case that secondary prosecution disclosure is triggered; and the material disclosed is selected according to the prosecutor's judgment of what might be relevant to the defence case.[30] This bears no resemblance to the

---

[24] For a discussion of the issues surrounding 'legal transplants' see Nelken and Feest (2001). Also, Zedner (1995).

[25] See eg, the debate between Golstein and Marcus (1977) and Langbein and Weinreb (1978). Also Pugh (1976); Weinreb (1977); Alschuler (1983); Mendelson (1983); Tomlinson (1983); Pakter (1985).

[26] See, eg Mansfield and Wardle (1993); Rose (1996). Also, those discussed by Field (1994:120). The Royal Commission on Criminal Justice (1993) considered the procedures of other jurisdictions, but (unsurprisingly) finding that none offered the perfect solution, rejected them all out of hand. The Auld Review (2001) also rejected the introduction of a *juge d'instruction* role.

[27] See eg Mendelson's (1983) comparison of the majority US procedure of plea bargaining, with the French minority procedure of *instruction*. The work of Goldstein and Marcus (1977) is a notable exception to this tendency.

[28] Major blunders in the investigation and prosecution of high-profile cases in England and Wales continue to prompt support for some form of judicial supervision.

[29] Together with the *juge d'instruction* and the trial judge, the *procureur* also enjoys judicial status as a *magistrat* and so is able to carry out the function of judicial supervision—see further the discussion in Ch 3.

[30] This procedure has been modified further by the Criminal Justice Act 2003, making the duty of disclosure yet more onerous for the defence but less so for the prosecution.

procedure in France, for example, where the accused is entitled to full disclosure of the case dossier once a decision has been made to prosecute and during the pre-trial investigation *instruction* procedure. Neither is such disclosure contingent upon the accused providing information: 'transparency' is neither partial, nor dependent on the actions of the accused.[31] Apart from the mongrel breed of procedure, which the introduction of measures such as those under the CPIA 1996 creates, this approach is dangerous in its misunderstanding and decontextualising of inquisitorial criminal procedure.

More recently, interest in things inquisitorial has developed in the context of the convergence, or otherwise, of European legal systems and the trend towards the 'Europeanisation' of criminal justice.[32] Intergovernmental co-operation was established between France, Germany and the Benelux countries under the 1985 Schengen Agreement[33] in visa, immigration and asylum matters. The Maastricht Treaty (the Treaty of the European Union, TEU), which came into force in November 1993, went further in establishing police and judicial co-operation in matters of terrorism and serious crime within the newly created field of Justice and Home Affairs.[34] The European Union's (EU) competence in criminal matters was then strengthened further by the 1997 Amsterdam Treaty (amending the TEU) creating an area of freedom, security and justice. Although one of the underlying principles of these structures of co-operation is that they should respect human rights and fundamental freedoms, the emphasis has been upon mechanisms of investigation and prosecution, rather than protection for the accused.[35] Europol,[36] for example, provides a basis for police co-operation in

---

[31] As one French prosecutor put it: 'Everything is debated, you cannot hide anything, you cannot produce something at the last moment: the final argument that will shake everything. In France, everything is transparent, everything is debated.' [A2] (See methodology section below for details on the coding of data.) In practice, disclosure is contingent upon the construction of the dossier by the police or *magistrats* and upon the point at which the suspect becomes the accused (*mis en examen*) during the *instruction*.

[32] The converse is also true: those in more inquisitorial jurisdictions have also been scrutinising the adversarial tradition to this end. For a broad reflection on the similarities between the two systems, see Lord Irvine (2003).

[33] The 1997 Amsterdam Treaty which came into force in May 1999, integrates the Schengen Agreement into the European Union framework, promoting the free movement of persons within the EU. The UK and Ireland, however, have retained their right to carry out frontier controls.

[34] This is in both civil and criminal matters. Examples of the latter include arrangements for extradition, mutual legal assistance and co-operation in the investigation of serious crime such as trafficking in drugs, arms, toxic waste and people. For further information, see the Justice and Home Affairs (JHA) website http://ue.eu.int/jai/pres.asp?lang=en.

[35] This is perhaps not surprising, given that the body which approves the relevant measures 'is (in effect) a convocation of all the Member States' home secretaries' Spencer (2002:57).

[36] The European Police Office, Europol, based in the Hague, became fully operational in July 1999 and its aim is to improve police co-operation between the Member States in order to combat serious forms of international crime.

matters of serious international crime; Eurojust[37] seeks to support and improve co-ordination between Member States in the investigation and prosecution of serious cross-border crime; and the development of the European Arrest Warrant (EAW)[38] and a European prosecutor have been high on the European criminal justice agenda. More recently, the Commission has turned its attention to the need for common standards of protection for suspects as a 'necessary counterbalance to judicial co-operation measures that [have] enhanced the powers of prosecutors, courts and investigating officers'.[39] The key areas identified are legal assistance; the provision of interpreters; special protection for vulnerable suspects; and consular assistance.[40] The fair trial guarantees under Article 6 ECHR formed the basis of the common protections for suspects put forward in the proposed Council Framework Decision,[41] as under the TEU, Member States are already obliged to give effect to the Convention. As the UK press release put it, 'Member States should in principle see the Commission's proposals as merely giving "visibility" to standards that they already adhere to'.

In practice, the different legal frameworks in which these guarantees operate in Member States have made it difficult to agree on the ways in which safeguards such as 'legal representation' should be provided: at what point the suspect should have access to legal advice (on arrest, detention or prosecution); and whether the lawyer should be permitted to be present during the police interrogation of the suspect.[42] There has been strong resistance in some quarters to the adoption of these relatively modest safeguards, notably from Member States in which they exceed the protection currently provided.[43] Further objection comes from the fact that in many

---

[37] Established in 2002, Eurojust is also based in the Hague. It describes itself as a key interlocutor with the European institutions . . . with a mission to be a privileged partner with Liaison Magistrates, the European Judicial Network and organisations such as the European police office (Europol) and the European Anti-Fraud Office (OLAF) . . . a legal melting-pot from which subsequent developments to strengthen the European judicial area will be defined.

See the Eurojust website http://www.eurojust.eu.int/index.htm.

[38] See Council Framework Decision of 13 June 2002 on the European Arrest Warrant and Surrender Procedures between Member States (2002/584/JHA).

[39] EU Commission Green Paper, 'Procedural Safeguards for Suspects and Defendants in Criminal Proceedings throughout the European Union' para. 1.4. The initiative is criticised by some (eg the French *Syndicat de la magistrature* in its response to the Green Paper) as being ineffective as a 'counterbalance', given its non-mandatory form.

[40] Other major areas, such as bail, will be dealt with separately.

[41] Following the Green Paper, the Commission published the Proposal for a Council Framework Decision on Certain Procedural Rights in Criminal Proceedings throughout the European Union COM(2004)3289 final (Brussels 28 April 2004).

[42] For the response of the UK government to the proposed Framework Decision, see the report of the House of Lords European Union Committee (2005).

[43] France, Ireland and Austria opposed the introduction of the Green Paper safeguards. In France, the suspect may consult with her lawyer for 30 minutes, but may not have her present during the police interview, contrary to the Green Paper proposals. In Scotland, also, suspects may have a lawyer informed that they are in custody, but may not consult with one as of right. Initial concern relating to the standard of safeguards available to suspects was in response to the adoption of the EAW procedures and the legal protection in place in the acceding Member States. It is therefore interesting to note

jurisdictions, any debate around the rights of the suspect will necessarily trigger consideration of corresponding rights for witnesses and victims. With the development of these new forms of co-operation, such as the EAW procedure and the assurance of common standards of safeguards for suspects, legal personnel will increasingly be in contact with their functional equivalents in neighbouring countries. If this is to be both meaningful and successful, a more practical knowledge and understanding of the functioning of other legal systems is required.[44] As well as methods of investigating and prosecuting crime, this will include the treatment of suspects and the different ways in which their rights are protected. Such informed understanding is essential to the mutual trust and recognition which is 'the cornerstone of judicial co-operation'.[45]

More broadly, there are those who argue that European legal systems are increasingly developing in concert and so converging. Markesinis (1994:30) writes:

> There is thus a convergence of solutions in the area of private law as the problems faced by courts and legislators acquire a common and international flavour; there is a convergence in the sources of our law . . . there is a slow convergence in procedural matters as the oral and written types of trial borrow from each other and are slowly moving to occupy a middle position; there may be a greater convergence in drafting techniques than has commonly been appreciated . . . there is a growing *rapprochement* in judicial views . . . This assessment . . . is also further justified by the underlying socio-economic similarities one finds these days in most of Europe . . . Increased travel, enhanced communications, greater urbanization, and closer interdependence of national economics, have all combined to make the kind of problems that have to be resolved by the law similar . . . All of these factors have . . . favoured growing assimilation—increasingly through court activity.

There is no doubt that European countries, like many other parts of the world, face common social, political and economic problems (mass unemployment, youth crime) and must respond to events which are perceived as having global significance (the events of 11 September 2001 in New York being the most striking recent example). The European Convention on Human Rights sets broad common standards and the jurisprudence of the European Court of Human Rights (ECtHR) is part of a slow process of approximation of the laws and procedural guarantees of

that assumptions about the standard of safeguards in place in the existing Member States may have been misleading, demonstrating the variety of ways in which international norms, such as the ECHR, are interpreted and applied at national level (discussed further below). In its response to the Green Paper, the French *Syndicat de la magistrature* refers to France's 'legal and political blindness' in assuming that the only danger comes from the 10 new Member States.

[44] Initiatives such as the 'Grotius' programme (1996–2000) have sought to improve judicial co-operation by improving the reciprocal knowledge of Member States' legal and judicial systems. See also eg the Council decision of 22 July 2002 establishing a framework on police and judicial co-operation in criminal matters (AGIS).

[45] Point 33—Presidency Conclusions—Tampere European Council 15–16 October 1999.

the signatory countries;[46] and the development of the European Union has more specifically, and with a greater degree of intervention, brought about the harmonisation of the laws of the Member States in a variety of areas. Yet, this is a long way from the assertion that the legal systems of those Member States are converging. Even the adoption of a common set of rules in some specified field includes no guarantee that they will be understood, interpreted and applied in the same way across different legal systems and political landscapes, such that the convergence thesis can be supported.[47] This exclusive focus upon rules, appears to deny the centrality of legal culture in the comparative enterprise and to adhere to 'a "law-as-rule" representation of the legal world' (Legrand, 1996:60). For Legrand, the convergence theory is misleading and over-simplistic: 'convergence, even if it were thought desirable . . . is impossible on account of the fact that the differences arising between the common law and civil law *mentalités* at the epistemological level are irreducible.' (1996:62).[48] The very nature of legal knowledge in civil and common law countries—what it is and how it is acquired—are fundamentally different, as are the bases for executive and judicial authority.[49] Historically, countries facing the same legal problems have adopted very different solutions—be it on account of their different legal cultures and histories, or the political order of the day.[50]

This study does not set out to measure whether the French criminal justice process is 'better' than that in England and Wales, nor whether it can offer ready-made solutions to the problems of UK criminal justice, nor whether legal systems with their roots in different procedural traditions are gradually converging—although these issues may inform the analysis at points. Rather, its objective is more broadly to provide a critical empirical account of pre-trial criminal justice

---

[46] Although there is also the important 'margin of appreciation' doctrine which militates against full scale convergence.

[47] See eg the discussion below of the different ways in which ECHR guarantees are understood and effected in France and in Britain, and above, relating to the different interpretations of Art 6 ECHR in the provision of safeguards for suspects. In France, the cultures and agendas of the Ministries of Justice and of the Interior are also relevant—discussed further in Ch 2.

[48] See also David (1980:20–21) below, who argues that fundamentally different approaches to statutory interpretation mean that the same rule would not operate in the same way in Britain and in France.

[49] Referring to Kahn-Freund's account, Legrand (1996:74) writes:

In all Continental countries there is to be found the notion that the government has the inherent power to govern. In England, however, the executive cannot justify any course of action unless it can rely on the conferment of a power by the legislature. Meanwhile, English law knows of the inherent power of the judiciary to adjudicate—a notion which civil law systems reject. As Kahn-Freund [1978:160] notes: 'That which is true of administrative action under the common law—that it must be based on a statutory grant of power—is true of judicial action under the "civil law" systems.'

[50] As an early example, when the Church condemned trial by ordeal in 1215, most western European countries responded by instigating a form of official investigation, or inquisition, which formed the basis of inquisitorial procedure. England, on the other hand, required a group of citizens to answer on oath as to the accused's guilt—a procedure that was basically accusatorial and formed the origins of the jury system. Spencer (2002:7).

in France and a more profound understanding of the forces by which it is shaped. This chapter describes the methodology of the study and introduces some of the more important themes which are developed in subsequent chapters and which act as a backdrop to later discussion.

Methodology

The majority of the data collected for this study was through direct observation,[51] followed up by lengthy semi-structured interviews and then finally questionnaires. Although more time consuming than other methods, direct observation is better suited to the study of complex processes: in this instance, the interaction of a range of legal actors involved in the investigation and prosecution of crime.[52] A clear benefit of ethnographic work is the ability of the researcher to immerse herself in the field in order to try to identify important and relevant issues, without the total constraint of precoded categories. That is not to say that research should be wholly unstructured (it can be systematically replicated in a number of sites or settings), but rather, space is needed to cross-check initial hypotheses and to generate new ones in the field. This open-endedness is of particular value in comparative work, where the researcher may wish to avoid predetermined (and possibly ethnocentric) categories and attempt to learn from the jurisdiction more directly.[53] Once the researcher has a framework within which to work, further data can then be gathered in a more focused way. In my own study, at the point at which interviews were conducted, substantial amounts of fieldwork had been carried out and preliminary analysis undertaken, allowing exploration of relevant issues in a thorough and informed way, avoiding the pitfalls of 'presentational' data.[54]

---

[51] I prefer this term to the more commonly used 'participant observation', as it more accurately describes the role of the observer who remains a researcher, rather than a participant in the sense of contributing to the goals of the organisation under study.

[52] As described by McCall and Simmons (1969:1), direct observation of this nature is less a single method and more a blend of techniques, involving:

> some amount of genuinely social interaction in the field with the subjects of the study, some direct observation of relevant events, some formal and a great deal of informal interviewing, some systematic counting, some collection of documents and artefacts, and open-endedness in the directions the study takes.

[53] For a discussion of the benefits of observational research in comparative work, see further Hodgson (2000).

[54] This refers to information presented by respondents which may be inaccurate, eg because they seek to mislead the researcher or have insufficient knowledge to give an accurate account. Where presentational or false information is provided in the course of fieldwork, this can be checked against recorded facts or observed practices and the discrepancies noted. Becker and Greer (1957:29). This then becomes a particularly interesting source of data, as people often lie about things which matter most to them—or which they think matter most to the researcher.

Some themes, such as the centrality of trust in the police–*magistrat* relationship, crystallised only once the fieldwork was complete and detailed discussion and analysis began.

Fieldwork was conducted initially during 1993–94, and in a subsequent larger study carried out between 1997 and 1999.[55] A total of 18 months observational fieldwork was conducted across these two studies by myself and two French colleagues (to whom I am greatly indebted), Geneviève Rich and Brigitte Perroud. The sites of research were Paris, two large urban centres, a medium-sized town and a small area of 170,000 inhabitants, referred to as sites A–F (interviews, but no observations were conducted in site B).[56] Observations were conducted concurrently by two researchers in site C and consecutively by two researchers in site D; other sites were observed by a single researcher. We spent between one and four months at each site, located in the offices of *procureurs*, *juges d'instruction*, police and *gendarmes*. Here we were able to observe how criminal investigations are conducted, directed and supervised on a daily basis, as well as the conduct of pre-trial and trial hearings and the questioning of suspects and witnesses. We observed legal actors of both senior and junior status, including the reception of newcomers into the organisation. By being placed in the office of the group being observed, we were able to follow cases through the process[57] and to supplement our observations with discussion of particular cases or decisions and the wider issues which arose out of them. We were also allowed access to case dossiers at each stage of the process.[58] At the end of the observation period we conducted 20 extensive semi-structured interviews (primarily with *magistrats*) and received 37 questionnaire responses from *procureurs* and 12 from senior police officers. We were greatly assisted in the process of designing and administering these questionnaires by staff from CESDIP (*Centre de recherches sociologiques sur le droit et les institutions pénales*) and the senior police officers' union, the *Syndicat des commissaires et hauts fonctionnaires de la police nationale* (SCHFPN).

Whilst the process of comparative research can be a difficult one[59] and, in particular, understanding subjects in their own terms, the methodology which we

---

[55] I am grateful to the Nuffield Foundation and the British Academy for funding the earlier project and to the Leverhulme Trust for funding the subsequent larger study.

[56] Interviewees are coded by the letter of the research site in which they work and a number. A brief description of each interviewee is included in Appendix C.

[57] In some instances, we followed cases through to trial (where they were dealt with by the rapid *comparution immédiate* procedure); in some, we observed them for part of their investigation under *instruction*; and in others, they were still ongoing when fieldwork ceased.

[58] Although observational work is often fascinating, it can also entail spending lengthy periods of time waiting for something to happen, only to find that, inevitably, the long-awaited activity takes place once you have left for home. The opportunity to discuss these fieldwork gaps with several officers or *magistrats* the following day, or to see what evidence was put on file as a result, was particularly useful.

[59] See eg Hodgson (2000) and other contributors in the collection edited by Nelken (2000).

adopted has a number of strengths.[60] A large amount of qualitative data was gathered over a relatively extended time period, providing a detailed and intricate account of the daily workings of the criminal process and the practices of key actors within it—across different locations and different time periods.[61] In order to avoid the premature narrowing of research issues and an excessively ethnocentric approach, data was cross-checked and challenged contemporaneously within the field (with the actors observed and on occasions, with the other fieldworker) and then subsequently across sites, as well as through interviews and questionnaires. The input of three different field workers (an English lawyer, a French lawyer and a French social scientist) also ensured that a variety of perspectives contributed to the development of the study.

The study was not without its problems. Organising access to the field is difficult in one's own jurisdiction; locating and negotiating access abroad is doubly so. In the absence of a tradition of empirical research, it was unclear to those we wished to observe why university scholars would wish to come and base themselves in the local police station or prosecutor's office. On the other hand, once the nature of the project was explained, there was much approval of our efforts to try to understand how things work 'on the ground' rather than relying on textbook accounts of criminal procedure. Like Zauberman (1997:328), we found that the police and *gendarmes* (and to a lesser extent, *magistrats*) were pleased to have someone from outside their organisation taking a serious and informed interest in their work. Whilst the police and *gendarmes* generally saw themselves as 'educating' us in the ways of French criminal justice,[62] some *magistrats* (notably *juges d'instruction*) were more defensive. One *juge d'instruction* in site C, for example, initially refused permission for us to be present during the questioning of the accused, claiming that this would violate the secret of the *instruction* process. She then relented once she realised that we had been sitting in her colleague's office for two months! There is also the danger that the researcher is cast in a particular role, or attributed with a particular motivation by her research subjects. As observers from another jurisdiction, it was sometimes assumed that in critically engaging with French criminal procedure, we were attempting to compare it unfavourably with that in England and Wales. For example, another *juge d'instruction* in site C

---

[60] Direct observation is particularly valuable in this respect. The aim is to 'use the culture of the setting (the socially acquired and shared knowledge available to the participants or members of the setting) to account for the observed patterns of human activity.' Van Maanen (1983:38).

[61] When fieldwork began, major changes such as the introduction of custodial legal advice had only just come into effect. By the end of the study, the government was proposing to strengthen this right and allow suspects access to a lawyer from the start of police detention, rather than after 20 hours as had been the case previously. The merits of strengthening the independence of the *procureur* from the hierarchical control of the Minister of Justice (a member of the executive) was a major concern addressed by the Truche Commission (1997) and was also being hotly debated at this time.

[62] For me, this included an education in French criminal slang, in drinking and in the delights of cèpes!

would frequently ask our opinion on cases and procedures. This generally led to fruitful and illuminating discussion, but on some occasions, the *juge* became exasperated with our responses. In the following extract, the researcher expressed concern that both the *juge d'instruction* and the court would see records of the suspect's arrest and detention, even where she had been released with no further action taken.

> Researcher: He is not convicted of things, but the accused will be prejudiced if the court sees this.
>
> *juge d'instruction*: No—I need it for my investigation.
>
> Researcher: . . . If I am arrested 10 times for selling drugs and they never find any proof and the eleventh time they do, the court will see the 10 times and think that I am guilty and was lucky to get away with it before.
>
> *juge d'instruction*: Yes, that's true, but the jury do not see it. And the court cannot **use** it.
>
> Researcher: Yes, but it is enough that they see it.
>
> *juge d'instruction*: [Shouting at this point and pacing up and down the room] But at least it is **written**! It is in the dossier and I cannot destroy things after me when I have requested them. It is better than in England where the judge or the prosecutor just phones up and asks the police what else they know about the person and he says he is a bastard! At least it is **written**!
>
> [original emphasis]

The strong culture of '*stages*' in France—placements in other organisations to gain experience of their operation—eased greatly the process of our assimilation into the organisation observed.[63] Once in the field, access to the next location was often made easier by the fact that we had spent time in another office without major incident. We began by making contact with the senior prosecutor in the area, the *procureur de la République*, who was then able to recommend us to the central *parquet*[64] and to authorise our presence at the police station. Police and *gendarmes* were a little suspicious of us, but this authorisation was generally accepted as proof of our bona fides. In general we were very well received by those in all research sites and those we observed and spoke to gave generously of their time and knowledge. Both police and *gendarmes* also allowed us to accompany them on operations, including those from which they might easily have excluded us on the grounds of risk to operational security or our own personal safety. The only problem we encountered in gaining access was in relation to the *gendarmerie* in site A. They were especially concerned with issues of security and confidentiality and we were required to sign in triplicate a formal contract, complete with wax

---

[63] Put in these terms, our presence was readily accepted as being like many other *stagiaires* who had spent time with the organisation.

[64] This is the collective term for *procureurs*, public prosecutors.

seal, detailing the conditions of the researcher's presence with *gendarmes*.[65] It was in the administration of questionnaires to the police, however, that we encountered our greatest hurdle. We had not anticipated the huge organisational difficulties of negotiating access through the many different police trade unions that exist. We had to be content with one union, which itself took several months of meetings and telephone calls to obtain names and addresses and a letter of recommendation (for which we were extremely grateful and without which we could not proceed), effectively authorising officers to respond to the questionnaire and reassuring them of the confidentiality of their responses. In exchange, we agreed to provide a short summary in French, of the questionnaire findings. We accepted this condition as it did not compromise the data in any way.

Understanding the French Criminal Process

By way of a backdrop to the analysis in the chapters that follow, this section considers the importance within the French criminal justice process of the French republican tradition, of codification and of the European Convention on Human Rights, as well as the different ways in which inquisitorial and adversarial procedure are characterised.

The French Republican Tradition

Although this study focuses on the description and analysis of contemporary criminal justice practice in France, the organisational structures and many of the key values which continue to influence both policy and practice, have their roots in the legal and political order established after the 1789 Revolution.[66] This was a time of great social and constitutional change and the brief account presented here can do no more than skim the surface and provide a broad idea of what

---

[65] It should be noted that once this formality was complete, the *gendarmes* were extremely open and helpful, allowing us to accompany them in all aspects of their work.

[66] This section focuses upon the centrality of the modern state within the French legal and political system. The specific histories of *magistrats*, police, *gendarmes* and *avocats* are discussed in Chs 3 and 4. For an account of the history of French criminal procedure and the continuities between pre- and post-revolutionary procedures, see Esmein (1913); Karpik (1999); Thireau (2001); Carbasse (2003). The Revolution reinforced many of the legal changes already in place (such as the growing centralisation of power, begun in the 17th century) and added the jury and institutions reflecting the centrality of the modern republican state, rather than of the monarch. Thus, the *Conseil du Roi*, became the *Conseil d'Etat*. Interestingly, the *procureur impérial* during the First and Second Empires became the *procureur royal* under the Restoration and the *procureur de la République* in 1870 (Martin 1990:145).

remains a contested history.[67] Under the pre-revolutionary *Ancien Régime*, the monarchy, the Church and the nobility provided the institutional foundations of society and the administration of justice was characterised by inequality, authoritarianism and feudalism.[68] Different laws applied to individuals depending on whether they were part of the nobility, the clergy, or others known as the Third Estate. Just as in England, before the idea of travelling judges was introduced to develop a common law system, there was also no centralised system of justice. Regional laws were administered in regional courts, with clearly discernible differences between the North and the South of the country. Whilst the *Ancien Régime* was neither static nor wholly opposed to reform (particularly during the 18th century under Louis XV and XVI) the state lacked the power and the unity to bring about effective change.[69] Inspired by the Enlightenment philosophers Montesquieu, Voltaire, Diderot, Mably and Rousseau, the revolutionaries sought to sweep away the old system of privilege and discrimination, establishing a new order in which the people, rather than the monarch, were sovereign.[70] The basic revolutionary principles of *liberté, égalité,* and *fraternité* were expressed in the 1789 *Declaration des droits de l'homme et du citoyen* (Declaration of the Rights of Man and of Citizens), which, since 1958 has become part of the French Constitution.[71] The First French Republic was declared in 1792 paving the way for the more effective political and legal centralisation[72] which was to take place under the leadership of Napoleon Bonaparte, who came to power in 1799. Although distinct from that of the revolutionaries, Bonaparte's role was of equal importance in shaping contemporary law and institutions.

At the heart of the French republican tradition, as it might broadly be described,[73] is the sovereignty of the French people and as the only body to enjoy the mandate of these citizens (through the election of politicians), this power is exercised in practice

[67] In considering political traditions and the ordering of the past Hazareesingh (1994:15) notes that ' . . . "history" was always a particular intellectual construct, a narrative which consciously blended imaginary elements with objective events in order to posit a precise relationship between past and present.' For a concise French legal historical account of this period see Thireau (2001); Carbasse (2003). For an alternative analysis of the role and nature of the modern state, see Kriegel (2003).

[68] Elliot and Vernon (2000:3).

[69] Carbasse (2003:254).

[70] In contrast with the revolutionary rhetoric of breaking away completely from the past and forging a new social, political and legal order, Thireau (2001:269–70) describes the concepts and solutions that emerged out of the Revolution as tending to follow and to accelerate changes that were already taking place.

[71] Legally, the Constitution consists of the 1789 Declaration; the preamble to the 1946 Constitution; the fundamental principles recognised by the laws of the Republic and referred to by the 1946 preamble; and of course, the text of the 1958 Constitution itself. Together, these sources are known as the constitutional block, *le bloc de constitutionalité*.

[72] Codification was a key part of this, as described below.

[73] There were, of course, three separate Republics declared during the 19th century, but the broad term 'Republican' is used here to contrast the ideals and structures which developed after the Revolution. The meaning and desirability of republicanism has been contested politically, especially by the Right. See Hazareesingh (1994) ch 3.

by the state, as the nation's representative. In this way, sovereignty of the people becomes sovereignty of the state. This has enormous significance for the moral and political legitimacy of the state as the representative and guardian of the public interest and for the wide powers it may exercise in the name of the people. In the 19th century, Napoleon's bold republican vision to make the ideals of the revolutionaries a reality, was to have a strongly centralised state with the power and technical competence to reconstruct a new political and social order which would fill the void left by the institutions of the *Ancien Régime*—the monarchy, the Church and the nobility.[74] The distinctive features of the early 19th century Napoleonic state, in which the military served as a model for the civil service and justice, therefore included:

> an emphasis on power, authority, and technical competence, a strict sense of hierarchy, a clearly delineated system of rules, which were applied in a uniform manner, and a scope of intervention in matters both public and private which was pervasive (in comparison with its predecessors). The most important and durable feature of the Napoleonic system was the principle of centralization, which Napoleon consciously adopted from the Jacobin heritage of the 1790s. (Hazareesingh, 1994:159)

In contemporary France, this centralised state tradition, or *étatisme*, remains an important feature.[75] The state enjoys the moral and political authority firstly, to become widely involved in areas which touch upon the public interest and secondly, to exercise significant powers in the protection of that public interest.[76] As Hazareesingh (1994:151) explains:

---

[74] Although 'the idea of an all-powerful State was firmly embedded in the intellectual landscape of the pre-revolutionary *ancien régime*' (Hazareesingh, 1994:167), executive power expanded rapidly after 1789.

[75] Georges Pompidou, de Gaulle's successor as President, stated that 'France would not exist without a State'—quoted in Knapp and Wright (2001:15). In both the pre- and post-revolutionary periods, there was a strong emphasis on state building and the notion of the state as the creator of the nation, as well as the autonomy and primacy of the state in relation to local government and to civil society (Knapp and Wright 2001:15–25). In discussing the shift of power from monarch to Emperor of the Republic, Hayward (1987:2) talks of infusing 'the cold monster of state authority with the hot blood of democratic nationalism.' See also the analysis of Kriegel (2003).

[76] There is, of course, debate as to the exact locus of state power. Although its role would be regarded by politicians as merely instrumental of political policy (and the purges within the high ranks of the administration following major political shifts would testify to this), there is no doubt that the bureaucratic elite (of which there is a strong tradition in France) is an important site of power within the French state (and a key component of *dirigisme*, 'the term coined to characterise the intervention of the State in the post-war economy,' Knapp and Wright 2001:18). There is an interesting relationship between the administrative and political elites in that the majority of high-ranking politicians (from the President and the Prime Minister, to government ministers) tend to come from the *Grandes Ecoles*, the institutions from which top civil servants are drawn. 'The *Grandes Ecoles* thus emerged not only as training schools for the bureaucracy, but as the breeding ground for current and ensuing generations of political leaders. This institutionalization of the process of elite formation remains significant (especially from a comparative perspective) in that France is one of the few advanced industrial societies which effectively recruits and trains its political elites to exercise power.' (Hazareesingh, 1994:171). See also Dorandeu (1994).

French government expenditure accounts for a considerably higher proportion of national income than its British or American counterparts.[77] This state activism is translated into a high level of territorial penetration, resulting in the establishment of vast state networks throughout the land. It is also reflected in a high level of functional complexity, as seen in the extent of its historical involvement in such spheres as agriculture, education, health and religion. Finally, the presence of the State is maintained through its self-image as the guardian of the long-term interests of the nation. This self-image is constantly projected to the population, reminding French citizens of the benevolent and paternalistic vocation of their State.

In this classical conception of the French republican state, the judiciary (as a body of non-elite public servants) has occupied an ambivalent space. Fearful that the judiciary might once more use the power which had helped to topple the monarchy (the spectre of a *gouvernement des juges*),[78] the early republican state ensured that the *magistrature* became subordinate to its political masters.[79] The role of the judge was envisaged as that of an automaton, declaring and applying the sacred text of the law literally and mechanically[80] and legislation passed in 1790 denied the courts any role in reviewing state action.[81] On the other hand, republican governments have been aware of the need to show respect for the rule of law and the judiciary was initially given an important role in the process of codification beginning in 1800 as well as in the supervision of state practice.[82] Napoleon abolished the brief revolutionary practice of electing judges,[83] replacing them once more with government nominated professional *magistrats*, arguably entrenching further the power of elected politicians (representing the will of the people) over the non-elected judiciary.[84] In comparison with their US

---

[77] Knapp and Wright (2001:40) note France's 'dense institutional architecture' demonstrated in the fact that '[I]n 1998, some 45.7 per cent of French GDP was represented by central and local government taxation plus social security contributions.'

[78] On the role of the wealthiest and most powerful *magistrats*, those in the *parlements*, see Martin (1990:161–62).

[79] See further the contributions in Magendie and Gomez (1986:17–29); Carbasse (2000).

[80] Carbasse (2003:252). eg, inspired by Montesquieu and Beccaria, the 1791 *Code pénal* stipulated fixed sentences, reducing the judicial role to that of applying the law mechanically without any power to moderate the sanction imposed.

[81] Article 13 of the Act of 16–24 August 1790 prohibited judges from interfering in any manner with the acts of the administration. Breach of this prohibition would incur criminal liability. A second law in August 1795 (and still in force today) contained an even wider prohibition on the criminal and civil courts having any dealings with the administration. This left the administration free from legal review as it was only later that the advisory function of the *Conseil d'Etat* expanded to develop an administrative court system.

[82] Hazareesingh (1994:66).

[83] The revolutionaries introduced juries in criminal cases and abolished the existing hierarchical *magistrature*, replacing it with judges elected for a six year period.

[84] This subordinate position was reinforced in 1958, since which time the *magistrature* have been referred to as a judicial authority (*autorité*) rather than a judicial power (*pouvoir*). This is said to recognise the fact that the judges apply the law which is made by the state. They are not a 'power' in their own right, which would rival that of the state and so challenge the sovereign will of the people.

and UK counterparts, the French judiciary have been granted only a limited degree of autonomy,[85] which some have argued, serves to legitimate, rather than to act as any real check upon, the actions of the state.[86] Within this ideology, the executive–judiciary relationship has been configured in a way which is quite different from that in the UK, where judges may be regarded as playing a role in protecting citizens from the excesses of the executive, most notably through judicial review. In France, on the other hand, the executive would claim to protect citizens from the excesses of a non-elected judiciary.

> Trust in the legislature, that is, the political powers, mistrust of the judge: such is the dual inspiration of the revolutionaries which continues with their successors. (Badinter, 1995:8)

In the case of the *parquet*, this gives rise to a paradoxical relationship, where the French judiciary is said to be independent of the executive, yet must also be democratically accountable to a government minister, the Minister of Justice.[87]

This traditional view has been challenged in recent years through phenomena such as '*les affaires*', in which politicians as well as business people have been investigated for fraud and corruption—not under an administrative jurisdiction, but in the ordinary courts.[88] This attack on the 'immunities' that servants of the state have enjoyed[89] is criticised by some as undermining the clear separation of powers that is such an important part of the post-revolutionary ideology. In the face of the judiciary's increasing independence from the executive, politicians in particular continue to invoke the pre-revolutionary spectre of the *gouvernement des juges*.[90] Garapon

---

[85] Hazareesingh writes of 'the French State's dismissive (not to say contemptuous) treatment of the principle of judicial autonomy.' (1994:171). Magendie and Gomez (1986:18–19) are critical of the state's assertion of its own unreviewable autonomy (on the grounds that it is the only power representing the sovereign will of the people), especially given its decision to cease judicial elections.

[86] See eg Magendie and Gomez (1986:18–20); Hazareesingh (1994:173). Also Karpik (1999).

[87] As well as the general hierarchical control exercised over the *parquet*, the Minister also has a powerful influence over the career of the *procureur*—see further the discussion in Ch 3. The executive's grip on the judiciary is also demonstrated by the 'purges' which have taken place with major shifts in political power. The largest of these was in1883 (694 *magistrats* were removed in the 'republicanisation' of the judiciary). More recently, 200 *magistrats* were removed under the Vichy regime and 363 (one-tenth of the whole corps) at the end of the war (Badinter, 1995:10–11). See further Breen (2003) for a discussion of the 'collaboration' of the executive and the judiciary in exercising a function of repression.

[88] Discussed further in Ch 3.

[89] Garapon (1996a:32).

[90] For example, proposals in 1998 to weaken the hierarchical control exercised by the Minister of Justice over public prosecutors, as well as the role of politicians in their appointment and promotion, were resisted as giving too much power to prosecutors and leaving them insufficiently accountable to democratically elected politicians. See Hodgson (2002a:235–40). Also Magendie and Gomez (1986:17–29); Bredin (1994); Badinter (1995); Pradel and Laborde (1997); Pradel (2000). Interestingly, the professional governing body of the French *magistrature*, the *Conseil supérieur de la magistrature* later called for the Minister of Justice to resume his temporarily suspended power to issue instructions to *magistrats* in individual cases. See the interview with public prosecutor and member of the *Conseil*, Michel Lernout in Rancé (2002d).

(1996a) suggests a different analysis. He argues that this new form of judicial activity is not born of any desire on the part of *magistrats* to 'attack' politicians, but is part of a wider process of change in which we are witnessing the mass juridification of affairs[91] and are turning increasingly to law and to the judiciary to make up the democratic deficit which exists in modern politics.[92] Together with the weakening of the state, the promotion of civil society and the power of the media, judicial activism is only one of several cogs in a more complex mechanism.[93] The executive–judiciary relationship is mutating[94]: a new model of law and of democracy is being born,[95] in which the judge is acquiring a symbolic role through the possibility of her intervention.[96]

Although flexing her judicial muscles a little more in recent years, the professional role and ideology of the judge continues to be informed by, and to some extent mirrors, her place within the wider political structure to which she remains largely subordinate. As part of the higher civil service as well as the judiciary, the *magistrature* is part of the state machinery to which the interpretation and application of the law is delegated and various mechanisms seek to ensure that government policy is translated into penal policy, particularly through the hierarchical structures of the prosecution service.[97] Investigating and trial judges enjoy a greater degree of independence from the executive, but the structure and professional ideology of the *parquet* is embedded within that of the state. It is strongly centralised and organised in a hierarchical structure, with clear lines of accountability from those at the base of the pyramid to the Minister of Justice at its apex. Within this model, the law, which is presented as fixed and with little or no scope for interpretation, is applied in a uniform manner with an emphasis upon technical competence rather than individual discretion. And perhaps most significantly, the *procureur* has as her overarching objective, the protection and representation of the public interest. Just as we saw above in relation to the state, this public interest orientation in the judicial context justifies the awesome concentration of power in the hands of one person. This contrasts with the dichotomy of interests represented in the adversarial tradition, which divides different functions between different legal actors—what Damaska (1975) terms a co-ordinate, rather than

---

[91] See also the comments of *magistrats* in Greilsamer and Schneidermann (2002).

[92] Jean de Maillard, president of the *chambre correctionelle* in Blois, considers that underlying the major '*affaires*' of the last 10 years, is the return to society's confrontation with its elites. Greilsamer and Schneidermann (2002:363).

[93] Garapon (1996a:22).

[94] Indeed Breen (2003:221) goes on to question the stark dichotomising of power between the judiciary and the executive, arguing that it is now more appropriate to understand this as a collaboration of powers.

[95] Garapon (1996a:24).

[96] Garapon (1996a:40). He describes (at p 44) the symbolic site of democracy shifting from the state, to justice. See also Guarnieri and Pederzoli (2002).

[97] See Hodgson (2002a).

hierarchical model of criminal procedure. In this way, the two potentially conflicting roles which the *magistrat* is required to perform—guaranteeing both the
effectiveness of the investigation and the rights of the defence—are successfully
reconciled within her wider professional ethos of representing the interests of
society. This is of interest and importance in the current study, as the way in which
'the public interest' is constructed and understood through the daily practices of
the *magistrat* becomes a central driver in the investigation and prosecution of
crime.[98]

The existence of a strongly centralised state and the constitutional position of
France as a republic also impact upon the state–citizen relationship and notions of
citizenship more broadly. Together with the equality of all citizens before the law, the
unity and indivisibility of the people has been a key part of the construction of the
French nation state.[99] Equality in the post-revolutionary period was concerned to
eliminate the systems of privilege and discrimination which had characterised the
Ancien Régime. In the modern context, it has tended to promote a homogenous and
monolithic model of citizenship,[100] preventing, for example, the recognition of
minority cultures and languages within France, such as those of the Breton people.[101]

In England and Wales, cases are prosecuted not in the name of the people, but
of the Crown. In France, as a republic, the judiciary acts on behalf of a state which
is not separate from, but which is a part of and represents the ordinary people.
This defines the relationship between the accused and those administering the

---

[98] Discussed more fully in Ch 5.

[99] Hayward (1987:21) argues that the dominance of the state is such that: 'France is a state-nation
rather than a nation-state. The nation is an artefact of the state.'

[100] See eg the mayor of Strasbourg's comments that the expression of Islam should be French and
republican. *Le Monde* 20 November 2003, p 10. 'Republican' values are frequently referred to by politicians when describing social and criminal justice initiatives. See eg Prime Minister Raffarin's comments on the need to bring republican values into the ghettos, *Le Monde* 19 November 2003, p 10.

[101] Zauberman and Lévy (2003:1081) describe it as 'an abstract conception of citizenship'. As recently as 1994, the Constitution was amended to express the fact that French was the language of
the Republic. Constitutional Act No 92-554 of 25 June 1992, *Journal Officiel* of 26 June 1992. In 1994,
the French language law (Loi No 94-665 *relative à l'emploi de la langue française*), whilst not opposing the
use of regional languages, affirmed French as the language of instruction, employment, the media,
commerce and public meetings. In 1991, the *Conseil constitutionnel* ruled that a government bill
designed to give greater autonomy to the island of Corsica could not contain the phrase 'the Corsican
people'. This would challenge the notion of the 'one and indivisible' French Republic. (*Conseil constitutionnel* decision No 91-290 DC of 9 May 1991, *Journal Officiel* of 14 May). Hayward (1987:21) writes:

> France is a unitary state superimposed upon a multinational society, the authority of Paris having
> been established under the monarchy, expanded by the Napoleonic Empires and reinforced by the
> Republics over *Alsaciens*, Basques, Bretons, Catalans, etc . . . A secretary-general of the Gaullist UDR
> (predecessor of the RPR) could complacently recall Michelet's claim that 'French France had
> attracted, absorbed, amalgamated the English, German and Spanish Frances with which it was sur-
> rounded. She had neutralized each with the other and converted them all into her substance . . . She
> had southernized the north and northernized the south.'

See also Rouland (2000).

criminal process in a different way. The judge is administering the law, representing the state and so, the people. The defendant is a fellow citizen who is seen to have failed in some way, to have let down both herself and the community and who now needs assistance in the process of reintegration into society. In contrast to the demeaning way in which accused persons are generally regarded in England and Wales (even by their own defence counsel)[102] where they are treated as an underclass beyond redemption, a criminological other outside respectable society, the accused in France is required to take responsibility for her actions, to reflect on the consequences of what she has done and to participate in the process. This model is played out in practice, as well as in theory: defendants are questioned by the *procureur*; they are questioned directly by the judge in court (though they are not required to take an oath and it is not an offence to lie to the court); there is a sense in which they are held to account as erring citizens. This contrasts with criminal procedure and practice in England and Wales, where the accused is marginalised in the trial process itself, treated as the object of the case, rather than the subject whose actions are on trial.[103] The accused in France is very much more present in the process than defendants in the UK, who may speak only a few words at a court hearing, whilst the case takes place around them, narrated and disposed of by professional lawyers. The degree of participation of the accused is also a function of the procedural model by which she is tried: in an inquisitorial system, she is expected to contribute to the process of discovering the truth, whilst in an adversarial or accusatorial system, her guilt must be established objectively and on the basis of evidence exterior to her.[104]

However, the notion of the *magistrat* administering the law objectively and impartially on behalf of the state, also provides an insulating distance between accuser and accused. Decisions are frequently prefaced by phrases such as 'I am obliged by the law to . . .' or 'I am required to . . . '. The law and its application are presented as fixed, rather than variable or discretionary. This normative moral standpoint suggests the uniformity of the law and its application and invites the defendant to buy into a homogeneous model of French society and values, where all citizens are equal and equally bound by the law. However, this image of the *magistrat* and defendant as 'fellow citizens', where the *magistrat* simply applies the pre-determined law, masks the real power relationship that exists. As described in later chapters, the *magistrat* does exercise discretion and make personal choices, but this discourse allows her to mete out tough decisions behind the veil of 'the requirements of the law'. Soulez Larivière (1995) describes the psychology of the *magistrat* and the ways in which she distances herself from the process and consequences of judgment. The *magistrat*, he argues, is able to exercise the power even

---

[102] See eg McConville *et al* (1994).
[103] Discussed further in Ch 4. See eg Bankowski and Mungham (1976); McConville *et al* (1994).
[104] Spencer (2002:24).

to condemn a person to death without it troubling her conscience, because of her belief that this is not by her own hand, but that of the law. To judge is to not comprehend: once the judge personifies and identifies with the accused, she can no longer judge. The independence of the judge, argues Soulez Larivière (1995:53), maintained by the 'fantasy' of belonging to something separate and apart from the rest of society, is not a positive attribute which guarantees fair treatment, but rather, manifests itself as an inability to identify with the accused and a 'freedom to exercise power whilst sheltering behind a legal logic which recodes reality.'

Codification

Debate around the codification of criminal law and procedure in England and Wales tends to assume a consolidation model, whereby existing common law and statute is rationalised into one central source. The French experience has been rather different, with codification originally conceived as part of a process of wider political and ideological change after the Revolution. The first code to be introduced was the *Code pénal*, in 1791.[105] Between 1793 and 1796, three drafts of a *Code civil* were also presented, but each was rejected in turn. With the coming to power of Napoleon Bonaparte, there was a need for greater stability after the upheaval and radical changes of the Revolution. Executive power was strengthened (Napoleon himself exercising the most effective authority in this respect) and the establishment of a *Code civil* formed a crucial part of the strategy of legal and political centralisation.[106] In contrast to the radicalism of the revolutionaries, the Napoleonic codes attempted a synthesis of the traditions and experience of the past, with the ideas of the Revolution such as the jury, divorce and greater equality in the laws of property and succession.[107] Introduced in 1804, the *Code civil* was written by four practising lawyers, two from the North of France and two from the South.[108] This is often referred to as the *Code Napoléon*, given his close involvement with the implementation of the project.[109] The text was intended to be practical rather than philosophical, and, in line with revolutionary ideology, to be written in language that could be understood by the ordinary citizen.[110] It was followed by the *Code de procédure civile* in 1807, the *Code de commerce* and *Code*

---

[105] Esmein (1913: Part III, Title I, ch III) refers to these as the Codes of the 'intermediary period', ie after the *Ancien Régime*, but before the Napoleonic era.

[106] Napoleon saw the *Code civil* as his real glory, an achievement that would live on forever (Thireau 2001:322).

[107] A synthesis already begun with the doctrine of the *Ancien Régime* (Thireau 2001:308–9).

[108] This is significant in that the customary law in France was different in the North and in the South. It should also be noted that these four authors were politically moderate.

[109] See further the account of this process in Thireau (2001:300–16)

[110] The greater part of the population remained excluded, however, as they could not read. Bell *et al* (1998:24).

d'instruction criminelle in 1808, and a *Code pénal* in 1810.[111] The essence of these codes was that they should formulate general principles of law:[112]

> The task of legislation is to determine the general maxims of the law, taking a large view of the matter. It must establish principles rich in implications rather than descend into the details of every question which might possibly arise. The application of the law belongs to the judge and the lawyer, steeped in the general spirit of the legislation.[113]

The aspiration was that these texts would simplify the law and provide an intellectually coherent legal framework in contrast to the fragmented nature of the laws and customs that were in existence at the time. However, although drawing on some established principles, the codes were not a mere consolidation of existing law: they were intended to be radical reforms instilling something of the ideology of the Revolution, creating new rights to own property, to contract freely and so on.

It is important, nevertheless, not to overstate the significance of codification. To say that French law and procedure is codified, whilst that in the UK is not, would be both an exaggeration and a simplification of the nature of the differences between the approaches of the two legal processes.[114] The original ideal of codification in the post-revolutionary context has been diluted. There is still a desire for a coherent and accessible body of law, but of the five original Napoleonic codes only the *Code civil* remains in its now outdated and original form and there is much which has been codified subsequently in a less radical and more consolidating format[115]—described by Bell (2001:57) as 'administrative restatement'.[116] The codes themselves have been added to and amended, such that in many instances the original coherence is lost and the original meaning difficult to

---

[111] The *Code pénal* returned to allowing the judges a discretion in sentencing, in place of the fixed penalty approach of the 1791 code. In criminal procedure, the *Code d'instruction criminelle* was inspired by the inquisitorial system of the 1670 *ordonnance*, but retained the jury as introduced by the revolutionaries.

[112] The Swiss scholar, Wieland, compares the written law to a theatrical play or piece of music: the text remains the same, but its interpretation may vary over time and in new settings. See David (1980:23).

[113] Portalis 1799 (one of the authors of the *Code civil*) *Discours préliminaire* cited in Bell (2001:57).

[114] David (1980) argues that the difference lies in the attitude towards statutory law. In France, legal rules are expressed at a broad level of generality, enabling the court to (re)interpret them to resolve any given case. In England, the tendency is to construe legal rules narrowly and to distinguish cases in the process.

> It matters little that we have codes in France and that the English have no codes. The point is that the English *cannot* have codes having the same significance as the French codes, as long as they will keep their traditional notion of a legal rule, maintain their notion of precedent and stick to their technique of distinctions instead of taking the broad continental view of the legal rule and resorting to the technique of interpretation which is used in civil law countries. (David, 1980:20–21).

[115] Eg the *Code pénal* of 1994. This is the task of the *commission supérieure de codification*, created in 1989.

[116] This is not true, however, of the 1975 *Nouveau Code de procédure civile* and the 1992 *Nouveau Code pénal*.

discern.[117] In the case of the *Code de procédure pénale* (CPP), this has led some commentators to call for root and branch reform of criminal procedure, rather than the constant addition of new and apparently contradictory concepts and provisions.[118] This tension has been felt especially in relation to changes enacted in response to the need for conformity with the requirements of the ECHR—as will be discussed in more detail below.

The place of case law in France, though formally quite different from that in a common law tradition, is not unimportant.[119] Any French lawyer would expect to be familiar with leading cases in order to know the law[120] and they are cited in the standard commentaries. This includes appeals made in the course of the *instruction*, as well as appeals following trial.[121] Further challenging this 'legicentric' view of law is the increasing importance of international treaties which require the judge to make reference to exterior sources (such as the EU or the ECHR) in order to state what the law is and to verify its compatibility with international norms.[122] Within the French republican model, however, we have seen that the judiciary occupies a subordinate position and judicial decisions are not treated as an originating source of law,[123] yet the interpretation of the codes by the higher courts is very influential. The apparent objectivity of judicial decisions as declarations of state decreed law is reinforced by their fixed format. The terse presentation of court judgments is very different from those delivered by the appeal courts of England and Wales. The French judgment is extremely short and expressed in one long sentence. Unlike the lengthy English judgment which seeks to explain, to justify and to locate the decision, there is no dialogue with the past or with the future, no discussion or acknowledgement that there may have been several plausible outcomes from which a choice was made. It is the language of assertion rather than argument, a definitive pronouncement, suggesting that the decision represents not a choice, but the only logical deduction from principles of enacted law.[124] This succinct form is a product of the status of judicial decisions which neither

---

[117] See Bell *et al* (1998:5–9). Lasserre-Kiesow (2002) argues that laypeople could never have the same level of understanding of the law as lawyers and this is now exacerbated by the complexity of legislation and judicial decisions which now supplement the codes.

[118] One of the most outspoken of these is Mireille Delmas-Marty, both in her own writing and the Commission she chaired in 1991. See eg Delmas-Marty (1990), (1991).

[119] Even at their inception, the Napoleonic Codes anticipated a clear judicial role in interpreting and applying the law (Thireau 2001:310) and 30 years after its publication, the *Code civil* was already transformed by the effect of judicial decisions (Lasserre-Kiesow 2002:1160).

[120] David and Jauffret-Spinosi (1992:51).

[121] Such decisions tend to be well known within the relatively small corps of *juges d'instruction* as they impact directly on their work.

[122] Garapon (1996a:36–38).

[123] The subordination of the judiciary to the supremacy of 'the law' has been expressed in strong terms. For Robespierre: 'The word jurisprudence should be erased from the language.' See Bredin (1994:79). The law-making role of the judge is not formally recognised and whilst moral and political philosophy are taught within French universities, legal philosophy is not. Garapon (1996a:30).

[124] Rudden (1974). This denial of legal discretion and choice is also part of the ideology of the *magistrat*, as discussed above.

make law nor set precedent. However, this rather mechanistic legal–scientific format masks the realities of the judicial reasoning process, which is not dissimilar to that of the common law judge.[125] Bell *et al* (1998:33) argue that in fact,

> Lasser's and Bell's observation of files and decisions reveals very clearly that the doctrinal, precedential and 'policy' arguments familiar to common lawyers are present in the deliberations of French judges, but they do not form part of the justification. The justification offered presents, as Lasser suggests, an 'official portrait' of the judge simply interpreting the legal rules and arriving at deductive results. The reality is that the 'unofficial portrait' reveals the judge much as his German or British counterparts, concerned to adapt the law to new circumstances.[126]

Furthermore, whilst codification is often thought to provide a greater degree of legal precision and certainty, in contrast to the common law contingencies of judge-made law, this is not always the case. Freed from the shackles of judicial precedent, the courts have potentially much more latitude in the interpretation and application of the law. In practice, there are often consistent decisions on the same point of law, but uninhibited by the requirements of precedent, there are also examples of radical changes in the way in which the law is interpreted.[127] This undermines the efficacy and certainty of legislation for citizens as well as lawyers, and underlines the contextual interpretation of the law which is not fixed and closed, but incomplete and constantly under construction.[128] Rudden argues that in not being bound by earlier decisions, together with the 'decision as statement' style of judgment, French courts can and do act more decisively and more boldly than their English counterparts. But, by always citing the Code as their authority (the only relevant source of law), they are able to deny the judge-made character of even a dramatic shift in the way in which the Code is interpreted.[129]

> The paradox is that a constitutional system which gives great power to the judges finds it necessary, by a doctrine of precedent, to make responsible the exercise of that power; while a system which denies the creative role of the judge sets him free to legislate. (Rudden 1974:1025)

---

[125] Rudden (1974:1018) also notes that it is in the submissions of the *procureur* that we see features more familiar to the common lawyer—reviewing previous cases and academic opinion, considering policy arguments such as insurance and making observations on the possible future implications of the course proposed. What remains hidden is the court's evaluation of these submissions and the reasons for their decision.

[126] See Bell (1991); Lasser (1995). This observation also reflects my own experience in observing the deliberation of the *Cour de cassation*.

[127] See eg *Rebboah* Cass. crim., 30 June 1999.

[128] Lasserre-Kiesow (2002:1158).

[129] David (1980:23), where he notes the emergence of strict liability, as the courts adopted a new interpretation of Article 1384 of the *Code civil* some one hundred years after its enactment. See also Troper (1981), who acknowledges the role of the judge in interpreting and creating law, but argues that the form in which the judicial function is exercised means that it cannot be regarded as a *pouvoir* in the same way as the executive and the legislature.

Inquisitorial and Adversarial Procedure

French criminal procedure is characterised typically (by those outside France) as being inquisitorial, in contrast to the system in place in England and Wales, which is generally described as adversarial. In fact, just as the system in England and Wales is not a pure representation of the adversarial model, so the French would describe their own criminal procedure as 'mixed', incorporating aspects of both models.[130] Adversarial procedure assumes a broad equality between the opposing parties—prosecution and defence—each of whom gathers evidence to support their case and argues it before a neutral judge. The proceedings are oral, public and argued by both sides. Inquisitorial procedure dates back to the 13th century and is the product of a more institutionalised and centralised state role, that does not rest upon equality between the parties. In its original 'pure' form the enquiry was conducted by a representative of the state who was not a party in the case, in the sense that she investigated, prosecuted, could instigate coercive measures and determined whether the case should go to trial.[131] The defence did not participate in any aspect of the pre-trial phase. The procedure was written, secret and not debated.[132] The different emphases within the two procedures mean that the inquisitorial model has a longer investigation period and the adversarial a longer trial. The two procedures have been characterised as being concerned with truth (the inquisitorial model, with its wide ranging pre-trial investigative powers) and proof (the adversarial model, dependent on the evidence presented by the parties).[133] Although relying upon different methods of legal proof, Jackson (1988) has argued that both models work within the

---

[130] '[T]he history of criminal procedure in Western Europe is in a sense the story of each tradition borrowing the other's ideas, either with or without attribution' (Spencer, 2002:3). See also Salas (1992). See too the recurring debates around the wisdom of introducing the jury system in France, described in Esmein (1913). For a more contemporary view, see further Munday (1995). Napoleon's 1808 *Code d'instruction criminelle* maintained some aspects of the English criminal procedure which had been introduced by the revolutionaries, whilst reinstating a broadly inquisitorial procedure which now separated out the functions of investigation and prosecution, as well as outlawing torture. For a more detailed description of the history of French legal procedure, see West *et al* (1998) ch 1; Spencer (2002: 5–20). The most detailed and authoritative account is provided by Esmein (1913).

[131] See Delmas-Marty (1991:19–20).

[132] Early French procedure in the 13th-century feudal courts, was in fact accusatory. The shift to inquisitorial procedure took place under the influence of the Church and the growth in royal power, controlled by ordinances in 1498 and 1539, the most significant codification being the Ordinance of 1670.

> The result was that a code of criminal instruction was now definitely established which lasted down to the French revolution and was rigidly followed in all its details of secret processes, variegated tortures, and cruel punishments by all the courts of justice in France. Back of it lay the royal authority, which could be exercised arbitrarily against the subject. (Trenholme, 'Introduction' to Esmein (1913) pp xxxvi–xxxvii).

[133] See eg Frank's (1949) analysis. He is extremely critical of the adversarial trial method, which he likens to throwing pepper into the eyes of a surgeon (p 85).

same epistemological tradition, seeking to arrive at 'the truth' using the classic scientific method of proof:[134] conclusions are reached by observation and experience using what might be termed a broadly empiricist approach.

Whilst remaining rooted in its inquisitorial tradition, French criminal procedure has incorporated a number of more adversarial features into its procedure: the *instruction* and trial phases are generally regarded as including a number of adversarial features, whereas the preliminary police investigation (by which over 95 per cent of cases are investigated) remains largely inquisitorial.[135] Firstly, in response to increasing concerns over the enormity of the power of the *juge d'instruction*, power exercised behind a shield of secrecy,[136] the 1808 code of criminal procedure was reformed in 1897 to allow the accused's lawyer a role during the *instruction* investigation: the defence lawyer was permitted to be present during the judicial questioning of her client and to consult the case *dossier* beforehand.[137] This marked a significant change to the procedure originally laid down in the 1808 *Code d'instruction criminelle* and the reform was widely criticised at the time as undermining the nature of the inquisitorial process and frustrating the *juge* in her search for the truth. Secondly, in order to separate out the functions of investigation and prosecution, the 1958 code established the independence of the *juge d'instruction* from the public prosecutor, the *procureur*. Thirdly, whilst criminal proceedings continue to be characterised by written, rather than oral evidence,[138] the trial and some pre-trial hearings are now conducted in public and the

---

[134] This method assumes firstly:

> that there is a world of fact which exists out there as part of reality, independent of the human observer, and the work of the scientist is to discover as much of it as he can by comparing this reality with his own theories and hypotheses, what has been called the correspondence theory of truth. Secondly, it is assumed that although many conclusions can only be stated with probability, given time the complete truth is in principle capable of being revealed, the principle of universal cognitive competence. Third, since knowledge of reality can be obtained by using as a foundation the empirical evidence of our sense-experiences which is value-free, science can be conducted in a value-free manner. (Jackson, 1988:552)

There are, of course, significant problems with this theory, in particular concerning the subjective way in which we perceive and interpret things and Jackson goes on to examine these.

[135] The French criminal process is classically defined in 3 stages, the *enquête de police*, *instruction*, and trial. Given that over 95% of cases do not involve the *instruction* procedure, this division appears outdated.

[136] The conduct of the investigation by the *juge d'instruction* was likened to a 'duel between the *juge* and the accused, a duel without witnesses and with weapons of which the *juge* alone had the mastery' (H Halton *Etude de la procédure criminelle* p 69, cited by Salas (1991:248)). There had been proposals for a more adversarial procedure to be adopted, but these were rejected out of hand by the high-ranking judiciary and by Parliament. See Salas (1991:248).

[137] Ironically, in order to avoid the presence of the defence lawyer, the *procureur* and the police began their own process of investigation which included the detention of suspects. This remained outside any formal legal framework until the 1958 code of criminal procedure laid down procedures for the regulation of this longstanding practice of *garde à vue* (the period of police detention).

[138] See eg McKillop (1998). Oral evidence is less significant in practice in England and Wales, given that very few cases are contested. In guilty plea hearings, no witnesses are heard and the court relies only on the written statements produced by the prosecution. This also highlights the key role of the

principle of *contradictoire*, where the evidence is debated by both sides, is more firmly entrenched.[139] This is part of the growing influence of the ECHR and the jurisprudence of the ECtHR which have inspired a number of recent reforms, notably those increasing further the participation rights of the defence,[140] allowing the suspect access to custodial legal advice (1993); obliging the police to provide greater information concerning the nature of the charges for which she is being detained (2000); and allowing the suspect a greater opportunity to participate in the investigation conducted by the *juge d'instruction* (1993, 2000).[141] Like the reform of 1897, the recent strengthening of defence rights also attracted widespread criticism as being likely to paralyse the police, whilst privileging the interests of the suspect (discussed further in chapter four).[142] Those sponsoring the reforms were careful to emphasise that whilst bringing France into line with ECHR requirements, they did not represent a move to a more adversarial procedure. For example, in addressing the *Sénat* (15 June 1999), the then Minister of Justice, Madame Guigou, said:

> The adversarial system of justice is by nature unfair and unjust. It favours the strong over the weak. It accentuates social and cultural differences, favouring the rich who are able to engage and pay for the services of one or more lawyers. Our own system is better, both in terms of efficiency and of the rights of the individual . . . I prefer, and I want to make this quite plain, an independent judge who investigates evidence both for and against the suspect, to police officers who carry out large parts of the criminal investigation without any judicial supervision.

In an interview with *Le Monde* (15 December 1999), she rejected the idea of the defence lawyer playing a greater role in the process:

> Lawyers are there to help their clients and to ensure the proper conduct of the *garde à vue*, but not to start getting involved in the case. I have chosen not to adopt the

---

defence in England and Wales: the guilty plea of the accused (with the benefit of legal advice) transforms the statements of prosecution witnesses into evidence on which the court will base its sentencing decision.

[139] See eg the views of the Delmas-Marty Commission (1991:13): 'There is no justice without both sides being debated and the earlier that this procedure is instituted, the better the chances of objectivity.' In *Rowe and Davis v UK* (2000, para 60) the European Court of Human Rights stated: 'It is a fundamental aspect of the right to a fair trial that criminal proceedings, including the elements of such proceedings which relate to procedure, should be adversarial and that there should be equality of arms between prosecution and defence.'

[140] This trend continues. One of the most common grounds for condemnation before the ECtHR in the last few years, has been the failure to disclose to the defence the report of those advising the appeal court—the *procureur général*, the *avocat général* and the *conseiller rapporteur*—information which is made available to the prosecutor and to the court.

[141] Loi No 93-2 of 4 January 1993; Loi No 2000-516 of 15 June 2000 *renforçant la protection de la présomption d'innocence et les droits des victimes*.

[142] The 2000 reform also obliged the police to inform the suspect of her right to silence. This has now been repealed in legislation sponsored by the Interior Minister (rather than the Justice Minister, see Ch 2) the Loi No 2003-239 of 18 March 2003, *pour la sécurité intérieure*.

adversarial procedure because it reinforces the inequalities of access to the law. It would lead ultimately, for example, to the use of private investigators in order to verify the investigation led by the police.

This tension between adversarial and inquisitorial procedure was again seen in the 2004 reform of the procedure for dealing with serious and organised crime.[143] In this instance, it was not the due process protections of the accused that came under fire. The legislation was seen by some as taking selected aspects of adversarial procedure (plea bargaining, and police rather than judicial investigations) though in this instance, without ensuring the corresponding defence protections necessary in order to respect the principle of equality of arms.[144] The then Justice Minister, Dominique Perben, rejected this claim and reaffirmed his commitment to the French inquisitorial system, denying any slide towards the 'Anglo-Saxon adversarial procedure'.[145]

Like those in my own research (described in Chapter 4), the senior *magistrats* interviewed by Greilsamer and Schneidermann (2002) were concerned to emphasise that the European framework was the natural context for France. Most favoured the clearer separation of judicial and investigative functions suggested in the Delmas-Marty Report (1991) as well as the guarantees of the ECHR. But whilst recognising an undeniable shift towards a more accusatorial procedure, this was not understood by them as a move towards 'Anglo-Saxon' or 'Anglo-American' procedure,[146] a change which they considered would be undesirable and ultimately, one that would offer less protection to individual liberties. Rather than the traditional dichotomy between inquisitorial and adversarial procedure, recent changes were characterised in the more 'European' terms of greater participation by the defence and the promotion of the principle of *contradictoire*.

The inquisitorial roots of French criminal procedure are significant for our understanding of the present day roles of legal actors, as well as the different ways in which investigations are undertaken and the rights of the accused protected.[147]

---

[143] Loi No 2004-204 of 9 March 2004, *portant adaptation de la justice aux évolutions de la criminalité.*

[144] *Le Monde* 10 April 2003.

[145] *Le Monde* 23 May 2003. This position was emphasised again in the Justice Minister's speech to the *Sénat* (1 October 2003), as the Bill passed through parliament: 'I reaffirm my commitment and the commitment of the government, to an inquisitorial type system. This system seems to me to be the best means of ensuring at the same time equal treatment of accused persons and respect for the rights of society, victims and the defence.'

[146] See eg interview with Gilbert Azibert, president of the *chambre d'instruction* in Paris (Greilsamer and Schneidermann, 2002:191–220).

[147]

Legal systems are in a constant state of flux and consequently the roles played by those who operate them must constantly be adjusted. Even when the continental systems borrow certain elements of the English model, as is the case in Italy for example, they cannot disregard the sociological burdens that they have inherited along with the inquisitorial system, a system rooted in a centuries-old tradition of State authority. (Salas, 2002:489)

Whilst the UK system focuses very much on the roles of the individual parties, the French legal process continues to have a state-centred conception of justice. During the pre-trial phase in particular, the focus of the investigation is the offence, rather than the suspect.[148] The judge maintains a central role during the investigation. As a *magistrat* representing the public interest (rather than that of the prosecution or defence) she is charged with searching for the truth, gathering evidence which might exculpate as well as incriminate the suspect. The defence rights of the accused have been somewhat neglected, in part because the public interest orientation of the *magistrat* is considered sufficient protection and also, because the accused has been seen traditionally as an object of the search for the truth, rather than a party to the proceedings.[149] This has been rectified to some extent during the *instruction*, but in the majority of cases investigated by the police under the supervision of the *procureur*, the defence has little opportunity to participate in the pre-trial investigation. One *juge d'instruction* we interviewed reflected on the fundamental differences between the two legal systems:

> It seems to me that in the English system . . . you can perhaps challenge the evidence, you can debate it, you can question the witnesses yourself, summons them to court. In France, that is not really the case. It is in the hands of the judge . . . everything has usually happened before the trial . . . everything is pretty well decided, the die is virtually cast . . . Everything depends on the conception of justice that you have. Here, we have a very state-centred conception. Justice is created by the state. We have to re-create what the parties do not say, research, establish the balance. In your country, you start from this ideal absolute that the parties are equal. It is for them to bring you the truth and you accept it. In your country, the judge stands back, he is very reluctant to intervene. Here, he can ask for additional information if he considers that the parties have not provided him with sufficient . . . In your country, the criminal law is restricted to that which offends against public order. Here, the scope is much broader. There is that, but there is also the regulation of social affairs . . . The history of our countries brings a different approach. Here, we criminalise more. Once there is a threat to the state, which binds together the national collective, we want to repress it. In your country, it is about things that threaten the individual. It is a fundamental difference. [B1]

Despite the historically state-centred approach to the investigation and prosecution of crime in France, paradoxically, the victim enjoys a more formal status and

---

[148] In practice of course, it is generally the identification of a suspect which triggers the investigation in France, just as in Britain (though an '*information contre X*' can be established where there is no suspect). Interestingly, on more than one occasion, we observed lawyers being highly critical of the investigation where it was felt that it had centred upon the construction of a case against the accused, rather than a broader search for the truth.

[149] Contrast this with her clear participation at trial, as described above.

role than in England and Wales.[150] At trial she may constitute herself as a party to the case (the *partie civile*) and claim compensation directly from the criminal court, and where no investigation or prosecution has been instituted, she may activate proceedings directly. This form of action has increased in recent years[151] and has been of particular significance in some of the most serious cases: the ability of the victim to start proceedings can be an important way of getting around the executive's influence (manifested through the inertia of the *parquet*) in political cases.[152] However, there are also concerns that this procedure is open to abuse, clogging the caseload of the *juge d'instruction* with minor affairs. Within an inquisitorial model, where the enquiry centres upon the offence rather than the suspected offender, the rights of the victim often go side by side with those of the defence.[153] During the investigation by the *juge d'instruction*, for example, the victim has gradually acquired the same rights as the suspect and this status is continually being strengthened.[154] This view of the accused and the victim as being on an equal footing has also been used to constrain the development of defence rights: the legal representation of the suspect held in police custody, it is argued, would create an imbalance, placing the interests of the defence above those of the victim.[155]

Another legacy from the inquisitorial tradition is the great emphasis which is placed upon written evidence within French criminal procedure. All official activity must be recorded in a standardised form and preserved for possible later

---

[150] The notion of the 'victim' in France also includes associations such as those representing consumers; those combating racial or sexual discrimination, sexual violence, drug addiction or crimes against humanity; those defending the disabled; or those protecting animals. See art 2-1–2-19 CPP. For a general discussion of the increasing participation in the criminal process of individual interests (including victims and organisations representing/supporting victims) see Pin (2002).

[151] Guéry (2003) suggests that it is not unusual for up to one-third of the dossiers being handled by a *juge d'instruction* to have been opened by the *partie civile* rather than the *procureur*. In the specialist section for the investigation of financial crime, located in Paris (the *pôle économique et financier* created in 1997), 77% of investigations originated with a complaint from the *partie civile*, rather than the direct instruction of the *procureur*. (Greilsamer and Schneidermann (2002:299)—Interview with Jean-Claude Marin, *avocat général* in the *Cour de cassation*).

[152] eg *magistrats* interviewed by Greilsamer and Scheidermann were critical of this tendency, viewing it as evidence of an increasingly litigious society, where people expect a remedy for the slightest of harms—50% of the investigations in the *pôle économique et financier* resulted in no action being taken. Greilsamer and Scheidermann (2002:262; 445–46). Guéry (2003) also links this tendency with the increasing criminalisation of social affairs and the desire publicly to attribute blame.

[153] This point has been raised in the context of common standards of safeguards for suspects in the EU, discussed above. This perspective has been used effectively by the then French Interior Minister, Nicolas Sarkozy, to argue that the accused enjoys protections which are (more than) adequate. As well as strengthening the rights of the victim directly, he also used this as a justification for increasing police powers, equating this with an increase in the rights of victims.

[154] See discussion of legislative change in Ch 2.

[155] Although victims have greater rights to participate in the investigation and trial of criminal offences in France than is the case in England and Wales, the then Justice Minister Dominique Perben described the criminal justice system's 'shocking anomaly which treats the victim less favourably than the accused' in his announcement to provide legal aid to victims. See *Le Monde* 13–14 October 2002.

review. The evidence collected during the investigation is placed in the case dossier (the organisation of which is provided for in the CPP), which then forms the centrepiece of the trial, the central point of reference from which the judge will question the accused. In most instances, the evidence of witnesses will be accepted in written form, with no need for live testimony.[156] Those accustomed to the oral tradition of adversarial procedure may mistrust a written statement, preferring to judge the evidence in the context of the witness presenting it.[157] For the French, on the other hand, there is a certain objectivity in the written form which avoids the manipulation of clever advocates. As a *juge d'instruction* told us:

> Here, evidence relates to what is written. In your country, it is about witnesses, with all of their subjectivity, if they are not manipulated. Here, we do not place much trust in what is said. [B1]

The European Convention on Human Rights

Madsen (2004:58) argues that when originally established in the post-war era as a means to help bring future peace to Europe, the ECHR was regarded as 'an external measure to an external threat', an international instrument modelled on the established legal traditions of countries such as France and Britain. For this reason, he suggests, neither country considered that compliance would be problematic. However, despite having a strong influence in the drafting of the Convention, both Britain and France sought to limit its impact by resisting incorporation and seeking to limit the scope of its application. Nevertheless, in the half century since its creation, the Convention has gained in strength and autonomy and its relevance and influence in matters of law and justice have also increased.[158] In France, the ECHR is now increasingly present in debate around criminal justice law reform[159] and it has led to significant changes in the major legislative projects of 1993 and 2000.[160] However, there is also resistance to this external influence (particularly from the political Right) and even among those in favour of such change, the translation of Convention guarantees into the French inquisitorial context can be problematic; the requirements of Articles 5 and 6 are often understood in adversarial terms, and are therefore not considered to be wholly appropriate to

---

[156] In the *cour d'assises*, where the most serious cases are tried, witnesses are called and may be questioned directly by the *procureur* and defence *avocat*.

[157] The adversarial trial has also been compared unfavourably with the French approach, as a storytelling exercise in which the jury must choose between two competing versions, rather than a more objective problem solving exercise. See Pollard (1996).

[158] For discussion of the development of the field of human rights in France and Britain, see Madsen (2004).

[159] See eg the Commissions preceding each of these reforms: Delmas-Marty (1991); Truche (1997).

[160] Discussed in detail in Ch 2.

French criminal procedure.[161] As outlined in the preceding section (and discussed further in Chapter 4), the development of pre-trial defence rights has been particularly challenging in this respect, creating tensions with prevailing legal cultures at the legislative, judicial and investigative level (Hodgson 2004b). Some commentators, (notably Delmas-Marty) have been critical of the hybrid procedure which has resulted from this carefully negotiated process of change, calling for more radical root and branch reform. Many of those we interviewed were also critical of the way in which the ECHR had impacted upon criminal procedure. One senior *procureur* told us:

> My personal opinion is that we have added so much [to our criminal procedure] that we have lost the essence . . . When I began my career . . . the prosecutor could remand someone in custody . . . in order to try the case the next day . . . 24 hours later, the person would **have** to be brought before a judge. People said 'This is scandalous, the *procureur* is placing someone in custody, when he is part of the prosecution, without going before a judge.' So, we had a huge change . . . so that only a *juge du siège* can place someone in custody . . . But instead of being for 24 hours, because it was the *procureur*, the chap could stay there for 2–3 days because it was a *juge du siège*. I am not convinced that the chap in prison will make this subtle distinction and that he would not prefer that it was the *procureur*, in so far as it was for a shorter time . . . all of the reforms have been like this, that is adding on, adding on, adding on . . . now it is the *juge d'instruction* . . . he has been criticised so much that he no longer carries out the actual investigation, because he no longer has the time, so he must delegate . . . it is all paperwork. And eventually, that will be the death of the *juge d'instruction*. (E4, original emphasis)

The ways in which the ECHR is understood and played out by key legal actors responsible for implementing Convention guarantees is explored in later chapters. This introductory section considers the ambivalence of the courts and the legislature towards incorporation of the Convention.

The UK operates a dualist constitutional system which requires the express enactment of Parliamentary legislation in order to incorporate international law, treaties or Conventions into domestic law. Thus, it was necessary to pass the European Communities Act 1972 in order that European law could be relied upon and applied directly in the domestic courts. The Human Rights Act 1998 achieves a similar (though not identical) objective in relation to the ECHR. France, on the other hand, has a monist constitutional system and under Article 55 of the Constitution, ratified Conventions such as the ECHR are automatically incorporated into French law[162] without the need for further legislation. Although there

---

[161] The protections under criminal procedure were indeed inspired by British law and Madsen (2004:64) suggests that this discouraged France from allowing the right of individual petition to the European Court of Human Rights.

[162] In the internal hierarchy of norms, they are considered below constitutional law but above domestic legislation.

are differences in their constitutional position, France exhibits many of the same anxieties as Britain and incorporation was initially resisted for several decades, until 1974, because of fears that this would result in a loss of sovereignty and that it would interfere unduly with France's domestic law in sensitive areas.[163] Once ratified, the superiority of the Convention (and EC law) remained contested and the issue was litigated in each of the supreme judicial bodies in France.[164] Despite the clear hierarchy of legal norms in France and the (officially) non law-making role of the judge, the judiciary has at various times been able to wield considerable power to facilitate and to frustrate the Convention's place within the French legal process. These are, of course, concerns with which commentators in the UK are familiar and in particular, the desire of the courts to retain an inherent power to determine the outcome of a case notwithstanding the Convention. For example, the English courts remain reluctant to hold that a breach of Article 6 ECHR will of itself result in a conviction being declared unsafe and so overturned under the Criminal Appeal Act 1995.[165]

France has a high rate of condemnation by the European Court, around half of the cases relating to criminal procedure. Furthermore, the condemnations relate not simply to one-off cases, but to faults which have been endemic to the French system, such as police brutality, the non-respect of defence rights and excessive periods of detention before trial.[166] The initial judicial and legislative response following the conferment of the right of individual petition was a positive one. Following a string of cases in which the European Court condemned practices such as the procedure for setting up telephone taps[167]; the absence of legal aid

---

[163] For example, the President's powers in times of war, the funding of religious schools and the treatment of people detained by the police which was, at that time, 6 days (now reduced to 4) for those suspected of offences against the state and terrorism. Sovereignty was also a sensitive issue given the involvement in the Algerian conflict in the 1950s. The right to individual petition was yet further delayed until 1981.

[164] The *Conseil constitutionnel*, the *Cour de cassation* and the *Conseil d'Etat*. See Steiner (1997:278–80).

[165] See eg *R v Chalkley and Jeffries* [1998] 2 Cr App R 79. The later decisions of *Mullen* [2000] QB 520, *Allie Mohammed v The State* [1999] 2 WLR 552 and *Togher, Doran and Parsons* [2001] Cr App R 457 are more concerned to ensure respect for the ECHR. Lord Woolf in *Togher* stated ' . . . we consider that if a defendant has been denied a fair trial it will be almost inevitable that the conviction will be regarded as unsafe.' However, two subsequent Court of Appeal cases have stated the position in more ambiguous terms. In *R v Alami and Botmeh* [2002] 1 Cr App R 28, Rose LJ stated that '. . . even if there were an assertable breach of Article 6, we would not regard that breach as, in itself, calling for any remedy other than a declaration of violation . . .' In *R v Skuse* [2002] EWCA Crim 991, Rix LJ stated that '. . . had we held that there had been a breach of Art 6(1), we consider that we would not have been bound to hold the conviction to be unsafe.'

[166] See also, the criticisms made in each of the last three reports of the European Committee for the Prevention of Torture and Inhuman and Degrading Treatment or Punishment.

[167] *Kruslin and Huvig v France* ECHR 24 April 1990. The UK was also condemned for its failure to have in place proper legal controls over the authorisation of telephone taps—*Malone v UK* (1984) 7 EHRR 14. This resulted in the 1985 Interception of Communications Act.

provision to instruct a defence lawyer[168]; the length of detention awaiting trial[169]; and the violent treatment of those detained in police detention (a period known as the *garde à vue*),[170] France responded with legislation[171] and the *Cour de cassation* took note of the European Court decisions in the development of its own jurisprudence. However, some were critical of the *Cour*, claiming that it was acting outside its legitimate role. For example, immediately after the *Huvig* and *Kruslin* cases, the Ministry of Justice issued a circular setting out the conditions under which telephone taps should be ordered and the *Cour de cassation* duly gave effect to this through its subsequent case law. Yet, in doing this, the court was criticised for usurping the legislative function by effectively adding conditions to article 81 CPP, the authority under which the *juge d'instruction* may order a telephone tap to be set up. This illustrates the tension in the judicial role, between giving effect to the Convention (a source of law which is constitutionally guaranteed to prevail over existing legislation) whilst not infringing the legislative function. A 'high point' in this positive reception of the Convention was reached in 1993, when legislation was passed[172] which put in place, among other things, a more detailed legal framework to regulate the *garde à vue* and the amount of time suspects could be detained during investigation under the *instruction* procedure.[173] However, even before the year was out, a change of Government ensured that the second half of the reform was not implemented and some of its provisions were repealed.[174]

After this first decade of enthusiasm, there then followed a period of retrenchment, leading to what the French commentator, Marguénaud(2000) describes as a 'disaster', where criminal procedure went adrift from the Convention and the attitude of the courts and legislators became increasingly one of 'arrogance'. The

---

[168] *Pham Hoang v France* ECHR 25 September 1992.

[169] *Letellier v France* ECHR 26 June 1991, *Kemmache v France* ECHR 27 November 1991.

[170] *Tomasi v France* ECHR 27 August 1992.

[171] Eg Following *Kruslin and Huvig v France* ECHR 24 April 1990, a law was passed regulating telephone tapping (Loi No 91-646). Anticipating the decision in *Pham Hoang v France* ECHR 25 September 1992, Loi No 91-647 reformed legal aid provision.

[172] This legislation was preceded by a Commission whose task was to examine the extent to which French criminal procedure was in conformity with the ECHR: chaired by Mireille Delmas-Marty (1991).

[173] The original legal framework dated back to the 1958 CPP. For discussion of the 1993 legislation see Hodgson and Rich (1993); le Gunehec (1993); Trouille (1994); Field and West (1995).

[174] Eg the *juge délégué* had been introduced in Spring 1993, responsible for determining whether or not to detain those investigated by the *juge d'instruction*. This was promptly repealed in August of the same year and the decision returned to the *juge d'instruction*. Lawyers were allowed access to suspects held in police custody, 20 hours after the start of detention. The plan had been to allow access from the start in the second stage of the reform, but this also was abandoned by the new (right wing) government. Interestingly, both of these reforms were finally legislated in the June 2000 Act, discussed below. These political legislative swings were again apparent, as the June 2000 reforms of the socialist Jospin government were overshadowed by the repressive measures introduced by the subsequent right wing administration, the then Interior Minister Nicolas Sarkozy being very active in this respect.

Cour de cassation, rather than incorporating the jurisprudence of the European Court within its own, contrived to limit the applicability of the Convention, either by distinguishing cases on tenuous and cynical grounds,[175] or holding that decisions which allowed the appellant to claim reparation had no effect upon the domestic law, so accentuating the 'declaratory' nature of European Court decisions.[176] Practices and procedures which had been clearly condemned by the European Court remained in place and unsurprisingly, this led to further findings against France.[177]

If the position of the *Cour de cassation* was ambiguous in its interpretation and application of domestic and European Convention law, this was not helped by the inactivity of the legislature: the CPP remained out of step with the Convention because of the reluctance of the legislature to effect the relevant changes required. This left a 'twilight zone' between the Convention and its jurisprudence on the one hand, and the CPP on the other, an interpretive gap which it fell to the *Cour de cassation* to fill. A clear example, is the legislature's failure to address the excessive delays highlighted by the European Court and which continued to blight the criminal justice process, resulting in a further three condemnations in October 1999.[178] The stubborn defiance of the French judges and legislators on the one hand, in contrast to the increasingly broad interpretation of the Convention developed by the new permanent European Court on the other, came to a spectacular head in July 1999, in a case of police brutality. In the case of *Selmouni,*[179] France was dealt a severe blow when the European Court unanimously held that France had violated Article 3 ECHR, not only on the grounds of inhuman and degrading treatment,[180] but more

---

[175] Resulting in another European Court condemnation, *Lambert v France* ECHR 24 August 1998.

[176] Despite the European Court's decision that there had been an unreasonable delay contrary to Art 6(1) ECHR in *Kemmache v France* ECHR 27 November 1991, the *Cour de cassation* (3 February 1993) held that the provision for reparation meant that the decision did not affect the validity of any of the procedures of the domestic law.

[177] See, eg, the line of cases concerning Art 6(1) ECHR beginning with *Poitrimol v France* ECHR 23 November 1993, the continued condemnation by the European Court and the eventual legislative response in the 2000 legislation, discussed in Hodgson (2004b). See also Massias (2000) for discussion of these cases and in particular, *Khalfaoui v France* 14 December 1999.

[178] In *Djaïd v France* ECHR 29 September 1999 the *Cour de cassation* had taken more than 2 years to decide an appeal on a point of law; in *Donsimoni v France* ECHR 5 October 1999 it took over 5 years to bring to trial an accomplice to fraud in the Tribunal Correctionnel; and in *Maini v France* ECHR 26 October 1999 the *instruction* took over four and a half years. Delay continues to be a problem: in *Rouille v France* ECHR 6 January 2004, the *instruction* took only one month short of 6 years before the case came to trial; in *Blondet v France* ECHR 5 October 2004, the delay was over 5 years; and in *Vaney v France* ECHR 30 November 2004, the accused had waited one month short of 4 years. France is not alone in this respect: German fraud proceedings took 18 years in *Eckle v Germany* [1982] ECHR 4; murder proceedings took 16 years in Italy in *Ferantelli and Santagelo v Italy* (1996) 12 EHRR 288. The UK has now also been condemned under this head in *Howarth v UK* [2001] Crim LR 229 for an unnecessary 2 year delay in dealing with an appeal.

[179] ECHR 28 July 1999.

[180] In addition to the case of *Tomasi v France* in 1992 and *Selmouni v France* 28 July 1999, France has been condemned a third time for inhuman and degrading treatment under Article 3 ECHR in April 2004. This again concerned police violence during the detention and interrogation of a suspect.

significantly, on the more serious ground of torture. This makes France only the second country (Turkey being the first) to have such a finding against it.[181]

Following the report of the Truche Commission (1997), the socialist Jospin government introduced important legislation strengthening the presumption of innocence and improving the due process rights of accused persons in line with ECHR jurisprudence. Following this, recent *Cour de cassation* decisions[182] are also indicative of a possible change in approach, which is again more receptive to the need for conformity with the Convention.[183] A number of important changes have taken place, ensuring better respect for the principle of equality of arms and a stronger commitment to open debate and public hearings through the development of a more *contradictoire* procedure. Whether this more positive approach to Strasbourg will be maintained under the current administration, however, is doubtful. The repressive reforms of the former Interior Minister, Nicolas Sarkozy, dominated the Justice agenda for several years, with the Justice Minister at that time, Dominique Perben, following in his trail with a reform project which increased substantially the powers of the police, whilst diminishing the protections in place for many suspects. The 2004 legislation extends the period during which suspects can be detained in police custody, from 48 to 96 hours in some serious cases, as well as delaying access to custodial legal advice until 36 hours after the start of the detention period, and has been described as a 'complete regression which goes directly against the European Convention on Human

---

Giovanni Rivas (a juvenile at the time) required surgical intervention after receiving a kick to the genitals by a police officer during his detention. The officer was acquitted on appeal, the French court finding that his actions were in legitimate self defence. The European Court of Human Rights rejected this explanation and awarded €15,000 damages to the complainant.

[181] *Aksoy v Turkey* (1996) 23 EHRR 553. Concern over the treatment of political detainees in Greece led to a Commission finding of torture against Greece, confirmed by the Committee of Ministers—*Greek Case* (1969) 12 YB 170.

[182] Eg *Dentico* Cass. crim., 2 March 2001, where the *Cour de cassation* held that there was a breach of Arts 6(1) and 6(3) ECHR. Reversing a long line of decisions where the defendant had been convicted in her absence under Art 410 CPP, the court held that denying legal representation to absent defendants breached their right to fair trial and to defence representation. See also *Karatas v France* ECHR 16 May 2003. The procedure in the *Cour de cassation* has also altered to enable the appellant to participate more fully. See eg *Voisine v France* ECHR 8 February 2000; *Meftah v France* and *Adoud v France* 2002; *Mefta v France* 2003.

[183] There is still criticism of what some see as the increasingly interventionist approach of the European Court. The *procureur général* of the *Cour de cassation* responded to a recent European Court decision *Dulaurans v France* ECHR 21 March 2000 (where the decision, not simply the procedure of the *Cour de cassation* was condemned) by questioning whether, just as the Franc has surrendered to the Euro, the *Cour de cassation* will have to make way for the European Court as the ultimate appeal court. Burgelin (2001). Note also the continuing line of cases in which France has been condemned for failing to allow the defence access to the reports of either the *avocat général* or the *conseiller rapporteur*. There were more than a dozen such cases in 2004. In *Cossec v France* ECHR 14 December 2004, the *avocat général*'s presence during the appeal court's deliberations was also held to be a breach of Art 6(1) ECHR. For a commentary on the role of the *procureur général* and the *avocat général* see Sainte-Rose (2003).

Rights'.[184] There are a number of factors that might account for these shifts from the earlier 'arrogance' towards Strasbourg, the subsequent softening of approach on the part of both the courts and Parliament, and the current security dominated agenda. These include changes of government; the desire to defend national sovereignty from the encroachment of an international body; concerns as to how France is regarded within the international community (notably following the shame of the *Selmouni* decision); the European Court's more robust interpretation of the Convention; and the inevitable repressive response to the events of 11 September 2001. Whatever the explanations, the fact remains that, just as the assimilation of ECHR principles into the UK legal system has been a very gradual process, so constitutional incorporation of the ECHR represents only the first stage towards bringing Convention rights into French criminal procedure. In France, as in Britain, the courts and Parliament may act to hinder, as much as to help this process.

---

[184] Representing lawyers, M Farthouat, president of the *Conseil national des barreaux*, *Le Monde* 27 September 2002, p 14. See also the opinion (27 March 2003) of the human rights body, the *commission nationale des droits de l'homme* (CNCDH) and the interview with the former Justice Minister Robert Badinter in *Le Monde* 28 January 2004.

2

Recent Legislative Trends

The relevant provisions of the *Code de procédure pénale* (CPP) and the course of their recent development are discussed in detail at relevant points throughout this book. It is useful at the outset, however, to provide a brief overview of some of the most significant recent legislative trends and the legal and political forces which shape them. The CPP is the core text governing French criminal procedure, but as governments change, criminal justice reform is characterised by swings between putting in place either greater due process protections or more repressive measures, depending on the political hue of each administration.[1] In this, the protection of the right to either *sûreté* or *sécurité* is variously invoked in support of legislative change. Inspired by the right of *habeas corpus*, the right to *sûreté* concerns the freedom from arbitrary arrest or detention and is established in the 1789 *Déclaration des droits de l'homme et du citoyen*. The right to *sécurité* is a more contemporary theme, firmly established in the legislation of 21 January 1995 (and then redefined in the statute of 15 November 2001), as a condition of the exercise of freedoms and the reduction of inequality. The reduction of inequality has now been dropped and the first article of the legislation passed on 18 March 2003 now declares the right of *sécurité* as a fundamental right and one of the conditions for the exercise of individual and collective freedoms.[2]

The need to demonstrate conformity with the ECHR has been an increasing feature of French criminal procedure over the last decade and the inspiration for two major commissions.[3] However, this has become a point of tension as law and order measures and strategies to reduce the fear of crime have come to dominate

---

[1] This dialectic has been apparent for over a century: the reform of 1897 allowing those before the *juge d'instruction* access to a lawyer provoked similar debate. The '*Sécurité et Liberté*' legislation of 2 February 1981 was revised and repealed in part by the law of 10 June 1983. A similar fate was visited upon the law of 4 January 1993 with the passing of legislation later than year, 24 August 1993. The 15 June 2000 legislation has been amended by the laws of 4 March 2002, 9 September 2002 and 18 March 2003. See also Gleizal (2001) for a discussion of the politics of *la sécurité*.

[2] Lazerges (2003:645–46).

[3] The Delmas-Marty Commission 1991 (*commission justice pénale et droits de l'homme*) and the Truche Commission 1997 (*commission de réflexion sur la Justice*), discussed below.

the political agenda of both the Left and the Right,[4] encouraged by the position of the far Right in French politics since the 1980s and particularly during the presidential election campaign of 2002. In this way, despite the apparent stability of a codified procedure setting out clear principles, in France as in England and Wales, short-term political policies impact significantly on criminal justice, resulting in an instability of direction.

The Strengthening of Due Process Protections

The reforms of 1993 and 2000 made important changes to French criminal procedure, strengthening the rights both of the accused and the victim; providing clearer legal regulation of the exercise of police power; and making the decision making of *magistrats* more accountable. Each was preceded by a commission charged with examining the criminal justice process and each was concerned to ensure better conformity between French criminal procedure and the ECHR.

The January 1993 Reform

The 1993 legislation[5] followed the report of the Criminal Justice and Human Rights Commission (*Commission justice pénale et droits de l'homme*), chaired by professor Mireille Delmas-Marty (1991). The approach of the commission was to avoid the traditional constraints of the adversarial/inquisitorial dichotomy and to move towards a criminal justice process that was more strongly based upon the requirements of the ECHR. It was hoped that this would respect better the principle of equality of arms than is the case in inquisitorial procedure, whilst at the same time being more effective than accusatorial systems.[6] Although rejecting the

---

[4] Within this debate, youth crime, inter-agency and community-based strategies (*justice de proximité*; *police de proximité*; *contrats locaux de sécurité* etc) and the perceived rise in anti-social behaviour have played an important part. Embracing all of these, a major focus of the debate around law and order, policing and fear of crime, is the problem of the *banlieues*, (literally suburbs) a term used to refer to 'deprived areas, generally on the outskirts of cities, which experience a combination of educational, economic, urban and safety problems' (de Maillard and Roché, 2004:131). Characterised by high levels of unemployment and social exclusion, the *banlieue* is seen as the heartland of France's disaffected youth. For a brief overview of the key literature in this area see de Maillard and Roché (2004). Alongside repressive measures, the Interior Minister has also recognised the need to address the marginalisation of those in deprived areas: 'It is our responsibility . . . if we want to fight for republican values such as secularity, we must ensure that republican values are accessible to all.' (*Le Monde* 19 November 2003, p 10). For a different perspective on the concerns of young people and their disillusionment with the state and the authority it wields, see Mucchielli (1999).

[5] Loi No 93-2 of 4 January 1993 (amended by the 'reform of the reform', Loi No 93-1013 of 4 August 1993). For further discussion of the reform, see Hodgson and Rich (1993); le Gunehec (1993); Trouille (1994); Field and West (1995).

[6] Delmas-Marty (1991:107).

commission's more radical suggestions of root and branch reform which would separate out more clearly the investigative and judicial functions of *magistrats*, the legislation introduced a number of important new measures, many of which were similar to those provided in England and Wales by the Police and Criminal Evidence Act (PACE) 1984, including some key rights for suspects. A new procedure aimed at reducing the number of people detained in custody during the *instruction* was put in place, as well as a clearer framework for the legal regulation of the police detention of suspects. This included an obligation on the police to inform the *procureur* of a person's detention at the start of the *garde à vue* (GAV) and new rights for the suspect to inform someone of her detention in custody; to see a doctor; and to see a lawyer, 20 hours after the start of the detention period.[7] There was much resistance to the appearance, for the first time, of the defence lawyer in the GAV, with mass demonstrations by *magistrats* and the symbolic burning of copies of the CPP. Plans to allow custodial legal advice from the start of the detention period were immediately dismantled by the new right-wing government which took office during 1993 and a number of the original provisions were removed in the amending legislation in August of the same year.[8] The defence role during the instruction was also strengthened in the earlier reform and in order to demonstrate more clearly the presumption of innocence, the term *inculpation* was replaced with *mise en examen* to describe the process whereby a person is under the investigation of the *juges d'instruction*.

The June 2000 Reform

In January 1997, in the wake of a number of *affaires* which had seen high-ranking politicians as well as influential business people implicated in financial scandals,[9] President Chirac established the *Commission de réflexion sur la justice*, chaired by the president of the *Cour de cassation*, Pierre Truche.[10] As well as the perennial concerns with the delays, cost and complexity of the justice process, the commission was alerted to the fact that 'our fellow citizens suspect the justice system of sometimes being subject to government influence and of failing to guarantee sufficiently the respect of individual rights, in particular, the presumption of innocence.'[11] There had been controversy surrounding ministerial interference in some matters, which it was felt had been designed to protect politicians and powerful

---

[7] This is discussed more fully in Ch 4.

[8] Eg the newly created *juge délégué* who was responsible for decisions re the detention of those under investigation in the *instruction* procedure was abandoned and the decision reverted to the *juge d'instruction*.

[9] See eg Godard (2002). Ironically, President Chirac himself later came under suspicion, but the *Cour de cassation* has ruled that he enjoys immunity during the period of his presidency.

[10] Truche had also sat on the 1991 *commission justice pénale et droits de l'homme*.

[11] *Lettre de mission* from President Chirac to the commission, January 1997.

business people.[12] The commission was required to work rapidly and reported in July 1997 on both the presumption of innocence and the relationship between parliament, government and the justice process. This resulted in the June 2000 reform which sought to strengthen the protection of the presumption of innocence and the rights of victims.[13] The legislation was part of a broader reform package which included measures already enacted in June of 1999 to simplify and clarify aspects of criminal procedure and to reduce delay,[14] as well as two related projects to strengthen the independence of the *procureur* from the hierarchical control of the Minister of Justice and to change the way in which *magistrats* are selected. These latter two reforms required a constitutional amendment and so a three-fifths majority vote in Parliament. Although enjoying broad political support to begin with, this was withdrawn at the last moment and the special sitting of Parliament due to take place in January 2000 was cancelled by the President, Jacques Chirac.[15] The projects were subsequently abandoned and the professional governing body of the *magistrature*, the *Conseil supérieur de la magistrature* declared itself no longer opposed to the Minister of Justice giving instructions in individual cases.[16]

Like the 1993 legislation, the June 2000 project introduced a number of bold reforms, many of them clearly designed to bring France more closely into line with the ECHR. A new preliminary article now sits at the head of the CPP, setting out the basic principles of criminal procedure such as equality of arms, the presumption of innocence, the right to a defence and the right for accused persons to know the nature of the charges they face. Avoiding the traditional adversarial/inquisitorial dichotomy, this article is grounded instead in the principle of *contradictoire*, the notion that all parties should have the same right and opportunity to

---

[12] For earlier examples, see Magendie and Gomez (1986).

[13] Loi No 2000-516 of 15 June 2000, *renforçant la protection de la présomption d'innocence et les droits des victimes*. For further discussion of this reform, see Hodgson (2002b).

[14] Loi No 99-515 of 23 June 1999, *renforçant l'efficacité de la procédure pénale*. This legislation establishes a wide range of alternatives to prosecution (France's so called 'third way') which the *procureur* can propose to the accused. They include measures such as the issuing of a formal warning; requiring the accused to carry out up to 60 hours of unpaid work for the community; suspension of a driving or hunting licence for up to four months; and paying compensation to the victim. The accused may consult with a lawyer before deciding whether or not to accept the suggested alternative to prosecution. Although no prosecution can be brought, if the victim is later identified, she may claim compensation before the criminal court in the same way as if a prosecution had been brought.

[15] See further the interview with Valéry Turcey, president of the *Union syndicale des magistrats* (USM), who attributes the failure of the reform, to the Justice Minister's attempt to sell it differently to politicians and to the *magistrature*. Greilsamer and Schneidermann (2002:424).

[16] See *Le Monde* 26–27 May 2002, p 10. This had been at the heart of many of the *affaires*. Since 1993, instructions were required to be given in writing and placed in the dossier and from 1997, the socialist Justice Minister Elisabeth Guigou voluntarily ceased the practice altogether, in anticipation of her proposed reform. The Raffarin administration has not sought to take up the proposals, but has instead underlined the hierarchical control exercised by the Minister of Justice in the controversial legislation of 2004, discussed below (known as Perben 2).

participate and be heard in the criminal process. More specific provisions were also introduced, such as the improvement of the due process rights of the suspect held in police detention. Building on the earlier reform of 1993, these changes included allowing custodial legal advice from the start of detention, rather than after 20 hours; requiring the police, for the first time, to inform the suspect of her right to silence (since repealed) and of the nature of the offence for which she is being detained. The power to detain witnesses in police custody was also removed; there were again measures to reduce the number of people kept in custody whilst being investigated under the *instruction* procedure; a new right of appeal from the *cour d'assises* was introduced; and provisions to assist victims of crime, both in their reception at the point of reporting and by providing them with the same opportunities as the accused to participate in the *instruction* procedure.[17] Of particular significance for the defence was the widening in scope of article 82-1 CPP, giving the parties the same right as the *procureur* (under article 82 CPP) to request that the *juge d'instruction* carry out any act which they consider would assist in the search for the truth. Whilst previously the parties were permitted to request that they or a named witness be interviewed, that a confrontation be held, or that the *juge* visit the crime scene, their requests may now include the conduct of searches, the interception of mail or placing a person under investigation. The *juge d'instruction* may refuse to carry out these acts, but she must give written reasons and her decision is subject to appeal. In the view of some *magistrats*, this gives the defence lawyer the opportunity to become a kind of co-director in the *instruction* process.[18]

The reform represented a major achievement in strengthening the due process aspects of French criminal procedure and promoted a discourse which takes more seriously the jurisprudence of the ECHR. Notions of equality of arms and of open debate were increasingly cited as guarantees of fairness and incorporated into the various stages of criminal procedure.[19] In introducing and defending her reform project, the then Justice Minister, Elisabeth Guigou, made frequent reference to the importance of the rights of the defence in any fair and equitable criminal process and the need to balance these against the effectiveness of the criminal investigation. These were not portrayed as mutually contradictory as had often been the case in the past,[20] but as complementary principles: affording the accused

---

[17] See further Hodgson (2002b: 792–93). For a broader discussion of the increasing participation of individual parties (including victims) in the investigation and disposition of cases, see Pin (2002).

[18] See Greilsamer and Schneidermann (2002:194). The defence role is discussed extensively in Ch 4.

[19] The principle of *contradictoire*, as it is known, is seen, for example, in the introduction of public bail hearings (for *détention provisoire* during *instruction*); public hearings before the *chambre d'instruction* (formerly the *chambre d'accusation*) at the request of the accused, unless this threatens the security of the *instruction* or a third party; and the ability of the lawyers representing the parties to question directly witnesses at court.

[20] See eg Vroom (1988), who describes the underlying values of the French criminal process in crime control terms: the freedom of the individual is best protected through the provision of broad legal powers for the repression of crime.

greater protections was seen to enhance the fairness of the procedure and so, ultimately, to legitimate the investigation and trial process.[21]

However, it is important to see these changes within the context of the very different process of criminal justice in place at that time in France: where the police were not obliged to tell the suspect either of her right to silence or of the nature of the enquiry in connection with which she was being held; where the suspect held in police custody had access to a defence lawyer only after 20 hours of detention, and then for only half an hour (an arrangement which meant that in practice, less than 10 per cent of people held in GAV were able to consult with their lawyer)[22]; where witnesses against whom there was no suspicion of having committed an offence could be held in GAV; and where there was no appeal against conviction for the most serious offences, *crimes*, tried in the *cour d'assises*. Even taking into account the different historical roots and legal culture of French criminal justice as a procedure dominated by the guarantee of judicial supervision, these were significant deficiencies. In many instances the reforms were essential to ensure compliance with the ECHR as required by Article 55 of the French Constitution. In others, they were clearly necessary to avoid further condemnation under the Convention.[23] The excessive length of time some suspects spend in prison while the investigation is ongoing and before any decision to prosecute has been taken has been the frequent subject of litigation before the European Court. Famously, in the case of *Tomasi v France* a detention period of over five and a half years before acquittal was held to be unjustified.[24] This has been a long-standing thorn in the side of Justice Ministers and the introduction of the *juge des libertés et de la détention* (JLD) to decide issues of detention during investigation, like its short-lived 1993 predecessor the *juge délegué*, was designed to go some way to alleviate the problem.[25] A second issue which has seen France brought before the European Court on a number of occasions, concerned the obligation upon the appellant to surrender into the custody of the *Cour de cassation* before the appeal hearing. Following a string of cases in which France was found to have breached Article 6(1) ECHR, failure to surrender into the custody of the *Cour de cassation* will no longer result in the automatic rejection of the appeal.[26] Thirdly,

---

[21] In contrast, the official Ministry of Justice circulars sought to reassure the police in particular, that their powers remained largely unchanged. See further the discussion in Ch 5.

[22] According to the then Justice Minister, Mme Guigou, in her address to the *Sénat*, 15 June 1999.

[23] See further Hodgson (2002b; 2004b).

[24] [1992] ECHR 53. For other examples, see Bell (1999:365, fn35); Marguénaud (2000); Bell (2001:111).

[25] This was the tenth time such a reform had been discussed in parliament (*Libération* 23 March 1999). See further Robert (1992). 80 % of those in prison were in pre-trial detention—around half of them on the order of the *juge d'instruction*.

[26] *Poitrimol v France* ECHR 23 November 1993; *Omar v France* and *Guérin v France* ECHR 29 July 1998; *Coquin v France* ECHR 15 February 1994. Also *Khalfaoui v France* ECHR 14 December 1999; *Papon v France* ECHR 25 July 2002. Contrast with *Rebboah* Cass. crim., 30 June 1999, where the *Cour de cassation* effected what one commentator (Delmas Saint-Hilaire, 2001) described as a u-turn in its jurisprudence. The European Court repeatedly made it clear that dismissal of the appeal in these circumstances was a disproportionate response which breached the fair trial provisions of Art 6 ECHR.

France has failed to take account of decisions of the European Court in individual cases, where the accused has been found to have been treated unfairly. France was heavily criticised for its refusal to re-open a case after it had been condemned in 1997 under the ECHR for failing to respect the rights of the defence[27]: Abdelhamid Hakkar was convicted in his absence and without defence representation, of murdering a police officer.[28] The only other European country failing to re-open a case considered unfair under the ECHR is Turkey. The June reform finally amended article 626-1 CPP to ensure that in future, such cases can be re-opened at the request of any of the parties involved.[29]

The Return to Repression

Whilst the 2000 reform represents something of a high point in the legislation of due process protections and ECHR guarantees, the right wing Raffarin administration which took office in 2002 pursued a wholly different agenda, making security and repression its priority,[30] through a legislative programme dominated by the Minister of the Interior, rather than the Minister of Justice. The political rhetoric has changed: the rights and freedoms of the individual are no longer protected by the provision of due process rights, but through the repression of criminal conduct. Security is now described as a 'fundamental right and the most important freedom'.[31]

---

[27] See eg the discussion reported in *Le Monde* 16 February 2000. See also *Reinhardt and Slimane Kaïd v France* ECHR 31 March 1998; *Slimane Kaïd v France* ECHR 25 January 2000; *Voisine v France* ECHR 8 February 2000.

[28] The right to legal representation, even where the defendant is absent, has now been accepted by the full chamber of the *Cour de cassation* in the case of *Dentico* heard on 2 March 2001 (00-81.388, No. 473 P). This reverses a long line of decisions and is significant in holding that Art 410 CPP (which allows the case to be heard in the defendant's absence) is contrary to Art 6 ECHR if the accused is tried in her absence and the court refuses to hear from her defence. See Pradel's case note (2001b).

[29] For a brief account of the process of deciding whether to refer cases for re-trial (including in the case of *Hakkar*) see Barberot (2002). For a discussion of some of the broader issues to be addressed in the process of re-opening a case see Doroy (2003).

[30] It is variously described as '*ultra sécuritaire*', '*tout-répressif*' and dominated by a perspective which is entirely *policière*.

[31] Presentation of the *projet de loi pour la sécurité intérieure* by the then Interior Minister, Nicolas Sarkozy, to the *conseil des ministres* (equivalent to the British Cabinet) 23 October 2002. This is a return to the discourse of the 1980s—see eg the description by Vroom (1988). For a detailed analysis of the politics of *sécurité* and *insécurité*, see Roché (1993) and also Dieu (1999). See also the interview of the former Justice Minister Robert Badinter (*Le Monde* 28 January 2004), who criticises the government's rhetoric of 'rights' and its policy of confusing *sécurité* (involving repressive powers for the protection of people and property) with *sûreté* (protected in the *Déclaration des droits de l'homme*, a fundamental right of the citizen not to be subjected to excessive or arbitrary state power). Whilst the latter can be described as a right, the former cannot. The pursuit of *sécurité*, he argues, must not be at the expense of the citizen's right to *sûreté*.

The November 2001 Reform

However, the genesis of this shift can be traced to a period which pre-dates the change of government. The move away from the aspirational rhetoric of the June 2000 project, towards a discourse increasingly concerned with law and order, was already apparent as the socialist Jospin administration drew to a close. In the face of widespread opposition to the June 2000 reforms from police and *magistrats*, the Ministry of Justice circulars accompanying the legislation sought to undercut the force of many of the changes and a 'reform of the reform' was legislated in March 2002, diluting some of the original measures.[32] In early 2001, with rising crime figures[33] and the prospect of local elections the government began placing increasing emphasis on *sécurité* rather than prevention[34] and Daniel Vaillant, the then Interior Minister, put forward a broad reform project, the *loi relative à la sécurité quotidienne*. By the end of the year, as thoughts turned now to the general election campaign as well as the inevitably repressive response to the events of September 11, the stakes were raised and government preoccupation became almost exclusively with 'law and order' and in particular the problems of youth crime.[35] In November 2001 the highly controversial *loi relative à la sécurité quotidienne* was passed.[36] Originally conceived of to deal with more mundane matters of domestic law and order, immediately following the events of 11 September 2001 13 'anti-terrorist' amendments were subsequently added through an emergency procedure, allowing no time for proper parliamentary debate. The legislation has been described as a 'contradiction in terms',[37] an inco-

---

[32] For more detailed discussion of these, see Hodgson (2002b) and Ch 4 below.

[33] The quantification of crime has continued to be a hotly debated, but nonetheless major influence on criminal justice policy and Interior Minister Nicolas Sarkozy set up the *Observatoire de la délinquance* in 2003. The Right pointed to the increasing crime figures and the inability of the Left to tackle the issue head on. The Left argued that the figures reflected the increase in reporting (a better reception for victims of crime being one of the measures taken in the June 2000 project) and that they needed to be seen in their proper context e.g 50% of robbery from the person in Paris concerned the taking of mobile phones. See e.g *Le Monde* 23 June 2001; 2 August 2001.

[34] In particular, through *contrats locaux de sécurité*. Launched in 1997, this initiative is designed to encourage local multi-agency co-operation. By June 2001, 500 contracts had been signed, with 200 more in the pipeline. These 700 cover 88% of the urban population of France—see *Le Monde* 25 June 2001. Linked to this drive to increase the local governance of law and order measures has been the introduction of a system of *police de proximité* across France (established by the 1995 *loi d'orientation pour la sécurité*). This is very much linked to the idea of community policing, having more officers on the ground, in greater contact with local residents. (See eg the discussion of this initiative in the Parisian context in Renaudie (2000)). The Left has traditionally favoured a policy of prevention and spoken only of the 'feeling of insecurity'. (See further Roché, 1993). These initiatives are designed to move away from the dichotomy between prevention and security, by combining aspects of both.

[35] The problem of youth crime was a major issue for all parties in the run-up to the elections. Not only were juveniles allegedly committing more offences, but it was claimed that these were increasingly violent and committed by increasingly younger offenders.

[36] Loi No 2001-1062 of 15 November 2001, *relative à la sécurité quotidienne*.

[37] Evelyne Sire-Marin, president of the *Syndicat de la magistrature*, interviewed by Rancé (2002a:220).

herent amalgamation of measures which ranges from road traffic matters, credit card fraud and offences dealing with rave parties, to terrorism, across its 70 articles.[38] Regarded by many as a smoke screen, enabling police powers to be increased in what would otherwise be considered unacceptable ways,[39] the 'anti-terrorist' measures have attracted the greatest criticism both in the scope of their application and the anti-democratic way in which they have been rushed on to the statute book, precluding any proper consideration of their constitutional implications. Those charged with applying the provisions note that they include measures which have been declared unconstitutional when presented in earlier legislative projects,[40] leading some *magistrats* to question their compatibility with ECHR principles of freedom of movement, protection of one's home and the right to privacy.[41] In recognition of their exceptional character,[42] the anti-terrorist measures were legislated initially for only a two year period, but critics point out that once in place, there is a process of acclimatisation whereby such temporary measures become 'normalised' and are unlikely to be removed from the statute book.[43] This has already proved to be the case: the measures have been extended for a further two years and powers such as those relating to the search of vehicles have been extended to cover non-terrorist offences.[44] Furthermore, measures such as these, concerning criminal procedure and the rights and liberties of the individual are generally the responsibility of the Justice Minister. Yet, it was the Interior Minister Daniel Vaillant who presented these initial reforms alongside those addressing security and public order,[45] leading to a more general criticism of the increasingly prominent role played by the Interior Minister in matters which are properly the domain of the Minister of Justice.[46] As one com-

---

[38] Gozzi (2002) argues that 'It is intolerable that such serious measures are incorporated into a "catch-all" text which does not distinguish between the person who commits a speeding offence and who plants a bomb'.

[39] See eg *Le Monde* 1 November 2001.

[40] The November 2001 law allows the police to search vehicles on a public road in a specified area and for a fixed time, with the written permission of the *procureur*. A similar provision was declared unconstitutional by the *Conseil constitutionnel* 12 January 1977. See Gozzi (2002:2).

[41] At the start of December, only weeks after the legislation was passed, the *Syndicat de la magistrature* (SM) invited *magistrats* not to apply the most 'arbitrary' provisions of the reform. See *Le Monde* 16–17 December 2001. See also the comments of Marin, president of the SM in Rancé (2002a).

[42] As evidence of the exceptional nature of these measures, a member of the *Sénat* is quoted as saying 'I am assured that after 31 December 2003, we will return to the legality of the Republic. I hope that we will return to this before then.' Gozzi (2002:1).

[43] Daniel Lochak, professor of law from the University of Paris-X-Nanterre, argues that the only justification for a temporary measure is when the law is of an experimental nature, such as that relating to the termination of pregnancies or more recently, bioethics. He notes that measures in 1981 re identity checks and 1986 re visa requirements were never removed. (*Le Monde* 1 November 2001).

[44] *Loi pour la sécurité intérieure* 18 March 2003.

[45] Similarly, it was the then Interior Minister, Nicolas Sarkozy, who presented the March 2003 reform.

[46] See also Ch 3 for discussion of the relative standing and relationship between these two ministerial posts.

mentator described it, 'this gives the impression that we have two Ministers of Police in France'.[47]

The Raffarin Administration: Sarkozy's Vision, Autumn 2002

This increasing preoccupation with repression (rather than prevention) which dominated the final year of Jospin's government and became the primary electoral battleground, has become the cornerstone of the Raffarin administration's approach to both home affairs and justice. *Sécurité* is the key issue driving a broad range of legislative reforms (described by one left-wing lawyers' union as a 'frenzy of repression')[48] which include increases in police numbers; a restructuring of the jurisdiction of competence of police/*gendarmes*; the widening of police powers; the introduction of new offences; new sanctions and procedures to deal with juvenile offenders; more offences dealt with by the rapid trial procedure; and the attenuation of suspects' rights. And just as we saw in the latter months of the Jospin government, despite the fact that the policies implemented through these projects impact directly on the *Code pénal* and the *Code de procédure pénale*, their discussion and presentation were dominated by the then Interior Minister, Nicolas Sarkozy.[49] In the government's 'war on crime', it is Sarkozy who prepared the battle plan.[50] This blurring of roles has been widely criticised: in defining new criminal offences and proposing changes to criminal procedure,[51] the Interior Minister is seen to be encroaching on the territory of the Minister of Justice and therefore threatening the balance of responsibilities.[52] For his part, the Minister of Justice is criticised for his timidity, his lack of engagement with justice issues and his deference to the policy initiatives of the 'omnipresent' Interior Minister.[53] There has been

---

[47] Sire-Marin, interviewed by Rancé (2002a).

[48] These were the words of the president of the *Syndicat des avocats de France*, Bruno Marcus. (*Le Monde* 12 July 2002, p 9).

[49] M. Sarkozy always described himself as working hand in hand with the Justice Minister, but he was clearly the driving force and the projects were first presented by him. Thus, although later split into 2 projects, the *projet de loi pour la sécurité intérieur* (sponsored by the Minister of the Interior and legislated in March 2003) and the *loi sur l'adaptation des moyens de la justice aux evolutions de la criminalité* (sponsored by the Minister of Justice and legislated in 2004), the basis of these reforms was originally set out in Autumn 2002 in a single proposal by the Interior Minister (discussed below).

[50] *Le Monde* 17 July 2002.

[51] In particular, by changing parts of the June 2000 legislation, the important balance ensuring conformity with the ECHR would be altered.

[52] Géraldine Thomas, speaking on behalf of the left wing judges' union, the *Union syndicale des magistrats* in *Le Monde* 12 July 2002, p 9.

[53] The president of the *Union syndicale des magistrats*, Dominique Barella, described the Justice Minister as the secretary of state to the Minister of the Interior. '. . . everybody in the government is interfering in criminal justice policy . . . moreover, your absence in the debates on the legal reform presented by the Minister of the Interior has concerned us.' (*Le Monde* 20–21 October 2002).

some public disagreement though. Immersed in a 'culture of results',[54] Sarkozy called repeatedly for harsher sentences for recidivists as a way of reducing the increasing number of crimes of violence against the person. This would reverse the trend in place since the 1970s, of making sentences more appropriate to the individual rather than operating a tariff system and the then Justice Minister, M. Perben, publicly opposed such a move and underlined the importance of retaining judicial discretion: 'Justice is not a multiple choice questionnaire'.[55]

Although subsequently divided into several pieces of legislation, Nicolas Sarkozy's overarching plan was first set out in one policy document in Autumn 2002. It specified new public order offences relating to prostitution, begging, squatters and travellers. It proposed allowing the police greater powers to access information from a range of public bodies and to take DNA samples. The detention of 16–18 year olds in GAV would be extended without any need to present the suspect before the *procureur*, as is the case for adults and the period during which offences could be investigated under the *flagrance* procedure (which allows the police greater powers) would be doubled from 8 to 16 days.[56] It was also proposed that coercive powers currently available only under the supervision of the *juge d'instruction*, such as searches at night or without the consent of the individual, or the use of telephone taps, would be available to the police directly. In this way, the police would continue to investigate serious offences under the more distant supervision of the *procureur*, without the need to pass responsibility for the case over to the more independent *juge d'instruction*. This has been criticised as an unwarranted interference with the judicial control of the police and the protection of the rights of the individual: increasing the powers of the police whilst

---

[54] The Interior Minister showed a keenness for quantitative accountability, with greater emphasis on crime figures and police clear-up rates. See also his announcement of the creation of an '*observatoire de la délinquance*' 14 January 2003. Interestingly, in his closing speech at the national meeting on *contrats locaux de sécurité* on June 25, Jospin announced a new measure of delinquency which would measure the extent to which feelings of insecurity (fear of crime) were reduced. See also the major press conference organised by Sarkozy on 14 January 2004, in which he announced the latest crime statistics. *Le Monde* reported (16 January 2004, p 10): 'The Interior Minster's taste for statistics also led him to cite the number of arrests connected with Islamic, Corsican and Basque terrorism (65119 and 48 people) as if that were an indication of quality, allowing one to measure the effectiveness of specialist services.' Although announcing increases in police activity (GAV rose by 12%) the corresponding rise in reported police violence (560 cases in 2002, 611 in 2003) was, of course, not discussed. See *Le Monde* 28 January 2004. The Justice Minister has also moved in this direction, recommending that *magistrats* should be paid a bonus for their 'productivity'. This has been opposed by the unions (*Le Monde* 3 December 2002) who claim that it threatens to undermine their independence (*Le Monde* 25 September 2003), but welcomed as a necessary form of modernisation and accountability by others (*Le Monde* 14 January 2004).
[55] *Le Monde* 15 December 2003; 13 January 2004.
[56] *Enquêtes préliminaires* are ordinary investigations; *enquêtes de flagrance* (defined in Art 53 CPP) are those concerning 'recently' committed offences and the police are afforded greater powers in these instances—for example, to search premises without the suspect's permission. Around 85% of offences investigated are classified as *flagrant*. This figure is in part an artefact as many investigations begun on police initiative *en préliminaire* will be unsuccessful and so will not appear in the official statistics—or some may be successful and may be turned into an *enquête de flagrance* if possible. See also Lévy (1987:56–61).

keeping more cases under the supervision of the *procureur* (who is hierarchically accountable to the Minister of Justice) would strengthen the influence of the executive, whilst further marginalising the role of the *juge d'instruction* and therefore weakening the control exercised by the independent judiciary.

It is the proposed changes to the GAV regime which perhaps demonstrate most clearly the repressive and authoritarian approach of this project and the government's determination to stifle the due process reforms of the previous administration. It was proposed that the extended detention of those suspected of terrorism and drugs trafficking (where they might be held for 96 hours, rather than up to 48 hours) would apply to a range of serious crimes and to all offences involving 'organised crime'. Custodial legal advice would be available not at the start of the GAV, but only after 36 hours in cases of rape, attempted murder, torture and aggravated violence and the obligation upon the police to inform the suspect of the right to silence would be removed. No evidence was advanced to support the need for these new measures, which many viewed as regressive and contrary to the ECHR, setting the GAV back some 20 years in terms of the progress made on individual rights and ECHR compliance. It would represent a return to the '*exception française*' whereby the GAV was a legal grey area which left the suspect to face the all-powerful police alone.[57]

Unsurprisingly, the reform agenda has been well received by the police—in particular, the financial commitment made in July 2002 to provide additional personnel and equipment. Increases in the investigative powers of the police and the diminution of the rights of suspects are seen by most as making criminal procedure more effective , 'redressing the balance' which was upset by the 'hybrid' 2000 reform.[58] There has been concern in some police quarters, however, at the government's increasing tendency towards criminalisation, rather than addressing the social and economic causes of anti-social behaviour.[59]

The September 2002 Reform

These proposals have now found their way into a number of legislative projects, with responsibility divided between the Minister of Justice and the Minister of the Interior. The Minister of Justice has presented two Bills to parliament. The first,

[57] See eg the editorial in *Le Monde* 27 September 2002, p 20, which describes the police vision of society adopted by the government: 'The approach to the *garde à vue* illustrates the ultra-security tone of the project, giving more elbow room to the police, marginalising *magistrats* and making the exception the rule.'

[58] See eg the comments of André-Michel Ventre, the general secretary of the *Syndicat des commissaires et hauts fonctionnaires de la police nationale* (*Le Monde* 27 September 2002, p 14).

[59] Nicolas Couteau, spokesperson for the *Syndicat général de la police*, considered the changes to be largely in the right direction, but criticised moves to punish beggars, rather than giving them the means to keep off the streets: 'After beggars, who next? The unemployed?' He also expressed concern over the new offence of gathering in building hallways: 'Putting young people in prison will solve nothing. What you need is to create a social mix in these neighbourhoods.' (*Le Monde* 27 September 2002).

the *projet de loi d'orientation et de programmation pour la justice* (LOPJ)[60] was passed in September 2002, using the more rapid 'urgency procedure'. Inevitably, this attracted criticism, given the profound changes proposed—the introduction of a new type of lay judge, the *juge de proximité*[61]; new types of incarceration for the young[62]; more offenders being remanded in custody for longer with a new right of appeal for the *procureur* against bail[63]; the extension of the more rapid *comparution immédiate* procedure to offences punishable by a sentence of imprisonment of between 6 months and 10 years[64]; and a new accelerated procedure for the trial of juveniles.[65] There was also concern that the balance of defence rights struck in the June 2000 reform (which received all party support) would be upset; and overturning provisions relating to pre-trial detention[66] at a time when the prison population is in crisis (and given France's poor record on this issue before the European Court) was, inevitably, seen as a retrograde step.[67]

The establishment of *juges de proximité*, lay judges with jurisdiction over relatively minor offences, was designed to relieve the pressure of increasingly high court caseloads and so to help speed up the justice process.[68] Although the concept of *justice de proximité* has been in place since the end of the 1980s, notably with the advent of alternative forms of case disposition such as mediation, this new form of judge was received unfavourably by *magistrats*, who regarded the initiative as introducing a sub-standard form of justice which offered little advantage over the existing system of the single professional judge, the *juge d'instance*.[69]

---

[60] Loi No 2002-1138 of 9 September 2002, *d'orientation et de programmation pour la justice*. Designed to 'simplify and to reinforce the effectiveness of criminal justice'—Ministry of Justice circular 10 September 2002, setting out the reform in tabular form.

[61] The first eight of these new judges took office in Paris on 15 October 2003.

[62] See Castaignède (2003) for a discussion of the impact of the reform upon juvenile justice.

[63] Significantly, this has the effect of suspending the decision to bail the accused, who must remain in custody until the appeal is heard.

[64] Art 395 CPP. Previously, it was only available for offences with a maximum sentence of between one and seven years. Compare Germany, where the accelerated procedure (*beschleunigte Verfahren*) allows cases to be sent directly to trial, without the need for the usual 'intermediate stage,' where the guilt of the accused appears straightforward and the offence carries a maximum penalty of less than one year in prison.

[65] Called *jugement à délai rapproché*, this procedure is applicable for juveniles aged 16 to 18, charged with *délits* punishable by at least three years imprisonment, or five years where *en flagrance* (Ord 1945, art 14-2, I–V). For those aged 13 to 16, the offence must be punishable by five to seven years imprisonment (Ord 1945, art 14-2, VI).

[66] The threshold of charges for which a person can be detained in pre-trial custody has been lowered to those carrying a sentence of three or more years imprisonment, Art 143-1 CPP.

[67] The widening of the *comparution immédiate* procedure and the increased role for the *procureur* in bail decisions was considered by the opposition senators to 'massacre the law on the presumption of innocence, which was both desired by Jacques Chirac and voted for unanimously in this Assembly.' (*Le Monde* 28–29 July 2002).

[68] For an account, see Moutouh (2002).

[69] Evelyne Sire-Marin, president of the SM (but speaking on behalf of 11 organisations), suggests that the introduction of the new *juge de proximité* will eventually replace the *juge d'instance*. She points to the plan to merge the two court levels of *instance* and *grand instance*, as well as the shortfall in the number of *magistrats* recruited. (Moutouh, 2002)

When the reform was introduced, *juges d'instance* in the *tribunal de police* (the court trying minor offences) could refer cases on to mediators as an alternative to trial and around half of these were successful. Ironically, it is just these cases that will be dealt with by the new *juge de proximité*, threatening to increase rather than reduce the caseload of the courts, by bringing to trial cases which would normally be diverted out of the system.[70] There was also some debate as to whether the government was empowered to interfere with the judiciary in this way; it was determined that the measure was not in itself unconstitutional, but a special *loi organique* was required, rather than an ordinary piece of legislation.[71] This has not allayed the fears of the *magistrature* who remain uneasy that the manner of their appointment provides insufficient guarantee as to the independence of the new *juges*: appointed locally, with little training and for a fixed term, there is a real concern that conflicts of interest will taint the quality of justice delivered.[72]

The provisions relating to the treatment of juvenile offenders have also aroused considerable controversy. The principal legislation governing the treatment of young offenders, the 1945 *ordonnance*, recognised the need to treat juvenile offenders differently from adults. Starting from the basis that the child is not an adult in miniature, but rather a person who is still developing (and therefore, who might be influenced and shaped) the philosophy was one of prevention and education. Penal sanctions were available, but as a separate response of last resort. The role of the specialist *juge des enfants* was at the heart of this approach, which was, through the development of a personal relationship with the young person, to focus on social rather than legal factors[73] and to move towards resolution rather than retribution.[74]

---

[70] Jacques Faget, researcher at the CNRS, quoted in *Le Monde* 20 November 2002. After the first *juges de proximité* took office late in 2003, *juges d'instance* described as 'surreal' the way in which the new procedure was put into effect. In the absence of sufficient *juges de proximité*, *juges d'instance* were required to cover their cases, resulting in a considerable increase of time spent on cases which they would ordinarily have handled themselves. (*Le Monde* 24 October 2003).

[71] Decision of the *Conseil constitutionnel*, Decision No. 2002-461 DC 29 August 2002. Loi organique No 2003-153 of 26 Feb 2003 *relative aux juges de proximité*. A *loi organique* is a particular type of legislation required when a statute does not amend the constitution (this would be a *loi constitutionnelle*), but 'fleshes it out'. See Elliot and Vernon (2000:34).

[72] The emerging profile of the newly appointed *juges de proximité* has further fuelled this concern: most are retired police and *gendarmes* as well as some former *magistrats* and lawyers. (*Le Monde* 21–22 January 2004).

[73] Garapon (1996b) characterises this judge-centred model as being paternalistic, rather than legalistic. 'Paternalism frees the judge by allowing him or her to personalize his action, while legalism imprisons the judge within the walls of tight procedural rules' (p 337). He goes on,

> What is important therefore in the paternalist model is the personal, ethical involvement of the judge. It is on him/her alone, for example, that respect for the principle of natural justice—that the participants should know the contents of the social enquiry reports—rests. In the other model, this is a function of the law and of legal guarantees. Reciprocally, what is feared in the former case is the arbitrariness of a particular individual, while in the latter, it is the coldness and rigidity of a mechanical system. (p 341)

[74] Bailleau (2002) questions the ability of the legally trained *juge des enfants* to perform this social role which takes a long-term view, in contrast to the legal approach which focuses on a single act at a single point in time.

Although not setting aside the 1945 legislation, this reform makes significant changes, which, many argue, shifts the ideology of juvenile justice away from education to repression[75] and blurs the important distinction between education and the penal sanction by creating 'educational sanctions'.[76] The resort to criminal sanctions and the rate of juvenile incarceration has been increasing steadily over the last 10 years and many fear that this legislation will simply encourage further this trend.[77] 13 year olds can now be remanded in custody[78] and children as young as 10 may be placed in GAV. The creation of closed educational centres[79] (in which children as young as 10 may be held),[80] announced within a fortnight of Dominique Perben taking office,[81] has been seen as a huge step backwards to the experimental establishments which were closed down in 1979 under the Justice Minister Alain Peyrefitte.[82] The government rejects this criticism, arguing that the new measures will lead to fewer children in custody: the threat of imprisonment for those held in the closed centres will reduce the rate of absconding and so the need for incarceration. This embodies the government's mantra that 'repression is the best form of prevention'. It is also argued that these measures do not treat juveniles as 'beings in the making' whom society can help to develop and make responsible, but rather, as

[75] The CNCDH (16 July 2002) considered the project to be contrary to the International Convention for the Rights of the Child. The Justice Minister pointed to the proposed appointment of 25% more *éducateurs* as evidence of his continuing commitment to education.

[76] These may, for example, prohibit the child from entering a specified area (rather like the UK anti-social behaviour order, but without the threat of a criminal sanction) or meeting her co-accused or the victim; confiscate an object used for the commission of an offence; or require some act of reparation to be carried out.

[77] This is criticised, not only as ignoring the more complex approach of tackling the causes of the juvenile's offending, but also of being counter-productive. Exposing children to the violence of prison makes criminals of them and excludes them further from society. It is of little value in preventing future offending—40% re-offend within 3 months and 70% within 5 years (*Le Monde* 1 August 2002).

[78] The apparently increasing numbers (though no figures are provided) absconding from closed centres will be threatened with pre-trial incarceration. Since 1987, 10–16 year olds can only be detained in relation to serious offences which carry an adult sentence of 10 or more years. This new measure has been criticised strongly as likely to increase further the tendency to incarcerate the young. Laws in 1987 and 1989 prohibited the pre-trial remand in custody of 13 year olds and limited that of those under and over 16. This rapidly halved the number of juveniles remanded in custody from 4,270 in 1986, to 2,238 in 1991. See Bailleau (2002).

[79] Again criticised as blurring the educational and penal pathways, these centres deprive the child of her liberty, but they are not prisons.

[80] Referring to the increasing tendency to repression and criminalisation, the senator Michel Dreyfus-Schmidt (socialist party) warned: 'At least wait for the construction of these places for juveniles before sending them there.' (*Le Monde* 28–29 July 2002). Philippe Chaillou, president of the youth appeal court in Paris, commented: 'I have the feeling that France is trying to copy England where the imprisonment of 3,500 juveniles has done nothing to halt the tide [of crime].' (*Le Monde* 18 July 2002).

[81] This measure was also announced by Chirac (28 March 2002) as part of his electoral campaign.

[82] This was because of their extremely violent nature, which rendered impossible any educational function they might aspire to. The measure is seen as archaic by those working in youth justice—unable to play any part in reintegrating the young person and simply aggravating their problems. It will also aggravate further the trend towards incarceration which has increased by 40% in 5 years—from 2,900 in 1995 to 4,200 in 2000. (*Le Monde* 16 May 02).

the enemy within which must be controlled in the fight for law and order;[83] instead of addressing the more complex social and economic causes of offending behaviour through prevention and education, the increasing criminalisation of young people will result in their further exclusion.[84] Together with the establishment of the *juges de proximité* who will have jurisdiction in some juvenile cases, the reform is seen to undermine the role of the specialist *juge des enfants* and the more holistic approach to French juvenile justice. However, despite the socialist party's opposition to these measures, when in power they too canvassed more repressive measures for dealing with young offenders. Jospin proposed, for example, the extension of the *comparution immédiate* procedure to juvenile cases,[85] despite the fact that it is designed as an exceptional measure in the sense that the accused is usually tried that day, without time to prepare her defence.[86] More repressive measures were in many ways inevitable,[87] as the problem of youth crime became core territory on the electoral battleground with both major parties continually outbidding each other on their proposed security reforms.

Whilst the reform does not seek to improve the rights of the accused, it should be noted that it does strengthen the position of victims of crime. Following on from the provisions of the June 2000 legislation, it aims to provide the victim with rights equivalent to those of the accused (articles 53-1, 75 CPP), making them equal parties in the case. The police are now obliged to inform the victim of her right to the assistance of a lawyer and in the most serious of cases, this will not be means tested. She must also be informed of her right to constitute herself as *partie civile* in the case (from which flow a number of rights during the investigative stage), to claim compensation and to have the assistance of victim support organisations.

The March 2003 Reform

Sponsored by the Minister of the Interior, the *loi pour la sécurité intérieure* (LPSI) was legislated in March 2003.[88] As well as increasing certain police powers, it sets out new offences relating to prostitution,[89] threatening or hostile gatherings,

---

[83] *Le Monde* 1 August 2002.

[84] See also interview with J-P Rosenczveig. Rancé (2002b).

[85] See eg *Le Monde* 4 April 2002. It is most often used in cases of drugs, aggravated theft, or assault. In 2000, some 7.9% of criminal cases were tried in this way.

[86] The defence can ask for an adjournment, but this is unusual and not the expectation. Only cases which the *procureur* judges to be ready for trial are tried in this way.

[87] These changes can be seen as part of the trend for juveniles to be dealt with with increasing speed and repression, by people increasingly less specialised in juvenile justice. Alain Brunel, former president of the *tribunal des enfants* in Paris (*Le Monde* 16 May 2002).

[88] Loi No 2003-239 of 18 March 2003, *pour la sécurité intérieure*.

[89] The number of foreign prostitutes (more than 60% of prostitutes in Paris are said to be from abroad) and the increase in those living off their earnings is the major concern, but in order to get to the 'pimp', prostitution itself must be sanctioned more firmly, according to the Interior Minister in his address to the National Assembly, 14 January 2003.

begging and travellers.[90] Opposition to the legislation was voiced in terms reminiscent of that seen in the UK around the passing of the 1994 Criminal Justice and Public Order Act (CJPOA), which was criticised for the criminalisation of particular lifestyles, particularly those of the young.[91] In France, the legislation's singling out of specific groups within society has been criticised as being counter-productive and contrary to the values of the Republic.[92] Instead of addressing the causes of crime, those already perceived to be at the margins of society are excluded further by the measures, making them into social enemies,[93] rather than assisting in their integration.[94] For many, this attack upon the weak and vulnerable in society shows no concern for anti-discrimination, representing instead a return to the 19th century ideology of criminalising poverty.[95] According to the text signed by some 30 organisations, including political parties, the human rights league and unions representing both lawyers and *magistrats*, 'We will no longer be equal before the law because it is not the 'well-to-do' who sleep under bridges or go begging.'[96] The measures are also seen as short-term populism, a well-choreographed gesture towards crime control, which will have little impact on either the day-to-day causes and incidence of crime, or the pitifully low clear-up rates.[97] The general secretary of the *Syndicat de la magistrature*, Ulrich Schalchi, considers that the measures will simply create a raft of minor offences, in most instances solved when notified: 'This will, of course, increase the clear-up rate, but also the crime level which will in turn justify the repressive powers of the police. Cases of begging will be solved, but not burglary.' For his part, the Interior Minister was undeterred in pursuing his agenda of repression. In a speech of stirring rhetoric to the *Assemblée Nationale*, he was critical of the previous government's obfuscation of

[90] The criminalisation of squatting, contained in the original proposal, was withdrawn.

[91] Lord McIntosh of Haringey described provisions of the CJPOA as 'an open invitation for the police and for authorities generally to interfere in the legitimate activities of people, and particularly of young people, in our country. . . These are repulsive extensions of police power in our society and at some stage they will have to be removed.' Hansard, HL, 7 July 1994, col 1490. See also discussion in Belloni and Hodgson (2000) ch 10.

[92] The CNCDH (15 November 2002) considered the reform an unjustifiable attack on certain sections of society without affording them the necessary legal protection. They insisted that access to data records should be under the control of the *juge des libertés* rather than the *procureur*. They also expressed concern that a number of the provisions would disproportionately affect young people.

[93] There have been reports of increased violence against and general harassment towards prostitutes since the Interior Minister's announcement that they would be targeted (*Le Monde* 6 June 2002) and increased police violence against foreigners, travellers and young immigrants (*Le Monde* 10 January 2003).

[94] Michel Tubiana, the president of the *Ligue des droits de l'homme*, put it: 'As far as I know, Jacques Chirac was not elected to apply the politics of Le Pen.' (*Le Monde* 27 September 2002, p 14).

[95] Bruno Marcuse, president of the *Syndicat des avocats de France* (*Le Monde* 27 September 2002, p 14).

[96] *Le Monde* 22 October 2002 p 11.

[97] Eg only 8% of burglaries were cleared up in 2002.

the 'real' issues behind debates around prevention or repression,[98] insecurity or the sense of insecurity,[99] arguing for immediate action in tackling crime—to reclaim every centimetre which has been abandoned by the previous administration and to prioritise the victim above all else. His approach was crystal clear:

> We should not be afraid of sanctions, repression, punishment. It is the state's duty to use these whenever necessary. . . . I want to say that I am not afraid of these notions and that the way in which I conceive of my duty is to use them for the benefit of the smallest, the weakest and the most fragile. . . . There has been too much talk of offenders and not enough of victims. . . . What our fellow citizens expect is no longer to be afraid and indeed more than that. It is a real turn around of values, a return to realism.[100]

By presenting increases in police powers and criminalisation as measures which are designed to improve the lot of the victim, the government manages to turn repression into a moral high ground: to be against the legislation is to be against the plight of the victim.[101] Similarly, he rejects explanations linking crime with poverty and unemployment as 'an insult to all who find themselves in an extremely precarious social situation and who are scrupulously honest'.

The legislation also contains measures designed to strengthen the role of local politicians in the co-ordination and direction of the police and *gendarmerie*, to extend the territorial competence of officers and to provide them with wider powers to search cars. There are a number of surveillance-type provisions which increase the types of information which might be stored and accessed (such as bail conditions, immigration status, driving licence and vehicle details) including taking DNA from suspects and making the refusal to provide a sample an offence. In this, the UK is held up as an example: if 1,700,000 samples are held in a country described as the 'cradle of individual freedoms', allowing the police to solve 60,000 cases each year from such evidence, why not in France?[102]

Alongside these increased powers, the legislation also makes one very significant change to the rights of those detained in police custody: it removes the

---

[98] M. Sarkozy does not reject the need for prevention, but clearly privileges the politics of repression: 'The repression of crime is indispensable, because without it, the politics of prevention can never succeed.' Speech to the *Assemblée Nationale* 14 January 2003. The repression/prevention dichotomy has also characterised modern French penal policy—see Gallo (1995).

[99] See Roché (1993) on the feeling of insecurity,

[100] Speech of Nicolas Sarkozy to the *Assemblée Nationale*, presenting his *Projet de Loi pour la Sécurité Intérieure*, 14 January 2003.

[101] Eg he is highly critical of those protesting against his proposals, who, he claims, are more interested in offenders than victims—as objects of study, objects of explanation, objects of social or sociological excuse, or of compassion. 'Once more they invoke as a fantasy the problem of insecurity, no doubt because they have the privilege of not being among the more than four million victims of the previous year.' Speech to the *Assemblée Nationale*, 14 January 2003.

[102] Again, he uses an emotive discourse which focuses exclusively on victims: 'In France, we must tell the families of victims of rape and of murder that we cannot do this [solve cases using a DNA databank]. Is that acceptable? I do not think so.' Speech to the *Assemblée Nationale*, 14 January 2003.

obligation upon the police to inform the suspect of her right to silence—an obligation only recently introduced in the reform of 2000. In the vast majority of cases, this means that there is no requirement to inform the suspect of her right to remain silent during the investigation against her. In the small minority of cases (less than 5 per cent) where suspects are investigated under the *instruction* procedure, they will be informed of their right to silence once brought before the *juge d'instruction*, but only after having been detained and interrogated by the police for up to 48 hours, or four days in very serious cases. As an established component of the Article 6 ECHR fair trial provisions, introduced only recently in the June 2000 legislation as part of an important reform ensuring better compliance with Convention obligations, it is astonishing, firstly, that this change has been made and secondly, that it has been done under the auspices of the Interior rather than the Justice Minister. It is disingenuous to separate the existence of the right to silence from the importance of informing the suspect that she has that right and may exercise it. It is not apparent that the provision was causing any problems to administer and furthermore, informing the suspect of her right to silence is included in the recent EU Commission Green Paper as one of the basic minimum safeguards which all suspects should be afforded. It seems strange that as Member States are agreeing minimum protections for suspects as a clear guide for those states joining the Union (whose due process safeguards they fear may be lacking), France is removing one of those very protections.

The March 2004 Reform

The second project to be presented by the Justice Minister, the *loi sur l'adaptation de la justice aux évolutions de la criminalité* (known as Perben II), focuses on the investigation and trial of organised and serious crime.[103] It includes many (but not all) of the most controversial measures set out by the Interior Minister in his Autumn 2002 policy document and the *magistrats'* unions criticised its police-centred nature as 'an Interior Minister's dream!'[104] It provoked much debate during its passage through the legislature[105] and the *Conseil constitutionnel* required two modifications to the final text.[106] The first addresses the concern that these

---

[103] Loi No 2004-204 of 9 March 2004, *portant adaptation de la justice aux évolutions de la criminalité*.

[104] The view of Dominique Barella, president of the *Union syndicale des magistrats*. See *Le Monde* 12 December 2002. Before the National Assembly, André Vallini, speaking for the socialists, accused M. Perben of presenting 'a reform initiated, elaborated, desired by the police hierarchy surrounding M. Sarkozy' (*Le Monde* 23 May 2003).

[105] The *Sénat* continually softened the measures (reducing the delay in custodial legal advice, or the range of offences for which a plea bargain might be struck) only to have the original provisions restored each time the bill went back before the *Assemblée*. The readings were also accompanied by frequent demonstrations against the reform.

[106] Décision No 2004-492 DC—2 March 2004.

exceptional measures should not be used in the investigation of ordinary crime. The original text prevented any challenge to the use of extended police powers if it was found that the offence investigated did not in fact concern organised crime. The *Conseil constitutionnel* rejected this, making it clear that evidence could be excluded in such cases. It also underlined the importance of defining precisely the offences which might justify the use of these exceptional investigative powers: they should be of a serious and complex nature, not simply ordinary crimes, such as theft, committed by an organised gang. The *Conseil* emphasised that it is the responsibility of those *magistrats* called upon to invoke these exceptional procedures to ensure that there exist one or more plausible reasons to believe that the investigation concerns one of the serious offences set out in the new article 706-73 CPP. The second modification concerned the guilty plea procedure. In order to conform to the 1789 *Déclaration des droits de l'homme et du citoyen* (which states that judgment leading to loss of liberty must take place in public), where the *procureur* proposes a sentence of imprisonment, the hearing in which this is confirmed by the judge must take place in public, rather than in private as envisaged originally in the text.

The reform will result in a greater number of serious offences being dealt with by the police under the more distant supervision of the *procureur*, rather than through the *instruction* procedure, with the most repressive measures requiring authorisation by the JLD. It extends the exceptional GAV regime, already in place for drugs trafficking matters and terrorism, to a wider range of offences (defined in the new article 706-73 CPP) including sequestration, procurement, extortion, and human trafficking, as well as to offences committed in the context of organised crime.[107] In these instances, suspects may be held in GAV for up to 96 hours[108] and access to custodial legal advice can be delayed for 48 hours, or 72 hours in cases of drug trafficking or terrorism (article 706-88 CPP). The period for investigating cases under the *flagrance* procedure is extended to 15 days after the commission of the offence, rather than eight days as was previously the case, again providing the police with greater powers in a greater number of cases. Other powers already available for cases investigated *en flagrance* are now available to the police in ordinary *préliminaire*

---

[107] Lazerges (2003:649–52) criticises the increasing number of derogations from existing provisions. She describes this differential treatment as creating a parallel criminal procedure, a kind of criminal sub-procedure or 'mark II'.

[108] Detention would be authorised initially for 48 hours, renewable for two further periods of 24 hours—unless it is apparent that the full 48 hours are required, in which case the JLD or the *juge d'instruction* may extend detention immediately for 48 hours. The *Conseil constitutionnel*, in paragraph 26 of its decision, considered that this decision would be given in writing and with reasons. Where an intial extension of 48 hours is not requested, the suspect must be presented to the *procureur* for the first extension of 24 hours, but in exceptional circumstances need not be for the final extension up to a total of 96 hours (art 706-88 CPP).

investigations:[109] officers are now permitted to conduct night time searches and are afforded greater powers of surveillance, such as being able to set up a telephone tap or install cameras and listening devices in both public and private locations and to infiltrate organisations undercover. In shifting investigative responsibility yet further away from the *juge d'instruction* and towards the *procureur*, whilst at the same time increasing police powers across the board, the cumulative effect of these measures is to weaken seriously the degree of judicial supervision to which the police are subject. For example, in contrast to the familiarity which the *juge d'instruction* may be expected to have with the dossier, these new powers of search and surveillance will be under the control of the JLD who will have no detailed knowledge of the case and will therefore be ill placed to challenge the police perspective. Investigations of complex and serious cases will be under the supervision of the *procureur*, within a legal framework which both expects and allows for a more distant and less involved form of oversight than under the *instruction* procedure (Hodgson, 2001a:346–47)—though in practice, a proportion of these cases will still pass to the *juge d'instruction*, especially where detention is required. Significantly, once an *information* is opened, the police may no longer question the suspect—only the *juge d'instruction* may do this. Under the new procedure fewer cases will be sent to the *juge d'instruction* and so this restriction will no longer apply in a number of serious cases; in fact, the police will have an extended opportunity to detain and question suspects for up to four days—twice the previous time limit.

Although France currently does not have a system whereby the defendant enters a plea at court, her confession being treated (technically, at least) simply as a piece of evidence like any other, there are various procedures in place to rationalise the disposal of trials: the *comparution immédiate* procedure is designed to deal rapidly with cases where the suspect has admitted involvement for example, and both the *juge d'instance* in the *tribunal de police* and the *procureur* may instigate alternatives to prosecution and trial, such as mediation.[110] Under articles 41-2 and 41-3 CPP, the *composition pénale* allows the *procureur* to propose a range of measures such as a fine,[111] community service or the suspension of the offender's

---

[109] Although night time searches during the *enquête préliminaire* are permitted only in cases concerning the serious offences listed in art 706-73 CPP, this is not a requirement of day time searches, which may now take place with the individual's consent where the investigation concerns an offence punishable by five or more years' imprisonment.

[110] There is also the *ordonnance pénale* (art 495 CPP), whereby the defendant is judged on the dossier alone. This procedure applies to those over 18, where the victim has not brought a claim and either the *procureur* or the accused may reject the proposed sentence. It is limited to driving offences only, initially at the level of *contravention*, but now also for *délits* since the September 2002 reform.

[111] For *délits*, this may not exceed 3,750 euros, or half of the maximum fine applicable for the offence. For *contraventions*, the maximum is 750 euros, or half of the maximum fine applicable for the offence.

driving licence, to an accused who admits the offence.[112] This is done in writing and the suspect must be told that she has the right to consult a lawyer before agreeing to the measure proposed. The agreement is validated by the court[113] after first speaking with the offender and the victim if the judge considers it necessary. If the offender complies, there is no trial—though the fact of the *composition pénale* is recorded on the person's criminal record. For the *procureur*, this is an important way of dealing rapidly with offences[114] such as assault, theft, criminal damage or driving with excess alcohol; defence lawyers, however, argue that it is difficult for the accused to refuse and so it does not represent a real choice.[115] Furthermore, since the legislation of September 2002, the *procureur* may propose such a measure to the suspect held in GAV, which risks putting further pressure for a confession on those detained in police custody. This procedure strengthens the role of the *procureur*, and whilst it remains different from plea bargaining (containing no provision for negotiation) it attaches a particular legal significance to the accused's confession.[116]

The new legislation goes further still. Without creating a formal procedure of entering pleas at trial, it introduces a system of plea bargaining where the accused (in the presence of her lawyer) is offered a lower sentence by the *procureur* in exchange for an admission. The procedure applies to cases with a maximum sentence of five years imprisonment (which covers more than half of all cases handled by the criminal courts)[117] and the *procureur* may propose a prison sentence of up to one year, or half of the maximum penalty for the offence. There is a 10 day period in which to decide and if the offer is accepted, this must then be confirmed by a judge. As noted above, the *Conseil constitutionnel* has ruled that the judge's ratification or rejection of the sentence must take place in open court, rather in private as set out in the original legislation. The *Conseil* also urged judges not simply to rubber stamp these negotiated agreements, but to continue to enquire fully into the facts, as is the duty of the trial judge.[118] However, the judge may not modify the proposed sentence; she may only accept or reject it—in which case the normal trial procedure comes into play. Such an 'all or nothing' approach may act as a disincentive to rejection, providing a certain momentum in favour of accepting

---

[112] Pradel (2002:211) notes that whilst these are punitive measures which sanction an offence, they are not technically regarded as a 'sentence'. They are not given by the court and the terminology is slightly different: a fine is an *amende*, whereas this provides for an *amende de composition*; community service is *travail d'intérêt général*, but this provides for unpaid work, *travail non rémunéré*.

[113] In December 1994, the *composition pénale*'s predecessor, the *injonction pénale* was created. This was struck out by the *Conseil constitutionnel* as there was no role for the judge and so this effectively turned the *procureur* into a judge by allowing her to hand down a sentence.

[114] The range of offences covered is described as '*la délinquance urbaine*' or '*la délinquance de masse*'.

[115] See eg *Le Monde* 21 January 2004.

[116] Pradel (1999:382).

[117] *Le Monde* 4 March 2004.

[118] See eg *Le Monde* 4 March 2004, p 12.

the agreement negotiated by prosecution and defence and so undermining the function and safeguards of the trial.

Whilst the expedited disposition of cases can be advantageous both to the accused and the victim, reducing unnecessary delay, lawyers are sceptical about the transplantation of a practice which has grown up in another legal tradition, pointing to important differences between the two legal systems.[119] In France, the lawyer and the prosecutor are not of the same professional status, making negotiation more difficult. Secondly, whilst the victim has no formal role in Britain and the US, she is part of the process in France, with full participation rights. It is unclear what role, if any, she would play in this bargaining process. The reform will also require a shift in professional legal cultures. The defence lawyer will be asked to agree to a sentence; the *procureur* will negotiate directly with the accused; and the judge will share her decision-making power with the prosecution. There is concern that in allowing the *procureur* to manage cases in this way, the role of the judge becomes increasingly marginalised, undermining the accused's right to a fair and public hearing of all the evidence. It might also be argued that this conflicts with the principle that the judge must base her decision upon the evidence debated before her, as set out in article 427 CPP.[120]

The immunity for defendants assisting in the arrest of those involved in organised criminal activity and those who provide information which prevents the commission of further offences (*les repentis*), has been even less favourably received. This process of denouncement, lawyers argue, has been problematic in Italy, particularly regarding the lack of credibility of some 'supergrasses'. They oppose the encouragement of a system of informing, whereby criminals may benefit from more lenient treatment in exchange for informing on their potential accomplices.[121]

The Justice Minister describes the reform as part of the process of 'simplifying criminal procedure',[122] but lawyers and others have protested at its increasingly repressive nature.[123] There is particular concern that the balance struck between

---

[119] Rancé (2003). As Cécile Prieur, *Le Monde*'s commentator, notes: 'in France, as in other Western countries, it is now less about the solemn rendering of justice than of managing the flux of cases' (*Le Monde* 10 April 2003).

[120] See also art 353 CPP.

[121] There is an interesting (if not disturbing) parallel here with the practices of 18th-century English criminal justice. Deals were struck with those prepared to 'turn King's evidence' (Spencer, 2002:17) and rewards were offered for information which led to the conviction of criminals, providing a dishonest income for some prepared to denounce innocent people and see them executed (L Radzinowicz (1948–56) *A History of English Criminal Law* vol II, 326–32 (Stevens & Sons, London), cited by Spencer (2002:17)).

[122] *Le Monde* 20–21 October 2002. The very poor attendance of *députés* when the Bill was presented to the National Assembly in May 2003, however, was attributed by the president of the *commission des lois* to its complexity. He argued that it was 'much too technical, people understand hardly any of it' (*Le Monde* 23 May 2003).

[123] Some 30 trades unions and political parties demonstrated against this law and the Interior Minister's LPSI across all major French cities on 11 January 2003.

d for an effective investigation and the rights of the defence is being inter-
_.._ with in an unnecessary and dangerous fashion.[124] The move away from (the
already very small number of) investigations supervised by the *juge d'instruction*
towards a criminal procedure dominated by the police-*procureur* partnership, is
seen to take only selected aspects of adversarial procedure without ensuring the
corresponding defence protection which the principle of equality of arms
requires.[125] It also alters the constitutional balance between the executive and the
judiciary. Wider investigative powers, which may only be delegated to the police
under the *instruction* procedure, are available without the need to open an *information*: they can be authorised by the *juge des libertés et de la detention* at the
request of the *procureur*. This marginalises further the role of the *juge d'instruction* in favour of strengthening that of the *procureur*, who is hierarchically
accountable to the Minister of Justice. Whilst the influence of the independent
judiciary in the administration of justice is diminished, that of the executive is
strengthened.[126] This is also seen in the growing importance of the *procureur* in the
disposal of cases, from the expedited *comparution immédiate* procedure to the
composition pénale and plea bargaining.[127]

Furthermore, as more cases are kept away from the *juge d'instruction* where the
rights of the defence (and the victim) are greatest, remaining in the hands of the
police and the *procureur*, the role of the defence is yet further diminished; and as an
increasing number of offences are subject to the exceptional GAV measures, there is
a return to a more closed and secret procedure and 'the religion of the confession'.[128]
The provisions of the 2000 reform are not repealed, but by enhancing police powers and enabling an increasing number of cases to be dealt with by the *procureur*—
where both the victim and the accused have fewer rights to be informed of or to participate in the investigation—many of the protections enacted in the June 2000 legislation are undermined. Similarly, the increased use of the *comparution immédiate*
procedure needs to be accompanied by corresponding defence protections in order
to prevent cases being railroaded through the system by inexperienced lawyers with
neither the time nor the expectation to prepare thoroughly the defence case.[129]

---

[124] See also the opinion of the CNCDH 27 March 2003.
[125] *Le Monde* 10 April 2003. During the second reading in the *Sénat*, M. Dreyfus-Schmidt accused
M. Perben of introducing a reform which sacrifices freedoms and contains all that is needed to constitute a police regime. He went on to compare the securitarian nature of the instant discussions with
those which took place around the war with Algeria. M. Badinter was also very critical of this project
which, after the almost unanimous support of the 2000 reform, represented a clear regression. It
would, he argued, upset the balance of the essential principle of criminal procedure: the equality of
arms within a fair trial (*Le Monde* 22 January 2004).
[126] See also the trend in Germany to transfer power to the public prosecutor, marginalising the judicial role and attenuating the rights of the suspect and the victim (Albrecht, 2000).
[127] The *procureur* may also decide that a case should not be prosecuted, thus eliminating the court's
role altogether. For a detailed study of the inter-relationship between the executive and the judiciary
in criminal matters, see further Breen (2003).
[128] See *Le Monde* 10 January 2003.
[129] Saint-Pierre (2002). See also Field and West (2003) on the part played by the defence lawyer.

The constant concern to reduce delays in criminal proceedings is as striking in French criminal justice as it is in England and Wales, although the focus in the latter has tended to be on more rapid methods of trial, whilst in France it has been upon speedier investigation. Neither is this a new problem facing the courts. In 18th-century England, most cases were disposed of by a form of jury trial. In order 'to prevent the riskiest kinds of prosecution from going forward' defence lawyers and some basic rules of evidence were introduced (Langbein, 1983:133), which had the effect, by the 19th century, of slowing cases down to the point where radical measures were needed. In response, parliament increased the scope of summary trial and the courts no longer discouraged guilty pleas, later positively encouraging them with the development of the sentence discount for those who admitted their involvement and so relieved the court from having to hear all of the evidence (Spencer, 2002:17). We see a similar response today, as measures are taken to decrease the number of cases dealt with by the more costly and time-consuming procedures of the Crown Court, whilst increasing the number dealt with (and dealt with ever more rapidly) by summary trial. In France, it is the *instruction* procedure (and particularly the delays of *détention provisoire*) which has been targeted as the cause of delays and the response has been to divert cases away from this more lengthy form of investigation, preferring instead to send more cases directly to trial. In the 19th century, as the *juge d'instruction* became overburdened with cases, the *procureur* responded by sending fewer cases to *instruction* and greater numbers directly to the court. This practice was extended further by a legal reform in 1863, which authorised the *procureur* to bring directly before the court those accused of *flagrant* cases. This achieved the desired result: between 1831 and 1880, the proportion of cases passed to the *juge d'instruction* fell from 50 per cent to 13 per cent, whilst those sent directly before the court rose from 13 per cent to 33 per cent (Lévy, 1993:172). Today, we continue to see measures designed to reduce the number of cases dealt with by the *juge d'instruction*. The authority of the *procureur* is increased, enabling her to retain cases which would otherwise have gone to *instruction* and to authorise wider police powers which would formerly have required the authority of the *juge*. The concern in both jurisdictions, however, is the extent to which these measures inevitably lead to the practical attenuation of the rights of the accused, as corresponding defence rights are not transferred across to the new procedures. The modern history of criminal procedure is that of marginalising those processes designed to deal with more serious cases, promoting instead, rapid, fast-track means of disposing of increasing numbers of cases.[130] The procedural guarantees of Crown Court trial in England and Wales and investigation by the *juge d'instruction* in France have come to be regarded as unnecessary bureaucracy which can be dispensed with in the majority of cases.

---

[130] There are, of course, a range of ways in which delays might be tackled, such as increasing resources, halting the upward spiral of criminalisation, attacking the social causes of crime and so on, but these are beyond the scope of this more limited discussion.

3

Police, Prosecutors and Judges

The Judicial Function

The functions of investigation, prosecution and trial exist in the criminal procedures of both France and England and Wales, but the ways in which these various
tasks are distributed between legal actors is not the same and the two legal systems
do not share equivalent legal personnel either in name, task or status. In France for
example, as a *magistrat*, the public prosecutor belongs to the same judicial corps as
the trial judge and the *juge d'instruction*.[1] The defence lawyer remains something
of an outsider, her professional status being that of an *avocat* rather than a *magistrat*. In England and Wales, the judge is part of a professional elite, separate from
and (professionally) superior to both the prosecution and defence lawyers, who are
members of the same legal profession. Perhaps the most celebrated difference is
that in France, investigations are supervised by either the public prosecutor or the
juge d'instruction; in England and Wales the police retain sole responsibility for the
investigation, the prosecutor has no supervisory role, and the office of *juge d'instruction*, or her equivalent, does not exist. Thus, when we begin to compare the
prosecution or judicial role, the concept of functional equivalence alone soon
becomes inadequate. It fails to capture adequately the structural and legal cultural
differences which shape the way in which these roles are played out, or the different interplay which exists between the principal functions. In both jurisdictions,
investigation, prosecution and trial have evolved through the dispersal of power
among newly created or adapted personnel, in response to the needs and circumstances of the time. The different constitutional histories of England and of France,
for example, the decline of trial by ordeal in 18th-century Europe,[2] the French

---

[1] This discussion relates to criminal judges, who together with civil judges are *magistrats judiciares*.
There is a separate corps of administrative judges whose training is different. See Bell (2001:41–42).
[2] This led to the establishment of a form of jury trial in England and the more state-centred inquisitorial system of investigation and trial in France and other European countries.

Revolution of 1789,[3] the creation of local police forces in England and Wales in the 19th century,[4] the continuous rise in criminal cases[5] and the challenges of the 'Europeanisation' of criminal justice[6] are among the factors that have contributed in some way to the form of present day legal structures. However, this redistribution of authority is neither complete nor uncontested. Traces remain of what has gone before; there is confusion, a blurring of roles, and tensions between new and old.

Judges, Prosecutors and Police: Overlapping Histories

Comparing the structures and practices of the judicial and prosecution functions is complicated by the different ways in which they are understood in the two jurisdictions. This in turn is a product of their historical development, the shifting distribution of legal authority and power, and the practices which have grown up around this. Salas (2002:534) identifies a discernible 'transnational core of judicial competences' which centres around the judge as guarantor of individual liberties, but there is a range of tasks which might be understood to be properly within the judicial function, including investigation, adjudication and the authorisation of coercive measures. To lawyers in the common law world, the judicial function centres upon the adjudication of issues, primarily at trial.[7] This is distinct from the two phases of investigation and of prosecution (which must themselves be kept separate) reflected in the relatively passive, umpire-like role of the trial judge. Thus, in England and Wales, the judge plays no part in the gathering or presentation of evidence and only rarely will question the witnesses or defendant. The parties are responsible for presenting their case and the court must reach its verdict on the evidence before it.[8] In France, however, the judicial function is a more broadly defined concept, encompassing as it does, the trial judge, the *juge d'instruction* and the *procureur*. The extent to which this respects the separation of powers is a point of tension. Most criticism has been levelled at the blurring of

---

[3] In the immediate aftermath of the Revolution, a form of English criminal procedure was introduced. This was then replaced by a reformed version of the previous inquisitorial structure.

[4] This led to the police taking on the function of prosecution on behalf of the victim.

[5] Both France and England and Wales have developed more rapid trial procedures. Reforms have also sought to reduce the number of cases tried in the Crown Court, and in France, the number of cases investigated by the *juge d'instruction*.

[6] This has had a direct impact on the strengthening of defence rights in France, and the Human Rights Act 1998 requires judges in England and Wales to give effect more directly to the jurisprudence of the European Court of Human Rights.

[7] Increasingly, the judge may also be required to rule in pre-trial hearings (eg under the CPIA 1996) and there are a number of coercive powers, the exercise of which require judicial authorisation.

[8] In the magistrates' court, lay magistrates determine issues of fact and, with the guidance of the court clerk, of law. They deliver both verdict and sentence. In the Crown Court, the judge determines any issues of law and guides the jury in this respect in order that their decision on the facts of the case can be translated into a legal verdict. The judge determines sentence.

investigative and judicial functions during the pre-trial *instruction*,[9] but the distinction between the judicial and investigative role at trial is also less clear cut than in England and Wales.[10] The court's function is not simply to pass judgment on the evidence presented by the parties, but to conduct its own enquiries into the case in order to satisfy itself of the guilt or innocence of the accused.[11] The trial judge adopts a more interventionist stance, questioning witnesses and the accused, and calling for additional information where necessary.[12]

However, although the *magistrature* includes judicial officers performing a range of tasks and there remains an historical overlap between these, the French model does differentiate between an adjudicatory and an investigative judicial role, what Salas (2002:491) has termed a secondary and a dominant function. A distinction is made within the *magistrature* between the standing judiciary (the *parquet*)[13] and the sitting judiciary (the *juge d'instruction* and the trial judge). Whilst the *parquet* is responsible for the prosecution of cases and works within a hierarchy headed by the Minister of Justice, the sitting judiciary is independent of this form of executive control. Only the sitting judiciary may try a case and perform the adjudicative role undertaken by the judge in England and Wales and most, but not all coercive measures which impinge directly on the liberty of the individual, such as remands in custody and telephone tapping, are also authorised by this kind of judge. Significantly, however, whilst investigation is the responsibility of a *magistrat*, in practice it is carried out by the police under the supervision of either the *procureur* or the *juge d'instruction*. As a result, one of the most intrusive infringements of an individual's liberty—the detention of a suspect (and

---

[9] There have been many attempts to reform or abolish the *juge d'instruction*. Serious proposals for abolition were made in 1949 by a Commission chaired by Donnadieu de Varbres and in 1991 by the Delmas-Marty Commission.

[10] The Delmas-Marty Commission (1991:178) pointed to the tension created between the judge's investigative role and in particular, the questioning of the accused, and the requirement that she remain an impartial arbiter.

[11] The most minor cases in France (concerning *contraventions*) are tried in the *tribunal de police* by a single judge, the *juge d'instance*. Most cases (the middle ranking *délits*) are heard in the *tribunal correctionnel* either by a single judge or a bench of three judges—one president and two *assesseurs*. The most serious offences (*crimes*) are tried in the *cour d'assises* by three judges (a president and two *assesseurs*) and nine lay jurors. Together, these twelve determine both verdict and sentence.

[12] The recent report of the working party set up in the aftermath of the 'Outreau' case (Viout, 2005) recommended that the president of the *cour d'assises* make greater use of this power to, for example, gain more up to date information on the development of the child victim. In the Outreau case, seven out of 17 defendants accused of rape and sexual assault as part of a paedophile ring were acquitted, most of them having spent nearly three years in custody during the investigation. Serious concerns were raised about the handling of the investigation by an inexperienced *juge d'instruction*.

[13] The collective term for *procureurs* who are also known as the *ministère public*. The original meaning of the word *parquet* was a small park or enclosure and in the 16th century it came to mean the closed space wherein justice was delivered—the courtroom. In the 18th century it took on a more specialised meaning, referring to the '*gens du roi*', the predecessors of the modern *parquet*. See Carbasse (2000:19–21). Carbasse notes that it is sometimes suggested that the name refers to the *parquet* floor on which lawyers and prosecutors stood. He rejects this explanation on the grounds that there would not have been *parquet* flooring when the '*gens du roi*' were separated form the *juges du siège*!

until recently, a witness) in police custody without charge—is authorised not by the sitting judiciary, but by the police, overseen (in the vast majority of cases) by the *procureur*.[14]

The historically state-centred nature of the judicial function within the wider context of the French republican tradition has been discussed in Chapter 1, and a more detailed account of the practices of the *procureur* and the *juge d'instruction* is the focus of subsequent chapters. The purpose of this section is to set out the broader position which these legal actors occupy both relative to each other and in comparison with the different structural and legal cultural understandings of judges and prosecutors in England and Wales. In all three of its incarnations, the *magistrature* remains inevitably intertwined with the investigation. There is a separation of functions but also an historically defined unity between them which can have important consequences for judicial independence.

The Judicial and Investigative Role in France

In France, the judicial function has been, historically, state-centred[15] and has included both a prosecution and investigative role, as well as one of adjudication. Under the *grande ordonnance* of 1670, the processes of investigation, prosecution and trial were dominated by a single person, the *lieutenant criminel* (Esmein, 1913). In this way, 'the history of criminal procedure in France is the story of the redistribution of these powers, which had initially been concentrated in one single pair of hands' (Salas, 2002:491). The office of public prosecutor, for example, was created by a transfer of the judge's power, enabling her to initiate investigations and to bring a prosecution.[16] But if these powers have been redistributed, they have not been separated out entirely and all three functions are still bound together structurally and ideologically through the common professional grouping of the *magistrature*. The separateness of the English/Welsh judicial function is reflected in the judiciary's position as a clearly defined and insulated professional elite, operating in an occupational sphere which is distinct from that of the investigation and prosecution. This has disadvantages as well as advantages:

[14] In England and Wales, this is also authorised by the police, but with no external supervision, unless a warrant of further detention (ie detention beyond 36 hours for serious arrestable offences) is required. This must be authorised by a magistrate (ss 42–43 PACE 1984).

[15] See the discussion under 'Republican tradition' in Ch 1. Some would argue that the judicial function is not only state-centred, but represents the subordination of law to the interests of the state, as demonstrated by the blatant executive interference in international as well as domestice law—eg the *Rainbow Warrior* incident; legislation passed to protect those guilty of atrocities during the Algerian war—see Hazareesingh (1994:173).

[16] For a detailed historical account of the development of the role of the *procureur* see the contributions in Carbasse (2000). For a brief overview see Dintilhac (2002). The development of the police and their role in investigating crime was to come later. It is significant that, in contrast to the position in England and Wales, the police function emerged out of and alongside that of the prosecutor. See further Lévy (1993).

What I think is of value in the English system is this total division between the people who sit in judgment and those who prosecute. Total division. They are not friends, they do not know each other and they have different interests and different backgrounds. The negative effect is that in your country, the judge is very often somebody of note, with his total lack of understanding of the social system in which he started out. He defends a social order and not an idea of justice. [B1]

France, on the other hand, like many other European legal systems, has a career judiciary, the *magistrature*. But unlike countries such as Germany, this includes not only the trial judge, but also the public prosecutor (the *procureur*) and the *juge d'instruction*.[17] Entrance to this career judiciary is by competitive examination, followed by a period of centralised training at the national school, the *Ecole nationale de la magistrature* (ENM).[18] Recruits go on to specialise in one of the three functions, but their common training and status as *magistrats* means that they can and do move between these.[19] Much importance is attached to belonging to this judicial corps, where, through the instilling of a universal professional ethos, the law graduate is transformed into a *magistrat*, a judicial officer entrusted with the protection of the public interest and the application of the law. The process of socialisation is a rapid one[20] and there is an almost familial bond, which the competitive entrance examination and demanding training creates between individuals who are already characterised by a strong social resemblance.[21] Bourdieu (1989) describes the status of such highly educated bureaucrats recruited by competitive examination, as 'the new nobility, the nobility of the State, products of the educational process, which has, in some ways come to replace the nobility of blood of the *Ancien Régime*'.[22] This common status (a relic from the time when all three functions were carried out by a single judge) and the resulting ties of collegiality and ideology which bind them together as *magistrats*, militate against a clear separation of prosecution and investigation roles from within a wider judicial function.[23] As one *juge d'instruction* explained:

---

[17] In Germany, for example, the *richterschaft* describes trial judges and the *staatsanwaltschaft* the public prosecution service, each with separate career structures.

[18] For details on the training of *magistrats* see Bell *et al* (1998:61–62). For a description of the training and career tradition of the *procureur* see Frase (1990:561–64).

[19] For details on the movement between functions, see further Bodiguel (1999).

[20] Students are eager to become part of the judicial corps: when asked whether they already felt themselves to be *juges*, 63% of the 450 trainees at the ENM replied that they did. 'Les Juges dans la Balance' cited by Soulez Larivière (1995:48).

[21] Bourdieu (1989) cited by Bell (2001:34). Note also the high number of *magistrats* who come from a family of judges and go on to marry a judge—Bodiguel (1999).

[22] Quoted in Bell (2001:34).

[23] This is demonstrated physically by the position of the *procureur* on a raised platform alongside the bench, whilst the defence lawyer stands on the floor with the accused. The Delmas-Marty Commission (1991:180) recommended that the *parquet* stand at the same level as the defence, symbolising the separation between prosecution and judgment and greater equality between the parties.

The unity of a single corps which includes the functions of prosecution, of investigation and of judgment. We are the same, we come out of the same school, we know each other. That is the real problem ... I am often shocked by the way in which people talk about certain cases before and after the court hearing. That is already an encroachment on the independence of each ... I once heard a judge say, 'but of course we must defend the police.' ... That is the real debate. It is all the product of the ideology of society, the profile of the state. Our problem is based on having multiple functions coming out of the same school ... Even I question myself: Do I work as a judge, investigator or partner of the police and *Gendarmerie*? I do not know. [B1][24]

Others, especially in the *parquet*, considered this common training and outlook to be an advantage and in particular, the opportunity to move between functions. For example:

Procureurs are *magistrats* and can become trial judges, or *juge d'instruction*. I think that this position is really a question of culture. That is to say that here, recruitment is by a single competitive examination and in this context, it is believed that all *magistrats* can be called on to carry out all of the three functions. This has the advantage that one can put oneself in the place of the *juge*, certainly to be less partisan and to understand the strict requirements of evidence ... many people have been *juges du siège* and in the *parquet* ... that has the potential to vary your viewpoint. [D3]

... *magistrats du siège* or the *parquet*, I make no distinction, because in reality, the approach is very similar. I have spent my entire career in the *parquet*, but tomorrow, I could be *au siège* and I would not change an iota. I have colleagues who were formerly *au siège* and we reason in the same way [or rather] the approach to problems is the same. [E4]

In addition to the ideological ties which bind together *juges d'instruction*, trial judges and *procureurs*, there remains an overlap of roles in the structural definition of the different functions. The most widely debated of these is the confusion of judicial and investigative roles performed within the office of the *juge d'instruction*, the *magistrat* charged with investigating the more serious and complex criminal cases. Since Napoleon's 1808 *Code d'instruction criminelle*, this role has been divorced from the trial of the case, but a significant judicial function remained alongside the investigative role of the *juge*.[25] She must conduct a neutral and wide ranging investigation and also review and evaluate the case against the suspect; she must determine whether the evidence and charges against the suspect are well founded, but also protect the rights and liberties of the individual in assessing whether to authorise coercive powers such

---

[24] Compare Samet's (2000:33) description below, of whether the *juge d'instruction* is Solomon or Maigret.

[25] In *Journal d'un juge d'instruction* (Diary of a *juge d'instruction*), Samet (2000:33) writes '[The very character of the role of the *juge d'instruction*] thus surprises and misleads, and it has become common to ask oneself whether the *juge d'instruction* is Solomon or Maigret, judge or investigator, defender of rights or pursuer of wrongs.' Quoted in Bell (2001:115).

as telephone taps. Until recently (and perhaps most controversially), she also determined whether to bail or remand in custody the suspect under investigation.[26] This blurring of the investigative and 'purely judicial' (in the sense of being adjudicative) function has been strongly criticised. From the French civil law perspective, the concern is that the independence of the judicial function is undermined by having the investigator in the same professional grouping as the trial judge. This point was tackled head on by the Delmas-Marty Commission (1991), which proposed a much clearer separation of powers, transferring responsibility for all investigations to the *procureur* (with a reinforced defence role to act as an additional safeguard) and transforming the *juge d'instruction* into a more narrowly defined 'judicial' role.[27] This was not adopted in the subsequent 1993 legislation, but a new procedure has been put in place under the 2000 reform,[28] whereby the recently created *juge des libertés et de la détention* is responsible for determining whether to detain in custody those under investigation during *instruction*.[29] From a common law perspective, this confusion of roles might be seen in a more positive light: rather than the investigator as judge undercutting the independence of the judicial function, it might instead be thought to strengthen the independence and credibility of the investigative function.[30]

At trial, the judicial role is more focussed upon the task of adjudication, but given the inquisitorial tradition within which the French system is located, there is also an important investigative aspect. This stems from the historically different part in the process which the criminal trial played, where under the *Code d'instruction criminelle* the court hearing was more closely linked to the investigation, serving effectively as the final stage in the *instruction*, the concluding examination (Salas, 2002:507–8).[31] Today, appeal court judges and those in the *cour d'assises*

---

[26] As the person most familiar with the case, she was considered to be in the best position to determine whether the risks of granting bail outweighed the necessity of maintaining the suspect at the disposition of the enquiry.

[27] Where she would, for example, authorise detention in police custody and the use of other coercive powers. Compare this with the German *ermittlungsrichter* who exercises only judicial powers during the intermediate stage of the case.

[28] The reform of the *juge d'instruction*'s role has been almost constantly on the government's agenda. As the newspaper *Libération* noted, this was the tenth time in 15 years that members of parliament were discussing a reform of the procedure for pre-trial detention (23 March 1999). The purpose of this reform was, above all, to reduce the number of people remanded in custody.

[29] See Huyette (2003) for a discussion of the possible conflict of interest were the *juge des libertés et de la détention* to sit in judgment in the *comparution immédiate*—a situation that has not been addressed specifically by the legislature.

[30] It is ironic that in separating out the investigative and purely judicial roles, it is generally proposed to transfer power from the *juge d'instruction* to the *procureur* (whose supervisory role over the police is very much more distant) with the result that the protection afforded the suspect may be weakened. This has been the case with the Justice Minister's 2004 'criminality' reform, for example, which transfers further power from the *juge d'instruction* to the *procureur*, giving the latter control over an increasing number of serious cases. See above, Ch 2.

[31] Salas (2002:507) quotes Faustin Hélie (*Traité d'instruction criminelle*, 1845 vol VI, 8) 'Inquiry (*l'instruction*) is the soul of the trial, which gives it both form and being . . . It is the inquiry that prepares the ground for the courtroom debate, which sets out its terms of reference and the framework within which it is to operate.'

retain these investigative powers and may request information or call a hearing.[32] The French trial judge is less passive than her English/Welsh counterpart: her job is not simply to adjudicate on the evidence presented by the parties, but actively to seek out the truth. Thus, she may call for more information and she questions the accused as well as witnesses, asking her to comment on and respond to the evidence presented.[33] The defendant does not enter a plea as it is not for her to determine the limits of the enquiry.

> Everything depends on the conception of justice that you have. Here, we have a very state-centred conception. Justice is created by the state. One must recreate that which the parties do not say, research, establish the balance. In your country, you begin from this ideal absolute, according to which the parties are equal. It is for them to bring you the truth and you accept it. In your country, the judge stands back, he is very reluctant to intervene. Here, he can ask for additional information if he considers that the parties have not provided him with sufficient. In your country, it's completely different. It is part of history. [B1][34]

The Prosecution Role in England and Wales

In England and Wales, the judge performs a relatively narrow adjudicative function which has grown up independent of the state. The locus of tension is not around the relationship between judicial and investigative roles, as in France, but around the tasks of investigation and of prosecution which, historically, have been more closely linked. There has been interest in the potential of French criminal procedure to provide some form of independent review of police activity[35] (usually imagined as the *juge d'instruction*) and so it is worth setting out in some detail the relationship between the police and the prosecutor in England and Wales. In the 18th century, private citizens in England and Wales would bring their complaints before a Justice of the Peace who collected evidence, arrested suspects and determined whether or not a prosecution was warranted. This continued until the establishment of the police service in 1829, when officers began to take on the role of prosecuting cases on behalf of victims, combining the functions of investigation and prosecution.[36] In 1879 the office of the Director of Public

---

[32] Under art 310 CPP, for example, the president of the *cour d'assises* has a discretionary power to take any measures which she considers useful in the search for the truth. A similar power exists in the lower courts. Under art 283 CPP the president of the *cour d'assises* may require additional information if the *instruction* seems incomplete or new evidence has emerged. A recent working party (Viout, 2005) has urged the court to use this power more effectively.

[33] Until the June 2000 reform, the judge could also require that all questioning of witnesses was conducted through her, but the procureur and defence lawyer are now permitted to put their questions directly.

[34] See also Garapon and Papadopoulos (2003).

[35] Although this has been rejected by both the RCCJ (1993) and the Auld Review (2001).

[36] In theory, the police prosecuted, not as agents of the state, but as individual citizens.

Prosecutions (DPP) was created (operating under the authority of the Attorney-General, a member of the government) with the objective of achieving a degree of uniformity in the treatment of the most serious cases. In the vast majority of instances, therefore, this left the role of the police unaffected. By the 1960s and 70s, prosecution arrangements became more formalised and many police areas employed their own in-house solicitors to deal with more complex cases and the increasing volume of work,[37] but the policing role continued to encompass the dual functions of investigation and prosecution. As these prosecuting solicitors were employed by the police in a lawyer–client relationship, they were constrained to follow the instructions of their client: they exercised no independent power of review and they were unable to discontinue cases on their own initiative where they considered there to be insufficient evidence. In essence, they acted in an advisory capacity only, the decision to prosecute being that of the police. The Royal Commission on Criminal Procedure (RCCP) 1981[38] was critical of this state of affairs and argued that, in principle, the processes of investigation and prosecution ought to be kept separate in order that an objective and dispassionate view of the evidence could be taken. It recommended the establishment of an independent public prosecution service to ensure a greater degree of consistency and uniformity in the prosecution of cases. In particular, there was evidence that police forces across the country were adopting different guidelines in deciding whether to prosecute or caution, and were proceeding with too many weak cases, in some instances against the clear advice of their own lawyers. As a result, the Crown Prosecution Service (CPS) was established in 1985 under the Prosecution of Offences Act.

Although a public prosecution service, the CPS is a rather different creature from her French counterpart. As salaried lawyers, under the DPP and the Attorney-General, it was hoped that crown prosecutors might perform a ministry of justice role in a similar fashion to public prosecutors in much of the rest of Europe. However, the structure of the organisation and its dependent relationship upon the police have militated against this.[39] The police retain sole responsibility for the investigation of crime and, until very recently, for the decision whether or not to initiate proceedings through the process of charging a suspect. Since August 2004, under the Police and Criminal Evidence Act 1984, code of practice (COP) C, the CPS may determine the initial charge other than for routine offences or

---

[37] Weatheritt (1980).

[38] The Commision was established after the Confait affair, where it was considered that, had there been some form of independent review of the police investigation, the wrongful convictions of the three people tried for the killing of Maxwell Confait might have been averted.

[39] Although formally a new body, the inculcation of a whole new ethos was problematic. The new CPS required over 1,500 lawyers and it made sense to recruit many of these from the existing prosecuting solicitors—giving the impression in some places that little had changed, other than the name plate above the office door.

where a 'holding' charge is brought in order to justify a remand in custody.[40] Where the police determine the charge, they must comply with any relevant guidance issued by the DPP.[41] Formerly, the police alone had the power to charge a suspect which meant that where no charge was brought, the investigation was closed and the CPS would have no involvement. It was only if charges were preferred that the papers would pass to the CPS to determine whether or not to prosecute and with what offence. Under the new COP, crown prosecutors have an initiating power of prosecution in some instances, but they continue to have no control over the gathering of evidence, nor any power to require further investigation and so remain wholly dependent upon the police file of evidence in making their decision whether or not to charge or prosecute. Thus, whilst there is a structural separation of the investigation and prosecution role, the functional autonomy of the police remains problematic. Police officers continue to be the gatekeepers to the prosecution process in most instances, exercising unsupervised control over the flow of cases between investigation and prosecution. Unsurprisingly, empirical research into the decision to prosecute has shown that it is difficult for prosecutors to come to radically different conclusions from those reached by the police, given that they base their decision upon the same set of evidence. They remain dependent upon, and unable (unwilling, some would argue) to go beyond the police constructed case.[42]

Initiatives for closer liaison between the two organisations has not been hugely successful.[43] The police have tended to view the CPS as historical interlopers who have usurped an important part of the policing function: 'Having conceded their power to prosecute, the police are unwilling to lose any ground on the matter of investigation' (Belloni and Hodgson, 2000:108). This tension is aggravated by the inherent conflict between the two functions. The CPS is required to review the evidence produced by the police investigation, to filter out weak cases and to determine whether or not any prosecution is warranted; but the police resent the downgrading or discontinuance of charges which officers have instigated and consider justified. Thus, we are left with a paradox: the CPS remains structurally dependent upon officers, but is forced to operate at a distance, preventing the development of a culture which would enable the CPS to reap the benefits of working closely with the police, without the disadvantage of being dominated by them.

---

[40] s 28 Criminal Justice Act 2003.

[41] COP C, para 16.1A and 16.1B.

[42] See, for example, McConville *et al* (1991). This lack of independent distance between the police and prosecution (or some other review body) has contributed to numerous miscarriages of justice both before and after PACE 1984.

[43] The RCCJ (1993) recommended closer consultation to reduce the number of weak cases prosecuted. The CPS report (CPS, 1995:24) that their advice was sought in only 5% of cases and a Home Office study found that rates of advice varied regionally from 1 to 14% (Crisp and Moxon, 1994: ch 4).

The Prosecution Role in France

Like the CPS, the *procureur* in France is responsible for reviewing the evidence and determining whether or not to pursue a prosecution.[44] But unlike the CPS, the *procureur* exercises a supervisory function over the police investigation. As a *magistrat*, she plays a more neutral and wide ranging role than that of a simple (more partisan) prosecutor: she is a judicial officer, responsible for directing the police investigation and overseeing the detention of suspects in police custody, including the protection of their due process rights.[45] Although the emphasis is different, as is the nature of the legally structured framework of supervision,[46] the *procureur* like the *juge d'instruction*, performs a dual investigative and judicial function.

> [For the *parquet*] the difficulty is in reconciling what is necessary in terms of the conduct of the investigation with what is necessary in terms of the judicial role. [A6]

To those familiar with a more adversarial-style criminal process which shares out these functions differently and, in particular, which anticipates that the defence lawyer (rather than the same person responsible for the investigation and prosecution of the offence) will play a role in monitoring the protection of pre-trial defence interests, this model of judicial supervision represents a remarkable concentration of power. But it is the *procureur*'s status and ideology as a *magistrat* (rather than just a prosecutor) which, in theory, justifies this position. Furthermore, as part of the *ministère public*, the *procureur* is part of a centralised hierarchy of authority, headed by a government minister, the Minister of Justice. Designed to ensure the legitimacy and democratic accountability of the *procureurs*, as well as a degree of centralisation and uniformity within the *parquet*, this hierarchical control defines and constrains the exercise of the *procureur*'s discretion.[47] Perrodet notes that, in theory, governmental control over the prosecution service appears to be similar in France and in England and Wales.

> In practice, however, there is an enormous difference, because in France, unlike in England, the minister's legal right to control the prosecution system has not been tempered by a constitutional convention that it should be exercised very sparingly, and not

---

[44] For a historical overview of the development of the functions of the *procureur*, see further Carbasse (2000).

[45] The broad nature of her function is underlined by her representation of the wider public interest in civil as well as criminal matters. A *procureur* in area D explained:

> I would act in society's interest if, for example, a large organisation was going into liquidation; I would consider the position of the employees. Or, if there was a take-over bid, I would scrutinise the offers made. Or, if a company wanted to replace all of their employees with machines.

See further Dintilhac (2002:39–40).

[46] Hodgson (2001a:346–47).

[47] See further, Hodgson (2002a).

used to further the narrow political interests of the government and its supporters. (Perrodet, 2002:422)

Whilst the prosecution in England and Wales is characterised as one of institutional dependence and functional autonomy, the position in France is one of institutional dependence and functional subordination.[48] In practice, the concern in England and Wales centres upon the independence of the CPS from the police, while in France, it is the *parquet*'s independence from executive control which has been the focus of attention.[49]

In theory, the independence of all *magistrats* is guaranteed by Article 64 of the French Constitution, which guarantees the independence of *l'autorité judiciaire*. However, Perrodet (2002:422) notes that this is not the sense in which the article has been interpreted and two attempts (in 1993 and 1999) to ensure that *procureurs* are expressly included, have failed. There are also differences in the way in which the professional development of the *procureur* is overseen, compared with other *magistrats*. Although all *magistrats* are subject to the same governing body, the *Conseil supérieure de la magistrature* (CSM), its composition is more political when regulating the affairs of the *parquet* and it plays only an advisory role in the appointment of ordinary ranking *procureurs*.[50] Senior appointments (to the posts of *procureurs généraux*) are made by the equivalent of the Cabinet and the CSM plays no part in this. Perhaps the most controversial threat to the independence of the *procureur*, however, is her subordinate relationship to the Minister of Justice. The Minister's ability to issue instructions in individual cases, together with the powerful influence she enjoys over the career of the *procureur*, has, historically, created a tension between the independence of the *parquet* on the one hand and the requirement that she be democratically accountable to a government minister on the other.[51] This has been demonstrated most clearly in a number of high-profile affairs, where the Minister has issued instructions in individual cases concerning politicians and business people.[52] Since 1993 any instructions concerning a case are required to be in writing and placed in the case dossier, but in practice this rule has been circumvented and the Truche Commission (1997:24–25) noted that less formal communications continue to be issued and are often treated as

---

[48] Perrodet (2002:417–25).

[49] Carbasse (2000:17–18) notes that the *parquet* of the early 19th century was narrowly dependent upon the executive in a way that had been hitherto unknown to the monarchy. In England and Wales, the independence of the Attorney-General in his advice to the Prime Minister concerning the war on Iraq has been questioned. See *The Guardian* 1 March 2005, G2 p16.

[50] Perrodet (2002:423).

[51] The notion that the *procureur* is free to develop her own oral arguments, but is constrained to follow the orders of her hierarchy in what she writes is reflected in the expression: *La plume est serve, mais la parole est libre*. See also art 33 CPP.

[52] This is part of a wider tension in which the proper role of the executive within the repressive function is ill defined, leaving a 'lacuna' in the law. Breen (2003:226).

instructions. The hierarchical culture of *instruction* and subordination is less easily broken,[53] in particular given the influence of the Justice Minister upon the
career progression and professional disciplining of the *procureur*.[54]

In 1998, a reform was proposed which would strengthen the independence of
the *procureur* by weakening both the hierarchical control exercised by the Minister
of Justice over the *parquet* and the role of politicians in their appointment and
promotion.[55] In anticipation of this measure, the then Minister of Justice,
Elisabeth Guigou, announced that she would cease voluntarily to issue instructions in individual cases. Removing completely accountability to the Minister of
Justice was rejected by the Truche Commission, but it was hoped that without a
determinative influence upon the career of the *procureur*, the Minister of Justice
would be less able to influence the course of investigations of political significance.[56] Many politicians expressed concern that these reforms would give too
much power to prosecutors and leave them insufficiently accountable to democratically elected politicians, raising the spectre of the pre-revolutionary *gouvernement des juges*.[57] *Magistrats* rejected such claims as a cynical means of politicians
protecting their own interests by retaining the power to intervene in politically
sensitive cases. The proposed changes in the selection procedure required a
constitutional amendment and so a three-fifths majority vote in Parliament,[58]
and although enjoying broad political support, the Bill ultimately failed. Having

[53] The strength of this culture of hierarchical subordination is demonstrated by the fact that one
form of indiscipline is disobedience to lawful orders issued by a hierarchical superior (Perrodet
2002:423).

[54] As well as playing a key role in the appointment and promotion of *procureurs*, the Justice Minister
is also responsible for their discipline, although she may only remove *procureurs* from office on the
proposal of their superior and following the advice of the CSM. Some *procureurs* considered that the
hierarchical ties would not be broken easily. 'Even if you cut off the hierarchy to the Minister of
Justice—if he wants to intervene and the *procureur* is eager for promotion, he still can.' [*Procureur*,
Area D]

[55] *Projet de loi relatif à l'action publique en matière pénale et modifiant le code de procédure pénale*
(Law reform relating to criminal prosecution and modifying the code of criminal procedure). See also
Pradel and Laborde (1997), who argue that greater autonomy for the *parquet* is an indispensable part
of its legitimacy.

[56] For an account of the Italian experience, where prosecutors are independent of the Minister of
Justice (what Perrodet (2002:429) classes as institutional independence with functional autonomy),
see Guarnieri (1997); Di Frederico (1998); and Perrodet (2002). Guarnieri contrasts the evolution of
mandatory prosecution in Italy, with that of the discretionary powers of the French *procureur*. After
the fall of fascism and in the context of low levels of political trust (which persist today), Italian prosecutors were made wholly independent of the Minister of Justice, both in terms of prosecution decisions and of promotion. In contrast, he argues, the centralised system in place in France reflects greater
levels of political trust. Like Di Frederico, he notes the paradox that despite the constraints of the hierarchical network within which French prosecutors operate, their Italian counterparts appear to enjoy
a wider margin of discretion.

[57] This alludes to the part played by the judiciary in overthrowing the monarchy in the 1789
Revolution and their alleged potential to use the same power against the Republic. See further Martin
(1990:161–62).

[58] The issue was considered too technical for the other mode of constitutional reform, a referendum.

previously supported the reform, the CSM then favoured a return to the issuing of written instructions in some cases, in order to ensure 'coherence in the application of the law and effectiveness in the fight against crime.'[59] However, they also considered that as a necessary corollary to this, there should be less political interference in the appointment of senior prosecutors, recommending that the *procureurs généraux* should no longer be nominated by *décret en Conseil des ministres* (decree of the president of the Republic having informed the *Conseil des ministres*, the Cabinet).[60] Recent legislation has underscored the hierarchy of the *ministère public*, and *procureurs* again appear resistant to increased interference through the Ministry of Justice.[61]

Procureurs we spoke to were strongly in favour of a greater degree of independence from the Minister of Justice. The *procureur de la République* in area D told us

> The *parquet* has a different role [from the *juges de siège*] but it is just as important that they are independent—they too are *juges*. The debate is whether the Minister of Justice should continue to have a role and the right to intervene in certain cases and institute proceedings . . . I personally agree that there is no reason for the Minister to intervene. I am responsible for my own decisions and they are regulated by the court and can even be challenged by the victim if they decide to act. It does not seem evident that my actions must be justified to the hierarchy of the *procureur général* and the Minister of Justice . . . There is a tradition of dependence. There have been special jurisdictions, such as during the war. But now *magistrats* want to distance themselves from the executive. [D4]

He went on to explain that the Minister's interventions might also be seen positively.

> *Procureur*: Last year we had something like Islamic terrorism. Also, if there are fraud cases involving politicians.
> Interviewer: It seems ironic that in the cases where it is most important that you are seen to be independent, the Minister intervenes.
> *Procureur*: Yes, that's true . . . but there are two senses — he can also make sure that cases are pursued, as well as preventing them from being pursued. [D4]

Although most *magistrats* are unlikely to experience the kinds of political interference seen in high-profile cases, attacks upon their independence manifest

---

[59] *Le Monde* 26–27 May 2002, p10. The 35 senior regional prosecutors in France (*procureurs généraux*) expressed a similar concern at their conference in October 2001. This is not the wish of those *procureurs* below them, however. This has also angered unions representing the *magistrature*, who argue that, instead of guaranteeing the independence of the judiciary, the CSM is seeking to make justice subservient once again to politics.

[60] See the interview with Michel Lernout, member of the CSM, with Pierre Rancé (2002d:2061).

[61] See *Le Monde* 7–8 March 2004.

themselves in more mundane ways. In particular, many are keenly aware of their dependence upon the hierarchy for the progession of their career.

> The greatest pressure, of course, which means that colleagues are not necessarily very independent, is career pressure. This is happening more and more than was formerly the case, because a few years ago, whatever you did, you had a good career . . . that has happened to me . . . [my *procureur*] put pressure on me . . . and that happens very frequently with young *magistrats* in the *parquet*. [E7]

> What is bad in the French system is this type of submission of *magistrats* to their career, which means surrendering their independence . . . Everything which helps your career, in France, does not encourage independence. [B1]

> You can be required to apply a *politique pénale* . . . that's absolutely normal that there would be such directives . . . On the other hand, I am very much in favour of the reform which envisages that the *parquet* would have certain career guarantees, which means that their attitude to certain cases would not be dictated by their personal situation. [A6]

Judicial Independence *versus* State-centred Authority

Within the wider political landscape, the extent to which the French judiciary is either subordinated to, or independent of, the executive, serves as an interesting barometer of state-centred authority. As we have seen in the preceding discussion and that set out in Chapter 1, the relationship between the state and the judiciary is a complicated one.[62] Judicial independence is a necessary guarantee of the fair and impartial administration of the law, but within the French republican tradition, the judicial role must be subordinate to that of those elected in the name of the people. This is demonstrated in a number of ways: the 'purges' of the higher-ranking judiciary which have accompanied major political change[63]; the judiciary's status as an *autorité* rather than a *pouvoir*[64]; its lack of power to review the operation of administrative bodies[65]; and the powerful executive control exercised over the career, discipline and functioning of *magistrats* through the Minister of Justice. In this way, the role of the law is seen as largely subordinate to the interests of the state[66] and

---

[62] For a comparative analysis of the political and constitutional position of judges, see Guarnieri and Pederzoli (2002), especially ch 3. The study covers England, France, Germany, Italy, Portugal, Spain and the United States—all countries with an independent judiciary, but representing both the common law and civil law tradition.

[63] This was most aggressive during the Third Republic, but was also apparent during and after the Vichy regime. See further Badinter (1995) and Royer (2000).

[64] See further Troper's (1981) interesting discussion on this. He argues that whilst judicial activity is political in character, the form in which it is exercised means that it cannot be called a *pouvoir* in the same way as the executive or the legislature.

[65] There do exist administrative courts to this effect, however.

[66] Hazareesingh (1994:66). This extends to international as well as internal affairs:

> When the French state protected and even sanctioned the criminal actions of its own agents at home and abroad (as with the sinking of the *Rainbow Warrior* in 1985 . . .) it demonstrated that international law was just as expedient a precept as domestic law. (Hazareesingh, 1994:173).

instrumental in promoting its values and ideals. Wright (1999:94) describes the position at the start of the Fifth Republic:

> Law was also seen as a mobiliser and legitimiser of the sociopolitical system. It was not neutral, but embodied 'technocratic normative justice': it was instrumental and output-oriented, intimately involved in social guidance and social engineering, and served as a tool for ensuring social integration (based on a legally constructed concept of citizenship), political centralisation and economic *dirigisme*. In short, law was a top-down system of homogenisation.[67]

During the course of the Fifth Republic, the pervasive nature of this state-centred authority has been challenged both internally and from developments outside France, in ways which have led to a strengthening of the place and therefore the role of the judiciary.[68] The scope of judicial intervention has expanded and *magistrats* have flexed their muscles, asserting their independence and autonomy. This is seen in the important role which the *Conseil constitutionnel* has come to play in judicially reviewing the executive/legislative boundary and in protecting public freedoms; in the juridification (sometimes as a result of ECHR litigation) of issues formerly regulated by politicians and administrators; in the increasing independence and autonomy of the judiciary in bringing politicians and powerful business people to account; and in the claims to greater independence from the political interference of the executive.[69] For the purposes of this discussion, it is the last two of these that are of particular interest.[70]

The hierarchical accountability of the *parquet* to the Minister of Justice is claimed as a form of democratic accountability, designed to ensure the consistent and impartial application of the law. Yet, it also offers the potential for political interference in a way which does not guarantee, but undermines, the independence of the *parquet* and serves to protect favoured individuals from legal scrutiny.[71] Article 36 of the CPP permits the Justice Minister to instruct the *procureur* to prosecute, but orders to discontinue a case are technically excluded. However, no further action has been taken in numerous serious cases which would otherwise cause political embarrassment and there are strong suspicions that this is the result of political pressure—in some cases reaching back as far as the President.

---

[67] He contrasts this with the role of law in the USA, which Cohen-Tanugi has described as 'a mechanism for managing a diverse and pluralistic society . . . [which] could not be the expression of the general will since the existence of such a will was denied' (Wright 1999:93–94).

[68] See also Renoux (2001).

[69] See further Wright (1999:98–105).

[70] For a discussion of the changing role of the judiciary in relation to the executive, in the context of 'les affaires', see also Roussel (1998), (2000) and (2003); Montes (2002); and more generally Garapon (1996a) and Bancaud and Robert (2001).

[71] See *Le Monde* 26–27 May 2002, p 10 for a summary of the major *affaires*.

Research suggests that Mitterand intervened routinely in justice matters between 1981 and 1984, including in sensitive matters. A confidential note of a senior member of the President's staff in 1981 indicated that 'it seems desirable that the president conserves—as he always has done—a minimum of control over what happens in judicial matters.'[72] In 1989, the Justice Minister, Henri Nallet, instructed the *parquet* to classify a case for no further action to prevent the opening of an investigation which would look into the financing of the socialist party, as such an enquiry would have 'unfortunate and unforeseen consequences for a number of political representatives' and such action was necessary to protect the interests of the state.[73] In other instances over the next 10 years, investigations were delayed, allowing ministers to resign and further attempts were made to block politically sensitive cases.[74] Respect for the justice system was undermined and the relationship between prosecutors and politicians questioned. The independence of the judiciary more widely was also in question, given their shared status with *procureurs* as *magistrats* and the Justice Minister's (albeit less pronounced) influence on their career. It is against this background that the Truche Commission was set up in 1997 to consider the relationship between the public prosecutor and the Minister of Justice and the extent to which the 'umbilical cord' between them should be cut.

More recently, there has again been suspicion of executive interference in the proper administration of justice. In February 2004 investigations began into allegations by those trying the case of former Prime Minister Alain Juppé (accused of unlawfully abusing his political position) that their offices had been visited, their computers hacked into and their telephones tapped, during the course of the trial. The *procureur* opened an *information* on the case and president Chirac set up an enquiry led by three of the highest-ranking *magistrats* in the country. However, the executive's reaction to M. Juppé's conviction was criticised in many quarters. The Prime Minister described the conviction as a provisional decision (given that an appeal was being lodged) and President Chirac (who as the head of state, guarantees the independence of the justice system) described Juppé as 'an honest man'. This clear support for a person condemned under the due process of law has been seen as an attack on the independence of the judiciary and a threat to the separation of powers.[75]

A second challenge to the traditionally docile part played by the judiciary came from the *juges d'instruction*. A relatively small group, including Thierry Jean-Pierre, Eric Halphen, Eva Joly, Renaud van Ruymbeke, Laurence Vichnievsky and Patrick Desmure, have been engaged in some of the most controversial and

---

[72] Research conducted by Alain Bancaud, described in Elliot and Vernon (2000:153).
[73] In Nallet's book *Tempête sur la justice*, described in Elliot and Vernon (2000:154).
[74] See Elliot and Vernon (2000:154).
[75] See reports of the affair in *Le Monde* 5 Feb 2004; 6 Feb 2004 and subsequently.

high-profile investigations.[76] Political and administrative officials have increasingly been investigated and held criminally responsible for acts of negligence in a new wave of judicial activism which Roussel (2003) likens to aspects of American 'cause lawyering'.[77] Three former ministers (including Laurent Fabius, the former Prime Minister) were tried for involuntary manslaughter for their part in the transfusion of HIV contaminated blood to haemophiliacs and one, Edmond Hervé, was convicted.[78] Politicians and powerful business people have also come under scrutiny in a series of corruption cases which have implicated players from both sides of the political spectrum. The list of convicted politicians includes the former socialist minister, Bernard Tapie, convicted of tax evasion and rigging football matches; Michel Noir, former RPR Trade Minister; and numerous mayors across France who have siphoned off municipal funds for their own and their families' benefit. Perhaps the most significant investigation, however, concerns the corrupt practices used by all parties for political funding before this area was regulated by laws in 1988 and 1990. Knapp and Wright (2001:398) note that 'it was estimated that some three-quarters of all business funding at the 1993 elections came from firms liable to bid for contracts with local authorities run by party politicians.' Kickbacks were paid by firms in return for contracts with municipalities controlled by politicians. The Urba network was set up as a front organisation to disguise this practice and when this came under investigation, the socialists were implicated and the party treasurer and former president of the National Assembly, Henri Emmanuelli, convicted. More recently, the activities of the RPR have been investigated, centring on the corrupt management of housing stock in Paris and tampering with the electoral register of the fifth *arrondissement*—where Chirac and his successor, Jean Tiberi, were elected as councillors. Powerful heads of business have also been investigated and wide scale financial corruption rooted out, some of it also implicating politicians.[79]

The media has played an important part in preventing these investigations from being sidelined by *procureurs* constrained to act on the instructions of the

---

[76] See also the interviews with Eva Joly and others conducted by Greilsamer and Schneidermann (2002).

[77] Roussel notes, of course, that the French *magistrat* is in a quite different position from the American attorney, as she is employed by the state and subscribes to a professional ideology which casts her role in neutral public interest terms (2003:93–94). The form of action is also quite different—those investigating the *affaires* of the 1990s are not political militants (in contrast to the '*juges rouges*' (red judges) of the 1970s) and do not use their cases as a platform from which to call for social change and legal reform. Instead, their behaviour is explained as simply 'doing their job' and 'applying the law' (2003:97–99). Their neutrality is their strength. One *juge d'instruction* told the author (2003:99): '[The judge] is the servant of the law, no more and no less. He does not create the law, he simply applies it. And he wants to have it applied to everybody, including those who have made it.' See also the comments of those interviewed in Greilsamer and Schneidermann (2002).

[78] See Elliot and Vernon (2000:101–10) for a detailed discussion of this case.

[79] See the description provided in Knapp and Wright (2001:399).

Ministry of Justice.[80] Despite the apparent secrecy of the *instruction*, key evidence has been leaked to the press and a number of *juges d'instruction* have adopted a high media profile. Many of the *juges d'instruction* and other *magistrats* interviewed by Greilsamer and Scheidermann (2002) acknowledged the valuable role played by the media in acting as a lever for change, a kind of 'fourth power' ensuring the proper democratic functioning of the justice process.[81] However, having strengthened their independence in this way, most *juges* considered that this strategy was no longer necessary and was, in fact, now counter-productive. They were anxious to move away from a highly mediatised and personalised image of justice, to one which focuses upon the case and the evidence. To do otherwise, they argued, risks undermining the independence of the *juge* investigating, such that the case becomes not about justice, but about the individual (and sometimes iconic) *juge*.[82]

Ultimately, whilst the debate around executive interference with the judiciary (through the hierarchy of the *ministère public*) and the increased willingness of *juges d'instruction* to investigate political and financial corruption through the oridinary channels of the criminal law have been significant, they and other changes around the judicialisation of public policy have not been sufficient to displace the state-centred authority of the French republican model, only to modify it.[83] Following the report of the Truche Commission (1997), the removal of the hierarchical accountability of the *parquet* to the Minister of Justice (as has occurred in Italy) has been rejected, as have been alternative solutions, such as the retention of a Minister of Justice (thus providing legitimacy and coherence) who is not party political.[84] The reform that was proposed sought to alter the nature of the judicial–executive relationship by strengthening the independence of the *parquet* and weakening executive control of the career of the judiciary, but this was never legislated. The Justice Minister remains free to issue instructions to the *parquet*, to move, promote or transfer *procureurs* and to nominate her own political

---

[80] See also Zemmour (2001) on the relationship between justice, politics and the media. Also Garapon (1996a:61–65 and ch III) who describes (at p 73) the 'dubious alchemy' which exists between the justice system and the media.

[81] Eg Jean-Claude Marin, *avocat général* in the *Cour de cassation*, Greilsamer and Schneidermann (2002:294).

[82] Eg Armand Riberolles, *premier juge d'instruction* in Paris; Jean-Pierre Zanoto, *juge à l'inspection générale des services judiciaires*; Jean-Claude Marin, *avocat général* in the *Cour de cassation*, in Greilsamer and Schneidermann (2002:124–25; 155–57; 291–92). *Juges d'instruction* such as Eva Joly, or *procureurs* such as Eric de Montgolfier became renowned for their pioneering approach and were happy to use the media to their advantage. In the case of Eva Joly, her publicity of the poor conditions in which she was obliged to work also contributed to the eventual establishment of the *pôle économique et financier* in Paris in 1997.

[83] See also Breen (2003) for a more detailed discussion of the administrative–judicial interplay. For a general discussion of the changing position of the judiciary see Bancaud and Robert (2001).

[84] See eg Jean-Louis Delvolvé, *Le Monde* 22 January 1997, 'Pour un veritable ministère de la justice' p 14.

allies. Caught in a historical dialectic of a strong state and a weak judiciary, the subordination of the *procureur* to executive power fails to reflect modern conditions; the *procureur* is increasingly implicated in the debate, stimulation and co-ordination of local penal policy, as well as in various forms of inter-agency co-operation.[85] She has the power to make use of a number of alternatives to prosecution and trial, including mediation,[86] and she plays an important role in local policy making, notably through *contrats locaux de sécurité* (CLS) which seek to promote active partnership between local organisations such as the police, *gendarmes*, schools, social workers, mediators and the mayor.[87] In this way *procureurs* have come to exercise 'a hybrid function, half executive, half judicial and [they] have become the necessary interface between the judiciary, the state and civil society.'[88] Dalle and Soulez Larivière[89] argue that the preferred solution would be if the *parquet* were not part of the same professional family as the judge (as is the case across most of Europe) and were not dependent on the executive in their career. In this way, the objections to hierarchical control would be removed.

Despite the establishment of an administrative court system two centuries ago, which sought to ensure that the judiciary were prevented from reviewing executive activity, high-profile investigations such as those described above have resulted in the investigation (and in some instances, trial and conviction) of politicians, often under the media spotlight. The judgment of political elites under the ordinary criminal law in this way may be seen by some as the expression of society's desire for an effective counter-power,[90] but it has inevitably led to the criticism that the judiciary have trespassed into political life and are acting as a *gouvernement des juges*, violating the *Loi* of 16–24 August 1790 prohibiting judicial intervention in administrative matters.[91] For this reason, their role continues to be scrutinised[92]:

> People are always complaining about the *juge d'instruction*, that they should not be young and inexperienced—but it's not about that. It's because *informations* have been

---

[85] See further Garapon (1996a:237–39).

[86] For an account of the alternatives to prosecution developed by the *parquet* (France's so-called 'third way') see the Truche Report (1997:26–29); Crawford (2000); Pradel (2000). Loi no 99–515 du 23 juin 1999 *renforçant l'efficacité de la procédure pénale* establishes a range of alternatives to prosecution which the *procureur* might propose.

[87] Through the exchange of information, this initiative seeks to develop a more precise picture of criminality and anti-social behaviour in an area, as well as more effective means of addressing it. See Ministry of Justice circular 28 October 1997; Dieu (1999:133–38); Bell (2001:136). Also, eg *Le Monde* 25 June 2001. For a more detailed discussion of the *procureur*'s role in *justice de proximité* generally, see Wyvekens (2000).

[88] Dalle and Soulez Larivière, *Le Monde* 30 May 2002 p18.

[89] *Le Monde* 30 May 2002, p18.

[90] See also Breen (2003:222).

[91] An accusation rejected by *magistrats*. See eg the response of Jean-Pierre Zanoto, *juge à l'inspection générale des services judiciaires* in Greilsamer and Schneidermann (2002:174–77). For a discussion of the factors leading to this changing judicial role, see Roussel (1998) and (2000). On the changing inter-relationship between justice and democracy, see Garapon (1996a).

[92] Most recently by the working party set up after the Outreau case, Viout (2005).

opened accusing political figures and businessmen. That's what bothers them.[*Juge des enfants*, site D].[93]

The role of the *juge d'instruction* and the guarantee of more independent investigation[94] continues to be marginalised as increasing numbers of offences are placed within the jurisdiction of the *procureur*.[95] Marking the end of an era by their action, several of the *juges d'instruction* involved in investigating the high-profile financial and political *affaires* of the 1990s have now resigned from their posts, disillusioned with the lack of support given to them.[96] Corrupt practices have been brought to the public's attention, but the cynicism remains, what Wright (1999:116–17) terms 'the lingering cultural aversion to the rule of law which affects many groups—from the ordinary citizens who evade and avoid taxation . . . to certain state officials who do not disguise their contempt for the "legal pedantry" of the courts.'[97] The implication of local politicians in corruption scandals has not prevented their re-election: for example, despite receiving an 18-month suspended prison sentence, Xavier Dugoin remained in office as a senator. This arrogance and contempt for the judiciary reaches to the highest political level. When Olivier Foll, head of the judicial police in Paris, instructed his officers not to assist the *juge d'instruction* Eric Halphen in his search of the apartment of Jean Tiberi, the mayor of Paris, Foll was suspended from office[98] and the Interior Minister who backed him openly, Jean-Louis Debré, was publicly rebuked by the *Cour de cassation*. President Chirac, however, despite his role as consitutional guarantor of the independence of the judiciary, supported both Foll and Debré.[99]

The Policing Function

Introduction

The policing function is similarly defined in England and Wales and in France, as the maintenance of public order and the prevention and detection of crime. The

---

[93] See also Valéry Turcey, president of the USM, in Greilsamer and Schneidermann (2002:427).

[94] Though see below for the conflicts of interest which arise when the police are placed under political pressure which overrides their judicial orders.

[95] See Ch 2.

[96] Eva Joly, Eric Halphen and Laurence Vichnievsky. See *Le Monde* 14 March 2002.

[97] In interview with Greilsamer and Schneidermann (2002:250), Jean-Pierre Dintilhac (then *procureur de la République* in Paris) describes politicians as being obsessed with a form of legitimacy which only comes through election: 'An elected politician is elected to pass laws, but an elected politican who breaks the law is not legitimate, whereas an unelected *juge* who applies the law is legitimate. The two types of legitimacy are of a different nature, but both are equivalent and valid.'

[98] See *Le Monde* 28 February 1997. See also the account of this incident in the *juge d'instruction* Eric Halphen's book (2002:91–95).

[99] Jean Tiberi was Chirac's successor as the mayor of Paris and the investigation into the finances of the RPR which this enquiry included, was of concern to Chirac.

overarching ideology, however, is presented in somewhat different terms. In France, the police act on behalf of the state,[100] whereas in England and Wales, they are said to act on behalf of the public—the notion of policing by consent. The range of activities assumed as part of the general policing function also differs: French police, for example, carry out work which would be undertaken in England and Wales by HM Immigration and by MI5. But perhaps most significantly for our purposes, there are also important structural and organisational differences between the corps of officers who undertake policing work in the two countries. In England and Wales there are forty three independent police forces, with overall accountability to the Home Secretary, but like many other European countries, the policing function in France is carried out by both the *police nationale* and the *Gendarmerie nationale*. The *police nationale* (comprising some 120,000 officers) tends to operate in and around cities and they are under the Minister of the Interior. The *Gendarmerie* (comprising some 85,000 officers) have tended to operate in less urban locations[101] and they are part of the army, under the Minister of Defence. In addition, there are some 3,000 small municipal police forces, employed, managed and paid for at the local level, accountable to the mayor.[102] Together with the further division between judicial and administrative functions discussed below, this makes the system of policing in France somewhat complex.[103] There has been some restructuring in an attempt to harmonise the corresponding grades between police and *gendarmes*, but each service is proud of its own tradition and the merging of the two to produce a single unified police service is strongly resisted.[104]

The Emergence of the Policing Role in France

The *Gendarmerie* enjoys a long history, dating back to the mounted military of the 14th century, known as the *maréchaussée*.[105] Initially concerned with military

---

[100] See Ch 1 for a more general discussion of the omnipresent role of the French state within the administration of justice.

[101] See the work of Renée Zauberman (1997) for an appreciation of the increasingly urbanised role of the *Gendarmerie*.

[102] The current trend towards local policing as a way of tackling the growing feeling of *insécurité*, particularly in 'sensitive' areas, is criticized by some as retrograde step. See eg *Le Monde* 16 March 2001, where André-Michel Ventre (then general secretary of the police union, the *Syndicat des commissaires et haut fontionnaires de la police national*) argues that prevention (the job of the municipal police, who lack the power of full national police officers) and repression (the job of the *procureur*) should not be separated, but should go hand in hand. The then Interior Minister, Nicolas Sarkozy, sought to reassure officers against the 'municipalisation' of the police. See *Le Monde* 28 June 2002.

[103] Comparing developments across 19th-century Europe, Emsley (2000:92) suggests a broad typology of three kinds of public police: state civilian; civilian municipal; and state military. Liang (1992) describes five national police styles that emerged in response to 'popular unrest' in the 19th century. See also Berlière (1996).

[104] In Belgium, legislation passed in 1998 merged the police and *gendarmes* into one unified service. See Pesquié (2002).

[105] See further Dieu (1999). Also Christine Horton's (1995) excellent study of policing policy in France. For a broader account of the *gendarmes* in 19th-century Europe, see Emsley (1999b).

offenders, by the 16th century they had acquired duties relating to civilians. The basic structure of today's *Gendarmerie nationale* stems from the reorganisation of the *maréchaussée* in 1720, although they did not become the *Gendarmerie nationale* until 1791. A decree in 1903 established the *Gendarmerie* as a local military force which must not, under any circumstances, intervene in political matters. As we shall see, this is an important defining characteristic which sets the French *gendarme* apart from her colleagues in the *police nationale*. The *gendarmes* are accountable to three different hierarchies: like the police, they are responsible to the Minister of Justice for criminal investigations and to the Minister of the Interior for public order, or administrative matters; but unlike the police, they are part of the army and for all other aspects of their work, they are responsible to the Minister of Defence.[106]

The *police nationale* has a more recent history and it has developed in response to political and social instability and in particular, to challenges to state power. The period following the 1789 Revolution which ended the absolute monarchy of the *Ancien Régime* in France and saw the birth of the First French Republic, was one of great social and constitutional change and upheaval. But even in the last century, France has had to deal with wartime occupation and the choice of resistance or collaboration; the struggle for Algerian independence (police discontent with the handling of which contributed to the fall of the Fourth Republic); and the general strike and student rioting of 1968, which nearly toppled de Gaulle's government and led to increasingly repressive policing legislation. Social stability and internal security have been key issues for government and this has resulted in the desire for a centrally controlled police which can maintain public order and gather political intelligence for the protection of the state.

The first non-military policing role in France was established in Paris in 1667, under Louis XIV.[107] Wide powers to ensure the welfare of citizens and to regulate aspects of food, housing, health and safety were provided for and exercised by the *basse police*. In addition, the political police (*haute police*) were concerned with wider surveillance and political security to protect the monarch's regime.[108] By 1699 this system began to be extended to the provinces. The monarchy was overthrown in the 1789 Revolution and Article XII of the *Déclaration des droits de l'homme et du citoyen* published in the same year asserted the role of the police in serving the interests of all citizens. As part of his drive to build a strong centralised

---

[106] There are a number of specialist groupings within the *Gendarmerie*. The *Gendarmerie Mobile* (similar to the CRS, described below) is a public order force with semi-military training, equipped with machine guns, water cannon, armoured vehicles, light tanks and helicopters. They are activated on the order of the Minister of the Interior, usually requested by the *préfet*. Also worthy of mention is the anti-terrorist unit, the *Groupement d'Intervention de la Gendarmerie Nationale* (GIGN).

[107] See further Williams (1979); Martin (1990) chs 2 and 3; Renaudie (2000).

[108] It might be argued that at this time policing represented a function rather than a coherent body of men or women. See further Williams (1979).

state, Napoleon established a network of mayors, *préfets* and *sous-préfets* to implement national policies, including that relating to policing. In 1829, just before the
establishment of the first police force in London, uniformed police were introduced in Paris, armed with a cane by day and a sabre at night. However, although
created to re-establish faith in the Paris police, they did not win wide public support and continued to be seen as the political tool of the *préfet* and the ruling
authorities.[109] Influenced by the apparent success and public support of Robert
Peel's beat officers, a similar system was introduced in 1854 under Emperor
Napoleon III and in 1871 the officers were renamed *gardiens de la paix*.[110] A gradual process of professionalisation began with the establishment of police training
in 1883 and trades unions from 1905.

However, despite the strongly centralised nature of France's political and
administrative structures, the policing function continued to be a local matter.[111]
It was not until 1941, under the more repressive powers of the Vichy regime in
occupied France that wide-scale change occurred, when the state declared itself
responsible for policing in every town with a population of over 10,000.[112] The
forerunner of the CRS (*compagnies républicaines de sécurité*) was also established
at this time—reserve groups of officers responsible for the maintenance of public
order and crowd control. A separate arrangement remained in place in Paris until
1966 when the Paris Prefecture of Police[113] was finally forced to merge with the rest
of the country's police (the *Sûreté Nationale*) within the newly named *police
nationale*.

A Two-Force System: National Police and *Gendarmerie*

Thus, we see that the two national services responsible for policing in France
have grown out of very different histories and traditions, traditions which continue to define the contemporary policing role. *Gendarmes* are part of the military
hierarchy, living on site in the *Gendarmerie* and very much a figure in the local

---

[109] Gleizal, J-J Gatti-Domenach, J and Journès, C (1993) *La police* (Presses universitaires de France, Paris) p 83, cited in Horton (1995:12).

[110] Emsley (1999a:36).

[111] Lyon was the first city outside Paris to have a central state police force in 1851, and the second, Marseille, did not succumb for another 50 years. There was considerable resistance to this process of centralisation and attempts to gain state control of policing in Lille, for example, were abandoned. See Horton (1995:13).

[112] As population centres have shifted since the original policing areas were drawn up in 1941, so the volume of work handled by police and *gendarmes* has become uneven in some places. In order to bring the 'policing map' into line with current needs, a two year process of redeployment was begun in 2003.

[113] A separate police *préfet*, appointed by the President of the Republic on the advice of the Interior Minister has responsibility for all the police forces of Paris. This arrangement, keeping the Paris police under the firm control of central government, is a function not only of the size of Paris as a capital city, but also of its importance as a key site in times of political turbulence. See further Fosdick (1915:84–91).

community.[114] This is their strength in terms of local knowledge, but the allegiance they have to 'their' community and their fixed view of people can also act as an obstacle. Mouhanna (2001b:39) found that for the *gendarme*, it is the outsider, the person living on the margins, who is often seen as the 'ideal' culprit.[115] A senior *procureur* in a larger urban location explained to us:

> The good thing about the *gendarmes* in the provinces is that they are omnipresent. When you need to carry out an investigation, you have a *gendarme* immediately and he is ready and willing, at your service, for whatever you need . . . It is interesting to work with the *gendarmes*, because they know everybody . . . For example, in straightforward cases of rape or incest, or things like that, they are effective because they know how to put people in touch with each other. But as soon as they have a more complicated case, first of all they bring you the case of the prowler. There is always a prowler. Let me give you another example. I have very rarely taken a case from the *gendarmes* and given it to the police. I did it once . . . a lady who had been found at home by her 12-year-old son, dead, with a rifle next to her. The *gendarmes* telephoned me at night, telling me 'the lady committed suicide' [because there was a bullet in her mouth] . . . I asked for another expert to check this . . . I was called an hour later to be told, 'the bullet entered at the nape of the neck' . . . it was now a *crime* . . . the *gendarmes* . . . they brought out the prowler for me, the famous prowler . . . There were problems with the timings which did not fit. That led me rapidly to think that the kid could be the culprit. I said this to the *gendarmes*, the *gendarmes* refused to accept this idea. Refused. A child of 12 does not kill his mother. So, I told them that the child should be taken when coming out of school, placed in *garde à vue* and interviewed. They refused. They refused, saying, 'No, we will try some other leads, some other lines of enquiry'. It was not a refusal, but it was a desire to wait. That did not suit me . . . the *gendarmes* refused, so I removed the case from them and passed it on to the police. [E7]

For the *gendarmes*, their work is more than just a job, it is a vocation and most are fiercely loyal and proud to be part of the army.[116] They point to their non-political role as evidence of their professionalism, reliability and commitment.[117] The police, in contrast, have always operated in larger conurbations and outside the

---

[114] Some *gendarmes* and their families are now living 'off site', putting some physical distance between them and the community they police. See Mouhanna (2001b). There are dangers in being such a close and potentially powerful part of a community. *Gendarmes* in Mouhanna's study described the way in which their dependence upon the mayor and others from whom they had received favours (such as free petrol, stationery, computers etc) meant that they felt obliged to turn a blind eye to some offences, especially road traffic crime. See also Zauberman (1998b).

[115] In our research, gypsies came in for especially harsh treatment in this respect, being blamed for the vast proportion of crime in some areas. See also Zauberman (1998c).

[116] Whilst police culture is largely limited to the professional life of the *police* (Monjardet 1994), that of the *gendarme* is more all encompassing and also permeates the private sphere (Mouhanna 2001b).

[117] The police, in contrast are highly unionised. Note, however, the somewhat shocking appearance of the *gendarmes* protesting on the streets in December 2001—see *Le Monde* 6 December 2001, p 36 'le visage Gendarme' P Georges: 'This really is the end. The *gendarmes* protesting. The *gendarmes* are on the street. In uniform. In anger . . . it is more than just the end, it is the end of a culture.'

military regime. The state has battled to gain a monopoly on the policing function and officers are now centrally accountable to the Ministry of the Interior. Although susceptible to political pressure from within their own hierarchy, they are more numerous and more specialised than their *gendarmes* colleagues, whom they consider to be less professional and too entrenched in the military, rather than policing function.

The difficulties of operating a two-force system, where there are conflicting loyalties and lines of accountability, has led to a hostile divide between the two police services, often referred to as '*la petite guerre entre la police et la Gendarmerie*'.[118] Most officers we spoke to considered themselves able to work reasonably well with their police/*gendarme* colleagues on a daily basis, believing any serious conflict to be confined to the most senior ranks. However, there was clearly a degree of mutual distrust and even resentment between police and *gendarmes*,[119] each believing themselves to be the more superior corps. As one senior *procureur* described the relationship:

> The *gendarmes* think that they are just as competent as the police, and the police take the *gendarmes* for a bunch of bloody idiots. [E7]

The police were critical of the *gendarmes*' loyalty to their military hierarchy, which they believed shielded them from scrutiny and prevented them from sharing information and collaborating in investigations. For their part, the *gendarmes* pointed to the political nature of the police hierarchy and the censoring effect this might have upon criminal investigations. Both believed themselves to be more open, more professional and more competent than the other. The professional rivalry between the two corps meant that on occasions, they were competing for the same investigation. The police, in particular, complained that the *gendarmes* would keep the 'best' cases for themselves, passing on more minor offences and those with no known suspect to the police.[120] In area A, for example, the police

---

[118] This is not a new phenomenon, it dates back to Napoleon I. See Lignereux (2002).

[119] The *gendarmes*, for example, often complained to us of the legal ambiguity surrounding their ability to work as plain clothes officers. (A decree of 1903 forbids *gendarmes* from working in plain clothes, but an *instruction* of 11 May 1987 provides for an exception to this, provided permission is granted from the competent authority within the hierarchy). The police, on the other hand, resented the fact that the *gendarmes* have greater authority to use arms: the police may only fire in self-defence; the *gendarmes* (provided they are in uniform and have issued the standard warning) may fire to prevent a person escaping. The legal immunity from prosecution for *gendarmes* opening fire in these circumstances (granted in 1903) has been challenged as being contrary to the ECHR by the family of Romuald Luffroy, who was accidentally shot dead in 1996 when trying to avoid a road check. See *Le Monde* 6 February 2003. The *Cour de cassation* (18 February 2003) ordered a re-trial of the case, as it was not established that the *gendarme's* use of force was absolutely necessary in the circumstances.

[120] This was resented as skewing the likely clear-up rate in favour of the *gendarmes*. The figures are indeed markedly different, the clear-up rate achieved by *gendarmes* appearing to be double the national average. See Zauberman (1997:325). There also appeared to be some difference in the recording of crime. *Gendarmes* kept only an informal note of offences which they did not intend investigating, thus inflating their clear-up rate. Crime statistics did not appear to be of huge importance to the *gendarmes*

were investigating a rape case involving five separate complaints. The neighbour-ing *gendarmes* were aware of this and had copies of statements gathered in the enquiry, but when they arrested a man in connection with the same investigation, they retained the case, preferring to interview the suspect themselves rather than pass the affair to those police already involved. This caused a great deal of bad feel-ing on the part of the police, who believed the *gendarmes* to have acted in bad faith, keeping hold of an 'interesting' high-profile case, rather than passing it on as is the usual practice. They also considered that the ultimate success of the case may be jeopardised because of inadequate preparation of evidence—notably the production of a confession of two short paragraphs which was likely to be chal-lenged by a defence lawyer should the case reach the *cour d'assises*.

> They have not played straight. We worked together from the start, we gave them every-thing, the statements are there . . . and what's more, it [the evidence] might end up being excluded. They have made a bad job of it—you've seen it —three lines for an interview. [Police officer, area A]

For the police, this incident typified the problematic nature of the military role of the *gendarmes*.

> We're completely open. They come here, we give them access to everything, and look what happens. As usual, it's totally one sided. They are full of secrecy, they hide every-thing. They're the army. [Police officer, area A]

This was also the view of a number of our police questionnaire respondents who disliked the military hierarchy of the *gendarmes* believing that it made them less accountable and less willing to share information, any collaboration on the part of the police not being reciprocated by the *gendarmes*.[121] Interestingly, the *gen-darmes'* opinion of police work mirrored almost exactly those of their police col-leagues:

> There are mistakes, terrible scenes, [the police] are like kids. And I'll tell you, they keep it all covered up. We can't do that. We are part of a hierarchy. You can't hide anything—it's the army. [*Gendarme*, area A]
>
> Our dossiers are well prepared, tight—everything is properly carried out and it is accu-rate. We do a thorough job. With them [the police], often there's no more than three words, nothing at all. [*Gendarme*, area A]

---

in the current study. In area A, for example, the *gendarmes* were praised for their good work by the senior commanding officer. The measure of success was not the results of investigations, but the high levels of activity in which they had been engaged: GAV, taking statements etc.

[121] Respondents talked of a 'different culture' and the tendency of *gendarmes* to 'hide' behind their military authority.

The incident observed in area A also demonstrates the importance of clear and co-ordinated direction in criminal investigations on the part of the *procureur*. A senior *gendarme* had taken advantage of the fact that an inexperienced *procureur* was on weekend duty, unaware of the ongoing investigations and the need to join the two cases together. A number of our police questionnaire respondents also complained that conflicts may arise through poor direction on the part of the *parquet*, when *gendarmes* were instructed to work on a matter which was within the territorial competence of the police. Although based broadly on geographical lines, the territorial division of responsibilities between police and *gendarmes* is not always clear. This can benefit an investigation, allowing *magistrats* to choose between the forces on the basis of skills, specialisation, available resources, competence, local knowledge and so on.[122] It also carries the risk that work and resources may be duplicated, with officers unknowingly working on the same investigation. As one *gendarme* put it: 'I've had a police gun pointed at me a number of times' (*Gendarme*, area A).

The current Raffarin administration is keen to bring the two policing corps closer together, in order that resources and intelligence can be shared more effectively.[123] Aimed at tackling the black market, the recently established *groupements d'intervention régionaux* (GIR) which bring together police, *gendarmes*, tax and customs officials, as well as *magistrats*, are directed jointly by police and *gendarmes*. Predictably, the then Interior Minister, Nicolas Sarkozy's announcement to integrate *gendarmes* into the central offices of the *Direction centrale de la police judiciaire* received a lukewarm reception from police unions. He continued to emphasise the importance of both corps working together 'against the common enemy' and the redeployment of *gendarmes* into more urban areas where the need is greater, as part of a wider restructuring of the policing architecture. For their part, the police have welcomed the extra resources promised and the determination of the present government to increase police powers. They remain troubled, however, by the prospect of amalgamating the two policing functions and in particular, the possibility that officers will lose status as a result of the conflation of ranks between the two.[124] Police and *gendarmes* have seen the inevitability of 'rationalising' the two services and expressed their concerns to us. Although the police were desirous of the better material resources that they believed were

---

[122] Eg in area F, the *procureur* wished to transfer a case from the police to the *gendarmes*, as they were better equipped to investigate the case because of their knowledge of the area. Aware of the need for diplomacy, the *procureur* first telephoned the police *commissaire* to explain why he was taking this action.

[123] As well as being the minister with responsibility for the police, under the Raffarin administration, the Minister of the Interior is now also the minister responsible for the employment of *gendarmes*.

[124] See eg *Le Monde* 12 July 2002.

available to the *gendarmes*,[125] the *gendarmes* feared that such a move would change fundamentally the nature of their job:

> The *gendarmes* will be absorbed by the police in the future. The police are militarising and the *Gendarmerie* is demilitarising. The grades are being standardised across both sides ... it was better as it was. The changes are less favourable and people will leave. We have to be mobile. It's terrible for the families. [*Gendarme*, area A]

The Double Hierarchy: Administrative and Judicial Policing

In addition to the existence of two policing bodies, both police and gendarmes have two distinct policing roles—administrative and judicial. The distinction is crucial as the officer's powers will depend upon the capacity in which she is acting. The administrative role is characterised as preventative, ensuring the maintenance of public order, whilst the judicial function concerns the investigation of a specifically identified crime. Put simply, one is before the commission of an offence (or concerning more general criminal investigation), the other is after (concerning a specific case). In practice, the distinction is not always clear and actions which begin as administrative (such as policing a public demonstration) may become judicial policing matters once offences are committed. In the *police nationale*, administrative policing will tend to be carried out by the uniformed branch, whilst the criminal investigation (*judiciaire*) work is undertaken by plain-clothes officers whose training and career structure are quite separate.[126] The *gendarmes*, who must wear uniform at all times (unless specifically authorised by a senior commanding officer), are organised in smaller *brigades* which are responsible for both administrative and judicial work (Horton 1995:27).

The judicial/administrative distinction is also significant and potentially problematic, given that officers depend upon a different hierarchy for each of the two functions. As *police judiciaire* conducting criminal investigations and so performing acts which impact upon the liberties of the individual, they are under the Minister of Justice, with day-to-day answerability to *magistrats*. In the most serious cases, the investigation is the responsibility of the *juge d'instruction*, who instructs the police to carry out specific enquiries through powers delegated to

---

[125] The *gendarmes* in our study were not well resourced and many bought their own copies of the CPP and even their own personal computers for use in the office. Zauberman (1997:346 fn 62) estimates that some 80% of computers used by the *gendarmes* in her study were the personal property of the officers.

[126] Officers must first undergo a period of training before acquiring the status of *officier de police judiciaire*, (OPJ), which then enables them to carry out arrests and to detain and question suspects in police detention (*garde à vue*), as well as authorising them to sign the all important statements of evidence (*procès verbaux*) which appear in the dossier, or case file. They are assisted by *agents de police judiciaire* (APJ) who may perform some of the same tasks under the supervision of the OPJ.

them by a *commission rogatoire*. In the vast majority of instances, however, it is the *procureur* who is responsible for the direction of criminal investigations, including the period of police detention and interrogation, the *garde à vue*. The nature of these two (different) forms of judicial supervision is explored in later chapters, but it is important to note here the relationship between the executive and the judiciary and the potential for political interference in the judicial control of police investigations.

As discussed earlier in this chapter, the *procureur*, as a *magistrat*, is part of the independent judiciary, guaranteeing the rights and liberties of the individual; and as part of the *ministère public* acting in the name of 'the people', she is democratically accountable to a government minister. To the common law jurist, such executive control or supervision of the judiciary would be improper; within the French republican tradition, accountability to the executive plays a crucial part in the guarantee of judicial independence.[127] However, there is a tension in this arrangement which has been demonstrated in a number of high-profile cases, where judicial independence has been overridden, rather than supported by the interests of the executive.[128] Ministers of Justice, often in consultation with the Prime Minister, have ordered investigations to be delayed or terminated altogether—resulting in one instance, in the extreme measure of dispatching a helicopter to Kathmandu in Nepal in order to get the prosecutor (who was there on a trekking holiday) to sign a document preventing the opening of an *information*[129] into the financial affairs of the mayor of Paris and his wife.

Most *procureurs* will rarely experience such interference, as it does not occur in the bulk of ordinary cases where those being investigated are of no political interest. The hierachical organisation of the *parquet*, however, ensures that superiors can keep a watchful eye over the business of those *procureurs* working on the ground.

> It's true that you can have political interference from within the hierarchy . . . There is nothing to stop the head of the local *parquet* from saying 'There is no need to deal with that case straight away, as it is not urgent'.[130] That's a way of sabotaging the investigation . . . it might happen in sensitive cases which implicate mayors and politicians, or business people who are linked to the government . . . I have never felt political pressure during my professional career. Perhaps because I have never had any political cases. You feel it a little in some very particular cases, where you can be questioned by superiors, or

---

[127] See also discussion in Ch 1, 'The French Republican Tradition'.
[128] See Elliot and Vernon (2000:153–55); Godard (2002); Hodgson (2002a:236–40) and the discussion above.
[129] This would be an investigation under the *juge d'instruction*, over whom the executive has no hierarchical control. Ironically, the more senior *procureur général* is not authorised to sign this documentation, only the *procureur de la République*.
[130] Conversely, we observed one case where the police were instructed by the *procureur* to deal quickly with a minor offence, as it related to an ongoing investigation into the affairs of a *juge d'instruction*.

required to report to the Minister of Justice, but I have never had the occasion to be told by the *procureur général* or the Minister that I must do this or that. [*Procureur adjoint*, D3]

In other aspects of police work, officers work within a different line of responsibility. The police organisation and administrative function (crime prevention; public order—notably the policing of demonstrations; traffic control; political intelligence gathering) is under the Minister of the Interior, with answerability to the *préfet*[131] (or, in some larger cities the *préfet de police*) at the level of *département*. This offers the potential for a government minister, either directly, or through the prefecture system, to exert political influence over the wider operation of the policing role, particularly in relation to the *police nationale*. At the local level, the *préfet* is responsible for the implementation of government policy and makes operational policing decisions affecting the types of offences and areas to be targeted and the mounting of particular police operations, as well as gathering political intelligence. Given the *préfet*'s accountability to the interior ministry, it is perhaps not surprising that Horton (1995:30–31) notes that a number of these policies are 'overtly political'. At the national level, the Minister of the Interior appoints the Director-General of the National Police (responsible for the day-to-day running of the police service) and plays a key part in the promotion and dismissal of senior police personnel.[132] Thus, there is a very close relationship between the *police nationale* and the political powers upon whom they depend, reflected in the accepted practice that a change of government will normally bring with it a change in most of the senior policing positions.[133] One *commissaire*[134] explained to us:

> At the level of *commissaire*, politics starts to manifest itself. It was scandalous how the previous government nominated *commissaires* who were their supporters, serious socialists. We are still dealing with this, clearing up the mess that resulted. They were politicians, not police. [Area A]

---

[131] As a local representative of the government, the *préfet* has a wide range of responsibilities, of which policing is only one.

[132] The *juge d'instruction* Eric Halphen (2002:162) writes of the influence of political power upon the police:

> When an investigation looks as though it might be awkward, and it is moving too quickly for their liking, nothing is easier or simpler than to silence those police officers who are too efficient, or to place at the head of their service, a senior officer loyal to his hierarchy or incompetent, or both. What better way to hinder an investigation and to stay informed of everything that happens?

[133] Horton (1995:38) notes the importance of the relationship between the mayor and the local police chief, both of whom have a vested interest in remaining in office. For this reason, close ties may develop which have an influence equal to that of the *préfet*—who is likely to have a weaker political affiliation and moves *département* every three years.

[134] A *commissaire* is a senior police officer, roughly equivalent to an English/Welsh superintendent. See Horton (1995) ch 4, especially pp 53–56.

Significantly, the functioning of the *Gendarmerie* is somewhat less implicated in this arrangement as many aspects of its organisation remain within its own military hierarchy. The Director-General of the *Gendarmerie*, for example, is selected by the Minister of Defence and the post is more likely to remain constant despite changing political administrations.

The division of responsibility between two equal (in theory, at least) and separate authorities is intended to ensure a balance of power, with each acting as a check on the other. The existence of this double hierarchy however, can lead to conflicts of interests between judicial and other policing priorities. These conflicts may be in the form of competition for resources and the allocation of officers to administrative or judicial tasks; or, more politically, to competing assertions of authority over the conduct of criminal investigations. In describing the nature of this dual system, *magistrats* were quite clear that whilst they could cultivate effective professional relationships with particular officers, at the general level, the judicial hierarchy would always be subordinate to that of the police themselves.[135]

> The problem is that they [the police] have their own hierarchy, which counts much more for them. 'The' reform, would be to place their hierarchy completely under judicial authority. If the police were wholly responsible to the Minister of Justice, then we would be able to master the situation completely. [A5]

> It is quite clear and every *magistrat* knows it, that in their [the police] organisation, in their ethos, in their culture, what counts for them—because it is their hierarchy, because it is their career, because it is the organisation of their daily work, what counts above all, is not the Minister of Justice, but the Minister of the Interior, that is plain. [A6]

> Ordinarily, the *parquet* directs the judicial activity of the police, but the police come under the direct authority of the *préfet* and it is from him that they take their instructions. If the *préfet* fixes his priorities, he gives a certain number of instructions which do not necessarily go in the same direction as those of the *procureur*, and it is obvious that the duty of the police will be to follow the *préfet* and not the *procureur*. [E3]

Although many *magistrats* suggested to us that having the judicial police wholly accountable to them would improve the quality and independence of investigations, they were under no illusions that this would be unacceptable to the police and unlikely ever to happen.[136]

> Senior *procureur*: The best solution would be . . . to have a direct attachment of the *police judiciare* to the *parquet* . . . that would be more effective . . . but . . . that would pose

---

[135] The way in which police and *procureurs* view one another is also of interest here. Neither saw the other as a colleague–85% of *procureurs* and 83% of police said this was never the case. But whereas OPJ were always or often considered subordinates by 79% of *procureurs*, and senior officers by 64%, 83% of senior police indicated that they would never regard the *parquet* as a superior. One senior officer interviewed told us, 'Sometimes, I get the feeling that they [the *parquet*] think of us as their auxilliary, that the OPJ is their housemaid.' [D5]

[136] See also Halphen (2002:160–61).

sociological questions . . . it seems obvious to me that someone who works on the instructions of a judicial authority should depend on that judicial authority. Now, they work on the instructions of a judicial authority, but they depend on their own hierarchy. Imagine what kinds of manipulation that can lead to?!

Researcher: Would that be possible in practice?

Senior *procureur*: Why wouldn't it be possible? It's a political decision . . . I think that the police are a much more powerful body than *magistrats* . . . If they wanted to, they could do it tomorrow. I don't believe that they want to . . . They [the police] do not want to be the by-product of *magistrats* . . . they do not want to be managed by *magistrats*. [E7]

This conflict of hierarchies was less pronounced in the case of *gendarmes* whose military regime of loyalty, discipline and obedience so disliked by the police, endeared them to *magistrats*.

In sensitive cases, there can be interference between the orders of the *préfet* (representing the state) and the judicial authority. This is less so with the *Gendarmerie* who seem to retain more autonomy. [*Parquet* questionnaire respondent 12b]

There is no equal measure between the judicial sanction and reward and that emanating from the interior ministry—only the genuine independence of the police investigator from the interior ministry would be a real guarantee of her work. It is the same with the *gendarmes*, but with one important difference, that they are part of the army, concerned to respect judicial authority. [*Parquet* questionnaire respondent 6]

The *gendarmes* will respect the order given, because of their military background . . . With the police: the failure to respect our instructions is partly due to the fact that they are very strongly unionised. [*Parquet* questionnaire respondent, 23f]

There are particular affinities which exist according to whichever investigator you work with (police or *gendarme*). But it is always easier to frame the work of the *gendarmes*, to get them to carry out a certain task by a certain time. [*Parquet* questionnaire respondent, 12b]

I prefer to work with *gendarmes* rather than then police. It is perhaps because the *gendarmes* are part of the military. There are things which bother me with the police. They have fixed hours—9am–12noon and 2–6pm—and even if they are working nights that always poses organisational problems. If you want them to bring a suspect to the office at 1.30pm, that's not always possible, whereas with the *gendarmes*, it's less of a problem. Also, for night time work such as surveillance, I find them much better. [A3][137]

---

[137] The diligence of the *gendarmes* was noted by several *magistrats*.

I am not happy with the statements of evidence, especially when there are several offences and [the police] make do with one overall interview. I find that there is a huge difference between statements taken by the police and those by the *gendarmes*. With the *gendarmes*, you have interviews of 15 pages, which include even the colour of the suspect's socks. That's also a waste of time in my opinion. But it's also their way of working. [A4]

More significantly, there may be political differences which compromise the independence and effectiveness of judicial investigations, such as happened in the Tiberi affair discussed above, when on the order of their police superior, officers accompanying *juge d'instruction* Eric Halphen, refused to follow his order to search the home of Jean Tiberi, a politician and mayor of Paris.

Accountability to more than one ministry is also unsatisfactory from the point of view of police officers and two-thirds of our police questionnaire respondents considered it problematic. The police function is complicated by having to work within different legal and organisational frameworks which sometimes work in co-operation, but which also come into conflict in the interests, approaches, cultures and priorities which they represent. Whilst many *magistrats* saw their role in the conduct of criminal investigations as complementary to police work, providing the necessary legal framework and guidance and representing the public interest, this was not the experience of all officers. Typically, respondents described the parquet as being disconnected from the reality of police work, with a vision which was limited to the understanding of issues in only judicial terms.

> *Magistrats*, for the most part, are disconnected from reality and often have no sense of the wider public interest. [Police questionnaire respondent 44]

> A city's crime and security problems cannot be reduced to the form of purely procedural matters which are the *magistrats'* only concern. [Police questionnaire respondent 31]

Two-thirds of our police questionnaire respondents did not think that the *parquet* appreciated the nature of and constraints upon their work, remaining ignorant of the different policing roles, as well as operational and resource issues. In particular, they were unaware of:

> The fact that investigating officers work much more than they do. The difficulties of dealing with large numbers of dossiers at the same time . . . [because of] the difference in culture. Many *magistrats* are closeted from reality and in their ivory tower. [Police questionnaire respondent 7]

> The multitude of tasks besides those done in our '*police judiciaire*' capacity . . . [because] that does not come within their sphere of competence. [Police questionnaire respondent 10]

> The budgetary constraints and the availability of men is not always taken into account by *magistrats* . . . [because] they are unaware of the entirety of the work carried out by the police which does not fall within *judiciaire* work. [Police questionnaire respondent 6]

> It is impossible for *magistrats* to understand or appreciate the realities and the constraints of police work . . . [because] they have a different culture and a restricted vision of the law. [Police questionnaire respondent 8]

One senior officer explained the different perspectives of the police and the *parquet* in allocating and managing work.

It is true that there are ambiguities because the *parquet* directs the investigation, but on the other hand, we direct the service. As a result, I generally try and avoid the situation where the *parquet* will say that a certain case should be given to a certain person. We are in the best position to judge the workload and the appropriateness of such a choice . . . OPJ are in regular contact with the *parquet* . . . and it has happened that a certain person has been given the case directly, which is not very good. It makes no difference to the *parquet*. All he wants is for the case to be dealt with. The first [officer] he comes across, he tells him that he must 'do that' and if that is a catastrophe then it's a lot of time and effort. What is urgent for them, is not necessarily urgent for us. [D5][138]

The maintenance of this balance between the two hierarchies within which criminal justice issues are implicated, is also important at the level of policy development as discussed in Chapter 2. Whilst the policing function is the responsibility of the Interior Minister, the Minister of Justice must ensure the judicial protection of civil liberties as guaranteed by the Constitution. Just as there are conflicts of power and accountability at the operational level, so there have been criticisms of the roles played by each minister in the development of policy and legislation. In the mass of reform proposals generated by the newly elected government in 2002, Dominique Perben was censured for his weak role as Justice Minister compared with the Minister of the Interior Nicholas Sarkozy, who was considered to be dominating the debate and legislative initiative on issues of justice, as well as policing and security. At the 2002 annual conference of the principal *magistrat* union, the USM, there was concern at '[t]he tendency of the police to want the creation of a police procedure detached from the judicial procedure, and without accountability' and criticism of the failure to maintain a proper balance between policing and justice issues[139]:

We want you to be a Justice Minister whose sphere of competence is respected at the heart of government. Whereas, in recent months, all members of the government have been meddling with criminal justice policy . . . In addition, we are concerned at your absence in the debates on the reform project presented by the Minister of the Interior.

---

[138] It shoud be noted that *magistrats* have no control over the allocation of police or *Gendarmerie* personnel and so cannot hasten their investigation by dedicating more officers to it. Conversely, the Minister of the Interior can slow down an enquiry by ensuring there are insufficient officers made available.

[139] See *Le Monde* 20–21 October 2002.

4

Defence Rights and the Role of the Defence Lawyer

Just as the policing and judicial functions have evolved in different ways, so too the role of the defence is different in England and Wales and in France. As one of those responsible for the investigation and presentation of evidence in the case, the defence plays a key part in England and Wales, both at the trial hearing and during the pre-trial phase. In France, the dominance of the judicially supervised investigation as the preferred procedural model has resulted in a less developed defence role. In recent years, under the growing influence of the requirements of the ECHR, the provision of defence rights has gradually moved on to the French criminal justice agenda, and reforms over the last decade have strengthened the rights of the accused in a number of ways. However, for the most part, these developments have concerned the role of the defence at trial and appeal, and during the pre-trial *instruction* procedure; in the vast majority of cases where supervision is by the *procureur*, the legally defined pre-trial defence role remains severely limited. This discrepancy is of increasing significance given the tendency within recent criminal justice reform to shift power away from the *juge d'instruction* (and even the trial judge) in favour of the *procureur*. Most crucially, suspects detained in *garde à vue* (GAV) continue to face their police interrogators alone, without the presence of either a lawyer or a *magistrat*.[1] This chapter examines the nature of the role played by the defence within a broadly inquisitorial model; the ways in which this is being redefined or developed through new legislation; and the ways in which the defence role is understood by legal actors. Chapters 5 and 6 then go on to examine in detail the ways in which the police enquiry is influenced or constrained by judicial supervision, and the extent to which the suspect's rights are guaranteed through this arrangement in practice.

In understanding the part that the criminal defence lawyer might play in the two jurisdictions, it is useful to separate out two issues contained within the

---

[1] Neither are police interrogations of adult suspects tape recorded, though those with juveniles are required to be video recorded. The safeguards present during the GAV are discussed in detail in Chs 5 and 6.

defence function which, although separate, are very closely connected. Firstly, there is the place allotted to the defence lawyer within criminal procedure: whether she may be present during the police interrogation of the suspect; whether she has access to the dossier; whether she is present during bail hearings; whether she may question witnesses in court, and so on. Secondly, in occupying that place, there is the role which she might properly be expected to play within the criminal process[2]: whether she is present in order to ensure that procedures are followed and respected; to contribute to a judicial enquiry; or to herself investigate and present evidence. The way in which each of these is defined and understood, affects the other.[3] For example, if the defence lawyer is expected to engage in defence preparation with her client during the pre-trial phase (as in England and Wales), we might expect her to be able to consult privately with the suspect held in police detention and to be present during the police interrogation of her client. If her role is to act only as an additional procedural guarantee to safeguards already in place (such as judicial supervision), with no investigative responsibility, we might expect more limited provision for custodial legal advice. Similarly, the defence might not be expected to play the same part during a pre-trial phase characterised by judicial investigation, as she might at trial, where the decision to prosecute represents a transition from investigation to accusation.

In this way, we might expect both the place and the role of the defence lawyer to be determined (at least in part) by the nature of the criminal procedure within which she functions and by the role and status of other legal actors such as the judge and prosecutor. This raises the question of whether there exists a core function that the defence lawyer must fulfil, irrespective of the particular criminal process within which she operates. This has relevance beyond the current comparative analysis; it is also an important issue in matters of international co-operation and in the ability of international instruments to provide meaningful and 'universal' guarantees of defence rights—which in turn may influence the development of domestic criminal procedures. For example, although Article 6 ECHR makes provision for a defence role, it does not specify at which point in the proceedings this becomes necessary, nor how this role should be played out. The former question has been resolved to some extent by the case law of the ECtHR (discussed below), but the precise nature of the role remains vague. To some extent, this will, of course, quite properly depend upon the ways in which defence rights are defined and understood within the wider criminal procedure in place in

---

[2] This may, of course, be defined differently by different legal actors or those representing different interests.

[3] The Delmas-Marty Commission, for example, recognised the need to respect the rights of the defence during the *garde à vue*, but was quite clear that the defence lawyer's role was primarily to inform the suspect of her rights. Thus, it was not proposed that the lawyer be present during interrogations, or that she have access to the dossier.

different jurisdictions (Hodgson, 2004b). However, this legal cultural and procedural tolerance can also serve to undermine Convention guarantees. The ways in
which defence rights are understood to be 'respected' differs across jurisdictions,
both in the legal procedural frameworks in place and the ways in which the rights
are put into practice.[4] This is demonstrated through the case law of the ECtHR
and also in initiatives such as the European Commission's recent framework decision on safeguards for suspects.[5] In order to promote 'mutual trust and recognition' of Member States' legal provisions, the objective of the framework decision
is to ensure more consistent compliance with the Convention (and now the
Charter of Fundamental Rights of the European Union), through a broad and
common agreement between Member States as to the safeguards that are necessary to ensure a 'fair trial'.[6] One key protection for suspects is the right to free and
effective legal advice.[7] Yet, although based upon the fair trial guarantees under
Article 6 ECHR (a standard, by definition, accepted by all the Member States),
there has been much disagreement around what constitutes 'defence assistance'
and at what point and for how long a suspect should receive custodial legal
advice.[8]

The Defence Lawyer as Adversarial Player

As discussed in earlier chapters, the adversarial model is characterised by two
opposing parties gathering, selecting and presenting evidence for trial. The court
has an adjudicative rather than an investigating function; it has no mission to go
beyond the evidence presented by the partisan parties (or increasingly, their representatives), either to seek out further information or to verify the probity of that
offered.[9] That is the task of the parties themselves. Accuser and accused therefore

---

[4] Signing the ECHR is not a sufficient guarantee that it is respected in practice. For example, in
R v Secretary of State ex p Ramda, 27 June 2002, the High Court said that France's status as a signatory to the ECHR could not be invoked as a satisfactory response to complaints about the fairness of the applicant's trial. Similarly, in its judgment of 16 May 2003, in the case of *Irastorza
Dorronsoro*, the French *cour d'appel* de Pau refused to accede to an extradition request from Spain
on the ground that there was a suspicion that a co-defendant had been 'tortured' by Spanish police
officers.
[5] EU Council Framework Decision on Certain Procedural Rights in Criminal Proceedings throughout the European Union COM(2004)3289 final (Brussels 28 April 2004) and discussed in Ch 1.
[6] Explanatory memorandum to the Framework Decision, para 9.
[7] Arts 2, 3, 4 and 5 of the Framework Decision.
[8] In its response to the EU Commission's earlier Green Paper, the *Syndicat de la magistrature* is critical of France's assumption that suspects' rights are only endangered in the 10 new Member States,
accusing France of a legal and political blindness with regard to its own legal reality. Their response
can be found on the Justice and Home Affairs website at http://europa.eu.int/comm/justice_home/
fsj/criminal/procedural/fsj_criminal_responses_en.htm
[9] There are, of course, rules of evidence concerning admissibility, which in turn relate to probity.

play a central role in adversarial procedure both in the trial and the pre-trial phase, controlling the nature of the evidence on which the court will base its decision. This is demonstrated in the defendant's decision to enter a guilty plea, which has the effect of short-circuiting the court's fact-finding role; the defendant's public admission becomes a formal judicial finding of guilt without the need for any further judicial scrutiny.[10] The inquisitorial model, on the other hand, entrusts the investigation and trial of criminal offences not to individual and opposing parties, but to a central judicial authority whose role it is to act in the wider public interest. Representing neither the interests of the prosecution nor the defence, the judicial investigator is charged with investigating evidence which exculpates, as well as incriminates, the suspect in the wider search for the truth. Investigation before and at trial is thus a public, rather than private, function, the responsibility of the state rather than the citizen; in this, the defence plays a subordinate role to the overall public interest oriented investigative function of the *magistrat*. There are no pleas of 'guilty' or 'not guilty'. An accused who admits the charges against her will still have her case heard by the court (though clearly in a more abbreviated form than in instances where the charges are contested) as it remains the responsibility of the court to satisfy itself that the offence has been fully investigated and the case against the accused made out.[11]

These two very different methods of investigation and trial suggest correspondingly different roles for the defence.[12] Within an adversarial procedure, the defence role is a necessary counterbalance to that of the prosecution before and at trial, especially given the relatively passive and distant role of the judge. Within French 'inquisitorial' procedure, the differently defined function of the prosecutor and trial judge as *magistrats*, together with the judicially supervised nature of the pre-trial investigation, mean that the defence is cast in a less essential and so subordinate role. Her participation in the process is mediated through that of the central player, the *magistrat*. In theory, the defence is not required to protect the interests of the suspect during the pre-trial phase, because the investigator is neutral, concerned to protect the rights of the accused as well as to gather evidence against her. It is only in adversarial procedure, where the investigation and prosecution roles are understood in more partisan terms and the judiciary has no

---

[10] A clear contradiction between the defendant's plea of guilty and any mitigation put forward which suggests a defence to the charges, is likely to cause the court to invite the accused to reconsider her plea. This is a rare occurrence in practice, as most defendants are represented . This in turn underlines the importance of the pre-trial defence role, as the defence lawyer's assessment of the case is generally accepted by the court without question.

[11] Arguably, the 2004 reform (Perben II) has introduced a form of guilty plea procedure. The *comparution sur reconnaissance préalable de culpabilité* permits the *procureur* and the accused to agree on a reduced sentence of up to one year's imprisonment in exchange for a formal admission, avoiding the need for a trial. This new procedure has been widely criticised as undermining the proper role of the trial court. See also discussion above, Ch 2.

[12] See also Merle (1970).

investigative function, that the accused requires her interests to be protected and advanced by her own representative.

The Rise of the Defence Advocate in 17th and 18th-century England

This view of the defence function defined relative to that of the prosecution and the trial judge is underlined in the historical work of Beattie (1986), Landsman (1983; 1990) and Langbein (2003). Drawing on the accounts provided in the Old Bailey Sessions Papers,[13] Langbein describes the rise of professional defence counsel as a direct response to increasingly zealous and partisan prosecutions, which a weak and passive judiciary was powerless to discipline. Early accusatorial procedure focused upon the accounts of the parties themselves. The presence of defence counsel was resisted for fear that it would detract from what Langbein terms (2003:35) the 'accused speaks' method of trial, thus depriving the court of an important information source, the defendant.[14] The role of defence lawyers at trial emerged during the 18th century, initially within the very specific context of treason trials. In such cases, the interests (and even the very existence) of the Crown were threatened directly, such that (in contrast to the trial of ordinary cases), prosecuting counsel was employed and the Crown's case was conducted with a partisan and excessive zeal which went as far as the suborning of perjured witnesses.[15] The trial judge was impotent to intervene: serving at the Crown's pleasure, the judiciary occupied a weak position, unable to provide adequate assurances of independence or impartiality.[16] The result of this wholly unbalanced trial method was a number of spectacular miscarriages of justice during the latter part of the 17th century.[17]

Langbein argues that an alternative and better approach may have been to move towards a criminal procedure based around judicial investigation, such as that existing in Europe. This would have required firstly, strengthening the role and the independence of the judiciary, enabling them to tackle prosecution practice in the court room directly; and secondly, institutional reform of both the trial and the pre-trial process, in order to ensure a greater degree of neutrality in

---

[13] These records are now available at http://www.oldbaileyonline.org. Note also that in Beattie's work, the 'central core of evidence comes from the Surrey assizes and quarter sessions, but a considerable body of material has also been drawn from the courts of Sussex . . . other courts, especially the Old Bailey, [are] also referred to occasionally' (1986:15).

[14] The trial process was something of a conveyor belt: 54 accused felons were tried in four days at Surrey Assizes in 1751, making the average hearing time around thirty minutes (Beattie 1986:378). See also Langbein (2003:18).

[15] Langbein (2003:98).

[16] The idea that the court acted for the accused (rather than 'their better client, the king') was ridiculed by some commentators discussed in Beattie (1986:358). See also King (2000:223-5).

[17] The Popish Plot (1678–80); the Rye House Plot (1683); and the Bloody Assizes (1685), all discussed in Langbein (2003) ch 2.

investigation and prosecution. However, the existing Continental model of a central investigative authority was unattractive, tainted as it was by the use of judicial torture to obtain confessions.[18] Instead, the response was the 1696 Treason Trials Act, which allowed defendants to engage their own counsel in cases of treason. In this way, Langbein argues that the criminal defence role developed in England precisely because there was no judicially controlled trial and pre-trial procedure. Although this marked the beginning of a more lawyer-centred adversarial procedure, it is important to note that treason trials were distinguished from ordinary cases in two important ways: the defendants were generally wealthy aristocrats; and the prosecution was partisan in the extreme. This meant that neither the cost of hiring defence counsel, nor the truth-distorting effect of defence representation which had previously troubled the courts, were considered problematic.[19] The procedure introduced was therefore specific to a very narrow band of cases, which involved a very specific and atypical type of defendant.

However, within the intellectual debate around the equality between Crown and defendant which took place towards the end of the 17th century and which was at the core of the Whig political agenda,[20] conditions became ripe for the extension of defence counsel provision to ordinary trials.[21] Once again, the main driver for this appeared to be prosecutorial practice, which made growing use of lawyers at trial and during the investigation, and which relied increasingly upon witnesses who testified in exchange for immunity or reward. 'Especially in London, prosecution was becoming ever more the province of lawyers and of a questionable corps of reward-seeking thieftakers' (Langbein 2003:4).[22] The judicial response was to allow defence counsel to examine and cross-examine witnesses in order that the reliability of the prosecution evidence could be probed,[23]

---

[18] Langbein (2003:338–43); Spencer (2002:8–10). It is ironic that judicial torture was a direct result of attempts to impose stringent standards of proof—standards that simply did not exist in England at that time. In order to restrain the power of the judge in the investigation and trial of offences in medieval Europe, a standard of proof was imposed which required either the testimony of two eye witnesses, or a confession. Judicial torture developed in order to ensure the conviction of those suspected of being guilty, but against whom there were not two eye witnesses.

[19] Langbein (2003:102–4). This was of similar concern in France. In debating the Ordinance of 1670 which fixed inquisitorial procedure in France, it was said of defence counsel:

> We know how fertile these kinds of counsel are in finding openings to frame conflicts of jurisdiction, how they often scheme to discover nullities in the proceedings and to give birth to an infinitude of side issues. It is therefore peculiarly in the interests of the wealthy that counsel is granted. (Pussort, quoted in Esmein (1913), Editorial Preface xxix).

[20] Shapiro (1993).

[21] Beattie (1986:356–59); (1991:224).

[22] Statutes offering rewards for successful prosecution led to what Langbein describes as a 'mercenary proto-police', the thieftakers, whose only interest was in getting a prosecution and so financial reward. See also Beattie (1986:50–59); (1991:224–25); (2001:226–56; 376–83; 401–17).

[23] Langbein (2003:109–10). Drawing on the work of Landsman (1990) and Beattie (1991) Vogler (2005) points to the wider factors which might also have contributed to this 'lawyerisation' process, such as the use of the courts for political campaigns during the latter quarter of the 18th century and the development of the law of evidence.

although not to address the jury, in the hope that the benefit of hearing from the accused directly would not be lost. The nature of counsel's participation in the trial appeared to vary between courts—some being allowed to question defence witnesses directly, others being required to leave this to the judge.[24] However, by the end of the 18th century, trial procedures had altered as rules of evidence developed and lawyers were increasingly present.[25] The extent to which the growth in evidentiary rules either encouraged, or was the result of the 'lawyerisation' of the trial is unclear. Landsman (1990:602) argues that the new rules of evidence encouraged the involvement of lawyers; Beattie (1986:362–76; 1991:233) that they were a consequence of lawyers' involvement; and Langbein (2003: ch 4), that they were a (misguided) judicial creation, designed to remedy the ills of an unsystematic and corrupt pre-trial process. Once their place was secured, however, it seems that the presence of defence lawyers changed the nature and objective of the trial, from a hearing which focused on the defendant's account, to one which largely silenced her voice, as counsel focused upon the enforcement of the prosecutorial burdens of production and proof.[26] In this way, the truth was demonstrated to the court rather than discovered or revealed.[27] Although the accused is implicated to a far greater extent in evidence gathering and in the court presentation of evidence within the adversarial model of procedure, paradoxically, her direct participation in the proceedings has been more pronounced in inquisitorial systems,[28] where the procedure is dominated by judicial investigation. As Spencer (2002: 23–24) describes it:

---

[24] Beattie (1986:359–61).

[25] Data from the Old Bailey Sessions Papers (Beattie 1991:227) shows that whilst 0.5% of defendants were represented in 1740, this rose to 7.3% by 1780, and then more rapidly to to 12.8% in 1782 and then 36.6% in 1795 and 27.9% in 1800.

[26] The accused was prevented from evidentiary participation in her own trial (to protect her from self-incrimination) until the 1898 Prisoners' Evidence Act finally made her competent to testify. Parallel, though less pronounced developments occurred in the pre-trial process (Langbein, 2003:273–77).

[27] See also Garapon (1996a:66).

[28] Whilst the accused in England and Wales will not speak until the close of the prosecution case and even then, may choose not to testify (although the nature of this choice has been compromised by the ability of the court to draw adverse inferences from the defendant's failure to testify under the CJPOA 1994), the French defendant is addressed by the court at the outset. She is questioned on the basis of her statements on file to the police and *magistrats*, as well as her criminal record and biography. She is asked to comment on the accusation against her, before any witnesses have been heard. The defendant has the right to remain silent, but psychologically, this becomes almost impossible to maintain within a trial structured around the judicial questioning of the accused (Spencer, 2002:24). The defence lawyer, the *avocat*, represents the accused, presenting factors in mitigation if the charges are admitted, or underlining the weaknesses in the prosecution's case and the factors supporting the accused if the charges are contested. Recent reforms allow the *partie civile*, prosecution and defence, to question witnesses in court directly, rather than having to direct any examination through the judge, but the trial remains a procedure dominated by the *magistrats* trying the case, rather than the lawyers representing those prosecuting and defending. See also the comments of Eric de Montgolfier, the *procureur de la République* in Nice (in Greilsamer and Schneidermann, 2002:343) on the continuing dominance of the trial judge in proceedings.

In an inquisitorial system the defendant is expected to contribute to the discovery of the truth, while in an accusatorial system his guilt must be established objectively and by evidence exterior to him.

The relative invisibility of the accused in the English trial, compared with her counterpart in France, was noted in 1820 by the French observer, Cottu, who remarked upon the wholly passive role played by the English defendant, such that 'his hat stuck on a pole might without inconvenience be his substitute at the trial'.[29]

According to Langbein, the dominance of lawyers in the court room distorted the trial process itself. Just as Frank (1949) has characterised the adversarial trial as being based upon a 'fight' (rather than 'truth') theory of justice, so Langbein criticises the 'combat effect' of increased lawyerisation.

> [L]awyerization was meant to be truth-enhancing by comparison with what had gone on before . . . Two-sided partisanship may indeed have been better than one-sided partisanship, but it was still a poor proxy for truth-seeking. Adversary procedure entrusts the responsibility for gathering and presenting the evidence upon which accurate adjudication depends to partisans whose interest is in winning, not in truth . . . The adversary dynamic invited distortion and suppression of the evidence, by permitting abusive and misleading cross-examination, the coaching of witnesses, and the concealment of unfavorable evidence . . . Adversary procedure presupposed that truth would somehow emerge when no one was in charge of seeking it. (Langbein, 2003:332–33)

The judiciary, accustomed to the processing of information generated by others (rather than having any investigative role themselves), 'found it easy enough to accommodate to the role of administering the truth-impairing norms of the evolving adversary combat' (Langbein, 2003:7)[30], such that the defence role was already entrenched when full rights to counsel in felony cases were legislated in 1836.[31] Vogler (2005) suggests that, in contrast to 'their continental brethren' English judges may have found it easier to relinquish authority over the trial to

---

[29] Quoted in Langbein (2003:6).

[30] The distant role of the judge during the examination and cross-examination of witnesses was also noted by the French observer, Cottu, in 1820: the English judge 'remains almost a stranger to what is going on' (quoted in Langbein 2003:6).

> [T]he failure to develop trial courts capable of truth-seeking criminal adjudication long predated the rise of adversary procedure. The judicial office had been shaped in the Middle Ages in essentially the form that it continued to manifest in the eighteenth century. In the trial of fact, English common law judges were administrators rather than adjudicators. They neither investigated nor decided disputes of fact. English judges merely process cases for jury verdicts. The primitiveness of the pre-trial process reinforced this stunted conception of the judicial function at trial. (Langbein, 2003:333).

[31] The Trials for Felonies Act 1836. Less serious offences were known as misdemeanours, more serious ones as felonies.

lawyers, given that they themselves are drawn from the bar and so 'they were sharing their authority with their own caste'.

Defence Lawyers and the Efficient Management of Justice

However, whilst the introduction of defence counsel in treason trials may not have been envisaged as a template for general criminal procedure, Langbein overstates the matter in arguing that no consideration was given to the benefits of adversarial trial, such that we 'live under a criminal procedure for which we have no adequate theory' (2003:9).[32] His analysis does not take account of the vigorous debate which took place around the six unsuccessful Bills introduced in the 1820s, which attempted to allow defence counsel a greater role in felony cases.[33] Interestingly, the different ways in which the function of defence counsel was characterised by those for and against legal representation, continues to be reflected within current debate around the nature of defence rights. Those opposing the changes advanced the now familiar arguments that they would undermine the truth seeking function of the trial[34] and would be of benefit only to the wealthy.[35] These are, of course, precisely the criticisms made by commentators such as Frank (1949) and Langbein (2003) and are the reasons advanced by those opposing the extension of defence representation in contemporary France. Whilst defence representation would undoubtedly assist some defendants in the presentation of their case, those in favour of the reform were not concerned to promote the interests of the accused, to benefit the defendant, nor to provide her with 'rights'. Rather, they saw the objective of the reform as being to provide greater certainty and to remove the discretionary practices which allowed defendants to evade conviction: 'Certainty of detection . . . certainty of conviction, certainty of punishment. No mercy and no escape. This was the logic of reform' (Cairns, 1998:63). The introduction of defence counsel was intended as a means of professionally managing cases in order to facilitate the court in convicting defendants. Supporters of the reform argued that the modern trial, with its rules of evidence and unreliable witness testimony, no longer represented an argument on the 'plain facts', but a 'lottery of justice' that allowed the guilty to go free.[36] The provision of fair representation would allow the court to dispense with the need for complex fictions and discretionary mercy and so be more professional and effective in uncovering the truth and, therefore, it was argued, in obtaining verdicts of guilt.

---

[32] See also Sedley (2003) who notes the importance of theoretical propositions such as the right to counsel and the right to silence.
[33] Hostettler (1992:46).
[34] Beattie (1991:250–58); Hostettler (1992:50–51).
[35] Hostettler (1992:52).
[36] See also King (2000:233–42).

Interestingly, this is the way in which contemporary commentators have characterised (and criticised) defence lawyers in England and Wales—not for being adversarial, distorting the truth and getting clients acquitted on minor technicalities, but rather, for their lack of adversarial practice and their role as bureaucratic managers, processing clients towards guilty pleas.[37] The argument that the provision of defence counsel might justify the removal of procedures designed to safeguard the interests of the accused, also continues to find favour within current criminal justice debate. The statutory right to custodial legal advice under section 58 of the Police and Criminal Evidence Act 1984 was introduced on the recommendation of the Royal Commission on Criminal Procedure (1981) to go some way towards redressing the imbalance between the suspect and the police, given the extended powers provided for the police under the same legislation. However, the availability of legal advice to suspects in police custody has been used to justify further inroads into the due process protections of the accused—most notably the ability of the court to draw adverse inferences from a suspect's silence under section 34 of the Criminal Justice and Public Order Act 1994. Other safeguards, such as the exclusion of evidence obtained as a result of police malpractice, are also more likely to be denied to suspects who are (or who have at one time been) legally represented.[38]

The benefits of legal representation in the 19th century were not, however, available to all, as most defendants could not afford to hire their own lawyer. As most criminal accused were indigent, the wealthy enjoyed the 'potentially outcome altering advantages' of defence counsel under the new arrangements, while the poor were denied the assistance considered necessary to counter the partisan investigation and prosecution of the accusation against them.[39] This disparity continued well into the second half of the 20th century, with numerous research studies pointing to the problem of unmet legal need and the inferior treatment of unrepresented defendants, most notably in the magistrates' court.[40] The Poor Prisoners' Defence Act 1903[41] provided legal aid to those of insufficient means on trial for indictable offences, if it was considered 'in the interests of justice' to do so, but it was only with the Legal Aid and Advice Act 1949 that provision was extended beyond just the poor, to include those who could afford to pay something towards the costs of legal assistance, through the introduction of a system of

---

[37] McConville *et al* (1994).

[38] Hodgson (1992); Sharpe (1998). This raises questions about the quality of legal advice and whether the suspect is credited with a benefit which she in fact never received. On the quality of legal advice in England and Wales, see McConville and Hodgson (1993); McConville *et al* (1994); Bridges and Hodgson (1995); Bridges and Choongh (1998).

[39] Bentley (1998:108) describes the 1836 legislation (providing for counsel in felony cases) as being 'cruelly irrelevant' to most defendants.

[40] Zander (1969); Borrie and Varcoe (1970); Dell (1971); JUSTICE (1971); King (1971).

[41] Extended by the Poor Prisoners' Defence Act 1930.

contribution. This scheme applied to criminal cases from the early 1960s and together with a number of other factors such as the establishment of the duty solicitor scheme, the requirement that defendants consenting to a 'paper committal'[42] be legally represented and the growth of the legal profession itself, the 1970s saw an expansion in the number of cases in which defendants were legally represented.[43] The scheme was modified under the Access to Justice Act 1999, under which legal representation in magistrates' courts is no longer means tested and only those defendants who are ultimately convicted in the Crown Court remain liable to make a financial contribution to the cost of legal aid in their case.[44]

This growth in legal representation in the latter part of the 20th century benefited defendants in matters such as bail and sentence, but it also resulted in the further 'professionalisation' of criminal justice, whereby the role of the accused in the magistrates' court became marginalised.[45] Although the defendant and her behaviour are at the centre of the trial, she is transformed from subject to object by a court room procedure which has been likened to a 'degradation ceremony' (Bankowski and Mungham, 1976:86–93).

> [T]he defendant comes to the courts as a case, a problem, not as an individual. Thereafter his identity is publicly co-opted by those who seek either to defend or attack him. Quite frequently details of his personal biography are discussed openly in court— but without reference to him. He is of interest only as a 'case'. The 'case', in turn, becomes the object of negotiation among the leading players in the courtroom. The defendant, although formally the focus of the bargaining is, in practice, excluded from participating. He is 'represented' and must wait patiently for the outcome of the deliberations of others. (Bankowski and Mungham, 1976:88)

Once again, the increased involvement of the defence lawyer has resulted in the silencing of the accused, and legal representation is favoured as an essential part of the efficient disposal of cases. In the court room ritual, court clerks, lawyers and judges are the 'repeat players', the legal actors who know the language and procedures of the process. Prosecuting and defence lawyers play the leading roles, while the accused must content herself with, at most, a walk on part. Her participation threatens to upset the smooth running of the ritual and so she is replaced, wherever possible, by her lawyer. Any unavoidable participation is minimised and carefully controlled. As the clients were repeatedly told in one firm observed in my

---

[42] Formerly, the prosecution case was tested out and the magistrates would only commit the case to the Crown Court for trial if satisfied that there was a case to answer. The Criminal Justice Act 1967 introduced 'paper committals' allowing the defendant to consent to her case being committed directly to the Crown Court 'on the papers', without the need for evidence to be heard. The option of holding what was referred to as an 'old style' committal was later removed entirely. See CJPOA 1994; CPIA 1996; CDA 1998.

[43] See McConville *et al* (1994:2–6).

[44] See further Bridges (2002); Cape (2004).

[45] See eg Bankowski and Mungham (1976).

own research, 'it's just name, address, date of birth and I'll do the rest' (McConville *et al*, 1994:172). In another example, the solicitor told the client:

> You'll go in and they'll ask you which court you want to be tried in and they'll warn you that the magistrates can send you to Crown Court for sentencing anyway. You say 'magistrates' court'. They ask you your plea, you say 'guilty' and then leave all the talking to me. (1994:172)

Appearing in court can be a nerve-wracking experience for defendants, and lawyers justified this approach as part of trying to make the process as painless as possible for their clients. However, addressing the alien nature of the court room procedure by seeking to exclude the defendant from it, raises questions as to how much the accused understands in practice and the extent to which she is truly 'represented' by her lawyer.[46] As criminal justice practice becomes increasingly professionalised and bureaucratic, the defence lawyer's objective becomes one of managing rather than representing her client (McConville and Hodgson, 1993; McConville *et al* 1994). This has led to a certain irony, in that the 'wealth effect' of adversarial trial has been mitigated to a great extent, offering potential benefits to the accused; the 'combat effect' has also been diluted, but in the absence of any alternative means of countering the investigation and prosecution, this undercuts the interests of the accused, reverting to 'one-sided partisanship'. The current concerns relating to the role of criminal defence lawyers in England and Wales do not mirror those voiced by Langbein in his critique of the development of the adversarial trial. In fact, they are just the reverse: lawyers have been criticised as being insufficiently adversarial or protective of their clients' interests, failing to challenge the prosecution case and so serving to legitimate the prosecution and conviction of the clients whose interests it is their duty to defend. The debate appears to have come full circle. In assuming that the accused has an adversarial and effective defence, the courts in many instances credit the defendant with an advantage that in practice, she does not have.

The French *Avocat* as Professional Outsider

The role of the French defence lawyer has evolved in a quite different way, within a profession which is independent of that of the judge and prosecutor. In the 13th century, lawyers in France were not established as a liberal profession, but a

---

[46] This was epitomised in a number of cases I observed during the fieldwork for my own PhD and later, the study which resulted in 'Standing Accused' (McConville *et al*, 1994). On numerous occasions, the defendant was asked by the court clerk whether she understood the charge. The accused turned to her lawyer, who, in full view of the court, mouthed 'yes'; the defendant then repeated, 'yes'. In other instances, we observed defendants going in to court, apparently to enter a guilty plea, only to discover that this had already been done on the previous occasion. The solicitor had failed to read the file with sufficient care and tellingly, the client was unaware of the significance of the previous hearing and the formal admission of guilt that she had made. See McConville *et al* (1994:172–73).

state-dominated organisation acting both in the exercise of state power and in the courtroom defence of ordinary citizens.[47] With the introduction of inquisitorial procedures in the 16th century and the removal of lawyers as the King's advocates (the Edict of Bois in 1579 prevented lawyers from acting in defence of the Crown, replacing them with magistrates of the public prosecutor's office, the *parquet*), the lawyer's territory was diminished and 'His was a history of loss' (Karpik, 1999:27). This opened up the professional distance between lawyers and *magistrats*, such that, 'by the end of the Ancien Régime, the *magistrat* won out over the bar . . . The least advantaged categories [of the robe] were still worth as much as the upper fraction of the Parisian bar'.[48] Excluded from the machinations of inquisitorial procedure, in the late 18th century lawyers took to publishing factums—legal briefs or pleadings—as a form of legal–literary rhetoric which denounced injustices and forced the courts to review their decisions.[49] Bringing cases to the attention of the public provided a way for lawyers to challenge the authority of the *magistrats* and the judiciary's protection of the vested interests of the old regime. Falconnet[50] formulated it: 'What is a judge? The voice of the King. What is the lawyer? The voice of the nation.'[51] The bar continued to struggle to retain its status against the Crown and the *Parlements* in the 17th and 18th centuries, whilst also campaigning for civil rights and individual liberties. In the 19th century, their commitment to political liberalism won them their independence and an important place within the apparatus of the republican state.[52] The economic and political crises of the First World War, however, resulted in a decline in the status and influence of the bar as law lost some of its power and standing.[53] There were now

---

[47] Karpik (1999:15).

[48] A Loisel (1986) *Les Magistrats du parlement de Paris au XVIIIe siècle* (Economica, Paris) p 91, quoted by Karpik (1999:34).

[49] Karpik (1999:72–74) describes the influence of Voltaire in this and his attacks on what he considered to be the two major vices of the justice system: the secret inquisitorial procedure which worked to the disadvantage of the accused and the damaging influence of prejudices upon witnesses, investigators and judges. Compare the pamphlet campaign conducted by the Whigs at the end of the 17th century, which criticised trial procedures and the inequality between Crown and defendant (Shapiro, 1993).

[50] Falconnet (1806–8) *Le Barreau français* 2 vols. (Cuchet et Garnet, Paris) vol. i p. xxxi cited by Karpik (1999:74).

[51] It is interesting to contrast this with the contemporary ideology of the *magistrat*, which sees the lawyer as representing the narrow interest of the accused and the *magistrat* as the representative of the wider public interest.

[52] Karpik (1999:136–37) writes of the 'symbiosis between bar and State' and the 'domination of the "legal mind" . . . in a vision of the world which gave law an essential role in the transformation of reality.' He goes on to argue that the limits of the lawyers' liberal model were demonstrated by their social conservatism in matters of social and economic change and their failure to challenge the state in the Dreyfus affair (1898), demonstrating the exclusion 'of individual freedoms the moment the defence did not fit into the dynamic of conflict between the State and a (relatively) unitary public . . . [showing] the particularism of an engagement entirely dedicated to the defence of a *rigid and strict conception of the moderate State and of political citizenship*' (original emphasis, 1999:139). See also Madsen (2004:65–68) for a discussion of the role of lawyers in the growth of political human rights organisations in France and Europe following both the Dreyfus affair and the war with Algeria.

[53] See also the discussion of the uncertain status of the legal profession in the post-war era in Madsen (2004:64–65).

new modes of expression, new public representatives and a 'change in the knowledge that appeared socially useful for dealing with public affairs. Law had to address economics as well as new extremist ideologies' and to adapt to a new type of politics which did not operate a narrow 'antagonistic dualism between the State and civil society' (Karpik, 1999:140–42). Developing an identity which was separate from both the authority of the state and the interests of the capitalist market, the profession re-established its status and independence, defining itself through courtroom defence and a personal clientele.[54]

The profession of *avocat* is thus separate from, and independent of, the *magistrature*. Karpik argues that the state has a powerful interest in maintaining the existence of an independent defence in this way; it has always been seen as a necessary condition of an independent judiciary, demonstrating and guaranteeing in turn the judge's separation from the state:

> [T]he State underwrites the bar's independence which, if it were to disappear . . . could only signify the end of the independence of the entire justice system . . . in liberal societies, a State that was to threaten the bar would only weaken its own power. (1999:148)[55]

This separation is further underlined by the different professional status of the defence lawyer, the prosecutor and the judge. As an *avocat* (rather than a *magistrat*), the defence lawyer is very much an outsider, separate from the professional group which encompasses the major functions of investigation and prosecution, as well as that of adjudication. In this way, what the *avocat* is not becomes as significant as that which she is. She is not a member of the judiciary, she is a lawyer; she does not represent the public interest, but the interests of suspected criminals; she is not part of the state-centred process of investigation and prosecution, she acts for the partisan interests of the accused. There is a different process of entrance and training for the *avocat* and for the *magistrat*.[56] Coming out of the same training school (entrance to which is extremely competitive), enjoying a common professional (judicial) status and sharing the same professional public-interest-oriented ideology, the *procureur*, the *juge d'instruction* and the trial judge

---

[54] Karpik (1999:154).

[55] He describes this arrangement, this inter-dependence, as 'a quasi-constitutional form' (Karpik, (1999:147). Historically, he argues, this has been the function of an independent defence in general:

> [The judiciary] set aside a space of its own and imposed an operating rule that was almost magical, in that it postulated the neutralization of the effects of real society, declared the equality of the parties, and guaranteed the impartiality of the judgment. If lawyers' independence was a constituent condition from the outset, it is because it was regarded as the condition, and soon as the sign, of an independent judiciary.' Karpik (1999:146–47).

See also Delmas-Marty (1991).

[56] The profession of *avocat* is not only separate from, but in the view of many *magistrats*, inferior to that of the *magistrature*. They claimed that many *avocats* had failed the entrance exam to the *école nationale de la magistrature* before going on to become *avocats*.

are bound together; and in being bound together as *magistrats* they are defined as separate from the *avocat*.

Furthermore, if *avocats* in general enjoy a lower status than *magistrats*, this is especially so of the criminal lawyer.[57] Of the 14 fields of law which Karpik (1999:198) uses for his analysis (based upon questioning lawyers), crime ranked only 12th in terms of prestige. Whilst some successful criminal lawyers in France have become celebrities, gaining their reputation through the representation of public figures or defendants appearing in high-profile cases, this is exceptional.[58] French criminal lawyers are characterised by Karpik (1999) as typically young solo practitioners or associates with an unstable clientele. The predominant model continues to be the individual generalist lawyer and even criminal law specialists are likely to undertake between 20 and 40 per cent non-criminal work according to Field and West (2003:270).[59] This contrasts with the profile of criminal solicitors in England and Wales, who tend to specialise to a far greater extent in criminal work.[60] In France, much criminal work is conducted by young and inexperienced *avocats* who act as duty lawyers, not because of any particular skill, commitment or experience, but because this is a required part of their training.[61] Unsurprisingly, like their counterparts in England and Wales, they receive lower incomes than colleagues practising in other fields of law,[62] as many of their clients are legally aided[63] and Field and West (2003:279) describe criminal specialists as

---

[57] This is true in England and Wales also, where the lawyer's status derives in part from that of her client.

[58] Badinter and Dumas, for example, though they too were very successful business lawyers.

[59] 'For a firm to have more than one partner practising widely in criminal law was wholly exceptional. And no *avocat* that we followed did wholly criminal work.' Field and West (2003:269–70).

[60] The structure of legal aid and specialist franchises militates towards this. In the mid 1980s, most solicitors' firms carried out some criminal work, but between 1986/7 and 1991/2 the number fell from 8,716 to 7,417. The requirement for firms to be awarded a contract to provide criminal defence services for magistrates' court work has had an even greater impact, the number of firms doing magistrates' court criminal work now standing at 2,900 by 2002/3. See Cape (2004).

[61] Field and West (2003:272). In some of Field and West's sites, experienced practitioners were prohibited from acting as duty lawyers—contrast this with England and Wales, where duty solicitor schemes were initially considered attractive to practitioners as a means of expanding their client base. In France (as in England and Wales) high-profile cases were likely to attract the more skilled criminal advocates. In area C, eg, after the defence lawyer had called to collect his permit to visit the accused in the case of a murdered young English woman, the *juge d'instruction* commented to us: 'That's a good lawyer, very experienced, who does not usually do legal aid work, but he wants this case.' Researcher: 'Because it will bring publicity and therefore more clients and more money in the future?' *Juge d'instruction*: 'Exactly!'.

[62] See also Milburn (1994) on the negotiation of lawyers' fees.

[63] Work was done on a wholly *pro bono* basis until 1983, and between 1983 and 1991 payments were derisory (Field and West 2003:275). Danet (2001:142) notes that the *Syndicat des avocats de France* calculate that criminal defence lawyers are paid around 150 FF (approximately £15) an hour. Although a little dated now, the Delmas-Marty Commission (1991:142) noted the huge disparity in legal aid expenditure between western European countries. Whilst the UK spent around 98FF per head, the Netherlands (whose procedure is closer to that in France) around 30FF, France spent only 7FF per head.

working very long hours in order to manage their caseloads. Their work is more court than office based and much of it is regarded as being routine and repetitive, rather than technical, leading to some standardisation of practices in order to keep down costs and to attract more clients.[64] Such routinisation may also be the result of much criminal defence work being undertaken by inexperienced *avocats*, and generalists who are little committed to engaging in the proactive defence of their client.[65]

In contrast to the English criminal lawyer whose role is enmeshed within the nature of adversarialism, the French *avocat* occupies a more marginal space within the criminal process. Purely inquisitorial procedure has no place for the defence lawyer and it is only with the growing acceptance of a more openly debated decision-making process (reflected in the principle of *contradictoire* discussed below) that the defence role has begun to develop in France's 'mixed' system of criminal justice. However, for legal actors and the legislature, the professional status and deontology of the *avocat* continue to act as something of a barrier to the lawyer's ability to participate more widely in the criminal process and in particular, the extent to which she might properly challenge the central role of the *magistrat*.

The Evolving Pre-Trial Role of the Criminal Defence Lawyer

Although the trial represents an important (and publicly accountable) hearing of the case, historically, much emphasis has been placed on the pre-trial phase in France. The investigation is regarded as a judicially supervised enquiry into the offence and the evidence surrounding it, rather than the gathering of evidence to support the prosecution of the accused.[66] In England, however, historically, evidence was not examined in this way prior to the trial hearing. The trial itself was the principal site of the accusation and the accused's response to it, pre-trial hearings emerging only very much later. This has important consequences for the way in which evidence is treated by the court (and in particular, the credibility that

---

[64] Competition revolves around cost because of the high proportion of simple cases, the over supply of lawyers and the low income of clients. Lowering prices is about survival, rather than expansion (Karpik (1999:186–88). For an account of the widespread practices of delegation and routinisation among criminal solicitors in England and Wales, see McConville *et al* (1994).

[65] See the broad typologies described in Field and West (2003).

[66] On a number of occasions, we observed lawyers referring to this explicitly in defence of their client. In one case in area A, for example, the lawyer told the court: 'In this dossier, right from the beginning, there is the impression of an enquiry which has been conducted in order to charge and prosecute' which, she reminded the court, is against the law. Although cast in slightly different terms, the construction of the case against the accused was recognised by lawyers as a form of police malpractice. Given the paramount importance of 'the search for the truth', this degree of pre-judgment is of even greater significance in a procedure understood to be centred upon judicially supervised investigation.

attaches to such evidence) as well as the role which the defence might be expected to play in testing out the prosecution case. In England and Wales, the prosecution presents the case against the accused, which must be tested and argued; in France, she presents evidence which is the result of a judicial enquiry.

Thus, the locus of power in the French criminal process tends more towards the pre-trial phase, the all important judicial investigation. In the 19th century, this was the *instruction*. Judicial torture had been outlawed after the French Revolution, but a broadly inquisitorial method of investigation remained intact[67] and by the end of the 19th century there was growing concern at the vulnerable position of the suspect, faced with the enormity of power vested in the *juge d'instruction* whose investigation was written, carried out in secret and denied the parties any opportunity to present their case. The conduct of the investigation was likened to a 'duel between the *juge* and the accused, a duel without witnesses and with weapons of which the *juge* alone had the mastery'.[68] In response, from 1897, the defence lawyer was permitted access to the case dossier 24 hours before any interrogation and to be present during the judicial questioning of her client. This represented a significant change to the procedure laid down in the 1808 *Code d'instruction criminelle* and a legal cultural shift that was widely criticised as undermining the very nature of the inquisitorial process and the search for the truth:

> [B]y obliging the *juge* to warn the accused at his first formal questioning that he is free to say nothing, by imposing the presence of a lawyer at all following interrogations, by, above all, constraining the *juge* to give the case file to the defence lawyer the day before every interrogation, this law paralyses the action of the judge who can barely hope, even himself, to discover the truth.[69]

As a result of these changes, a new form of pre-trial phase evolved at the end of the 19th century. In order to avoid the presence of the defence lawyer, the police and the *procureur* established a practice of official enquiries which existed outside any formal legal regulatory framework and which often resulted in the arbitrary detention of individuals.[70] In this way, the improvements to the *instruction* procedure led

---

[67] There was a brief period of adversarial procedure, introduced immediately after the Revolution, but the inquisitorial model was reinstated in the 1808 *Code d'instruction criminelle*.

[68] H Halton *Etude de la procédure criminelle* p 69, cited by Salas (1991:248). There had been proposals for a more adversarial procedure to be adopted, but these were rejected out of hand by the high-ranking judiciary and by Parliament. See Salas (1991:248). Compare this also with the criticisms of the trial in England at the end of the 17th century, of the 'fundamental unfairness that arose from the accused having to defend himself against charges that he had had no certain knowledge of beforehand, that were supported by what might be hours of oral testimony in court and to which he was expected to respond immediately' (Beattie 1986:357–78). Quoting the commentator Sir John Hawles, Beattie (1986:358) goes on to note that 'Very often, [Hawles] argued, the truth was not immediately apparent and required demonstration; keeping a man in prison before trial and then denying him the help of a lawyer in court, [Hawles] concluded, was "downright tying a man's hands behind him, and baiting him to death."'

[69] M Lemonde (1975) *Police et justice* 71–72, cited by Salas (1991:249).

[70] Feuillée-Kendall and Trouille (2004:17). Danet (2001:36–37).

to the informal development of what we now know as the GAV. In the century that followed, the role of the *juge d'instruction* as investigator declined as that of the police and *procureur* grew[71]: currently, less than five per cent of cases are the subject of an enquiry by the *juge d'instruction*, the overwhelming majority being investigated by the police under the supervision and direction of the *procureur*—including the police detention and interrogation of suspects in GAV. The GAV attained a formal (legally regulated) status with the 1958 CPP, but it was another 35 years before the defence lawyer was allowed access to the suspect held in police detention with the passing of the major legislative reform of 1993.

The Growing Importance of the ECHR in the 1993 and 2000 Reforms

The last decade has seen both trial and pre-trial defence rights strengthened in a number of ways, including those affecting suspects detained in GAV. The principal driver for the eventual recent change has been the ECHR and a growing recognition of the need to ensure that French criminal procedure reflects better the guarantees of Articles 5 and 6,[72] an issue specifically addressed by the commissions chaired by Delmas-Marty (1991) and Truche (1997), which preceded the key reforms of 1993 and 2000. The 1993 legislation set out a detailed legal framework for the regulation of the GAV which, for the first time, allowed suspects to have access to custodial legal advice,[73] 20 hours into the detention period,[74] as well as to have a friend or family member informed of her detention and to be examined by a doctor. The *procureur* was to be informed at the start of the GAV of any suspect detained, but officers were required to furnish the defence lawyer with only the minimum of information concerning the nature of the offence investigated, and not of the precise reason for the suspect's detention. The suspect, for her part, had no right to be told of the offence in connection with which she was being held, nor of her right to silence. This meant that for 20 hours, she was detained and interrogated with little or no knowledge of how or why she came to be a suspect, of her right to remain silent under questioning, nor of the length of time she might remain in detention. The 2000 legislation made a number of additional improvements to the rights of the defence, allowing suspects access to custodial

---

[71] Lévy (1993).

[72] Madsen (2004:64) argues that the UK's influence in the drafting of Art 6 was one of the factors discouraging France from ratifying the ECHR. In the context of recent assaults by the ECtHR upon the procedure of the *Cour de cassation*, one lawyer interviewed by Madsen reports that the ECHR was described as 'that text of Anglo-Saxon inspiration' (2004:78).

[73] The lawyer's presence during the GAV was not part of the government's original reform project, but was introduced as a parliamentary amendment. See Le Gunehec (1993:493).

[74] This meant that less than 10% of suspects in GAV were able to consult with a lawyer according to the then Justice Minister Mme Guigou in her address to the *Sénat*, 15 June 1999.

legal advice from the start of the GAV,[75] though the period of consultation remains limited to a maximum of 30 minutes. The police must now also inform the adviser of the date and the nature of the offence concerned, rather than simply the nature of the enquiry, though the accompanying Ministry of Justice circular seeks to place a narrow interpretation on this provision.[76] No provision was made to allow lawyers access to the dossier or to be present during the interrogation of their client and despite the Truche Commission (1997:64) considering it essential that GAV interrogations be tape recorded, the government also declined to adopt this recommendation. Police interrogations of the suspect continue to be recorded only as a signed statement.[77]

Suspects and accused persons in France enjoy the right to silence in the sense that they are not compelled to answer questions or provide self-incriminating evidence,[78] but only those suspects appearing before the *juge d'instruction* are informed of the right. The June 2000 reform required the police, for the first time, to inform the suspect of the nature of the offence for which she was being held and of her right to remain silent—if necessary through a sign language interpreter,[79] but this proved to be a highly controversial reform which was modified in form and then repealed. Even during the short time that it was in force, the impact of the requirement was undermined by the manner of its implementation.[80] The

---

[75] This was to have been the second phase of the original 1993 project, but it was abandoned by the new administration that took office later that year. Matters of organised crime, drugs trafficking and terrorism were treated as exceptional, with access to legal advice being delayed for 2–3 days under Art 63-4 CPP. The March 2004 legislation has now introduced a more complex 'exceptional' regime for serious and organised crime under Art 706-73 CPP, discussed above in Ch 2.

[76] Para 1.2.2.4 of the 4 December 2000 circular makes it clear that this obligation arises only at the start of the GAV. If the nature of the enquiry and the possible charges change, there is no obligation to inform the lawyer of this on her return after 20 or 36 hours. If the suspect is held initially on a minor charge, but the nature of the detention and investigation then changes and relates to more serious and more recent offences, the coercive powers of the police may alter significantly. Denied access to the dossier and police interrogations of the suspect, the lawyer will remain unaware of this and so be disabled from providing both proper advice to her client and noting the procedural regularity of the GAV. It would clearly be in the spirit of the provisions to keep the lawyer informed, given their objective of enabling her to provide more pertinent advice to her client and to ensure the legal regularity of the investigation.

[77] Since 2000, the questions put should also be included in the statement.

[78] It was, of course, in the case of *Funke v France* A.256-A (1993) 16 EHRR 297, that the European Court first recognised the privilege against self-incrimination (later described as the 'right' not to incriminate oneself in *Sanders v UK* (1996) 23 EHRR 313, 1996-VI) within Art 6(1) ECHR. M. Funke had been ordered to produce bank account details and was fined for not doing so. This was held to be in breach of of Art 6 ECHR.

[79] Art 63-1 CPP

[80] Initial plans to introduce a warning that silence may harm the defence were dropped. Given the existence of such a warning in the police caution administered in England and Wales since the curtailment of the right to silence under the CJPOA 1994, it is interesting that the CNCDH denounced the proposed clause as placing pressure on the suspect, hindering the proper organisation of her defence and (in the case of France, where there is no legal provision for the drawing of adverse inferences) resting upon no legal basis.

official Ministry of Justice circular which accompanied the legislation instructed police officers that they should not remind the suspect of her right to silence at the start of interrogations, on the grounds that it is neither desirable nor legally required according to the document and to do so would be 'pointless' and an encouragement to the suspect to remain silent, which would be against her own interests. The effectiveness of a requirement to inform the suspect of one of her most basic rights (and a fundamental aspect of the presumption of innocence and the Article 6 ECHR fair trial requirements) was to be doubted, given the clear concern to dissuade her from exercising it. The reform was widely opposed and it was claimed that coupled with the earlier access of suspects to custodial legal advice, many more would exercise their right to silence and so hinder the investigation and the search for the truth.[81] Unsurprisingly, just as was the case in England and Wales, these fears were not realised and silence continued to be exercised only rarely.[82] Despite this, the 'petite loi' of March 2002 modified the way in which the suspect was informed of her right to silence,[83] and the new Raffarin administration went further and repealed the requirement altogether in March 2003.[84]

The rights of those investigated under the *instruction* procedure have also been strengthened during this time[85]—again under the increasing influence of the ECHR discourse of defence rights and of equality of arms: lawyers have gained better and earlier access to the dossier[86]; this right has also been extended to the accused who may now have a copy of the contents of the dossier[87]; and the accused

---

[81] See also the cynical comments of Pradel (2001a) who dismisses this aspect of the reform as having little effect: the right to silence already existed and seasoned criminals have always known this. He does not countenance the value this might have to the first time or innocent suspect.

[82] See eg the report on the implementation of the 2000 reforms, Collomp (2001) para 1.4.2; *Le Monde* 19 June 2001. Interestingly, those who are silent are likely to be disciplined for their non co-operation—see *Le Monde* 13 February 2001. The number of suspects exercising their right of silence in England and Wales has always been low, even before the changes under the CJPOA 1994. The courts have also shown a willingness to discipline unco-operative suspects—see eg *Daniel* [1998] The Times 10 April 1998.

[83] Mirroring the way in which the *juge d'instruction* provides this information to the *mis en examen*, the suspect was no longer advised that she 'has the right not to respond to questions put', but that 'she has the choice to make a statement, to respond to questions put to her or to say nothing'.

[84] Whilst the original provision introduced under the 2000 legislation was sponsored by the then Justice Minister, Elisabeth Guigou, it is perhaps indicative of the then Interior Minister's dominance over the justice agenda that it was he, rather than the Justice Minister, who sponsored the reform repealing the provision. Furthermore, at a time when EU Members States are concerned to ensure that all suspects receive the basic defence rights implied within Art 6 ECHR, it is surprising that France should implement a measure which places it out of step with its European partners. See discussion of this in the context of the European Arrest Warrant and the EU Council Framework Decision on Certain Procedural Rights in Criminal Proceedings throughout the European Union COM(2004)3289 final (Brussels 28 April 2004) discussed in Ch 1.

[85] Principally since 1993. See art 114 CPP.

[86] The *avocat* must be informed five working days before any judicial questioning of her client and she has access to the dossier at least four working days beforehand.

[87] The right of access to the case file was originally that of the lawyer, rather than the accused, but since 1996, copies of the dossier can be given by the *avocat* to her client, provided that the latter signs an agreement not to disclose any evidence to third parties. The *juge d'instruction*'s written consent for the copying of each piece of evidence must be obtained in advance.

may request the *juge d'instruction* to carry out any act of investigation which might assist the discovery of the truth.[88] At the same time, the courts have been forced to respond to the jurisprudence of the ECtHR on the issue of defence rights at trial; in a number of instances, changes in practice have followed directly from ECtHR findings against France. For example, in the case of *Foucher v France* (1997),[89] the ECtHR held that the right to consult the case dossier was not just that of the defence lawyer, but should also be afforded the accused in cases where she conducted her own defence. To do otherwise was in breach of the accused's right to a fair trial and the principle of equality of arms. In the case of *Voisine v France* (2001),[90] the ECtHR held that the conclusions of the *avocat général* in the *chambre criminelle* of the the *Cour de cassation* must be communicated to the defence as well as the prosecution and the court.[91] After the ECtHR findings in *Poitrimol v France* (1993)[92] and again in *Van Pelt v France* (2000),[93] the *Cour de cassation* has adapted its own jurisprudence to accept that in trying a defendant who is absent without excuse, the refusal to hear her lawyer fails to respect both the right to a fair trial and to the assistance of defence counsel.[94]

Thus, we see a strengthening of the defence role across all aspects of French criminal procedure, but during the pre-trial stage, the defence rights of those held in GAV remain nevertheless very much more limited than those afforded the accused during the *instruction*. This restriction is not imposed by the jurisprudence of the ECHR, but is a function of French criminal justice policy and procedure. Although under the head of the right to a fair trial, the protections under Article 6 ECHR arise well before the accused ever reaches the courtroom, and so might be applied to the GAV procedure as well as to the trial and *instruction*.[95] Article 6 guarantees are expressed as having application to those facing a criminal charge—a concept that has been interpreted by the ECtHR in a 'substantive' rather than 'formal' way[96]: once

---

[88] Under art 82 CPP, the *procureur* may request that the *juge d'instruction* carry out any investigations which the former considers will assist in discovering the truth. The accused and the victim now enjoy the same right under art 82-1 CPP, and both they and the *procureur* may appeal against any decision refusing such request. For a discussion of the increasing participation rights of the individual (the 'privatisation of criminal procedure') see also Pin (2002).

[89] ECHR 18 March 1997.

[90] ECHR 8 February 2000.

[91] See also *Reinhardt and Slimane Kaïd v France* 31 March 1998; *Fontaine and Bertin v France* 8 July 2003 concerning the *Cour de cassation*. Also *Kress v France* 7 June 2001 concerning the *commissaire du gouvernement* in the *Conseil d'Etat*. These offices are held by *magistrats* independent of the parties and are considered valuable in synthesising the relevant jurisprudence and offering an independent opinion to the court. The decisions have been criticised as a grave misunderstanding of the French legal and judicial culture on the part of Strasbourg. These cases continue. In 2004 the ECtHR found against France in another dozen such cases.

[92] ECHR 23 November 1993.

[93] See also *Krombach v France* 13 February 2001, discussed in Massias (2001).

[94] In the case of *Dentico* cass. ass. plén., 2 March 2001, JCP.II.10611, note Ch LIEVREMONT.

[95] For discussion of this point and related case law, see Emmerson and Ashworth (2001:171–74).

[96] *Adolf v Austria* (1982) 4 EHRR 313 at para 30.

the individual is under investigation, her position has been substantially affected[97] and she is, at that point, in need of and entitled to the protection of Article 6 ECHR[98]—even if a formal charge or indictment is never brought.[99] This protection includes access to custodial legal advice as it is 'fundamental to the preparation of [an accused person's] defence'[100] which in turn forms part of the fair trial requirements which are relevant before trial 'in so far as the fairness of the trial is likely to be prejudiced by an initial failure to comply with them'.[101] Like defence assistance, the right to silence is also a central pre-trial protection guaranteed under Article 6 ECHR, as set out by the European Court of Human Rights in *John Murray v UK* (1996)[102]:

> Although not specifically mentioned in Article 6 of the Convention, there can be no doubt that the right to remain silent under police questioning and the privilege against self incrimination are generally recognised international standards which lie at the heart of the notion of a fair procedure under Article 6 . . . By providing the accused with protection against improper compulsion by the authorities these immunities contribute to avoiding miscarriages of justice and to securing the aims of Article 6. (para 45).

The jurisprudence of the European Court recognises that the trial cannot be treated as a discrete phase in the criminal process, unaffected by the processes which precede it, and a denial of defence rights at the pre-trial stage is likely to prejudice the preparation of the defence case and so the fairness of the trial. For those investigated under the supervision of the *procureur*, including those detained in GAV, these guarantees have been interpreted and applied in the narrowest possible sense. The suspect has the right to remain silent, but is not to be informed of this right.[103] Custodial legal advice is available to suspects held in GAV, but the ability of the lawyer to engage in any form of meaningful defence assistance is curtailed by the brevity of the consultation (no more than 30 minutes), the paucity of information on which to base any advice and her continued exclusion from the police interrogation of the suspect.

---

[97] This may be at the point of arrest (*Foti v Italy* 1983 5 EHRR 313 para 52) or formal police charge (*X v UK* (1979) 14 D.R. 26.

[98] Set out in *Eckle v FRG* [1982] ECHR 4; *Deweer v Belgium* (1979–80) 2 EHRR 439 at para 46.

[99] As in *Allenet de Ribemont v France* (1995) 20 EHRR 557 where the court held that the person was 'charged' at the point of arrest.

[100] *Bonzi v Switzerland* (1978) 12 D.R. 185 at p 190.

[101] *Imbroscia v Switzerland* (1994) 17 EHRR 441 at para 36. See also the current work of the EU Commission on achieving common standards of procedural safeguards for suspects throughout the EU.

[102] 22 EHRR 29.

[103] It is assumed, presumably, that the defence lawyer will do this. See Delmas-Marty (1991:120–1) and discussion below.

This discrepancy between the two main pre-trial investigative routes is significant not only because the *instruction* is increasingly marginalised and has now become a minority procedure, but also because, as described in detail in subsequent chapters, the role of the *procureur* and the *juge d'instruction* represent two very different models of investigation and judicial supervision, providing different levels of protection for the accused. During the *instruction*, the suspect may only be interrogated by the *juge d'instruction* herself, after having first been informed of her right to silence. This will normally take place in the *juge*'s office and her secretary, the *greffier*, will type the statement in the presence of the suspect and her lawyer. The defence lawyer is given notice of such questioning and has the opportunity to consult the dossier beforehand. In the majority of investigations, however, (that is, those carried out under the supervision of the *procureur*) the suspect is interrogated not by a *magistrat*, but by the police. She may be detained and interrogated in police custody for up to 48 hours, or four days in the most serious cases, seeing the *procureur* only at the close of the detention period. The defence lawyer may consult with her client for 30 minutes, but is denied access to the case dossier and neither she nor a *magistrat* will be present during the interrogation. Thus, the defence rights enjoyed by the minority of suspects investigated under the *instruction* procedure do not extend to those detained in the more hostile environment of the GAV, where the suspect is very much more vulnerable to the pressure to confess. *Procureurs* were well aware of this strategic advantage and frequently held on to cases for up to five days[104] before opening an *information* for this very reason. One senior *procureur* explained:

> The reason it's five days is because that is the limit for *flagrance*. That way, the police still enjoy wide powers and we can carry out the investigation . . . we want to get the culprit . . . The *juge d'instruction* is not going to interview the suspect three or four times, sit across the table from him and say 'Are you going to admit this?' The police station is a hostile environment. It's unpleasant and the police will use more pressure. And that does not make it unlawful—sometimes you need some pressure. [D3]

The *Avocat* as Auxiliary to the *Magistrat*

It is perhaps not surprising that, in France, custodial legal advice was not permitted before 1993, given that in the more adversarial procedure of England and Wales, the suspect's right to see a lawyer was only placed on a statutory footing in

---

[104] This limit has gradually been extended, most recently from eight to fifteen days under the March 2004 reform.

1984.[105] Yet, the secrecy surrounding the police investigation stands somewhat in contrast to the provision made for defence scrutiny of, and later participation in, the investigation of the *juge d'instruction*. Historically, the GAV has been regarded as procedurally less significant, part of the preliminary police enquiry preceding the more formal and important judicial investigation.[106] Any significant role for the lawyer is permitted only once the case is under the direct control of the *magistrat*— either at trial, during *instruction* or after the *procureur* has initiated a prosecution. However, it is important to recognise that even in this context defence rights are not understood in adversarial terms, but are part of the wider principle which seeks to promote the ability of the parties to participate in the procedure[107]—the principle of *contradictoire*, now enshrined in the preliminary article to the CPP.

The Defence Role during *Instruction*

During the *instruction*, defence participation focuses upon influencing the construction and content of the dossier which, as the product of a judicially supervised investigation, forms the evidential centrepiece of the trial. Conceived of in this way, the defence role does not challenge the basic principle of judicial supervision, as the *avocat* engages with the investigation through the *magistrat*, who is then able to mediate and control the influence which the defence has upon the enquiry, and so the dossier. The lawyer is not cast as a primary actor in the process (as she is in adversarial procedure), but rather, functions more as an auxiliary to the *magistrat*: she may scrutinise the results of the investigation, challenge irregularities in the procedure, request that certain investigations be carried out and be present during the interviews of her client and other witnesses.

> [Defence lawyers] do not bring anything to the case—it is not their job to. I investigate the affair and their role is primarily to ensure that the correct procedure has been followed and to challenge any irregularities. [*Juge d'instruction*, area D]

For *magistrats*, the defence often serves as a useful counter-reflex, ensuring that all angles are covered during the enquiry.[108]

> The accused can be an actor in the investigation through her lawyer . . . before, the police and the *juge d'instruction* were beyond reproach but not now—the defence can ask questions. The police and the *juge d'instruction* must be diligent in their investigation,

---

[105] Before then, the treatment of suspects was governed by the 1912 Judges' Rules.

[106] See also Le Gunehec (1993:495–96). A significant number of people are detained in GAV each year—426, 670 in 2003.

[107] Rights accorded the accused are also accorded the victim or *partie civile*, as both are considered 'parties' in the case. See also Pin (2002).

[108] See eg Leigh and Zedner (1992:73) who underline the defence role in stimulating critical reflection on the part of the *magistrat*.

they pay more attention; it is nearly always all in order. It is rare to have any problems—the quality of work is better. [*Juge d'instruction*, area D]

[The defence lawyer] is a good thing. Everything that goes against our natural tendency is a good thing. It places demands upon us. [D2]

I think the American system of state-paid lawyers is good. Here, they are all young and inexperienced. It is better to have good defence lawyers in the case. Then, they too can look at the dossier and point out anything I have forgotten. Now, lawyers never read the dossier properly. Out of all these 150 dossiers, maybe five or ten are read properly by the lawyers. [*Juge d'instruction*, area C]

The recent reform of article 82-1 CPP has expanded this role yet further, allowing the defence and the *partie civile* to request the *juge d'instruction* to carry out any investigations which they consider will assist in the discovery of the truth (rather than those of a previously limited nature), placing them on a more equal footing with the *procureur*. Whilst this offers the potential for the defence lawyer to play a greater part in the conduct of the *instruction*,[109] there are a number of obstacles to the realisation of this role in practice. Firstly, as noted above, all defence involvement in the investigation is articulated through the *juge d'instruction* who therefore exercises an important control over the extent to which the defence is able to participate effectively. Those *avocats* who sought to engage more directly with the investigation process were left in no doubt as to the *magistrat*'s authority over the case. Field and West (2003:301) describe the *juge d'instruction* as using various tactics to ensure that the *avocat* does not 'disrupt' the investigation, such as controlling the nature of the lawyer's interventions during interrogation. We also observed that lawyers who attempted to intervene during the *juge*'s questioning of the accused were usually given short shrift. In one instance, when a lawyer in area C tried to clarify something his client had said when questioned by the *juge d'instruction*, the *juge* cut him off mid-sentence, saying (condescendingly): 'Yes *maître*, I have understood perfectly, and I will note what your client says.' On other occasions, the sidelining of the lawyer's role was more subtle: statements were not put in the file until after the lawyer had consulted it (or sometimes not at all), in order that the accused remained ignorant of the evidence against her.[110]

We have to work from the dossier, but we know things which are not in the dossier. We should therefore not use them, but sometimes we know things and keep quiet to be more efficient in the enquiry. It is not unfair . . . it can really help in interrogation. [*Juge d'instruction*, area D]

---

[109] Gilbert Azibert, the then president of the *Chambre d'instruction* in Paris, argues that this change is fundamental: 'That means that a criminal lawyer, who now knows how to do his job, can participate in the conduct of the *information*. It is the beginning of an accusatorial system.' (Greilsamer and Schneidermann 2002:193).

[110] Field and West (2003:279) also describe an instance of a *juge d'instruction* misleading an inexperienced lawyer as to her rights of access to the case dossier.

Secondly, increasing the degree of defence participation will require a change in the legal professional cultures of both the defence lawyer and the *magistrat*. In most instances, the *avocat* does not challenge the pre-trial dominance of the *juge d'instruction*, accepting the subsidiary role allotted to her within the inquisitorial model.[111] Field and West (2003) describe a defence culture of re-reading the dossier in a way that is most favourable to the client, rather than engaging in the outright challenge of issues or evidence which go to culpability.

> There was wide agreement across a wide variety of *avocats* and magistrates as to the 'core' defence function—even our most adversarial lawyers saw this as establishing the client's account and offering an alternative 'reading' of the case on the basis of the elements already established in the dossier. (Field and West, 2003:280)[112]

The way in which the defence sought to 'reread' or deconstruct the case dossier followed fairly universal[113] conventions as to what constitutes a solid case,[114] mirroring the nature of the *procureur's* concerns in supervising the investigation and reviewing the file[115]: insufficient detail suggested weak and insufficient evidence; certain factual statements required standard supporting documentation such as medical certificates for injury or alcohol readings for drunkenness. Given the heavy reliance placed upon written evidence at trial and the absence of oral testimony in most instances, the most fruitful lines of enquiry (and bases for courtroom advocacy) for the defence were weaknesses and inconsistencies in the witness statements, forensic evidence or expert reports. It is only the criminal specialist[116] who is likely to go beyond this reactive process of deconstruction, to seek to influence the conduct of the investigation and to engage in an effective defence strategy before and at trial[117]—though such lawyers were very much in the minority as both the organisation of the Bar and the structure of the legal aid system

---

[111] As one lawyer told Field and West (2003:281–82): 'One is involved in an inquisitorial procedure, a procedure in which the *avocat* has in principle only a very secondary role. The principal role is that of the examining magistrate . . . As a consequence the *avocat* can only speak when he is invited.'

[112] Only the most adversarial specialist lawyer in their study qualified this by adding that proactive work on the raw material of the dossier may be required if the police and *juge d'instruction* had not done their job properly.

[113] See eg the comments by police and *gendarmes* on the necessity for more than a 'five line confession', discussed in Ch 3.

[114] Field and West (2003:293).

[115] See further Ch 5.

[116] During the financial and political scandals of the 1990s, many of the suspects (politicians and business people) were represented by commercial rather than criminal lawyers, whose more professional and competent engagement with the case placed greater demands upon the *juge d'instruction*. Roussel (2003:107). The way in which investigations were conducted in the financial section in Paris came to mirror the strengths of this different form of representation, where suspects were often represented by a team of lawyers with different specialisms. See Greilsamer and Schneidermann's (2002) interview with Jean-Pierre Zanoto, *Juge à l'Inspection général des services judiciaires* at pp 162–63.

[117] It is the minority of criminal specialist lawyers who are more likely to call and question witnesses at trial and to adopt a more adversarial posture in defending clients (Field and West, 2003:283–84).

militate against legal specialism.[118] But even for those specialist lawyers adopting a more proactive posture, the most successful approach was achieved through a subtle process of informal requests and careful manoeuvring, establishing and then exploiting doubts and ambiguities. The centrality of the case dossier at all stages of the criminal process and the lawyer's dependence upon the *juge d'instruction* as the investigator upon whose evidence the court will base its decision mean that outright challenge and confrontation would be inappropriate and the establishment of a wholly separate defence case risky. In England and Wales, the defence may seek to dispute evidence produced by the police by bringing their own witnesses to contradict the prosecution case. To do this within an inquisitorial procedure (without channelling such claims through the pre-trial enquiry), where investigations are understood to be judicially supervised, is to challenge the integrity of the judiciary itself. Furthermore, in its subsidiary role, the status of the defence in France as a party to the proceedings is inferior to that of the *magistrat* and the lawyer is trusted less than the (judicially supervised) police. This places a clear constraint on her ability to engage in any form of proactive defence. For example, when I asked whether the defence would call witnesses independently at trial, a *juge d'instruction* in area D told me:

> The lawyer can produce a witness statement, yes, but that has less validity than if the statement was taken by a police officer because we do not know the circumstances. It could have been taken with a gun to the witness' head. If taken by the police, we know that it was taken under proper conditions.[119]

This view was also supported in Field and West's study (2003:296–97) in which lawyers told them that they would not generally interview defence witnesses for fear of tainting their testimony.

The recent Outreau case (2004) in which seven out of seventeen defendants were acquitted of charges relating to child sexual abuse, also demonstrates the limitations of this participation model. One of the defendants, who was later acquitted, told the court how the *juge d'instruction* was not interested in her account, but only in explanations that supported the initial accusations, becoming angry and threatening in the face of her denials.[120] In one instance, her own defence lawyer left the *juge*'s office in tears. Six of the seven acquitted had spent nearly three years in custody on the basis of accusations that were withdrawn at trial—and the seventh, although on bail, had her son removed from her care. As the trial progressed, there was serious concern that the *juge d'instruction* investigating the case, who was young and inexperienced, had worked not to *charge* and to *décharge*, but to construct a case against the accused. Compounding this were

---

[118] See Karpik (1999); Danet (2001:119–47).
[119] Given the fact that several suspects were shot during police interrogation in the 1990s, this statement struck me as particularly ironic.
[120] See *Libération* 24 May 2004.

the psychology experts in the case, who were also found to have been insufficiently neutral in their professional assessments. As a result, immediately following the acquittals the Minister of Justice announced the establishment of a working party to look at the process of *instruction*, detention and the treatment of evidence from child victims. The objective was to see what lessons might be learned from the case, in order to avoid such a situation reoccurring. The report was published in February 2005 (Viout, 2005) and recommended the appointment of two *juges d'instruction* in complex and sensitive cases, in order that the workload could be shared and theories and ideas cross-checked, thus avoiding the 'tunnel vision' of case construction. Implicitly, this recognises the limitation of the defence role. The lawyer is unable to participate in a way that might effectively displace the case theory and assumptions of the *juge d'instruction*.

In cases supervised by the *procureur*, it is very much more difficult for the defence to play any part in the investigation, or to have any impact on the construction of the dossier. Her role during the GAV is limited to a 30 minute consultation with the suspect (the nature of which is discussed below), and many cases are then listed for trial shortly afterwards, effectively closing the investigation. In non-*instruction* cases, the *avocat*'s role tends to focus on accompanying the accused if she is brought before the *procureur*[121] and representing her in bail hearings. Field and West observed some informal exchanges resulting in mutual concessions, but this depended upon the *avocat* having a degree of trust in, and some form of personal relationship with, the *procureur*. Such exchanges were the exception rather than the rule:

> Any image of a dossier constructed on the basis of real dialogue between prosecutor and defence with the latter using a reading of the dossier and client interview to prompt the prosecutor to order further investigations was a long way from reality. (Field and West, 2003:295)

The Defence Role at Trial

This narrow understanding of the defence function also extends to the *avocat*'s role at trial, where she was considered by many *procureurs* to have little effect upon the case outcome. Instead, her value was more in giving the appearance of representation both to the defendant and the outside world:

> I think that, unfortunately, the lawyer does not know a great deal. Sometimes there are aspects of the accused's personality which they might play on. A defence on the facts,

---

[121] This occurred where the case was passed to the *juge d'instruction*. In some sites lawyers were present as duty lawyers waiting to pick up the case (but playing no role in the proceedings) when the case was sent for trial that day. Some *procureurs* also brought the suspect before them in other instances, in order to mark the gravity of the affair, even if it was being treated more leniently.

strictly speaking, I am not sure that that achieves a great deal. In my view, the accused would be dealt with in just the same way[122] . . . There is also the social role of the lawyer. Someone who is sentenced to imprisonment and has a lawyer will at least feel that they have been defended. That role exists. It is very important. [A4]

In many instances, this may well be true. The majority of cases in France, as in England and Wales, are not contested and the growing number of defendants dealt with through the rapid trial procedure are usually represented by duty lawyers who have received the case papers only hours before the hearing. The presence of an effective lawyer at trial was not, however, wholly without consequence. Just as the *avocat*'s participation in the *instruction* was considered a useful counter-reflex in the judicial enquiry, so too the value of the defence in keeping the *procureur* on her toes was also recognised.

> Generally speaking, the defence lawyer plays an important role at court. Depending on the personality of the lawyer, we will prepare our submissions to the court more thoroughly. [A2]

> The problem [in the French system] is the defence . . . the defence is too weak. I see this at court, for example. When I know that there is going to be a good lawyer, I need to make sure that my submission to the court is well prepared. Most of the time I make very few submissions because I know that there will not be much of one in response and I do not want to unbalance the criminal process yet further by making a scathing submission in the face of what will be a weak defence. [E7]

What is less acceptable (and, it is claimed, less effective) is a defence that seeks to challenge the core of the case or the procedure more directly.

> There are two types of defence . . . there are those who work at the margins, engaged in damage limitation and there are those hoodwinked by their clients: 'I was not there. It was not my hand. It was not the jam etc' and who accept that. That is unacceptable. Those who play on the margins win in general. Those who play on the client lose. I do not know if you understand what I mean. They can still be effective at the margins. They can gradually win a suspended sentence, although I am asking for six months in prison. They can mitigate the sanction, but in no case can they modify the sanction . . . otherwise, nobody listens to them. That is a totally ineffective defence. [E7][123]

However, this narrow account of the part played by the defence lawyer is based upon an idealised view of the *procureur*'s own role and a refusal to countenance a

---

[122] This limited role for the defence was confirmed by a lawyer in area C who considered that cases were essentially 'pre-judged' on the basis of the dossier beforehand.

[123] See also the criticism of the '*défense de rupture*' in which the judicial institution itself is attacked, rather than the dossier. The *magistrats* interviewed by Greilsamer and Scheidermann (2002:61, 106, 146–48) described this as an increasingly popular phenomenon where politicians and business people were under investigation. See also Danet (2001:111–12). Also the discussion of the resistance of elites to being investigated under the ordinary criminal law, above in Ch 3.

more active form of defence lawyering. In some instances, where the accused was represented by an experienced criminal lawyer, defence representation had a significant impact upon the case. For example, in one case we observed in site C, the co-defendants had protested their innocence from the outset, but the police and *procureur* preferred the evidence of the complainant to that of the accused. At trial, the lawyer was able to demonstrate the weakness in the complainant's testimony and both defendants were acquitted. Such examples were very rare in our study, but demonstrate the potential importance of effective defence scrutiny and representation; the *procureur* alone cannot always be relied upon to weed out weak cases.

The role which the defence is expected to play is particularly problematic in the increasing number of *comparution immédiate* hearings and in the new process whereby the *procureur* may propose a reduced sentence in exchange for a guilty plea, so avoiding trial altogether.[124] Although the disposal of cases in these instances depends upon the presence of the defence lawyer, the investigation of such cases will in most instances have been supervised by the *procureur* where there are no structures in place to enable effective participation, and the defence is therefore absent from the dossier.

The expedited *comparution immédiate* procedure is available in offences with a maximum sentence of between six months and ten years imprisonment, where the *procureur* considers the case ready for trial. Most defendants are represented by a duty lawyer (who, by definition, is likely to be young and inexperienced) who will also have a number of other cases to represent that day. The *avocat* has access to the file once the decision to prosecute has been made, but as the case is heard later the same day, there is insufficient time to prepare anything more than a basic plea in mitigation. In such cases, court representation is considered by *procureurs* as likely to have little impact on either the verdict or the sentence.

> For cases which are dealt with by *comparution immédiate* there are duty lawyers. We think that the cases are straightforward. We have a personal knowledge of the cases. A lawyer is pleading before the court for nothing really. It is rare that he will provide more weight to an argument, in a way that we have not already considered . . . The defence is more effective [during the *instruction*] . . . I do not see the need for the duty lawyer in the French system. It's a waste. It is an absurd and grotesque comedy. [E1]

> When the case is dealt with by *comparution immédiate* and they are duty lawyers, they only have a relatively short time in which to see their client and read the dossier . . . here, we suggest they take a little more time if they need it. We try to respect the rights of the defence. [A3]

The difficulties of respecting the principle of *contradictoire* are acutely demonstrated through this procedure which takes place within hours of the GAV, relies upon the availability of duty lawyers who have no opportunity to engage with the case and who are unlikely to have had more than 10 or 15 minutes during which

---

[124] Described in detail in Ch 2.

to discuss the evidence with their client. Without corresponding changes to the way in which *avocats* are organised, paid and trained; a greater opportunity to participate in the pre-trial process (notably during the GAV, given the rapidity with which these cases come before the court); and a more responsive attitude on the part of the *parquet* (which may also have resource implications given the high caseloads of most *procureurs*), respect for the principle of *contradictoire* in these cases will continue to be illusory. Yet, recent reforms have expanded yet further the number of cases which may be dealt with in this way.[125]

The defence role is also key to the implementation of the new 'guilty plea' procedure introduced in 2004. Although the accused is given 10 days during which to consider the *procureur*'s sentence offer, the defence will have had little or no opportunity to contribute to the construction of the case and the safeguard of scrutiny of the dossier by the trial judge is largely removed. The reform represents a significant shift in legal culture and the roles that legal actors are expected to play and, although not acknowledged explicitly in the surrounding debate, the procedure will make new demands upon the defence lawyer in particular. A greater degree of vigilance will be required of the *avocat* in order to assess the worth of the *procureur*'s offer, to protect the interests of the accused and to engage in negotiation over the case outcome. These are new roles which represent a departure from the relatively passive and reactive ways in which the defence function is currently understood. In addition, it might be argued that the *procureur* is acting very much in her narrow role as prosecutor (rather than as a *magistrat* supervising a police investigation), yet there is no 'independent' judicial supervision of this crucial part of the pre-trial process and no trial judge to be satisfied.[126] This casts the defence role in more adversarial terms as, by implication, the protection of the accused will fall to the defence lawyer, requiring her to act in a more proactive way. Furthermore, this is not a shift that will necessarily be restricted to a minority of cases. Applying to offences punishable by up to five years imprisonment, over half of the cases tried in the courts will be eligible to be dealt with in this way.

The Defence Role During the *Garde à Vue*

This final section scrutinises more closely the role of the *avocat* during the GAV, as despite the centrality of the initial police enquiry to the case investigation,[127] it

---

[125] It applied previously to offences with a maximum sentence of between one and seven years imprisonment, but under the reform of September 2002 (discussed above in Ch 2) this was increased to those with a maximum sentence of between six months and ten years' imprisonment.

[126] Although the case must be heard in open court, the judge may only accept or reject the sentence proposed and it is unlikely that she will examine the case in the same detail as she would at trial. If she were to, there would be no time saving element to the procedure.

[127] See Chs 5 and 6.

is here that resistance to increased defence rights is strongest. The police investigation is crucial in providing the initial evidence against the suspect, in informing the *procureur* in her decision on how to proceed with the case,[128] and in setting the parameters of even the investigation of the *juge d'instruction*. Yet, despite calls from a wide range of bodies such as lawyers' associations,[129] the *Syndicat de la magistrature*, the working group of the *Cour de cassation*[130] and external bodies such as the European Committee for the Prevention of Torture and Inhuman or Degrading Treatment or Punishment (2001:para 34), lawyers continue to be allowed only a brief consultation with their clients and to be excluded from the police interrogation of suspects. Resistance is based upon a desire to retain the current *magistrat*-dominated structure of judicial supervision, an antipathy to all things adversarial and a general mistrust of the profession of *avocat*.

During the pre-trial stage, the inquisitorial basis of French criminal procedure (including the professional status, function and ideology of the *magistrat*) remains a defining feature of the defence role even during the *instruction*, limiting it to a carefully managed 'dialogue'[131] between lawyer and *magistrat*. In contrast to this choreographed *avocat–juge d'instruction* relationship, however, the nature of any defence engagement with the enquiry during the GAV would be directly with the police and so less susceptible to judicial regulation and containment of this sort. In this way, custodial legal advice represents a departure from the existing forms of defence role and is seen to pose a more direct threat to the ideal of judicial control and supervision. In terms of the analysis set out at the start of this chapter, the defence lawyer is allowed a place in the GAV, but it is clear that she is not expected to play any role that might impact upon the procedure or the conduct of the enquiry, beyond reaffirming the rights of the suspect and preventing some of the more blatant physical abuse. During the *instruction* (and together with the *partie civile*) the lawyer has access to the dossier, the right to request that particular investigations be carried out and she may accompany the accused at all stages of the procedure including judicial interrogations. Whilst the nature of the criminal bar (with its few experienced specialists) together with the occupational culture of the *juge d'instruction* (whose working practices remain entrenched in the inquisitorial model) tend to militate against the full exercise of these defence

---

[128] See further Chs 5 and 6. Also the response of the *Syndicat de la magistrature* to the EU Commission Green Paper on procedural safeguards for suspects at http://europa.eu.int/comm/justice_home/fsj/ criminal/procedural/fsj_criminal_responses_en.htm

[129] In evidence to the Truche Commission (1997). See P Leleu, *Président du Conseil national des Barreaux*, in Truche (1997) *Annexes* 243 and B Vatier, *Bâtonnier de l'ordre des avocats à la cour d'appel de Paris*, in the same, at 274.

[130] See responses to the EU Commission Green Paper on procedural safeguards for suspects at http://europa.eu.int/comm/justice_home/fsj/criminal/procedural/fsj_criminal_responses_en.htm

[131] 'Dialogue' being the term adopted by Field and West (2003) as the ideal to which the French system aspires.

rights, her increased ability to participate in the investigation provides a procedural opportunity (and some might argue, an expectation) for the *avocat* to influence the judicial construction of the dossier. During the investigation supervised by the *procureur*, however, and especially during the GAV, no such role is envisaged. Absent from the police interrogation of her client, with only a limited period of consultation and scant knowledge of the details of the offence for which the suspect is being held, the lawyer's role, both in participating in the investigation and in assisting her client in police custody, is limited by its narrow procedural definition.[132]

The Lawyer at the Police Station: Moral Support, Not Legal Advice

In recommending the establishment of the right to custodial defence advice, the Delmas-Marty Commission (1991) proposed that the lawyer be given the opportunity to intervene earlier and more actively in the procedure,[133] but it was stated explicitly that this would not extend the principle of *contradictoire* to the GAV[134] and so would not include the right to be present during interrogations or to request that witnesses be heard[135]—the lawyer's principal function was to inform the suspect of her legal rights.[136] Similarly, in discussing the reform that was legislated in June 2000, the then Justice minister, Elisabeth Guigou told *Le Monde*:

> Lawyers are there to help their clients and to ensure the proper conduct of the *garde à vue*, but not to start getting involved in the case.[137]

This view of the defence was also held by police and *magistrats* in our study, who defined the defence role during the GAV in ways that did not challenge the current model or practice of criminal investigation. The lawyer's function is not understood in terms of 'defending' the suspect, or engaging in any form of active defence, but rather, as reinforcing and supporting the role of the *procureur*. Just as the lawyer's role during *instruction* is mediated through the *juge d'instruction*, police and *magistrats* whom we observed and questioned consistently described the lawyer's role in procedural terms. This was not considered an opportunity to

---

[132] See also Danet (2001:40); Field and West (2003:287).

[133] (1991:142).

[134] (1991:120–21; 207–8).

[135] (1991:141).

[136] (1991: 120–21). Contrast this with the much stronger position taken by the *Conseil constituionnel* in its decision of 11 August 1993, when considering the legislative proposal to deny access to legal advice to suspects held on suspicion of terrorism or drugs trafficking. The *Conseil* stated that a person's right to see a lawyer during the GAV was part of her right to a defence and whilst the exercise of this might be varied according to the nature of the offence, to deny the right altogether offended against the principle of equality of arms.

[137] Interview with Mme. Guigou in *Le Monde* 15 December 1999, quoted further in Ch 1.

engage in defence work, to participate in the enquiry, but simply to check that the GAV was being conducted without major incident and to enhance the credibility of the process. [138] For many, the role was no more than one of emotional support.

> In France, the lawyer is not there to advise the person, but to signal any problems in the conditions of the *garde à vue*; not so much to provide legal advice as moral support. [D3]
>
> [Having a lawyer during the first interrogation by the *juge d'instruction*] reinforces the defence, but at the same time, reinforces the word of the *magistrat* as it makes it more difficult for things to be denied later and easier to prove that nothing undue happened. For the most difficult cases, the three per cent of cases, it is very important to have a lawyer. It has been the same for the police with the lawyer at the 20th hour. It was against their culture, but now, on the contrary, it provides an additional guarantee to the process. [*Juge d'instruction*, area D]

For this reason, (questioned before the June 2000 reform), police and *magistrats* were opposed to the lawyer having access to the client from the start of the GAV rather than after 20 hours.

> The reason that the lawyer is allowed in the *garde à vue* is to ensure that conditions of detention are complied with. You cannot know that at the start: you can at the 20th hour, but not the first . . . that would change totally the nature of the lawyer's role in the *garde à vue*. In my view, that would not be a good thing. In some cases, that would hinder police activity. [E7]

Whilst not seeing themselves as supporting the role of the *procureur*, lawyers in Field and West's study (2003:286–87) considered the scope and purpose of their role to be circumscribed by the limited time they were able to spend with the client and the absence of any reliable case-related information on which they could base any meaningful advice.[139]

> They saw their primary roles as to provide reassurance and support, to reduce the isolation and psychological pressures of detention, to provide general legal advice on suspects' rights in police custody, to explain the broad lines of what might happen next and, by monitoring the prior conduct of the police custody phase, to try to ensure that the client's rights were not violated . . . The role was seen by some as more that of a social worker or psychologist with little need or opportunity to exercise complex lawyerly skills and thus rather frustrating. (Field and West 2003:287–28).

---

[138] See also Danet (2001:39–42).

[139] This accounted for the widespread use of inexperienced and non-specialist lawyers in the provision of custodial legal advice.

For the police, the presence of the *avocat* during the GAV was largely of no interest[140]. It was regarded as a procedural requirement which was largely unnecessary and at times, inconvenient to administer. Like the *procureur*, the police also considered it as a means of affirming their actions.

> This is not a time set aside specifically for preparing the defence but for the lawyer to have a first look at the events and to check the conditions of detention, to protect the suspect from abuse, but essentially, to protect the police from false accusations. There is no longer any violence—in the 1970s, yes—but not now. [Police officer, area D].

Resisting a More Effective Defence Role

Claims that the introduction of custodial legal advice would hamstring investigations and result in large numbers of suspects remaining silent appear to have been misplaced—just as was the case in England and Wales a decade earlier. In practice, the reforms have had a more modest impact[141] and in some instances, have been experienced very positively.[142] However, despite the fact that the lawyer's presence during the GAV has been accommodated with relative ease, its legitimacy was initially (and in some senses continues to be) contested. Both the 1993 and 2000 reforms were greeted by extreme opposition from police and *magistrats*, as was the 1897 reform allowing lawyers into the *instruction* and aspects of the 1958 CPP that initially regulated the GAV.[143] At the heart of much of this resistance is the fear of a slide towards a more adversarial process, in which the fate of the accused is understood to depend upon the quality of her legal representation[144] and the procedure itself becomes an obstacle to the truth. Policy makers have therefore promoted defence rights in a way which is grounded in the requirements of the

---

[140] 83% of our questionnaire respondents described it in this way. Two thirds said that it was also inconvenient and bothersome.

[141] Although no specific figures are provided, the government's evaluation of the 2000 legislation noted only a slight increase in the number of suspects attended by a defence lawyer. See Collomp (2001) para 1.4.1. In refuting any link between the availability of custodial legal advice and the decline in the clear-up rate, Danet (2001:39-40) also notes the very small number of affairs in which the lawyer becomes involved.

[142] See eg *Le Monde* 19 June 2001. One police officer told the reporter: 'I have also noticed that the arrival of the lawyer, straightaway, that releases the tension of really furious suspects who would sometimes take three or four hours to calm down. And for us, that is real progress.'

[143] The nature of the protections which the suspect should be afforded during the GAV seems always to be contested. The initial regulation of the GAV in the 1958 CPP was condemned by some as resolutely preferring the rights of the individual over the necessity for repression, encapsulating its authors' hatred of the police (Bredin, 1958) whilst others deplored the fact that the suspect could neither consult with a defence adviser, nor have her present during interrogation (Merle, 1969). For discussion of the introduction of custodial legal advice proposed by the Delmas-Marty report (1991) see eg Sauron (1990); Waquet (1991); Gendrel (1992).

[144] See eg the concerns expressed by the Delmas-Marty Commission (1991:141–43) and the arguments of those opposing the commission's suggestion of any role for the defence lawyer during the GAV (1991:293–97).

ECHR, but which is also explicitly non-adversarial and does not challenge the central principle of judicial supervision.[145]

For the police and *magistrats* we observed, interviewed and questionnaired, the objections to expanding the defence role during the GAV were also rooted firmly in the inquisitorial principle of judicial supervision. The extension of pre-trial defence rights is seen by many as usurping the proper role of the supervising *magistrat*,[146] privileging the interests of the accused over those of the victim[147] or the effectiveness of the investigation and so, to have a distorting effect upon French criminal justice.[148]

> Regarding the presence of a defence lawyer during the *garde à vue* . . . I am fiercely opposed to it because, firstly, I think that it is a fundamentally inegalitarian measure. Furthermore, it can be part of a gimmick . . . Now, it is at the 20th hour; tomorrow from the beginning. What will be the role of the lawyer from the start of the *garde à vue*? What is going to be his role of assistance? Either, he is going to be useless because by definition he does not know what it is about, or, it is going to be to say, 'say this' or 'say nothing'. That is no longer a job of assisting, it is a job of hindering . . . In Anglo-Saxon countries, the *garde à vue* bears no relation to what we have in France . . . no relation at all. [E4]

> So, supervising or verifying confessions . . . What does that imply? That implies an *a priori* mistrust of everything that the police do, because the only way to effectively check on confessions and statements, is to have a third party present the whole time, whether that be a *magistrat* (and at that precise moment, what would her role be in relation to the interrogating officer?) or whether it be a lawyer, guaranteeing the rights of the defence; he would be present during the whole of the questioning. That really is not our system at all. [A6]

These views are predicated upon an image of the *magistrat* as representing all things good (and in particular, the public interest) and the lawyer, all things bad (notably, the interests of suspected criminals, rather than the truth).[149]

---

[145] See eg the speeches of Justice Ministers discussing the 1993 and 2000 reforms, set out in Ch 1.

[146] A police officer in area C explained that it was very important to have a good relationship with the *parquet* and it was felt that the presence of a lawyer acted as an extra check on their work and so undermined this.

[147] The victim has increasingly been afforded the same rights as the accused—to be represented, to consult the *instruction* dossier, to request that certain investigations be carried out by the *juge d'instruction* and so on.

[148] These were the same concerns expressed to the Delmas-Marty Commission (1991:293–97): those opposing the presence of lawyers in the GAV claimed that it would lead to financial discrimination in a way that would benefit major criminals This also echoes the objections of opponents of the introduction of defence counsel in England in the 18th and 19th century, as well as of later commentators such as Langbein (2003) and Frank (1949)—that the introduction of defence lawyers would benefit only the wealthy and would have a truth distorting effect upon criminal procedure.

[149] Garapon (1996a:66–67) notes that these images are also reflected clearly in French cinema, where adversarialism is denounced simply as a game. The lawyer is generally portrayed as a womaniser who will sink to any depths to block the truth and to benefit his client. The *juge* is portrayed as the antithesis to this (often contrasting both in the same film), in some instances sacrificing even his life in the interests of truth.

These 'Anglomaniacs' claim that equality of objectives is the same as equality of arms. But lawyers and judges are not the same. The lawyer wants to acquit the person who pays him. The judge wants to deliver justice to protect society. [*juge d'instruction*, site F][150]

[Lawyers] are auxiliaries of justice and I do not expect them to participate in the search for the truth, because the truth can be terrible for their client. They are not paid to condemn their client. It is the lawyer's role to search for what is most useful to his client, as against the interests of society, which is the responsibility of the *procureur*. [E4]

The Delmas-Marty Commission noted (1991:294) that whilst *magistrats* proclaim themselves in favour of equality of arms, they are opposed to any measures that seek to put this principle into practice. We also found that any attempt to enable or encourage the exercise of rights, rather than simply informing the suspect of their existence, was criticised, as was the proactive assembling of the defence case or the adoption of a posture benefiting the suspect, rather than the enquiry.[151] As one *procureur* in area D explained:

Procureur: I would not be happy with [the lawyer's] presence in more serious matters. They will tell the suspect to say nothing because people will feel better if they say nothing, than if they confess.
Researcher: But people have the right to remain silent?
Procureur: Why yes! Of course!

I am totally hostile to the lawyer being present at the start of the *garde à vue* . . . a lawyer who tells his client 'you will be in *garde à vue* for 24 or 48 hours, in your own interest, try and say nothing'—from the start, that defeats the whole object and the effectiveness of the *garde à vue* is no longer important . . . We know full well that if someone does not admit their guilt in *garde à vue*, they never will do after that. [E3]

The protection of the suspect's interests was considered, by definition, to be opposed to those represented by the *procureur* and so to undermine the proper function of the investigation—the search for the truth. This senior prosecutor had a cynical view of the effects of the defence role:

[W]hen all the lawyers at the first hour [of the *garde à vue*] tell their clients 'say that you have been beaten up and do not say anything else to the police' . . . they will have succeeded in convincing everybody that even though they have done something, they must never confess . . . to tell a person 'never confess, you will be fine', that creates a state of mind, a state of mind that is completely amoral. [E6]

---

[150] This was just how one court area described it to the Delmas-Marty Commission (1991:294) in rejecting the notion that there could be equality of arms: '[T]he interests defended by the prosecuting *magistrat*, which are those of society, cannot be put on an equal footing with the strictly personal interests of the accused.'

[151] This mirrors the view of the defence role at trial and during *instruction*.

When asked whether the defence lawyer should be allowed to see the case file and permitted access to the suspect throughout the GAV, all of our police questionnaire respondents replied 'no' to both questions. Again, their responses were clearly rooted in an understanding of the French criminal process as an inquisitorial procedure, in which it was not appropriate for the defence to have such a role:

> Our system is not your system. [Police respondent 1]

> That does not correspond to the French inquisitorial system, but to the accusatorial Anglo-Saxon system which favours wealthy suspects. [Police respondent 2]

> Only the *parquet* should be able to check on the dossier of evidence and have access to it. Only the *parquet* should have access to the suspect if necessary. [Police respondent 11]

> Supervision of the *garde à vue* is the job of the *parquet* and not of the lawyer. [Police respondent 5]

Interestingly, some of the most senior *magistrats* in France take a quite different approach to that inscribed within criminal justice practice. In contrast to this narrow and negative view of the *avocat*, the *Cour de cassation* working group, chaired by the *Premier President* of the *Cour*, Guy Canivet, was strongly in favour of a more effective pre-trial role for the defence lawyer.[152] They considered that suspects should have access to a defence lawyer, who in turn should have access to the case file, 'as soon as a public authority (whether police or judicial) makes the accusation to a defendant that he has committed a crime, as perpetrator or accomplice . . . whatever stage the proceedings are at' (p 4). In contrast to those who oppose any extended role for the *avocat* during the GAV on the grounds that it will impede the proper functioning of the investigation, favour the suspect unduly and so create an imbalance in the system, they argue that:

> This requirement, far from establishing an imbalance that is too favourable to the defendant, aims to compel the investigating authorities to establish sound foundations on which to build the prosecution case. Too many proceedings collapse because the case is essentially based solely on the defendant's initial statements, made without a lawyer present . . . it should be specified that the right to genuine assistance from a lawyer should not be reduced to just an interview as currently established under French custody law, particularly at the start of the measure. This interview . . . mainly aims to protect individual freedoms and provide psychological support to the person

---

[152] This was in response to the EU Green Paper on procedural safeguards for suspects. Their and other responses can be found on the Justice and Home Affairs website at http://europa.eu.int/comm/justice_home/fsj/criminal/procedural/fsj_criminal_responses_en.htm.

held in custody. It in no way enables them to exercise genuine 'rights to defence',[153] which in order to be effective, are required by the European Court not only at the beginning when the indictment is notified but also to be part of an organised strategy and to be implemented each time that the person is questioned, confronted with witnesses or when a court decision is made that he could appeal against. (pp 4–5)

Mistrust of the Defence Lawyer

The Delmas-Marty Commission (1991:294) commented on *magistrats'* lack of understanding of the lawyer's role and the harsh picture which they painted of the *avocat*, as representing only the personal interests of the accused (rather than the wider interests of society) and of being dishonest.[154] In our research too, some *magistrats* were critical of certain lawyers' ethics.

> In that gipsy case, the lawyer charged £18,000 for one case and one visit to prison was charged at £800! This was paid by the 'penniless' clients. It is obviously dirty money. He has become their lawyer and is now rolling in money while they steal to pay him extortionate fees. [*Juge d'instruction*, area F]

Others showed a general mistrust of lawyers. For example:

> [W]hat is surprising is that people say 'we must have the lawyer present from the start [of the *garde à vue*]'. Well, I think about that, saying to myself that there are two areas in which, curiously, there is a mistrust of the bar—these are drugs and terrorism. Why, when the lawyer has been allowed in after 20 hours, is it desirable that he should not be allowed in until 72 hours in drugs and terrorism cases? ... What does that mean? That means that in some areas, the lawyer is viewed with suspicion. [E4]

The picture of lawyers painted by the police was almost always one of an untrustworthy profession, tending towards corruption.

> [Access to the dossier would] lead to a risk of communicating with witnesses or accomplices before the investigation is complete. [Police respondent 4]
>
> A lawyer lives from his clients and in the past, we have often observed that the deontology of the lawyer comes after his own interests and those of his client. [If allowed

---

[153] A footnote appears here: This is how it was understood by the Constitutional Council, which announced that 'an individual's right to see a lawyer during custody is a *right to defence* which is exercised during the investigation phase of the criminal proceedings' (Dec. No 93-326 DC 11 August 1993). The *Conseil constitutionnel* was considering here the original proposal to deny access to legal advice to suspects in drugs and terrorism cases. The *Conseil* held that the right could be delayed, but it could not be denied altogether. See also Le Gunehec (1993:494–96).

[154] See also Hodgson (2002b:788–91) for a discussion of the way in which lawyers have been regarded.

greater access to the suspect there would be a] risk of accomplices fleeing, of searches rendered useless after friends had been informed. [Police respondent 6]

Some lawyers don't want to be searched. They are searched when they go to prison, but they don't want to be searched by the police . . . There are a minority of bad lawyers who will alert the family and friends. I have proof that has happened. [Senior police officer, area C]

We don't like lawyers, because they are hooligans too. A lawyer in Paris stole a piece of evidence from the file. He was paid 33,000 francs to do that. Some people pay each month so that when they are in trouble and need a lawyer . . . [Police officer, area C]

Perhaps the most frequent objection to custodial legal advice is that in contrast to the neutral judicial investigator whose task is the search for the truth, the presence of the lawyer during the GAV is seen to promote inequality of treatment, a means by which the wealthy (politicians, business people and organised criminals) could buy themselves an unfair advantage over the ordinary citizen:

To systematically have lawyers present during the *garde à vue* is to privilege the most intelligent and the most wealthy criminals. If the Mafia have the chance to have a lawyer during *garde à vue*, they will get one immediately and he will be the best, because he will be paid . . . On the other hand, the poor boy who has never been in trouble before will ask for a lawyer immediately—will he come? Not necessarily. If he comes, will he have the necessary ability? By no means sure. [D3]

In a road traffic offence, or theft of a car radio, the lawyer allocated by the *bâtonnier*[155] will just go through the motions. He will come and will say, 'Have you anything to say? Nothing at all?'—that will be of no use. On the other hand, when you have a gang of armed robbers or a fraud case . . . you will have an effective and useful defence . . . the presence of a lawyer at the start of the *garde à vue*, in reality, it is not designed for the majority of ordinary offenders . . . but for a socio-professional category who might be involved in financial crime or major trafficking . . . who will immediately call their lawyer (whose number they will have in their pocket) telling them to, 'Get down here' . . . I believe that one should try and deal with people on the basis of what they have done and not on the basis of who they are. [E4]

All the changes in terms of rights for the suspect are a cover for manipulating the system to the advantage of the few—the elite and the well-to-do. [Police officer, area A]

Lawyers are not officers of justice. They are like greengrocers, they are business people. They only do things for money. In the USA and the UK you have the problem that those with more money get a better lawyer. [*Procureur*, area D]

[The introduction of lawyers at the police station] is done for two reasons. To protect criminals and to help lawyers earn more money! . . . They will always warn the other people that we are looking for, or at least the family . . . Those who have more money can get a better lawyer and be better protected. [Police officer, area C]

---

[155] The local head of the bar, responsible for organising the duty lawyer system.

In line with Field and West's (2003) findings that criminal specialists are more likely to engage in an active defence strategy (in contrast to the generalist or inexperienced *avocats* who tend to act as duty lawyers), the distinction between *avocats* named (and paid for) by the suspect and those assigned as duty lawyers was drawn clearly in both *procureur* and police questionnaire responses.[156] Whilst 83 per cent of police respondents said that duty lawyers would rarely or never be there to prepare the defence, one-third said that named lawyers would always or often do this and a further third considered that this would sometimes be the case. Of *procureur* respondents, three-quarters considered that named lawyers would always or often engage in defence preparation, but only one-quarter in relation to duty lawyers. Similarly, duty lawyers were thought less likely than named *avocats* to check the conditions of detention and more likely to be there simply to fulfil a legal requirement. This difference might also have an impact on the conduct of the enquiry, as one *procureur* explained:

> If, for example, we need to conduct a search during an *enquête préliminaire*, we need the agreement of the suspect. If the suspect agrees and then the lawyer intervenes, telling him that he absolutely must not, then you might find yourself obliged to open an *information* and then you have to carry it out under *commission rogatoire*. Fortunately, that does not happen very often. I think you find this situation when it is a named lawyer, rather than a duty lawyer. [A3].

Having examined the role that defence *avocat* might properly play in French criminal procedure, both in theory and in practice, the following chapters go on to examine the way in which judicial supervision is characterised during the preliminary investigation and the *instruction*.

---

[156] Interestingly, the working party established after the March 1993 reforms, whose report preceded the August 1993 legislation, recommended that only a duty lawyer should be able to attend suspects in GAV.

5

Judicial Supervision of the *Garde à Vue*

This chapter examines the legal framework governing the detention and questioning of those held in police custody in France (*garde à vue*) and the ways in which the *procureur's* supervision of the police investigation is understood and played out in practice. Just as in England and Wales, those suspected of crime are arrested, detained and questioned by the police, but in France, the conduct of criminal investigations is also the responsibility of a *magistrat*. In more serious and complex cases, it is the *juge d'instruction* who conducts or supervises the enquiry, but in the majority of investigations, including the detention of suspects in *garde à vue* (GAV), supervision is by the *procureur*.[1] As well as defining differently the roles and relationships of police and prosecutors,[2] this structure of accountability also implies a pre-trial defence function which is very different from that in England and Wales.[3] The principal guarantee of the proper treatment of accused persons and the respect of defence rights is not through the involvement of the defence lawyer (although this is also important), but by the judicial character of the investigation, placing the *magistrat* very much at the centre of criminal procedure.

When compared with the more iconic model of judicial investigation and supervision by the *juge d'instruction*, the regulation of the GAV appears as something of a paradox. Both in practice and in the text of the law, the nature of the *juge d'instruction's* supervision of criminal investigations is defined differently from that of the *procureur*. Whilst the latter is required to oversee the GAV[4] and to direct the police initiated investigation,[5] the *juge d'instruction* is characterised as being more directly involved: she is required personally to conduct the investigation and any delegation of this function represents a significant transfer of

---

[1] Over 450,000 people are detained in *garde à vue* each year.
[2] For a discussion of the broader role of the *procureur* see Ch 3.
[3] Discussed in Ch 4.
[4] Leigh and Zedner (1992:3) describe the word *contrôle* as signifying oversight and accountability. The (Collins-Robert) dictionary definition is to inspect, to control, to check, to verify, to supervise.
[5] Art 41 CPP.

authority, rather than the supervision of an existing police power. Furthermore, whilst all aspects of the GAV are conducted by the police under the supervision of the *procureur*, including the interrogation of the suspect, once an *information* has been opened officers are no longer permitted to question the accused; only the *juge d'instruction* may do this. In practice, as described in more detail below, the *procureur* remains office bound and has many cases to supervise at any one time, allowing for little active involvement during the 24 to 48 hour GAV period. The *juge d'instruction* also has a heavy caseload, but as most cases last several months and even years, she has more time to review the evidence collected by the police and to liaise with investigating officers. Thus, there is much closer judicial involvement during the *instruction*, yet the defence enjoys far greater rights to participate in the investigation than she does during the GAV: the defence lawyer has access to the case dossier; she may be present during the questioning of her client by the *juge d'instruction*[6]; she may request that investigative acts be carried out and that expert and other evidence be obtained.[7] During the GAV, she enjoys no such rights.[8] Thus, where judicial supervision is weakest, so too are the rights of the defence.

This is explained in part by the fact that, historically, the GAV has been regarded as being procedurally less significant than the *instruction*, but this view is not supported in practice. In all aspects of her decision making, the *procureur* is dependent upon the information provided by the police,[9] including that obtained during the GAV. The detention of suspects in police custody is not, therefore, an unimportant part of the process preceding the more formal stages of either *instruction* or trial, but is a central part of the 93 per cent of investigations supervised by the *procureur*. This will be increasingly the case, as more cases are dealt with by rapid trial procedures (affording little time for defence preparation) and a decreasing number fall to be investigated by the *juge d'instruction*.

In France as in Britain, criminal justice is prime political territory and as described in Chapter 2, reform over the last decade continues to be characterised by the political Left–Right dialectic, swinging between due process and repression. It is the rights of victims rather than the accused which appear on the current government's agenda and the trend is towards the widening of police powers, rather

---

[6] Neither are these recent innovations: the defence lawyer has enjoyed these rights since 1897.

[7] The accused is also questioned, not in the hostile environment of the police station, but in the office of the *juge*, where a legal secretary makes a written record of the interview.

[8] Contrast the rather more exaggerated description of defence rights during the GAV presented by Bück (2001:326) who writes that, since the 2000 reform 'the GAV is also the official act whereby a person is informed that she is a suspect in the eyes of the police and from which point she may exercise her rights of defence (in parallel with being *mis en examen* by the *juge d'instruction*).'

[9] In determining whether to ratify detention in GAV, to prolong the GAV, to open an *information*, to seek a remand in custody, to prosecute (and with which offence), to suggest an alternative to trial/prosecution or which trial procedure to invoke.

than their constraint. With the introduction of a range of measures which provide for the differential treatment of non-terrorist, as well as terrorist, suspects,[10] the rights of those detained in GAV have been attenuated and an increasing number of cases are governed by an exceptional legal framework in which those suspected of more serious offences may be detained for longer (up to four days) and be denied access to custodial legal advice for 36 hours. Such provisions have been criticised as a backwards step, placing France out of line with the rest of Europe in the provision of even the most basic due process protections.[11] At the same time, police powers have been widened and measures which formerly might only be taken during the *instruction*, can now be requested by the *procureur* during ordinary investigations.

The Legal Framework Regulating the *Garde à Vue*

The French *code de procédure pénale* (CPP) sets out the powers, duties and responsibilities of those conducting and supervising criminal investigations, together with the rights of all parties involved.[12] Like all criminal investigations, the principal means of regulating the GAV period of the police investigation is supervision by a *magistrat*. In most instances, this will be the responsibility of the *procureur*, whose duty it is to investigate and prosecute crime and to supervise the conduct of the GAV.[13] The initial decision to detain a suspect is made by an *officier de police judiciaire* (OPJ), but the *procureur* must be informed at the outset,[14] and her express authority is required for detention beyond 24 hours;[15] in a range

[10] See further the discussion in Ch 2.

[11] The EU Council Framework Decision on Certain Procedural Rights in Criminal Proceedings throughout the European Union sets out the basic safeguards which suspects might be afforded, drawing on those developed under the ECHR. France falls short of these in a number of respects—most notably in the provision of custodial legal advice and informing the suspect of her right to silence.

[12] The French criminal process might be thought of as tripartite in many ways, including the *magistrat* representing the public interest, the victim and the accused. During the *instruction*, the victim, for example, is able to see the case file and request that investigative acts be carried out in the same way that the suspect may.

[13] Art 41 CPP sets out the *procureur*'s responsibility to '*dirige*' the police in pursuing her duty to investigate and prosecute crime. The 1993 reform made clear that this also included a responsibility to '*contrôle*' the GAV.

[14] There were complaints, however, that informing the *procureur* at the outset placed a heavy burden on the police (see *Le Monde* 19 June 2001; *Le Figaro* 9 March 2001 and the reports of Collomp (2001) and Dray (2001)) and there was a (failed) attempt to change this to 'as quickly as possible' in the 2002 legislation.

[15] Arts 63, 77 CPP. Juveniles aged 14 and over may be detained in GAV. On the prior authority of a *magistrat*, those aged between 10 and 13 may also be detained if there is evidence that they have committed or attempted to commit serious offences (*crimes*, or *délits* punishable by five or more years imprisonment). The initial GAV period for juveniles is 12 hours. Exceptionally, the young person may be brought before the *magistrat*, in order that detention may be extended for a further 12 hours.

of serious offences, detention may be extended for a further two periods of 24 hours, up to a maximum of 96 hours. The purpose of advising the *procureur* in this way is to enable her to ensure that the GAV is conducted properly and the Commission nationale consultative des droits de l'homme (CNCDH) has underlined the significance of the *procureur's* intervention as part of the constitutional guarantee that individual liberties must be judicially protected.[16]

Informing the *procureur* marks the beginning of the judicial supervision of the GAV, the primary safeguard ensuring both the proper treatment of the suspect and the effective conduct of the investigation. However, the way in which this supervision should be effected is not stipulated by the law[17]: there is no obligation beyond the provision of information by the police to the *procureur*, which may be done by telephone or by fax.[18] Neither is there a requirement that the *procureur* will attend the GAV,[19] monitor closely the way in which it is conducted or take measures to ensure the reliability of the evidence gathered. France has been heavily and repeatedly criticised by the European Committee for the Prevention of Torture and Inhuman or Degrading Treatment or Punishment, for its poor treatment of those held in GAV.[20] As a result, although not concerned with the investigation and treatment of individual suspects, there has been some attempt to encourage visits to police stations and *gendarmeries* in order to inspect the material conditions in which detainees are held. The 2000 reform established a requirement that the *procureur* make quarterly visits to each police station or *gendarmerie*, to signal any problems in the conditions of detention, such as poor heating or lighting. In the face of strong opposition from the

---

[16] In their opinion, the proposal (which was ultimately withdrawn) to allow a delay of up to three hours in informing the *procureur* of a person's detention in GAV was constitutionally unjustified. See Opinion on the 'petite loi' complementing the June 2000 reform, adopted by Parliament 24 January 2002. However, the importance of this form of judicial supervision appears to be undercut by the Ministry of Justice circular (10 January 2002, para 2): it describes the purpose of informing the *procureur* as being to allow judicial control of the GAV, yet, it emphasises that this does not transfer to the *procureur* the right to decide or to validate the measure. If she does not have the power to determine the legality of detention (and therefore to authorise or terminate such detention), it is difficult to see what the *procureur's* role as judicial supervisor is, or in what way she can be said to guarantee the liberty of the individual.

[17] There is no requirement even that the original copy of the fax informing the *procureur* of a person's detention in GAV appear in the final dossier. (Decision of the *Cour de cassation*, 3 April 2001, 01-80939). The terms in which the *procureur* was initially informed of the detention and the information on which she based her initial decision is not necessarily, therefore, on the file. This is surprising given the centrality of the case dossier during both investigation and trial and the importance of its review as part of the process of judicial supervision. It seems to suggest that the duty to advise the *procureur* is little more than a formality, rather than the provision of key information upon the basis of which decisions can be taken regarding further police action and the liberty of the detainee.

[18] The original 1993 formula 'without delay' was modified later that year to 'as soon as practicable' because of problems experienced by the police in getting hold of the *procureur* and to enable contact to be made by fax.

[19] Though, arguably, there is an expectation of some personal attendance. See Ministry of Justice circular, 1 March 1993, para 2.

[20] See, for example, the Report (2001), para 22, which criticises the meagre progress made by France in this respect over the last 8 years. Poor conditions of detention were also highlighted in the reports following both the 1991 and 1996 visits.

parquet, however, on the grounds that there simply were not the resources to effect such visits, the provision was amended to require only annual inspection.[21]

Prior to 1993, anybody could be placed in police detention 'for the necessities of the investigation', though in the case of witnesses, this was permissible only for the time necessary to take a statement. In 1993 the power to detain witnesses was removed in the case of ordinary investigations (*enquêtes préliminaires*) but it persisted for other types of investigation (*enquêtes flagrantes* and *instruction*) until 2000.[22] Although witnesses may still be detained by police for up to four hours[23] in order to take their statement[24] (by force if necessary), this was a significant curtailment of the powers of detention and the reported decrease in the number of people placed in GAV has been attributed largely to the removal of this power.[25] Now, only those suspected of having committed or attempting to commit an offence may be detained, a position which conforms more closely to Article 5(1)(c) ECHR. However, as with a number of the June 2000 provisions, the advances made by the reform were undermined somewhat by the Ministry of Justice circular addressed to *parquets* and detailing the application of the law. Keen to assuage the fears of the police, it sought to reassure officers that 'repression' was still very much on the agenda.[26] It goes on to remind officers of the variety of situations in which a person might be considered a suspect, as well as the fluidity of definition between 'suspects' and 'witnesses'.[27] In addition, the supplementary legislation passed in March 2002[28] went on to broaden the very definition of a suspect.[29]

---

[21] The amendment was part of the March 2002 '*petite loi*'. The 2001 Collomp report (para 1.4.2), charged with evaluating the success of the reform, noted that in the first three months after coming into effect, of the 10 *parquets* inspected, only 4 had complied fully with the requirement to visit and 3 had made no visits at all. The number of stations to be visited and the distances between them was of particular concern.

[22] *Enquêtes préliminaires* are ordinary investigations; *enquêtes de flagrance* (defined in art 53 CPP) are those concerning 'recently' committed offences. In practice this extended to 8 days but it has now been extended to 15 days under the 2004 reform (described in Ch 2).

[23] The Ministry of Justice circular, 10 January 2002 (para 1.2) suggests that this is an appropriate time by analogy with the four hours allowed to conduct an identity check under art 78-3. If a witness becomes a suspect, the time already spent in custody should be added to the GAV time.

[24] This is justified under art 5(1)(b) ECHR as the lawful detention of a person in order to secure the fulfilment of an obligation prescribed by law.

[25] See *Le Monde* 19 June 2001.

[26] Ministry of Justice circular, 10 January 2002.

[27] Witnesses who refuse to answer questions, for example, may then become suspects. This would suggest that witnesses do not enjoy an unfettered right to silence.

[28] Often referred to as '*la petite loi*', this is described as legislation 'complementing' that of June 2002, ironing out some minor points, rather than making any fundamental changes.

[29] It altered the criteria for suspicion from someone relating to whom there is 'some evidence suggestive of' to 'one or more plausible reasons to suspect' having committed or attempted to commit an offence. In quite specifically requiring only one reason to suspect, this amendment has been criticised as unnecessary and failing to follow properly the standard set in art 5(1)(c) ECHR, which talks only in the plural of '*des raisons plausibles*' to suspect criminal involvement, not the singular of '*une ou plusieurs raisons plausibles*'. This preferred interpretation had already been set out in the Ministry of Justice circular 10 January 2002, para 1.1, making clear that, 'There need only exist one single piece of evidence' against a person to detain them in GAV.

Immediately upon detention, the suspect must be informed of her rights[30] which now include having her employer or a member of her family informed of her detention within 3 hours[31]; to request a doctor[32]—also within 3 hours[33]; to see a lawyer for 30 minutes 'without delay'[34]; and to be informed of the nature of the offence in connection with which she is being detained.[35] The police must inform the lawyer of the date and nature of the offence for which the suspect is being held. Lawyer–client consultations must be in private, but the defence lawyer is not permitted access to the dossier of evidence, nor to be present during the interrogation of her client. Interviews are not tape recorded, but are noted down in the form of a statement. A formal record of detention must be kept, detailing the duration of the GAV, interrogation times, rest periods, meal times, when the suspect was told of her rights and whether she wished to exercise them. The requirement that the police inform the suspect of her right to silence was introduced in June 2000, but was then repealed by the following government in March 2003.

The provisions of the Police and Criminal Evidence Act (PACE) 1984, provide a range of safeguards designed to ensure the reliability of evidence and to protect suspects held in police custody in England and Wales. It has been criticised, however, for the absence of clear sanctions in the event that these provisions are breached.[36] Thus, for example, there is no requirement that evidence should be excluded where the suspect has not been told of her right to legal advice, despite the fact that this safeguard has been described as a fundamental right of the suspect.[37] Confessions obtained either by oppression, or in circumstances likely to render a confession unreliable, must be excluded,[38] but otherwise, it is within the discretion of the court

---

[30] Art 63-1 CPP. These provisions are also discussed in Ch 4. Officers responsible for detaining suspects in GAV in Lemaître's Lyon study (1994:80) were initially afraid that their obligation to inform the suspect of her rights would set the wrong tone—reassuring her, rather than psychologically isolating her. In practice, they found that it did not make a great deal of difference.

[31] Art 63-2 CPP. The June 2000 provision to ensure that the suspect was told 'without delay' of her right to have someone informed of her detention was changed in the 2002 legislation. This was criticised by the CNCDH as likely to introduce a norm of a three hour delay, which in many instances will be excessive.

[32] Art 63-3 CPP.

[33] In the case of juveniles, the doctor must be requested immediately.

[34] Art 63-4 CPP.

[35] Art 63-1 CPP. Telling the suspect that there is evidence suggesting that she has committed or attempted to commit an offence is not sufficient (Cass. 2e civ. 22 mai 2003, *Chiang Jiao Z*).

[36] See eg Sanders (1988).

[37] See eg *Samuel* [1988] 2 WLR 920, where evidence was excluded and the later cases of *Dunford* (1990) 91 Cr App R 150 and *Dunn* (1990) 91 Cr App R 237, where it was not.

[38] Section 76 PACE requires the exclusion of confession evidence where the prosecution cannot prove beyond reasonable doubt that the confession was not 'obtained (a) by oppression of the person who made it; or (b) in consequence of anything said or done which was likely, in the circumstances existing at the time, to render unreliable any confession which might be made by him in consequence thereof'.

having regard to all the circumstances.[39] In France, the position is open to the same criticism. Garé and Ginestet, (2002:234) note that despite providing a number of additional guarantees for suspects, the framework put in place by the 1993 legislation fails to make provision for the exclusion of evidence obtained in breach of these safeguards. The original January 1993 text required the automatic exclusion of evidence where the new rights of the suspect were not respected[40]; this was promptly repealed, however, in the new government's legislation in August of the same year.[41] In the absence of *nullités textuelles* (where the CPP makes express provision for the exclusion of evidence where certain procedures are breached)[42] any exclusion of evidence must be on the basis of a *nullité substantielle*. In these instances, article 171 CPP (concerning the *chambre d'instruction*), article 385 CPP (concerning ordinary cases before the *tribunal correctionnel*) and article 802 CPP (of general application) state that evidence can be excluded if a provision of criminal procedure has been breached, prejudicing the interests of the party concerned.[43] This may concern general/public[44] or private/individual interests. The kinds of breach in criminal procedure which amount to a *nullité substantielle* are not easy to categorise and they have been decided on a case by case basis[45] and the extent to which some prejudice must be shown has been the subject of inconsistent case law.[46] The *Cour de cassation* developed a novel approach by treating breaches concerning the public interest (*d'ordre*

---

[39] Evidence may be excluded under s 78 PACE where, 'having regard to all the circumstances, including the circumstances in which the evidence was obtained, the admission of the evidence would have such an adverse effect on the fairness of the proceedings that the court ought not to admit it'.

[40] It is interesting that in order to prevent the court from avoiding the enforcement of these provisions, there was no requirement to show any prejudice. These provisions were mostly repealed in August 1993. Some remain, eg art 59 CPP where the formalities of conducting a search between 6am and 9pm have not been respected—though the *Cour de cassation* has interpreted this as requiring some prejudice to the party.

[41] The exclusion of evidence has been the subject of what Spencer (2002:606) calls a political tug-of-war, with the Left legislating to sanction irregularities in the GAV, promptly followed by a reversal of the law by the Right. This happened with Loi No. 81-82 of 2 February 1981, which extended the range of *nullités*, only to be reversed by Loi No. 83-466 of 10 June 1983, then again with Loi No. 93-2 of 4 January 1993, which was reversed in this respect later the same year by Loi No. 93-1013 of 24 August 1993.

[42] In practice, the court has also required that some prejudice to the party's interest be shown.

[43] See further Guerrin (2000).

[44] This refers to provisions which protect the wider interest, whose importance goes beyond the individual in the instant case—general legislative provisions, those which are necessary for the procedure to fulfil its purpose, such as the requirement for public trial hearings or the territorial competence of a *magistrat*. Breaches include, for example, where the papers opening an *information* are not signed or dated (Crim. 4 Dec. 1952: *Bull. crim. No. 290*; 23 Apr. 1971: *Bull crim. No. 115*); or the dossier of evidence is not attached for the *juge d'instruction* when opening an *information* (Crim. 6 Jul. 1955: *Bull. crim. No. 339*); or when the person held in GAV is not informed that the custody period has been extended (Crim. 30 Jan. 2001: *Bull. crim. No. 26*).

[45] The qualification 'substantial' seems to refer in part to the provision breached and in part to the prejudice caused to the interests of the party (Garé and Ginestet, 2002:309).

[46] Guerrin (2000) is critical of the absence of any coherent theoretical approach to the exclusion of criminal evidence in France.

public), as causing prejudice by definition. This reasoning was applied successfully to the GAV, holding that any unjustified delay in informing the suspect of her rights would necessarily prejudice the party's interests. Evidence properly obtained prior to the GAV remains valid; that obtained after is excluded only if the search for the truth has been vitiated. However, more recently, the *Cour* appears to have reverted to a stricter reading of article 802, requiring some evidence of prejudice even in cases where the breach is unquestionably *d'ordre public*, such as the obligation for a court hearing to be held in public.[47]

The exclusion of evidence and, in particular, of confession evidence can be an effective sanction for breaches in the procedure relating to the detention and interrogation of suspects, sending out a clear message as to the required standards of compliance. However, the reluctance of the French courts to exclude evidence,[48] coupled with the absence of clear guidelines relating to interrogation practice, make this an ineffectual sanction in practice. Although the appeal courts are showing signs of taking more seriously breaches of procedure during the GAV,[49] the exclusion of confessions is rare. The difficulties in challenging evidence obtained during the GAV highlight further the importance of mechanisms such as judicial supervision, designed to ensure the credibility of evidence.

Understanding Supervision in Practice

There are now a number of safeguards in place as part of the legal regulation of the police detention of suspects and witnesses, bringing France into line with most other European countries and ensuring compliance with the ECHR. For example, the reform of article 63-1 CPP requiring the police to inform the suspect of the reasons for her detention in police custody is necessary in order to comply with Article 5(2) of the European Convention, which states that: 'Everyone who is arrested shall be informed promptly, in a language which he understands, of the reasons for his arrest and of any charge against him.' Similarly, the provision of translators at all stages of the criminal process is a basic ECHR requirement. However, whilst representing important advances in the provision of due process

---

[47] Decisions of the *Cour de casssation* 15 June 1999. Garé and Ginestet (2002:310).

[48] This is an issue even where there have been clear breaches of the ECHR. For example, excessive delay in bringing a case to court, whilst in breach of Art 6 ECHR, does not result in any evidence being struck out. Crim. 7 Mar. 1989: *Bull. crim. No. 109*; 29 Apr. 1996: *D. 1997. somm. 148, obs.* Pradel.

[49] See eg Pradel (2002) paras 510–15. Also Bück (2001). It is interesting to compare this with the situation a decade ago, when professor Pradel (1993) described the *Cour de cassation* as being 'hostile' to excluding evidence and he concluded that in stark contrast to the strict legal regime and jurisprudence concerning the *instruction*, the notion of unlawfully obtained evidence in relation to the GAV, in effect, did not exist: it was virtually impossible for the suspect to demonstrate that her statements could not be relied upon as a result of breaches in GAV procedure.

protections, these modifications to the legal framework regulating the GAV period do not displace the model of judicial supervision in any significant way. It
remains at the heart of French pre-trial criminal procedure and continues to be
the central mechanism by which the proper treatment of the suspect, and the reliability of confession and other evidence, are guaranteed. Additional safeguards
such as the tape recording of interrogations or the extended availability of custodial legal advice have been rejected as unnecessary on the grounds that the existing
system of judicial supervision provides adequate protection. In presenting the
June 2000 project, the success and desirability of judicial supervision was underlined repeatedly, contrasting it with adversarial procedure in particular, which is
considered to protect neither the suspect, nor the interests of justice.[50] In evaluating the treatment of the suspect detained in GAV and the extent to which her
interests are protected, it is central therefore, to interrogate the ways in which judicial supervision is understood and carried out.

The appeal of judicial supervision to observers from an adversarial jurisdiction, is its potential to effect a wider investigation, ensuring that the police might
follow leads which exculpate, as well as incriminate, the suspect.[51] In this way, the
'stronghold' which the police in England and Wales have historically exercised
over the conduct of the investigation, the resulting premature fixation upon the
guilt of the suspect and the tendency to 'construct' the case against her, (the hall-
mark of so many miscarriages of justice)[52] can be avoided. Key to this alternative
model is the involvement of a judicial officer whose status, ideology and objectives
are independent of those of the police and who, therefore, is able to challenge and
go beyond the narrow confines of a police-dominated investigation. However, the
way in which the *procureur* understands her role in supervising the police investigation (and indeed, the legal model of supervision set out in the CPP) is rather
different from this expectation.[53] Her principal objective is not to monitor closely
the work of the police, but to provide a more general 'legal orientation' in order
to ensure the construction of a legally coherent dossier that will withstand the
scrutiny of the court. In this way, supervision is perhaps best characterised as
being concerned with the *outcome* and the *form* of the police investigation, rather
than with the *method*. This is done quite literally by monitoring the output of the
investigation, ensuring that basic evidence is collected and that compliance with

---

[50] See Ch 1, extract of the speech of the then Justice Minister, Elisabeth Guigou, presenting the
reform project to the *Sénat*, 15 June 1999.

[51] See Mansfield and Wardle (1993), Rose (1996) and those discussed by Field (1994:120).

[52] See, for example, the treatment of Stephen Miller (one of the 'Cardiff Three') discussed below in
Ch 6.

[53] Given the very different history and legal culture of the French criminal justice process, we would
not expect the role of the *procureur* to conform to the needs of the legal system in England and Wales.
Historically, her function has not developed in this way, out of a need to counter an excessively police-
dominated investigative process. Instead, the roles of the police and of the *procureur* have evolved hand
in hand (Lévy, 1993) their contemporary relationship characterised by trust and teamwork, rather
than conflict or hierarchy. See also Ch 3 above.

procedural safeguards has been documented. In a busy duty office, this will involve dealing with a wide variety of cases, from shoplifting to murder. The types of issues on which the *procureur* may be required to provide advice or a decision range from basic evidence and mode of trial points, to jurisdiction issues and the implementation of mediation. During the GAV, officers are prompted to take witness statements and reminded of the need to gather basic probative evidence such as a specimen of blood to measure the alcohol levels of the suspect; a medical certificate relating to the victim's injuries; a death certificate; or vehicle insurance documents. When reviewing the dossier, the *procureur* will check that statements are signed and in triplicate; that the *garde à vue* documentation records times, medical visits and the communication to the suspect of her rights; that the *procureur* has been informed of the suspect's detention and any extension authorised. The emphasis is upon procedural conformity and the absence of any probing for information beyond the standard details provided was demonstrated in this typical account, given by a senior *procureur*:

> [A] person is in *garde à vue* . . . the *parquet* must be informed as required by the CPP, that is, as soon as possible, and then, the investigator reports on the progress of the investigation. To begin with, the investigator will relate the essential information in order that the *magistrat* knows what is going on, the nature of the offence, the identity of the suspect, how long and finally at what time he was placed in *garde à vue*, so that he can place this in a legal framework on the one hand, and on the other, gather information about the suspect, notably, for example, asking for his criminal record and any previous convictions he has in this region and then . . . [the investigator] will call back the *magistrat* to tell him how that investigation is going and if the case arises, he will call back . . . to get advice and . . . at the end of the *garde à vue* . . . the *magistrat* must decide how to proceed. [A6]

This bureaucratic form of supervision, although relatively passive, has the potential benefit of filtering out obviously weak cases where the basic elements of an offence are not made out or where there has been a failure to comply with or document basic procedural safeguards. As one *procureur* told us: 'Our job is to shake out the dossier to bring out anything which does not stick.' [C1].

In most instances that we observed, the *procureur*'s supervision of the police concerned the detention of suspects in GAV, but the *procureur* might also be involved in overseeing an ongoing investigation before a suspect has been identified. A senior *procureur* in area E explained his role in these instances as guarding against the dangers of searching for 'a culprit', rather than searching for the truth. In his view, the investigation became more of a process of case construction when the police were acting under pressure[54] and he described to us the way in which

---

[54] This has also been identified as a key ingredient in many of the miscarriages of justice in England and Wales. See Belloni and Hodgson (2000).

the *procureur* herself might unwittingly contribute to this. In this particular case, a number of rapes had been committed in the same area and it became apparent that they had more than likely been carried out by the same person. Therefore the *procureur* asked the *gendarmes* to put a team together to try to find the rapist. They were unsuccessful:

> So, they said to themselves, 'We will make the *procureur* happy, we will find him, we will bring him the culprit.' They searched the records of sex offenders, they found me a guy who lived not far from the place where the victims had been raped . . . they showed the photo of the person they thought was the rapist to one or two of the victims . . . and afterwards they put together a photofit. They reversed the facts . . . So, obviously, the photofit was a perfect match with the photo and they arrived in my office with a dossier, saying, 'We have found your rapist.' Luckily, I looked very carefully at the evidence, as I always do, to make sure that there are no errors . . . The date on which they had pulled out the photo records was before that of the photofit. I asked them why and they were put out. To them, they had uncovered the truth for me . . . It was a manipulation. That happens very, very often, if I put pressure on the police or the *gendarmes*. When there are major miscarriages of justice, is it the *gendarmes* . . . they are not trained specifically for criminal investigations. They are the military.[55] [E7]

This case demonstrates the potential value of the *procureur* as a safeguard, but also the critical importance of the accuracy of the written record. The *procureur* is dependent on the case file in order to judge the strength and credibility of the evidence. If the *gendarmes* had not recorded the dates of their work so meticulously, this error might not have come to light.

In the more hurried context of the GAV, this focus upon the outcome and the legally documented form of the investigation, rather than the process and the method by which it is conducted, cannot of itself provide a sufficient guarantee as to either the treatment of the suspect or the credibility of confession and other evidence. Supervision is reduced to an essentially bureaucratic (and largely retrospective) process of review.[56] During the GAV, the initial telephone conversations between the police and the *procureur* are important in shaping the case and its subsequent treatment, but great reliance is placed upon written evidence and authenticity of form is equated with a wider guarantee of legitimacy in relation to how the evidence was obtained. As one *procureur* we observed warned an accused who wished to correct something in his statement taken by the police: 'I am paid to read the dossier of evidence. I believe what I read . . . This is written and signed.'[56] Increasingly, the efficacy of even this level of bureaucratic review may be

---

[55] See further this interviewee's comments on the working methods of *gendarmes* in Ch 3.

[56] See Lévy (1987) for a similar account of the *procureur*'s oversight of the GAV in Paris in the 1980s.

[57] The importance of the construction of the written record is discussed in Ch 6. Lévy (1987) describes the police as constructing written evidence in order to influence the decision of the *magistrat*, whereas Mouhanna (2001a:124–25) characterises the police and *magistrat* as complicit in producing a version of events that will avoid future complications.

reduced by the requirements to deal with cases more rapidly. Under the *traitement en temps réel* procedure, officers are required to report all cases to the *procureur* and a decision as to case disposition is taken immediately on the close of the investigation.[58] This has the advantage of rapidity, avoiding a build up of cases dealt with through the post,[59] but in an environment of already stretched resources,[60] it has increased the pressure upon the *procureur* to turn cases around as quickly as possible, without full consideration of the case dossier.[61]

This relative disengagement of the *procureur* from the case investigation may not accord with the expectations of commentators and would-be reformers from more adversarial traditions, but neither is it necessarily deviant behaviour. The way in which the *procureur* carries out her role needs to be understood within the legal cultural expectation of what constitutes supervision. The legal text is framed such that the *procureur* could undertake personally large parts of the investigation, but for a number of reasons, there is no expectation that this will take place. In many instances, there are simply insufficient resources for *procureurs* to engage in a more proactive way with the police investigation during the GAV. In my own study, most were responsible for the detention of suspects in GAV across a wide area[62] and had too many cases in progress at any one time to allow for anything more than minimal involvement via telephone or fax. In smaller locations (as described in the typologies below), *procureurs* had fewer GAV cases to supervise and enjoyed closer contact with police and *gendarmes*, although involvement in monitoring the detention of suspects remained distant. This disengagement is a result not only of meagre resources, but also of the paradoxical structural relationship between the *procureur* and the police, in which, as a *magistrat* the *procureur* is an authority over the police, yet at the same time she is wholly dependent upon officers in order to carry out her duty to investigate and prosecute crime. In our questionnaire survey, although most *procureurs* (85 per cent) said that they would never see the police, whatever their

---

[58] Under this procedure straightforward cases which are not serious enough to require the suspect to be brought before the court are now dealt with over the telephone, immediately at the close of the GAV. The *procureur* will indicate the charge to be brought and the court date, and the police will issue the official summons to appear.

[59] Dealing with cases in this way is time consuming (some *procureurs* spent one week in four dealing with their 'post' dossiers) and can result in long delays. In the dossiers we examined, the *procureur* would review the dossier and send the police instructions for further investigations (typically interviewing key witnesses). Officers, often many months later, would then transmit the result of their investigation. This may result in further requests and so on, until a decision to prosecute or discontinue the case was finally made. Since the notion of *traitement en temps réel* was first encouraged in a circular (2 October 1992) from the Ministry of Justice, the number of cases dealt with through rapid trial procedures has increased and the time taken to bring a case to trial has decreased.

[60] See generally Haenel and Arthuis (1991); Jolibois and Fauchon (1996–97); Mouhanna (2001a).

[61] It has also resulted in more paperwork for the police, discussed in the next chapter.

[62] In one urban centre, for example, this included 660 officers (OPJ) and over 2,000 APJ supervised for the most part by 3 *substituts*.

rank, as colleagues and 79 per cent described officers as subordinates, there is a recognition that co-operation and trust are more likely to foster a good working relationship than assertions of rank or authority.[63]

> I think that, really, I direct [the investigation], but equally, so do the police ... Fine, you can assert your authority, but that is not an effective way to get things done. [E2]

> I think you need to be aware that you cannot work without the police. Then, if you want to do a good job, there needs to be a relationship of trust and mutual respect. Legally, hierarchically, we give them orders, but anyone who thinks that it just needs to be written in the law to work like that is mistaken. [D1][64]

The nature of the authority which the *procureur* might exercise over investigating officers is further limited by the competing structures of authority in which both police and *gendarmes* operate.[65] Although under the Minister of Justice in the conduct of criminal investigations (with day-to-day answerability to *magistrats*), in all other matters—most notably the organisation and availability of personnel and resources—the police and *gendarmerie* are under their own administrative hierarchy.[66] Justice is the poor relation in this as the Ministries of the Interior and of Defence 'are very jealous of their authority and carry much more weight in the state than does the Ministry of Justice' (Lévy, 1993:179). This can be problematic at the local level also.

> The *procureur* can say, 'Stop everything now and go to [a town 50km away]' which could take a whole day. The *commissaire*, the head of section, can say, 'No, I cannot send three men to [a town 50km away] on an investigation.' That can be a problem. That can create tensions. [D3]

It can weaken considerably the control which the *procureur* is able to exercise over officers: 'In a difficult inquiry, a police officer is likely to follow the advice of his police boss, rather than that of the magistrates' (Guyomarch, 1991:321).[67] If her

---

[63] When we asked the police to describe the nature of their working relationship with the *parquet*, 83% of officers answered that they would never see the *procureur* as a colleague or a superior. Most saw her as an authority and sometimes a specialist and 83% considered her to be sometimes or often an ally. 50% said that she was rarely an adversary; 25% that she sometimes was. A good *magistrat* was someone with whom they had a relationship of trust and who was there to provide advice when needed. These findings accord also with those of Mouhanna (2001a).

[64] See also Mouhanna (2001a:96) who notes that when describing their relationship with the police, *magistrats* did not talk of ordering, but of convincing, advising, explaining, motivating and assisting.

[65] Discussed in more detail in Ch 3.

[66] The police are under the Minister of the Interior and the *gendarmerie* is a military force under the Minister of Defence, but is now under the operational authority of the Minister of Interior.

[67] Quoted in Horton (1995:36).

directions are ignored, she has few means of sanctioning the police. This was a source of frustration for some *magistrats*.[68]

> The problem is that they [the police] have their own hierarchy, which counts much more for them. 'The' reform, would be to place their hierarchy completely under judicial authority. If the police were wholly responsible to the Minister of Justice, then we would be able to master the situation completely. [A5]

> It is quite clear and every *magistrat* knows it, that in their [the police] organisation, in their ethos, in their culture, what counts for them—because it is their hierarchy, because it is their career, because it is the organisation of their daily work, what counts above all, is not the Minister of Justice, but the Minister of the Interior, that is plain. [A6]

> It is odd giving orders to the police when they are not really our subordinates. They are in their own hierarchy and are under the Minister of Defence or of the Interior. That is awkward and not always very comfortable. [*Procureur*, area D].

The Importance of Trust: The GAV as Police Business on Police Territory

In this relationship of mutual dependence and ambivalent authority, trust is central to success, and is described by Mouhanna (2001a:82) as a pragmatic response to the irreconcilable demands of justice. Lemaître (1994:81) also notes that in the absence of adequate resources, trust can come to take the place of real supervision and oversight. The centrality of trust was emphasised to us over and again by *procureurs*, police and *juges d'instruction*. A model of supervision based on challenging and verifying the investigative work of the police would create antagonism and undermine this trust. For most *procureurs*, their preferred approach to promoting good police practice is by strengthening the police–*procureur* relationship and improving the level and quality of contact between them. When asked about ways of controlling the GAV, one *procureur* told us:

> It would be better . . . to improve this collaboration [between police and *procureur*] in this climate of confidence, it is much more meaningful it seems to me . . . than to develop systems of control which . . . one way or another, can go wrong. [A6]

---

[68] See also the views of respondents A6 and A5 quoted above in Ch 3 'The double hierarchy: administrative and judicial policing'. The potential for conflict between these authorities is perhaps greatest in more politically sensitive cases, which will often involve the *juge d'instruction*, with the police acting on her direct orders under the *commission rogatoire*. This was seen quite clearly in an affair in Paris in 1996 when a number of officers, on the orders of the head of judicial police in Paris, refused to follow the orders of the *juge d'instruction* Eric Halphen, to search the home of Jean Tiberi, a politician and mayor of Paris. As a result, the head of the judicial police, Olivier Foll was stripped of his status as a judicial police officer for six months. See *Le Monde* 2 February 1997; Gaetner (2002); Halphen (2002); also Ch 3.

For those at more senior levels this contact is cultivated through meetings to discuss local policy initiatives and visiting the different police squads where possible, as one *procureur* explained:

> Going to see the *gendarmes* for the meeting with the head of the division each month, going every four months or so, just to spend an hour, letting them know in advance . . . that enables you to be in touch with the heads of each division . . . When an investigator comes by to deposit a dossier, that gives us the chance to chat a little . . . that is very useful. There are things like that which need to be done systematically, but they take time . . . but it is a necessary investment and it is also done as part of our role in supervising and monitoring the police. [E5]

In other instances, the *procureur* may be able to strengthen contact by visiting officers at the police station, where distance allows. This was the case in area A:

> There are all the judicial means of assuring the effective direction of the police, provided by the CPP. What is the most significant, at base, is the concrete relations we have with them . . . When I need to go and see . . . an investigator, an inspector . . . I open my door, I go down the stairs and I am two minutes from the office. That helps the nature of our contact enormously. [A6]

Officers confirmed the value of personal contact and regretted the fact that *procureurs* appeared to be almost entirely office bound. Increased contact was not perceived as increased surveillance, but as a means of improving knowledge and understanding of police work.[69]

The extent to which trust, rather than authority, is engrained within understandings of supervision is demonstrated in the approach of the *parquet* to police station visits during the detention of suspects. Although judicial supervision by the *procureur* represents the central safeguard ensuring the proper conduct of the GAV, there is no legal stipulation or minimum threshold requirement as to how this should be effected.[71] In supervising the detention of suspects in practice, there is neither a norm nor an expectation of personal attendance at the police station. Any visits which do take place are agreed in advance and are designed to improve police–*parquet* contact, representing an act of support rather than surveillance. Of our *parquet* questionnaire respondents, 87 per cent reported that they sometimes or rarely visited the police station; 69 per cent said that this was always or often announced in advance; and 25 per cent that this was sometimes the case. The principal reasons for attending were to strengthen relations with the police and to

---

[69] See also Mouhanna (2001a:79–80), whose police and *magistrat* respondents also shared this view of their relationship.

[70] Art 41 CPP requires the *procureur* to oversee the GAV and the accompanying circular (1 March 1993) anticipates that some visits will be made, allowing the *procureur* to ensure the proper conduct of the GAV and that formalities are observed (para 2).

deal with practicalities such as extending the GAV period. Fifty-six per cent said that such visits were rarely or never to assert their authority and only 31 per cent reported that they were often or always to effect some check. During our observations, only *procureurs* in area D expressed any interest in attending the police station in a supervisory role. Whilst this did not include sitting in on interrogations, they were aware of the need to see the suspect alone; to visit at night, as this was when injuries typically occurred; and to ensure that those dependent on drugs were not in a state of withdrawal by the end of GAV. Unfortunately, this remained an aspiration, as they considered that they had insufficient staff at that time to implement their plan.

All visits to the police station or *gendarmerie* which we observed were signalled to officers in advance and took place in an atmosphere of congeniality—designed to strengthen the nature of the contact between police and *parquet* rather than to exercise any control. *Procureurs* described the reasons for their visits:

> When I arrived here, I only had telephone contact [with the police], I did not know any-thing of the conditions in which they were working, which is a shame. Using the pre-text of a serious case I was dealing with, during a *garde à vue* of little importance, I went to see them at 7pm one evening. They were so pleased. That really helps in our relations with them. [A2]

> There is not any violence here. It's more to make contact . . . I try and visit them there as it can be easier than trying to find an escort and it allows me to see the police or the *gendarmes* in their own environment—on their own territory. [Area F].

To do otherwise is considered inappropriate. A visit designed to check on the GAV, for example, is less well received:

> I have some colleagues who went to visit the station in their area and it is an initiative which did not arouse enthusiasm from their hosts . . . they went to check on the *garde à vue*. [E3]

> There used to be a woman in the *permanence* who did go down to the police station and it caused a terrible rumpus. The police were furious that she just turned up. You have to be careful when you go down—so that the police don't think it's because you're suspi-cious of them. (*Procureur*, area D)

Despite the absence of defence lawyers or the tape recording of interrogations, there was no question of the *procureur* sitting in on the police questioning of a suspect or a witness.

> That would make me ill at ease. If I realise that there are questions that should have been asked, I ask the police to put them to the suspect, but I am not actually present. I can go to the scene and make sure all the evidence is seized after a search, yes. But I do not sit in on interviews. [A2]

The police station is the site of the GAV for which the *parquet* is legally responsible, yet it remains firmly police territory. Any attempt to challenge this is unlikely to be tolerated by the police. For example, we observed a *procureur* in area C when she visited the station in order to prolong the GAV of a young man and his girlfriend who were being held on suspicion of the burglary of a pharmacy.[71] The *procureur* went first to visit the man, a heroin addict. She commented on his slurred speech and was told that it was on account of his medication. He was thin, gaunt and constantly on the verge of falling asleep. It was clearly very hard for him to concentrate and he seemed barely aware of what was happening. Yet, the *procureur* made no note or comment on this, nor raised any question as to his fitness to be questioned or the reliability of his evidence.[72] She then went into the office of the investigating OPJ where the young female suspect had been questioned and was waiting. The girl's boyfriend appeared to be the principal offender, having admitted this and a number of other offences, and there was no obvious evidence against her.

> *Procureur*: You've seen the doctor?
> Suspect: Yes, but he didn't give me any medication.
> *Procureur*: You live with someone who keeps committing offences.
> Suspect: I know—do you mind me smoking?
> *Procureur*: No, not at all. Did you profit from these burglaries?
> Suspect: Yes and no.
> [The policeman comes in and tells her to put her cigarette out.]
> *Procureur*: Any remarks about the *garde à vue*?
> Suspect: I've seen the doctor, but he won't give me any epilepsy tablets and I'm cold [she is wearing shorts].
> *Procureur*: [To the officer] Can she have more blankets?
> Officer: No—no blankets for security.
> *Procureur*: Can you make the room warmer?
> Officer: Perhaps.

The *procureur* made little effort to ascertain what evidence there was against the girl and agreed to extend the GAV for convenience, in order that the detainee

---

[71] This was in the first stage of the 1993 reforms, when all suspects were required to be brought before the *procureur* before the GAV could be extended. In most instances, the police brought the suspect to the *procureur's* office, but in this instance, she went to the station on her way home from work. This short-lived requirement for presentations provided an insight into how *procureurs* behaved when they did have the opportunity to monitor more closely the GAV. In most instances, the presentation was perfunctory, with forms granting the GAV extension already filled out before the suspect's arrival.

[72] Perhaps predictably, the man was persuaded to confess to a string of other burglaries in exchange for the release of his girlfriend, against whom there was no evidence other than the fact of her living with him.

could be brought before court the following morning. Neither did she enquire further into the potentially dangerous refusal to allow the suspect her epilepsy medication. The whole tone of the encounter and the body language of the officer (who sat up on the desk alongside the suspect's chair, one foot on the desk, facing the *procureur*) made it quite clear who was in charge.

The wide discretion afforded officers in the conduct of their investigation as a result of this relationship of trust and confidence, can also be seen as part of the ideology of the *juge* in which the functions of *magistrat* and of police should be kept separate. There is a distance between the two which cannot be bridged.[73] This is recognised by both the *procureur* and police.

> There is a part of [the police's] work that I cannot evaluate. I can only talk of their role in the legal procedure, how they report on the telephone. We inhabit different worlds. They do not know the world of judges and I do not know the world of nightclubs. [*Procureur*, D2]

> It is impossible for *magistrats* to understand or appreciate the realities and the constraints of police work . . . [because] they have a different culture and a restricted vision of the law. [Police questionnaire respondent 63]

> [The *parquet*] has a lack of realism and knowledge of the kind of environment in which we live. [Police questionnaire respondent 76]

> Our work is different. They are in their offices and we are outside on the ground. [Senior police officer, D5]

The police and *magistrat* respondents in Mouhanna's (2001a) study expressed themselves in almost identical terms to those we observed and interviewed. One senior police officer explained:

> I think that there are two separate worlds—that of the police officer and that of the *magistrat*. Trust is at the point of contact of these two worlds. In his work, the *magistrat* can take refuge behind his *code*, behind the law . . . and they [*magistrats*] must not dirty their hands or they will lose their credibility . . . They must be respected, but they must also understand that a police officer is not a *magistrat*, that we are confronted with social situations for which there is little or no legal provision. The reality that they see is a pre-digested legal reality. (Mouhanna, 2001a:125–26).

---

[73] The different views of what represented a good commanding officer also illustrated to some extent the different professional worlds which each occupies. The police *commissaire*, who was tall and stocky, wore jeans and visibly carried his gun, was liked by the police. The younger *commissiare*, who wore a suit and whose strengths were intellectual rather than physical, was disliked by officers, but favoured by the *parquet*.

Lévy (1993:181) explains:

> [T]here is a professional ideology which opposes the magistrate, incarnation of the law whose hands must remain clean, to the policeman, who inevitably soils himself by contact with the underworld and who must as a result be kept at a distance.

This professional distance between *magistrat* and police has clear functional benefits to the *magistrature*. Based in her office and insulated from the realities of investigation and interrogation (described further in the next chapter), the *procureur* deals with the relative 'moral certainties' of legal procedure. Provided her dossier is in order at the end of the day, she is largely unconcerned with the investigative methods employed by the police, leaving officers to do what is necessary in order to obtain the evidence which the *magistrat* requires to do her job.[74] In the event of a major police transgression, however, she remains free to condemn the offending officers and sufficiently distanced from events to emerge unscathed.

Two contrasting examples illustrate this point. In the first case (also discussed in Chapter 7), the accused appeared before the *procureur* at the end of his GAV, before being sent to trial that afternoon. He did not contest any of the charges made against him, but protested at the rough treatment he had suffered on arrest (he had cuts to his face and nose) and claimed that the police had stolen some of his personal property. The *procureur* ignored these complaints without further enquiry and simply told the suspect to 'Stop talking rubbish' and to 'Tell it to the court'. It was left to the defence lawyer to raise an official complaint before the court that day. When asked about his approach to the suspect, the *procureur*'s lack of commitment to due process rights was clear: 'You have to bear in mind that he has several convictions and does not respect the law, so his word counts for less than that of the police.' In the second case, a juvenile suspect had been held on suspicion of assaulting a police officer. In the dossier, there was a medical certificate relating to the injuries of the suspect, but not the police. In contrast to the first example above, this clear documentary evidence prompted an immediate response from the *procureur* who instructed the police to ask the suspect's father if he wished to lodge a formal complaint, before then instigating an official enquiry into the affair. Although responsible for supervising the police investigation in both of these examples, there is a sense in which the *magistrat* does not want to delve too deeply into 'police work' unless compelled to do so.

Typological Models of Supervision

In addition to the legal framework set out in the CPP, the work of the *procureur* is also shaped by her position within the *parquet*, with hierarchical accountability to

---

[74] Mouhanna (2001a:124–25) goes further and describes the *magistrat* as complicit in creating a record of events that simplifies reality, eliminates doubt and so avoids future complications.

the Minister of Justice (Hodgson, 2002a). In theory, government policy is disseminated through Ministry of Justice circulars and implemented locally under the
supervision of the *procureur général*[75] and the *procureur de la République*.[76] However,
the effect of this highly centralised hierarchy, as described above in Chapter 3, whilst
designed to ensure coherence and democratic accountability, has at times operated
to achieve quite the reverse. At the local level too, hierarchical control is unable to
ensure the degree of coherence across areas which many would argue is a necessary
part of guaranteeing equality before the law.[77] In some instances, this is a result of
unwillingness on the part of the *procureur de la République* to implement national
policy, in others, it is a function of insufficient resources to meet the demands of
high levels of criminality or wide areas of geographical competence. The disparities
in practice which may co-exist and the varieties of interpretation which the law may
allow, despite this hierarchical arrangement,[78] are illustrated by the different ways in
which *procureurs* across the country undertook their legal duty to supervise the
GAV period. As described above, supervision of the majority of investigations across
most areas we observed was conducted with little direct intervention, but there were
also some variations in practice in terms of the level of contact between the *procureur* and police. In general, this depended upon the gravity of the offence and the
caseload of the *procureur*. We observed what might loosely be termed three typolog-
ical models of supervision.[79] At one end was the 'hands on' model where *procureurs*
were relatively closely involved in investigations. At the other, the 'fax' model, where
officers had no contact with the *parquet* until the close of the GAV. In between, the
'throughput' model (representing the majority), where only the most serious cases
receive close attention, while the majority are handled quickly, entailing little
involvement beyond the receipt of information.

The Hands-on Model

In some instances, there is close contact between officers and the *procureur* during the supervision of the police investigation and GAV. This is both area and case

---

[75] Operating at the level of the *cour d'appel*.

[76] Operating at the level of the *Tribunal de Grande Instance* (TGI).

[77] This was noted by the Truche Commission (1997:24). Ministry of Justice figures show a wide
regional variation in cases where some form of action (prosecution, mediation etc) was taken: from
93.4% of cases in Guéret to 42.9% in Thonon-les-Bains. For additional figures see special edition of
L'Express 29 November 2001.

[78] See also Mouhanna (2001a:112–20).

[79] Based on his interviews with police officers, Lemaître (1994:76–77) suggests four typologies of
procureurs supervising GAV: the passive type, who listens carefully, does not know the file and asks the
police what to do, leaving them feeling insufficiently protected; the aggressive type, often young, who
wishes to direct the whole investigation, does not listen to officers and seeks to reinforce her status by
placing a distance between herself and the police; the police type, who conducts her own investigations, wants to run the enquiry and does not know what role the police should play; and the good
procureur who is well informed, asks the right questions, provides direction, but leaves a degree of
autonomy to officers and with whom there is a genuine exchange or dialogue.

dependent. In contrast to most cities and large urban areas, *procureurs* in smaller sites, such as areas A and F, had a smaller caseload and tended to know personally most of the officers in their jurisdiction. It was not uncommon for police and *gendarmes* to visit the *procureur* to seek advice and to discuss more generally cases on which they were working. In contrast to busier locations with higher levels of crime, officers frequently telephoned to inform the *procureur* of even the most minor offences. As the *procureur* in area F (by far the smallest of our research sites) explained to us, 'Some squads do not have a lot to do. It keeps them busy, it reassures them.'

Supervision of the GAV in these areas was conducted over the telephone, but the *procureur* was also able to visit the police station in person on occasions, to extend the detention period. This was possible in area F because it was a small jurisdiction served by few police stations and *gendarmeries*, all of which were within easy reach. Area A was larger, but contact was greatly facilitated by the fact that the main police station adjoined the court building, the *Palais de Justice*. Visits were always agreed in advance and this personal contact was appreciated by officers, conducted as they were in the spirit of support rather than scrutiny. The relaxed nature of the visit was apparent in a case we observed in area F, where the *procureur* arranged to visit the GAV to extend the detention of the suspect and joked with the police:

> We will come and do it now, we'll come to you—then we can check you out at the same time!

The higher the local level of criminality, the busier the office tended to be and so the greater the degree of case seriousness required before the *procureur* would become more closely involved in directing the investigation. Thus, in area F, a quiet rural location, the *procureur* would discuss most GAV instances with officers. In area A, a medium-sized location, major intervention was restricted to the more serious or complex cases, particularly those which might be investigated under the *instruction* procedure. In these instances, the *procureur* would have extensive discussions with the interviewing officers during the GAV period, directing that specific questions be put to the suspect to ensure that evidence was gathered to demonstrate all the legal elements of the offence. For example, the police in area A were holding a suspect in GAV on a simple theft charge, but the *procureur* wanted to characterise the case as one of fraud and instructed the police to ask quite precise questions in order that the more serious charge might be made out and the opening of an *information* justified.[80] In the larger, busier locations such as areas C and D, it is only in the most serious and complex cases, or those

---

[80] In this case, the *procureur* followed this up by speaking with the *juge d'instruction* and emphasising the gravity of the case.

which will attract media attention, that the *procureur* has the capacity to become more closely involved in the case.

> You try to orient the investigation, to shape it in the way that you would like it to be carried out. This is not an objective that is always easy to achieve. It is true that it is somewhat theoretical, because you cannot be involved in all cases. You cannot follow all cases. But, we follow the most serious cases. [D3]

In these instances, the officer may not be known to the *procureur*, but they will be in relatively close contact during the GAV. For example, in area D, a doctor was held on suspicion of indecently assaulting a number of his female patients. Wishing to open an *information*, the *procureur* was anxious to ensure that sufficient evidence was gathered to justify the more serious charge of rape.[81] She instructed the police to ask specific questions about the ways in which the doctor had examined his patients and then later discussed his response to them, his reaction to the accusation and his general demeanour. She also asked for statements to be faxed through to her so that she could review the evidence and direct the police more precisely.

In these instances, supervision conformed more closely to a model of 'directing' the police enquiry, in contrast to the majority of instances where the *procureur* acted as the passive recipient of information. Yet, even where contact was frequent or exchanges detailed, the concern of the *magistrat* was with shaping the nature of the evidence produced and getting the most out of the suspect, rather than scrutinising the methods by which it was obtained.

The Throughput Model

In most areas and for the majority of cases, the *procureur* knows few of the officers with whom she has contact,[82] rarely or never visits the police station or *gendarmerie* and her involvement is limited to basic evidential and procedural prompts. Typically, there will be three or four *procureurs* in the *permanence*,[83] one of whom will spend most of the day on the telephone, receiving calls from officers reporting the placement of suspects in GAV. As such offices cover tens of stations and hundreds of officers, personal attendance at the police station or *gendarmerie* is simply not feasible and there is often insufficient time to do anything more

---

[81] The *procureur* has a discretion in how she characterises the offence. In this instance, digital penetration might result in a charge of either indecent assault or of rape.
[82] The exception is in specialist squads such as vice, drugs or those dealing with juveniles, when there is a much smaller corps of officers and relationships may develop.
[83] The main duty section of the *parquet* is usually referred to as the *permanence* or STIP (*section de traitement immédiat des procédures*). Larger sites also had specialist sections such as juvenile (interestingly, this may include victims as well as offenders), drugs, fraud or vice.

than gather basic information. For the police, it can be frustrating waiting to get through to a single line and the requirement to inform the *procureur* is increasingly being effected by the transmission of a fax, in order to avoid excessive delay and a potential breach of article 63 CPP.[84] For the *parquet* the constant turnover of cases is hectic and stressful. As one *procureur* put it: '[A]t times it feels as though you are working on a production line.' [D2]. Another complained,

> It is about figures, about making large numbers of decisions and making them quickly. And in the future, nobody will ask you about the basis of what you do, but only the quantity . . . When you have learned to work like that you won't be satisfied with what you have done, but in the end you will be considered to be good at managing your office. [E3]

This impacted on a variety of the *procureur*'s functions and obligations:

> We should go and visit the *garde à vue* and check the register. We should go to the scene of a murder. Or when there is a suicide or a riot in prison. But we don't leave the office because of the workload here. [*Procureur*, area D]

The police were aware of the burden of work on some *magistrats*:

> The problem is the number of staff. If you calculate the ratio of the population to the number of police, [area D] is not as well served as [other nearby towns and cities]. The *magistrat*'s job is not as easy. You are waiting on the telephone, it rings incessantly in his office, you have to put yourself in his place. Going from one case to another is not easy. [D5]

In most instances, the *procureur* will note the basic facts and then ask the police to telephone back towards the end of the 24 hour GAV period in order that a decision can be made on how to proceed. The legal basis of the GAV can be verified and some lines of enquiry suggested, but little direction is provided. Although most *procureurs* did not consider the level of their (non) intervention to be problematic, some (notably those in the first few years of their post as *magistrat*) recognised the limitations of their total dependence upon the police for information, a dependence likely to be increased by the *temps réel* procedure described above, where decisions are made without first seeing the dossier of evidence. As Lemaître (1994:76) notes, the *procureur* can only oversee that which she is informed of by the police. One such *procureur* explained the dangers:

---

[84] *Procureurs* in small and less busy locations could be contacted with relative ease. In larger cities, such as areas D and C, officers had to wait up to 30 minutes before finally getting through to the *procureur* on the telephone. Of our questionnaire respondents, one-third said that there were always or often difficulties in reaching the *procureur*, 58% that this was sometimes the case . There was sometimes a queue of officers at the same station waiting to speak to the *procureur*, in order to try and avoid the obligatory waiting time 'on hold'.

On the telephone, you can be completely manipulated. You decide to bring the case immediately before the court and then when you see the evidence, it is totally crap. There are omissions . . . The police officer says that X has admitted everything, there are no more problems . . . and then the file arrives with crucial mistakes and omissions. That can be deceptive. In terms of the gravity of the offence, you can be manipulated quite easily. [D1]

His colleague also told us,

That is the difficulty in the way in which they [the police] relate to us. They can manipulate us. We only know what they want to tell us. [D2]

A more experienced *procureur* cautioned:

We must not delude ourselves, we can be manipulated. So, it is for us to ask the questions, to obtain the information, to take the decisions. [C1]

Although this was not fully recognised by the *magistrats* interviewed in Lemaître's study (1994:75), the police explained that they were able to exaggerate or diminish the gravity of a case when presenting it to the *procureur*. In my own study, the police expressed similar sentiments[85]:

Researcher: I think you may have the same problem here as in England—it is you who gives the information to the *parquet* and so you can influence their decision.
Officer [smiling]: Yes, it can depend on how you present it. But don't forget that we see them and speak to them after that and they see the suspect and the written procedure the next day. [Area C]

[The *parquet* is] an authority which must be respected and which has the last word, but we have a great deal of influence. The *magistrat* bases her decision on our account, so we can influence her on the objective facts, but also on subjective things. [Area D]

Inexperienced *procureurs* may be more vulnerable to police influence and we observed officers exploiting this.[86] For example, in area C, when a *procureur* from the financial division acted as duty *procureur* during the holiday period, she was unfamiliar with the procedures for regular cases. Aware of her lack of confidence, the police persuaded her to deal with several offences as *en flagrance* (thus widening their investigative powers) when this should not have been the case. In area A,

---

[85] Mouhanna (2001a) also notes the filtering role of the police, encouraged by the local policies of taking no further action.

[86] Ironically, their inexperience may also result in closer supervision of the police: 'Ah, the new ones, the young ones, when they arrive it is difficult. Sometimes there are no problems, but that is rare . . . they do not know enough, they make you check everything and they have no trust in you.' [OPJ, Area D].

it was again an inexperienced duty *procureur* who allowed the *gendarmes* to retain a case which they knew was under investigation by the police, resulting in a string of errors and the mistaken release of a suspected rapist. In serious investigations, officers ensured that newcomers were under no illusions as to the value of experience. As the police told one young *procureur* in area D:

> Ah, you're new? Welcome. Don't you worry. I've been in the job for 30 years. I know what I am doing. [OPJ, Area D]

He then proceeded to insist that authorisation be given for the arrest of a suspect's father, in order to put more pressure on him. The *procureur's* reservations as to the absence of any evidence against the father were brushed aside and, as a relative novice, he felt unable to challenge the police view.

In area F, in cases investigated as an *enquête préliminaire*, suspects were always brought before the *procureur* in order that the GAV could be extended, as required by the law (art 77 CPP). Only in exceptional circumstances does this procedure not apply. In larger areas however, such as sites C and D, the practice was quite different. Detention was always prolonged over the telephone, with written authorisation being faxed through and the original appended to the dossier at the close of the GAV. The lack of resources available to both *procureurs* and police meant that it was never anticipated that suspects would be seen beforehand and 'exceptional circumstances' in fact represented institutionalised practice.

The Fax Model

In most areas, the *procureur* is informed of a person's placement in GAV during the night by fax, unless it requires urgent attention. In the general section[87] of one observation site, area E, however, information of those held in GAV was also transmitted by fax during the day. The practice was for the police to then telephone some 12 hours into the detention period in order to receive instructions on how to proceed. In this way, the *procureur* systematically disabled herself from any degree of contemporaneous supervision. The faxes appeared to serve only the purpose of ensuring formal compliance with the law, as they generally lay in a pile, unread. There was very poor contact between *parquet* and police, resulting in little mutual understanding or communication of policy and good practice. *Procureurs* in other areas spoke of the importance of their pedagogical role vis-à-vis the police and of grooming officers in the correct procedures and the implementation of national and local penal policy. For most, this was a central part of their day-to-day supervisory role. One *procureur* explained:

---

[87] Area E was a large office with a number of specialist sections who enjoyed closer working relationships with the police.

I consider that there is a pedagogical role to play vis-à-vis the police . . . I call the investigator who has conducted the investigation and I tell him, 'There is a slight difficulty here and this is how I see the problem for the future, so try to avoid it and let your colleagues in the division know'. [A6]

Such contact was largely absent in area E and the communication of information was left to the initiative of the police, without even the usual prompting from the *procureur*. The result was a string of procedural errors, for which the police were continually reprimanded. Minor offences were prioritised over more serious ones; sometimes the *procureur* was not contacted to extend the GAV until after 24 hours, making the final hours of detention unlawful; crucial documentary evidence affecting the level of charge to be prosecuted, such as medical certificates and records of previous convictions, were missing from the dossier. The *procureurs* never tired of criticising the police for this, yet, it was a predictable result of their own failure to liaise more closely with officers. One *procureur* complained:

I tell them, it is not what you think, but what the law allows. *Garde à vue* is a deprivation of liberty. They [the police] don't always understand that. It's a problem of training. You always have to remind them. We are the guarantors of human rights. They do not understand that, although we tell them. We bawl them out when we have to, we note it on their record, we kick them out if necessary, we ask their superiors to do something. Twice a year something really serious happens. [Area E].

In an amazing twist of irony, the next telephone call concerned a GAV where the 24 hour limit had passed by nearly an hour. The officer did not seem unduly perplexed.

OPJ: What time shall I put for the *garde à vue*? We can sort that out?
Procureur: Absolutely not! You put the correct time and take your responsibilities.
[To the researcher] He is not doing his job. And what is more, he wants me to take part in his bloody stupidity. And an OPJ, a *commandant*. [Area E].[88]

Interestingly, the head of this section began by presenting an idealised account of its functioning when interviewed:

It is the *procureur* who directs the *police judiciaire*. In practice, it is probably in [this] section that relations are the most permanent, most constant, most consistent and I would say, on the whole, of good quality. There is a real mutual trust and confidence. I am not exaggerating. I think you have been able to witness this. They [the police] call

---

[88] It is, of course, interesting that the officer assumed that the time could simply be altered. The effect of the observer's presence may well have influenced the *procureur's* response, as well as his earlier outpouring on the deficiencies of the police.

us not simply to tell us, 'We have *Monsieur Dupont* in *garde à vue* for a theft on the train', but often to tell us, 'We have to ask your advice, we are not sure how to proceed, we wonder how to frame the offence'. That means that there is real confidence and a real dialogue, a real exchange. [E6]

When pressed more specifically, he then described some of the problems which needed addressing:

I constantly have to remind certain officers . . . there is sometimes a lack of understanding of the texts, especially concerning identity checks. You have to constantly re-remind them of the legal requirements . . . they do not even know that [the ECHR] applies . . . there is some real work to be done in that respect . . . we spend a fair amount of time telling them, 'Be careful, you should have notified the [suspect of her] rights earlier. The *Cour de cassation* requires this to be done immediately, the CPP says this. You should have checked that you were actually investigating *en flagrance* . . . you should have checked your territorial competence.' These problems, these technical errors could sometimes mar the whole case. And then errors of availability, when they stop somebody at night . . . I think the [GAV] investigation, where at all possible, should begin immediately. [E6]

The high turnover of officers, which was a feature of area E, might have made more difficult the dissemination of good practice, but the failure to engage with cases early on at even the most basic level, ensured that this did not happen, regardless of personnel arrangements.

The Ideology of Supervision

In England and Wales, the independence of the CPS from the police is hamstrung by their total reliance upon the police file and their inability to influence its construction.[89] In France, investigations are conducted or supervised by a judicial officer, whose role and position is quite separate from the police and who is charged with acting in the wider public interest. Unlike the CPS, those supervising the police have the authority to direct the investigation and the powers of the *magistrat* are the same or greater than those of the officers they oversee. However, the structural context in which the police-*procureur* relationship operates, as we have seen above, makes control and direction both complex and problematic. In particular, the *procureur*'s functional dependence upon officers to conduct the investigation for which she is responsible makes almost impossible a model of supervision in practice, which challenges or goes beyond the case paramenters set

---

[89] See Ch 3.

by the police. Furthermore, the nature of their working relationship means that the interests of the *procureur* become almost inevitably intertwined with those of the police, undercutting the ideology of the impartial *magistrat* in a way which sees the public interest being defined in largely crime control terms. A former *juge d'instruction* entering the *parquet* in area C reflected on the parallel nature of police and *procureur* interests:

> The philosophy of each person in the system is very important . . . The police are there to catch people and they look to charge them. The *procureur* will supervise, but thinks in the same way really. He is there to represent and to protect the public interest and looks, really, to charge.

Another *procureur* contrasted his former position as *juge d'instruction* with his current role in the *parquet*:

> One has to realise that you are no longer in the same position and a *procureur* who does not ask for a remand in custody when for many people, custody would appear to be jus- tified, will be criticised. He is there to protect society, of course, but you could consider [not requesting a remand in custody to be] a professional fault. . . . The *procureur* will be excused for being too harsh, but he will be excused much less for an error, a lack of severity.[90] [E1]

In theory, the *procureur*'s responsibility in representing the public interest encom- passes ensuring both the effective conduct of the investigation and the proper respect of the rights of the defence. This is core to the notion of judicial supervi- sion and its opposition to adversarial procedures which operate a clearer separa- tion between pre-trial investigative and defence roles. This neutral posture which requires the *procureur* to both direct and judge the investigation, to be both involved and detached from it, is almost impossible to maintain.

> What is the role of the *parquet*? Is it to immerse yourself completely in the direction of the investigation, or is it to maintain a quasi-Olympian detachment, waiting for it to happen, for it to deliver the results ready-made . . . ? Of course, I think, it is something between the two. [A6]

In practice, this is easier to operate within the framework of the *instruction*, where the *juge d'instruction* is able to maintain a greater distance from, and degree of objectivity towards, the investigation. Although most *juges d'instruction* have case- loads of one hundred or more dossiers, investigations last months and sometimes

---

[90] A distinction should be drawn between (i) the *procureur*'s role in determining herself what is in the public interest when overseeing police detention, or deciding whether to prosecute and (ii) her role in putting a case before another *magistrat* who will make the final decision (such as at trial and in bail hearings), after also hearing representations from the defence.

years, providing ample time for reflection and analysis. The defence lawyer also has access to the dossier and may request that investigations be carried out and evidence gathered, as well as scrutinising the evidence as it appears in the dossier. All of this has the potential to act as a counter-reflex to the *juge d'instruction* being caught up in a single (police constructed) thesis. The *procureur*, on the other hand, must act quickly and once the GAV has commenced, she has (in most cases) a maximum of 48 hours within which to assess the case. The defence plays no role in this, all communication being exclusively between police and *procureur*. As a result, there is little time for reflection and no input other than that from the police. It is perhaps unsurprising, therefore, that the *procureur's* outlook tends to reflect that of the police.

This has important consequences for the nature of judicial supervision of the GAV and the kind of guarantees which it is able to provide in practice. The instigation of a broader set of enquiries is neither possible in the time available, nor desired by the *procureur*, who, in most instances, quickly adopts the case theory of the police. Thus, for most *procureurs*, as for the police, the principal function of the GAV is to obtain a confession.[91]

> The *garde à vue* is a constraint which can last 48 hours, or four days for drugs cases. It is to put pressure on . . . With people who resist, it breaks them down. [A2]

And despite 40 per cent of our *procureur* questionnaire respondents reporting that they suspected that violence or excessive pressure was sometimes used during the GAV,[92] the *procureur* is generally tolerant of the kinds of pressures which the police may need to exert in order to make the suspect tell 'the truth', that is, to confess. Even questioning which might be classed as overbearing or oppressive by a British court is considered acceptable, and at times necessary, to get at 'the truth'. One *procureur* told us that when he spent some time at the police station as part of his training, he saw a suspect slapped across the face:

> It's not shocking, it was just to move things on. It was a drugs case and the officer wanted to know the truth . . . I wouldn't call that 'violence'. [D1]

Other *procureurs* explained the pressure that might be necessary in order to obtain a confession:

> In principle, there should never be forced confessions, with psychological pressure . . .
> In theory that is all very well, that is great, but in practice you realise that many cases

---

[91] One *procureur* described the central place which the confession occupies in French criminal procedure: 'For us, the confession, in countries with a Latin tradition, has always had an extremely important place, whereas the Anglo-Saxons have always tried to restrict it. The origins are historical and are, I would say, almost ideological and religious.' [A6]

[92] See also the account in *Le Monde* 19 July 2001. The number of complaints of police violence during criminal investigations to be upheld has been relatively stable since 1999. See *Le Monde* 2 February 2005.

require explanations which only the accused can provide . . . Pressure to confess, yes, that exists, of course, because it is linked to the very nature of the interrogation, such pressure exists, and . . . this pressure to confess . . . also allows the investigation to progress. [A6]

It's true that the *garde à vue* exerts a certain psychological pressure and for some people that pressure may lead to slightly ill-considered admissions . . . But that is not the point of view of a *procureur*—there are no innocents in *garde à vue*. [D3]

Although the psychology of false confessions does not feature in discussions around the detention and interrogation of suspects in France, for those who choose to look, it is clear that problems exist. The dangers of psychological pressure in producing unreliable confession evidence were demonstrated in recent miscarriages of justice such as those concerning Pierrot and Dils (both discussed in Chapter 6). The violent treatment of suspects detained in police custody in France has also been the subject of public and international attention. In the case of *Selmouni*,[93] the ECtHR found France to have breached Article 3 ECHR, not only on the grounds of inhuman and degrading treatment, but also of torture. Selmouni, a 49-year-old man who had never been arrested or questioned before, was brutalised and degraded during his 72 hour detention in order to obtain a confession. A search of his person and his room had revealed nothing; the only evidence against him was the accusation of another man questioned in the course of an *instruction* investigating drugs trafficking.[94] Like the previous two before it, the recent report of the European Committee for the Prevention of Torture (2001) was also highly critical of the conditions of police detention in France. As well as insanitary conditions and prisoners being provided with little or no food, they also found evidence of kicking and punching, overly tight handcuffs, people violently thrown to the floor and in particular, the maltreatment of foreigners. All of this is said to take place during interrogation and affected some five per cent of those seen by police doctors. The anti-terrorist division came in for especial criticism. Two people detained in the prison hospital in Paris recounted their maltreatment. One had been allowed only six hours rest out of 60 hours of interrogations—allegations supported by the detention records. The other had been the subject of written instructions not to allow him any bed covers and to keep the light on in his cell.

The *procureur's* supervision of the detention and interrogation of suspects does not act as a constraint upon the conduct of the GAV, but is frequently directed at facilitating or encouraging officers in obtaining admissions from the suspect. This

---

[93] ECHR 28 July 1999.

[94] Four police officers were convicted of assaulting Selmouni. Three (Gautier, Staebler and Hurault) were initially sentenced to three years imprisonment, reduced to suspended sentences on appeal. The fourth man (Hervé) was the divisional inspector and was sentenced to 4 years imprisonment, reduced on appeal to 18 months, of which 15 were suspended.

is done in two ways—either by shaping the interrogation strategy, or more commonly, adopting a strategy of perseverance. Sometimes officers are directed to pursue a particular line of interrogation (as demonstrated in the 'hands on' model described above) or to use a different approach to try to win over the suspect with threats or promises. For example, the police in area A had arrested the suspect for possession of an offensive weapon (a knife) and together with others, for assault. The suspect had made no admissions and the police had no evidence that it was he who had inflicted the knife wound. The *procureur* advised the police on the approach they might take to move things on:

> The victim cannot say anything, saw nothing? So what are we going to do, we have nothing, we can do nothing . . . There is a risk that the *juge d'instruction* will not remand him in custody. He has no previous convictions in any event. This is a delicate case. We have to find something. You have no evidence which would enable you to say who struck out? This is about the psychology of your job. Perhaps you need to play the incident down a little to get the evidence. You need to explain that clemency does exist, and that the attitude of a person will be taken into consideration. You get the idea of how I see this going?

In most cases, the favoured strategy of the *procureur* was one of simple perseverance: to extend the GAV period to allow another 24 hours of detention and interrogation.[95] Not only was it extremely rare for the *procureur* to refuse such an extension, but in the majority of instances, the idea came from her rather than the police.[96] These were typical of the telephone conversations which the *parquet* had with investigating officers.

> He's not going to spit it out in two hours. I will extend the *garde à vue* then you can question him again and try and get a confession. Then we'll see . . . [Area A]

> Let the *garde à vue* do its job. We can always prolong it. Keep interviewing him from time to time to refresh his memory. [Area D]

> Keep him in for the moment and try and get him to confess. Interview him again this afternoon. [Area D]

---

[95] In some instances, the GAV was extended simply for convenience—when there was not a court sitting until the following day, there was no transport available to bring the suspect to the court building or the *juge d'instruction* was not yet ready to see the suspect. This was especially problematic in small areas, such as site F, where *magistrats* had to play a form of musical chairs between functions. In busy jurisdictions, there was often a delay of several hours between the end of the GAV and the presentation of the suspect before the *magistrat*. Although this 'limbo' was neither GAV nor a remand in custody, the courts have refused to condemn such delays as unlawful detention. For a discussion of recent case law condoning considerable delays between the end of the GAV and presentation before the *juge d'instruction* (delays which effectively amounted to a further GAV—of 20 hours and 33 minutes; 19 hours and 44 minutes; and 18 hours and 32 minutes, *Cour de cassation* 25 November 2003) see Maron (2004); and for delays of nearly 20 hours between the end of the GAV and presentation before the *procureur* (*Cour de cassation* 21 January 2003), see Rebut (2003).

[96] A *procureur* in site D told us that in another *parquet* where she had worked, her colleagues had asked for a rubber stamp for authorising GAV extensions—as a custody officer was reported to have done in the UK, authorising the detention of suspects.

> He denies it, so there's no rush. We can extend the *garde à vue*. This is a bit serious and I think I will send it straight to court, but we'll prolong it to be more thorough. [Area D]

For juveniles detained in GAV, detention can only be extended by bringing the suspect before the *procureur* or *juge des enfants*. As with adult suspects, prolonging the GAV was used frequently when suspects refused to make an admission (or, as in this case, a sufficient number of admissions) and contact with the suspect was often used as a further opportunity for the *procureur* to make clear the need for a confession. The following example concerned a case in which complaints had been received that two North African youths had demanded money from boys on the bus, pushing one and punching the other before taking pens and other items from their bags. There were no medical certificates and no witnesses. The two suspects were arrested, some of the stolen items found at their home and then they were placed in GAV. The *procureur* framed the holding charge as one of gang robbery in order to justify extending detention, even though she had no intention of prosecuting them with such a serious offence. The following is the conversation with the first boy; the second was dealt with in just the same way.

> *Procureur*: You are before the *substitut du Procureur de la République*. You could have seven years in prison for what you have done—committing robbery with others.
> Suspect: But. . .
> *Procureur*: Be quiet for now. You can speak later. Normally, the *garde à vue* is 24 hours, but I am authorised to extend this—the law allows this when the offence is particularly serious. You will be sent back for another 24 hours. It is in your interests to tell everything.
> Suspect: I have.
> *Procureur*: OK—we'll see. I am not convinced. You have only admitted two. The investigation is still continuing. I tell you, you must co-operate, it's in your interests because if you do not tell all, it will come out and then it will be worse. [She enquires about the conditions in the *garde à vue*].
> Suspect: I am cold. I want some blankets.
> *Procureur*: Well, if you had not done this in the first place, you wouldn't be cold. So, the *garde à vue* is fine?
> Suspect: No.
> *Procureur*: Why not? Did they hit you?
> Suspect: No, I don't like it.
> *Procureur*: This is not the Club Med. You're not meant to like it. If you told us what happened, I would not need to prolong your detention. But I have. There is no point in telling stories.

In the files we examined and the cases we observed, this strategy of perseverance did indeed appear to be successful in obtaining admissions. For example, file notes on a case in area C show that the suspect was interviewed four times, twice very late at night, in a case of burglary. He was arrested at 2.15pm, but not interviewed until 11.45pm that night, when he denied the offence. The GAV was extended at 11.30am the following day. He was interviewed a second time at 4.30pm and again denied involvement. During the third interview at 8pm, he admitted stealing, but not breaking the window to enter the house. Finally, when interviewed at 12.30am, he admitted breaking the window and being with another man (whom he named) who broke the door locks to get in. He also admitted having committed burglaries before with the same man. Interestingly, some files also showed evidence of the kinds of tactics which we observed the police using and which are described in more detail in Chapter 6. For example, in this case of burglary, tactics included the police establishing the criminal lifestyle of the suspect (no drugs were found on the suspect, but he admitted to smoking 'shit' (cannabis) in the first interview) and threatening to implicate the girlfriend (in the third interview, he states that his girlfriend did not know or do anything).

The psychological pressure which prolonged detention exerted upon the suspect was understood perfectly well by *procureurs*, this being the precise reason for its use. One *procureur* explained her approach:

> The 48 hours can be used to get him [the suspect] to crack. I systematically prolong the *garde à vue* to ensure this. Frequently, it's the first interview in the morning after they've spent the night in custody that they crack, because they're tired and vulnerable and realise that we will keep them in custody . . . It's not an environment where the police hit them—it's more psychological. [Area D]

In directing the police enquiry, the *procureur*'s objective is not a neutral assessment of the case, but is focused upon enabling the police (through the application of pressure if necessary) to obtain a confession from the suspect. Understood in this way, the *procureur*'s parallel role in the protection of defence rights is at odds with her representation of the public interest. Most *procureurs* we observed and interviewed did not perceive such a conflict, but some did and were troubled by the contradictory roles they were required to perform:

> There are two things which do not seem to me to go in the same direction. On the one hand, the need to protect the rights of the defence of the accused, his access to the dossier. On the other hand, the effectiveness of the police investigation. Sometimes, the measures taken [for the defence] can seem to go against this concern with effectiveness. [E3]

Supervision acts less as a constraint upon the police conduct of the GAV and more as a shield, enabling the police to gather evidence against the suspect unhindered. This raises important questions about the role of the *procureur* as a neutral judicial supervisor and the extent to which an independent defence role might be desirable in the GAV. Despite the recommendations of the European Committee for the Prevention of Inhuman or Degrading Treatment or Punishment, and of the 1994 Truche Commission, both the tape recording of interrogations and any extension to the suspect's right to custodial legal advice continue to be opposed by both police and many *magistrats*. Although resistance is often expressed in neutral terms, appealing to a model of judicial supervision which protects the public interest and ensures the effectiveness of the investigation, such safeguards are disliked because of the constraints they would place upon police methods of investigation and interrogation, and the pressures which are considered necessary to 'get to the truth'. As one *juge d'instruction* in area C explained to us on hearing that tape recording police interrogations was standard procedure in England and Wales:

> It's unbelievable! And to think that we might end up doing that here . . . You should just leave the police to do their job. When you're dealing with difficult people like drug addicts and hooligans, you need to put the pressure on. I don't mean hitting them, but you have to make them talk. [*Juge d'instruction*, area C]

The *procureur's* role supervising the GAV and ensuring the protection of the suspect, cannot be understood as a substitute for the function which a defence lawyer might properly fullfil[97] in enabling the suspect to exercise her 'rights to defence'.[98] The *procureur's* action is driven not by a concern with the proper treatment of the accused or any guarantee as to the reliability of the evidence produced, but with ensuring that compliance with due process protections is properly documented, in order to avoid the case being challenged on the grounds of procedural irregularity. Furthermore, the crime control perspective which, in practice, characterises the *procureur's* understanding of 'the public interest', means that breaches of procedure frequently go unchallenged and the suspect's interests are not actively protected by the *procureur*: that is left to the defence lawyer.[99] This was clearly explained by one *procureur*:

> I am staggered by what goes on here. I see piles of cases with improperly obtained evidence. Not mistakes—nullities![100] Nullities in the *garde à vue*. A lawyer who did his work properly would have the case thrown out in five minutes and I see cases arrive which are

---

[97] One senior *procureur*, for example, told us: 'There is an imbalance between the defence and the police, to the detriment of the defence . . . when there is too much of an imbalance, something needs to make up for that. This is done by the *juge d'instruction* . . . or sometimes . . . the *parquet*.'

[98] See discussion in Ch 4. Some commentators argue that the provisions for custodial legal advice do not constitute 'defence rights', but 'pre-defence rights', since 'defence rights' presupposes the existence of an accusation and of the right to challenge based upon access to the dossier (Garé and Ginestet, 2002:233).

[99] On the rare occasion when police activity is censored, this is resisted and resented. The head of the *permanence* in site D told us that she had thrown out a case because the officer had made a mistake early on in the procedure: 'The police were furious and phoned me and said, "You want war? You will have it."'

[100] ie evidence improperly obtained which the court should strike out.

completely useless, interviews which are completely useless and lawyers just don't see it and they don't have the evidence thrown out. It's a shame. That does not encourage us to do our job well. [A4]

Inadequate resources together with the often crime control ideology of the *mag-istrat*, mean that police supervision by the *procureur* remains distant and bureaucratic, designed not to interfere in the method of the investigation or the conduct of the GAV (which remains quite firmly police territory and police business), but rather, to ensure the legal coherence of the ouput, preferably in the form of a confession. The independence of the *procureur* is constrained by her structural and material dependence upon the police and additional safeguards, such as record keeping and the provision of custodial legal advice, remain peripheral, concerned to bolster the legal bureaucratic form of the dossier, rather than the ways in which the evidence is constructed and produced. The rhetoric of due process safeguards within the professional ethos of the *mag-istrat* encompasses the protection of rights in only the narrowest procedural sense and the culture of legal bureaucracy means that compliance with such protections is a matter of form rather than content, which serves only to authenticate, rather than actively to regulate, the enquiry. It is by no means sure that supervision of this nature, especially given the absence of defence lawyers or tape recorders during interrogation, would be able to prevent the kind of misconduct which led to the wrongful convictions of those such as the Cardiff Three. The dangers of such 'arm's length' supervision have been powerfully demonstrated in a number of French miscarriage of justice cases, where detainees have been persuaded to make false confessions to offences such as armed robbery[101] and child murder,[102] through a process of detention and interrogation which places no effective constraints upon the ways in which the police construct the evidence of suspects.

---

[101] See the case of Joël Pierrot, whose conviction was quashed in May 2002.
[102] See the case of Patrick Dils, whose conviction was finally quashed in April 2002.

6

Inside the Police Station

The previous chapter described the centrality of judicial supervision in the legal regulation of the *garde à vue* (GAV) and the way in which defence interests are understood as part of a wider concern with procedural regularity. The *procureur* is the judicial officer entrusted with oversight of the GAV period and the ways in which she understands the nature of the police–*procureur* relationship within which supervision is played out were described—a relationship characterised by trust and the need to work alongside the police, placing their practical investigatory work within a legal framework. The structural dependence of the *parquet* upon the police militates towards such a model and makes ambiguous the nature of the authority which the *procureur* is able to exercise over officers. Visits to the police station are rare and when they do take place, they are part of a system of formal procedural checks. They are not designed to check upon the conduct of the GAV, the general treatment of suspects, nor upon the methods of interrogation. There is no real concern to verify the means by which evidence is obtained through engagement with the enquiry while it is still ongoing. Understood in largely procedural terms, the principal objective of supervision is the production of a legally coherent dossier which will withstand the scrutiny of the court.

To the observer from a jurisdiction with a more adversarial tradition of criminal procedure, this seems a limited form of supervision, based upon trust and paperwork, rather than active verification or challenge—and all the more so, given the diminished role of the defence. In England and Wales, several decades of critical empirical research and numerous miscarriages of justice have demonstrated the vulnerability of suspects and the unreliability of confession evidence—even when obtained as a result of interrogations quite properly conducted. The police station remains an inherently hostile and coercive environment, but a number of safeguards are in place in England and Wales, designed to ensure the greater reliability of in particular, confession evidence. These include the establishment of the post of custody officer to oversee the detention period and to ensure the suspect's welfare; the tape recording of interviews with the suspect; custody reviews to prevent unnecessary and excessive periods of detention; the availability of custodial legal advice before and during interrogation; and the presence of appropriate adults for those suspects considered especially vulnerable.[1] Although the failure to respect these safeguards does not, in itself, result in the striking out of evidence, the court does have a discretion under section 78 of the Police and Criminal Evidence Act 1984 (PACE) to exclude evidence (including confessions) which it considers it would be unfair to admit. This may, for example, allow the trial judge to exclude confession evidence obtained in the absence of a defence lawyer or an appropriate adult. Under section 76 PACE, if a confession is found to have been obtained by oppression, or in consequence of anything said or done which is likely to render the confession unreliable, it cannot be admitted as evidence and its exclusion in these circumstances is mandatory.

In France, however, the danger of unreliable confessions is not a central concern in the judicial regulation of the GAV, neither in the legal procedural requirements, nor in the ways in which supervision is effected in practice. Judicial supervision is unable to go beyond the police account of the investigation—both during the GAV (over the telephone) and after (in the dossier statements taken by the police). Features such as the *procureur*'s dependence upon the police, the potentially conflicting structures of hierarchical accountability between the Ministries of Justice and the Interior, as well as stretched resources in many areas, place very real constraints upon the kind of control which can be exercised over the GAV period in practice. Yet few aspire to a different or more interventionist model of supervision, content in most instances to leave the 'dirty work' of criminal investigations to the police. Neither is there any incentive to do otherwise given that the *procureur*'s disengagement from the investigation remains unproblematic in legal procedural terms. As we have seen, supervision as practiced is not designed to constrain and challenge officers, so much as to support and guide them. The public-interest-centred ideology of the *magistrat* (the primary justification for such a concentration of power in the hands of one individual) poses little threat to that of the police when the search for the truth becomes universally understood as the search for a confession. Thus, the *procureur* will restrain the occasional over-zealous officer who has misunderstood the extent of police powers but in many instances, she acts to encourage and facilitate the police in pressing for an admission from the suspect and she is generally tolerant of the kinds of pressures which are considered necessary to get to 'the truth'.

Additional safeguards put in place more recently to protect the due process rights of the suspect are limited in scope and, as with supervision more generally, tend to be understood in procedural rather than substantive terms. Custodial legal advice, for example, satisfies Article 6 ECHR requirements and serves to

---

[1] There are, of course, problems in implementing these provisions as evidenced by the findings of independent research studies such as Dixon *et al* (1989); McConville *et al* (1991); McConville and Hodgson (1993); McConville *et al* (1994). See also generally Belloni and Hodgson (2000); Sanders and Young (2000). The curtailment of the right to silence under the 1994 CJPOA has also undermined some of the existing protections.

legitimate the detention period, but it is not designed to assist the suspect in the early preparation of her defence. For most *procureurs*, control and oversight of the investigation is best achieved through trust and a close working relationship with the police, rather than through other verification measures which can ultimately go wrong. One *substitut* was deeply cynical about what he described as an 'excess of formalism' which was reducing everything to a series of check boxes:

> Eventually, the cause of evidence being struck out will be a police officer having forgotten to tick a box . . . Formalism, to be precise, is about external scrutiny, it's about paper . . . The machine prints it out and you sign without reading it . . . it no longer has any meaning . . . personally, I am not convinced that this is necessarily very protective of a person's rights. [E4]

This chapter considers the view from the other side—the conditions of the suspect's detention and interrogation and the constraints which legal regulation and judicial supervision place upon the conduct of the GAV. What is quite striking is, firstly, the similarity in approach between the interrogation strategies of officers in France and their counterparts in England and Wales; and, secondly, the extent to which, as in England and Wales, the French police are able to construct a dossier of evidence centring upon the guilt of the suspect. The evidence from recent miscarriages of justice (*erreurs judiciaires*), which have come to light, demonstrates the extent to which officers in France are able to elicit a confession from a detainee with the same ease as those in England and Wales.

Miscarriages of Justice

The inability of judicial supervision to exercise effective control over the police conduct of the GAV was demonstrated in the recent case of Patrick Dils, whose conviction for murder was quashed in April 2002. Interrogated by *gendarmes* in April 1987, Dils initially denied any involvement in the offence, but after spending the night in GAV, he finally admitted to the grotesque murder of two 8-year-old boys in Montigny-lès-Metz. He maintained his GAV admissions before the *juge d'instruction*, retracting them one month later in a letter to his lawyer. It was 15 years before his conviction was finally overturned in a dramatic hearing which had as its star witness, a self-confessed serial killer. This case and others demonstrate the gaping holes in the protection of the suspect and the inadequacy of judicial supervision in controlling the investigation and, particularly, the interrogation activities of the police.[2] The circumstances of the case carry the familiar

---

[2] The French courts have overturned very few convictions—only eight between 1945 and 2001. In some of these cases too, the appellant had initially confessed (including during the *instruction*) before later retracting the admission. See *Le Monde* 21 June 2001.

hallmarks of the miscarriages witnessed in the 1980s and 1990s in England and Wales.[3] The victims were two children, making the offence a particularly high-profile case, attracting maximum media attention and public sympathy. This in turn placed the police under considerable pressure to find the culprit. Dils was a vulnerable suspect, aged 16 at the time, with a social age of 8. He was interviewed alone and was (unlawfully) not provided with a lawyer when questioned by the *juge d'instruction*. Psychiatrists also noted his suggestibility and tendency to give the answer desired by his interrogator. At his appeal hearing, he described the questioning technique of his interrogating officer as highly suggestive of the 'right' answers, a technique which also produced admissions from two men arrested earlier and held in GAV in connection with the same murders. And finally, the police failed to follow up important evidence which might have prevented Dils from ever becoming a suspect: the appeal hearing heard how a 16-year-old youth told the police the day after the crime, of having seen someone close to the scene, spattered with blood. Although informed that he would be asked to come to the station to create a photofit of the person seen, this was never done.

At the appeal hearing, Dils attempted to explain how he came to make a false confession to such an awful crime. He described the interrogation strategy of the police—how the answers were given in the questions and how he felt that the only way to escape further detention was to give the police 'their truth'.[4] His account is lent added credibility by those of the two other men detained earlier, both questioned by the same officer as Dils and from whom similar confessions were also obtained before being discarded as not credible.[5] Like Dils, the confession of one of the men, Henri Leclaire, aged 38, was repeated in front of another officer. Both men were unable to explain why they had confessed, saying only that the police asked so many questions 'until your head was full' and that they 'harrassed you until you would would say anything'.[6] Dils' confession was, of course, obtained in the absence of a lawyer, an appropriate adult, or a tape recorder. He had been 'prepared' by officers, who had a number of preliminary conversations with him, none of which were noted down as they were conducted unlawfully outside the documented interrogation times, during the suspect's rest period.[7] On appeal, the lack of credibility of Dils' alleged account was underlined: it was noted that crucial facts as to the murder were not included in his 'confession' and that parts of his statement were vague and incoherent.[8] After a number of unsuccessful attempts, his conviction was finally overturned in April 2002. A re-investigation of the case by the

---

[3] See Belloni and Hodgson (2000) ch 1.
[4] *Le Monde* 12 April 2002.
[5] A further suspect had also 'confessed' to his psychiatrist.
[6] *Le Monde* 19 April 2002.
[7] *Le Monde* 13 April 2002.
[8] *Le Monde* 13 April 2002.

gendarmes unearthed evidence that a convicted serial killer, Francis Heaulme, was working 400 metres from the scene of the killing. He admitted to being at the scene and seeing the boys dead, though not to having killed them, but his presence was ultimately enough to raise serious doubts as to the involvement of Dils.[9]

This case and other instances of false confessions, raise important questions about the conditions under which suspects are interrogated in police custody in France and the safeguards in place to ensure the reliability of confession evidence—both during the GAV and subsequently.[10] Some commentators will argue predictably that such a case would not happen today with the procedural safeguards[11] put in place in the 1993 legislation—just as it was argued that the miscarriages of justice witnessed in England and Wales in the last two decades of the 20th century concerned cases investigated prior to the safeguards legislated in the Police and Criminal Evidence Act 1984 (PACE). However, neither police malpractice nor miscarriages of justice ceased with the passing of PACE.[12] Among the most notorious of the later cases were the 'Cardiff Three' who were convicted in 1990 of the murder of a Cardiff prostitute. Miller, one of the appellants, had his police interviews tape recorded and his solicitor present, yet these safeguards in no way deterred the police from conducting an oppressive interrogation: 19 separate interviews continuing for more than 13 hours over a 5-day period were conducted, with the police constantly asserting Miller's guilt and offering no respite even when he was crying and sobbing for extended periods. It was only after Miller had denied involvement more than 300 times that he finally admitted to being at the scene. In the course of his questioning, Miller was 'bullied and hectored' by the police and the Court of Appeal was 'horrified' on hearing the tape of the interrogations, describing how officers

> were not questioning him so much as shouting at him what they wanted him to say. Short of physical violence it is hard to conceive of a more hostile and intimidating approach by officers to a suspect. It is impossible to convey on the printed page the pace, force and menace of the officer's delivery.

Yet, Miller's own solicitor did nothing, but sat 'passively through this travesty of a [police] interview'.[13]

---

[9] *Le Monde* 19 April 2002.

[10] For example, after 30 hours in GAV, Jacques Hoffmann confessed to killing his ex-wife Marthe. He then retracted his confession, but remained in custody for 18 months before DNA evidence finally showed that he was not the killer. See *L'Express* 31 May 2004.

[11] See Ch 5.

[12] For example, in 1994, the Court of Appeal quashed the conviction of Ivan Fergus, a 13-year-old boy convicted of attempted robbery. The case revealed a string of errors on all sides. Despite repeated requests from the Crown Prosecution Service, the police had refused to interview four alibi witnesses. The defence failed to prepare the case properly, failed to call key witnesses and to submit that there was clearly no case to answer. There were further errors at trial, when the trial judge failed to warn the jury of the dangers of convicting on the basis of identification evidence alone.

[13] *R v Paris, Abdullahi and Miller* (1993).

The Dils case cannot be simply swept away as an aberration of police malpractice, a relic of former times and a relatively unregulated GAV regime. Once made,
it is almost impossible to retract a confession.[14] The Dils case was investigated
under the more thorough *instruction* investigation procedure, yet this (and two
trial hearings) failed to uncover the truth and probe sufficiently the credibility of
this young man's confession.[15] More recently, Joël Pierrot also maintained his false
admissions before the trial judge. After initially denying involvement during his
GAV interrogation in December 1997, Pierrot admitted committing an armed robbery and two days later was tried, convicted and sentenced to four years
in prison (three suspended) by the rapid *comparution immédiate* procedure.[16] Notwithstanding the judicial supervision of the police and the further enquiry of a
trial court where no guilty plea system exists, the young man's admissions were
never questioned—despite the fact that he stated that he had used a plastic gun,
in clear contradiction to the evidence of witnesses. He maintained his admission
before the court, as it had been indicated to him that if he retracted it, he would
face certain incarceration, whereas admissions demonstrating remorse would
attract clemency. He appealed and was again convicted in February 1998 and it
was only when he learned that two other men had admitted to and been convicted of the crime for which he had been imprisoned, that he finally succeeded in
having his conviction overturned.[17]

Both cases underline the centrality of evidence gathered by the police and the
importance of ensuring its credibility given the absence of clear due process protections; subsequent judicial scrutiny cannot be relied upon to verify or challenge
such evidence. Furthermore, whilst it is hoped that the reforms of 1993 and 2000
have brought some improvements in regulating the detention of individuals held

---

[14] See also the comments of Serge Portelli, the vice-president of the *Tribunal de grande instance* in
Paris, interviewed by Pierre Rancé (2002c). The appeal process is also narrowly circumscribed. Until
recently, there was no appeal from the *cour d'assises* (the court trying the most serious cases, such as
murder) and the *Cour de cassation* is generally restricted to hearing issues on a point of law. Only rarely
does it act as a full appeal court, if there is new factual evidence and a prima facie case that there has
been a judicial error.

[15] The recent Outreau case (2004) has also been criticised for failing to investigate with sufficient
thoroughness and impartiality. Six out of the seven accused who were acquitted of child sexual abuse
had spent nearly three years in custody during the *instruction*. This case is discussed further in Ch 7.

[16] This procedure and its increasingly extensive use are discussed in Chs 2 and 4.

[17] In another false confession case the suspect was more fortunate. In the summer of 1998, Patrice
Padé was persuaded by *gendarmes* to confess to the rape and murder of the British schoolgirl, Caroline
Dickinson. Described by *Le Monde* (9 June 2004) as an 'ideal suspect', Padé had previous convictions
for child sexual assault, was a vagrant, had been near to the youth hostel where Caroline was killed at
the time of the murder and was unable to provide an alibi. He initially denied involvement, but after
40 hours in GAV, he confessed. He later retracted his confession and DNA tests demonstrated that the
sperm found on the girl's body could not have been his. After 18 days in custody he was released and
two years later he received 10,000 francs in compensation. In 1988 Richard Roman confessed to the
rape and murder of a 7-year-old girl, after only four hours of GAV. His co-accused, who had originally named him, retracted his accusation at trial in 1992 and Roman was acquitted. See *L'Express* 31 May
2004.

in GAV, it cannot be assumed that legal change alone is sufficient to transform the practices of legal actors—as the Miller case pointedly demonstrates. There needs also to be a more profound shift in the occupational cultures of these players. Research has demonstrated that unless addressed directly, these factors are likely to transcend mere changes in legal rules[18]. Thus, it is to the ideologies and practices of those responsible for the interrogation of suspects, as well as to the legal framework governing the GAV, that attention must be directed.

Police Accountability to *Magistrats*

Although both police and *procureurs* recognised that, for a number of reasons, supervision was effected in a relatively distant and bureaucratic way, police and *gendarmes* were conscious that they were increasingly accountable to *magistrats*. The findings of the current study support the research conducted in Lyon by Lemaître (1994:79). He found that more senior police officers were the most hostile to the reforms of 1993, especially the introduction of the defence lawyer into the procedure. They were critical of the police obligation to inform the suspect of her rights, claiming that this would now reassure suspects instead of destabilising them through isolation. They also resented the mistrust of the police, represented in the the obligation to report to the *parquet* at the start of the GAV. Officers working on the ground shared these concerns to begin with, but soon came to realise that the new legal regime did not alter things in quite so drastic a way as they had feared (Lemaître 1994:80); the presence of a lawyer for 30 minutes, for example, changed little. In addition, contact with the *parquet* came to be viewed positively as offering officers a form of protection.

In the present study, senior police officers were vehemently opposed to the presence of the defence lawyer and resented their accountability to the *procureur*. Lower down the hierarchy, some older OPJ, especially *gendarmes*, were resentful and slow to adapt to the new procedures and we observed numerous errors, but for most OPJ, reporting to the *procureur* was not in itself problematic.

> We are in frequent contact with the *parquet* and we have a positive relationship with them. They like to be kept informed of what is happening—there has been a change in this respect since the reform some 10 years ago. They are implicated in our work to a much greater extent. That does not pose any particular problem for us. [*Gendarme*, area A]

However, there were complaints that this increasing accountability to the *parquet* was symptomatic of a wider trend of eroding officers' autonomy and further bureaucratising the policing function.

---

[18] For discussion of police practices, see eg Dixon *et al* (1989) and McConville *et al* (1991). For discussion of the organisation and practices of defence lawyering, see eg McConville *et al* (1994).

Before, we took all the decisions and, except for the most serious cases, we made a judgment. Now, we have to inform them of everything. We are moving closer and closer to the justice system. There is more and more contact. [Police officer, area A]

There is too much work, more and more work and less and less room to act on our own initiative, investigating new cases. We respond to [the demands of the judiciary] all the time. [Police officer, area A]

I have the impression that the climate of trust is disappearing. The *parquet* is becoming very active in its instructions. There is an increase in judicial power in France compared with political power. There is a greater degree of independence and *magistrats* see themselves with more responsibility . . . Now, the work is not easy. Giving a telephone account is not always easy, especially if it is an obscure case. The way in which the *magistrat* intervenes on the telephone . . . sometimes he asks lots of questions which totally loses the officer . . . there is more trust with the *juge d'instruction*. [D5]

The concerns of officers were similar to those raised by the police in England and Wales after the introduction of PACE: they resented having to account for everything and spending so much time in the station completing paperwork, rather than engaging in 'real' police work. In France too, the universal complaint was that changes are inevitably accompanied by increasing amounts of paperwork or *paperasse*. After the 1993 changes requiring the police to inform the *procureur* of those held in GAV and to keep a custody record, they told us: 'We are drowning in paperwork.'

Since '76 we are on the ground less and less. It is all paperwork, paperwork. Before, we had much more individual initiative. Now we are doing the work of the justice system, as well as policing. [Police officer, area A]

We need less paperwork so that we have more time on the ground. [*Gendarme*, area D]

The COPJ (*comparution par officier de police judiciaire*) procedure passes the burden of summoning the accused to court on a specified date from the *procureur* to the police. The *procureur* simply tells the police the relevant offence and court date and then leaves the officer to complete the paperwork and give it to the suspect before her release.

[COPJ] makes more work for us. If in one day, you type out a COPJ that is not a great deal. But multiplied by the number of officers, by the number of days, that represents time saved for *magistrats* and time lost for us. It is an additional burden. The procedure is getting more onerous as the law changes. [D5]

This was also the case with the more recent changes towards the *traitement en temps réel* (TTR) procedure.[19] Most officers in our questionnaire survey agreed

---

[19] Also discussed above, Ch 5. Police resentment at the additional work was fuelled by the corresponding decrease in resources available.

that whilst TTR was a more effective way of dealing with cases, it was more complicated and represented a greater burden of work; half considered that it required the police to do the work of the *parquet*. This was also the view of those we observed, especially in area A, where TTR was already in place for juvenile cases, and was set to expand to all investigations.

> [TTR] takes time, but it is a good thing. You know straightaway if there is going to be a prosecution or not and that accelerates the process. It is a good thing for the justice system but it is a lot of work for the police—and yet more paperwork. [OPJ, area A]

The *parquet* was generally in favour of TTR, as it allowed cases to be dealt with more quickly and shifted paperwork from the *procureur* to the police. They were conscious, however, that it may be experienced differently by the police.

> It will be a good thing once it is fully in place. We will have better control over the case and less paperwork to do because we will not have dossiers arriving through the post to deal with—the decision will have been made there and then . . . At present [the police] are not for it . . . they will make fewer decisions as everything will be dealt with by telephone and they will lose the freedom to deal with minor cases themselves. They will have more work, but less responsibility. The *procureur* will also be more difficult to contact, because the telephone will be even busier. [*Procureur*, area A]

The obligation upon officers to inform the *procureur* of a suspect's detention as soon as possible was initially regarded as an indication of society's mistrust of the police by officers in Lemaître's (1994) Lyon study. However, once the practice was established, they came to see that it could have clear benefits for them, providing them with a degree of protection for their acts, as well as enabling them to be better informed and so to keep the victim better informed.[20] The police in Mouhanna's (2001a) research described their relationship with *magistrats* in similarly positive terms.[21] The involvement of the *procureur* was understood less as an intrusive authority and more as a source of legal advice; and when difficult decisions had to be made, officers were happy to pass responsibility for the case to someone else. In the present study too, the *procureur*'s authority was not only experienced as a feature of police accountability, but also, as a source of advice and protection.[22] Most frequently, officers would seek clarification on a point of law or procedure, but on some occasions

---

[20] Jankowski (1996:26) also notes that the police consider this to be a positive aspect of the procedure.

[21] Whilst the internal police hierarchy was understood as a disciplinary structure, the interdependent nature of the relationship between OPJ and *magistrat* was viewed as one in which the officer's status was elevated from that of simple police officer, to that of auxiliary of justice (Mouhanna 2001a:83). Jankowski (1996) also characterises police working relationships with other officers as conflictual, whilst those between OPJ and *magistrats* were positive, based upon trust and a mutual respect.

[22] In practical matters such as ensuring the co-operation of doctors in providing medical certificates, officers relied upon their own police hierarchy.

they looked to the *parquet* to 'regularise' matters where an error had been made: for example, the officer in area E, described in the previous chapter, who asked whether he should change the times on the custody record to hide the fact that the GAV had overrun the 24 hour period. In a case in area D, the officer to whom the case had been assigned was horrified to discover that his colleague had gone to the suspect's house shortly after 10pm, had entered the premises and seized the firearm used in the offence. In France, searches may not be conducted after 9pm[23] and the officer feared that the search would be discounted as unlawful and the evidence lost. The *procureur* was contacted immediately and after much consultation with her colleagues (the fax originally sent after the arrest contained only rudimentary details), she was able to provide a satisfactory resolution: as the suspect had invited the officer in and agreed to hand over the firearm, it would not be classed as a search, but a voluntary act on the part of the suspect.[24] The police were obviously relieved that responsibility had passed to the *procureur*, who had been able to reconfigure the procedure in a way which ensured its legitimacy. In another case in area D, the process of 'regularisation' was more difficult to resolve. The police telephoned at 11am to report that a man was stopped at 4pm the previous day, carrying a small cheese box which was found to contain 20g of herbal cannabis. His house was searched and a further 70g found and he was then placed in GAV. The *procureur* warned that some reason was needed for the original stop, telling the officer: 'The original stop is fragile. What offence was he suspected of?' The officer telephoned later to report:

> OPJ: I have changed the statement re the original stop and questioning, to say that the box fell open onto the floor.
> *Procureur*: OK, I heard nothing.

Later that afternoon, the *procureur* became concerned about the way in which the evidence was being presented and determined to speak to the police again.[25]

> *Procureur*: The stop must be for good reason, but you cannot make up what happened. All this nonsense about the box happening to fall on the floor and then they questioned him.
> Researcher: What will you tell them?
> *Procureur*: I will tell them to tell the truth.
> Researcher: Which was?

[23] Other than in exceptional circumstances, eg under the provisions of the 2004 legislation.

[24] This adopts the same reasoning as 'consent searches' in England and Wales, whereby searches of the person conducted with the individual's consent, are not searches conducted under s 1 of PACE and so are not subject to the safeguards of that section such as recording etc. See Dixon *et al* (1990). Interestingly, this practice is widespread in England and Wales. As one officer told Dixon *et al* (1990:349): 'I have never had any problems with anyone refusing to be searched ... so I have never had to fall back on proving my reasonable suspicion.'

[25] It is, of course, possible that the presence of the researcher influenced the *procureur*'s behaviour.

Procureur: That he went to hide the box in his jacket when he saw the police. I do not want to be implicated in some sort of cover-up.

He then telephoned the police and told them:

Procureur: He was going to hide the box, fine. You can say that it is in an area where many drug offences are committed, that you had just stopped someone for buying herbal cannabis.

The police hierarchy itself can also be a source of advice and the senior officers who allocated casework were often at hand to check how the investigation was progressing. There is also an increasing amount of delegation from OPJ (*officiers de police judiciaire*) to the lower ranking APJ (*agents de police judiciaire*). Whilst OPJ are the principal officers authorised to arrest, detain and question suspects, they are assisted by APJ who may carry out some of the same tasks, under the supervision of their OPJ colleagues. Their role is becoming more important as their numbers are increasing: when OPJ leave, they are often replaced by APJ. This was resented by some, especially in area E, where there was quite a high turnover of personnel. There was a feeling that time and effort was devoted to training APJ, who then generally left once qualified. Supervision was also an onerous task in some instances, to prevent APJ from exceeding their powers and jeopardising an investigation. In the following example from area E, the suspect was being questioned in the course of an investigation *en préliminaire*, so that his consent was required before his home could be searched. During the course of the interrogation, the OPJ was firm but civil; the APJ shouted and adopted a bullying manner which served only to antagonise the suspect and make him unco-operative.

OPJ: Can you write this out and sign [the consent form].
Suspect: No. I'm not signing anything until I have seen my lawyer.
APJ: Fine, we will just telephone the *procureur* and he will give us permission anyway. It doesn't bother us.
OPJ: No, no, we can't do that. The *procureur* cannot.
APJ: But he already did it for me.
OPJ: No, that was the *juge d'instruction*.
APJ: No … that [pointing to the CPP], that doesn't cover everything. The *parquets*, they are all different.
OPJ: No, you cannot do that.

In her interviews with OPJ, Jankowski (1996:24) found that the investigative discontinuity between officers was sometimes problematic. When APJ begin an investigation, it is then passed to an OPJ to be presented to the *procureur*, and OPJ resent having to be accountable for the errors and deficiencies in their colleagues' work.

Inside the *Garde à Vue*

The Interrogation Environment

There are many aspects to the police station environment in France,[26] such as its overwhelmingly white, male personnel,[27] the visible presence of guns and the obligatory two hour lunch, which differ from that in England and Wales. Most notable for the purposes of this discussion are the very different conditions under which suspects and witnesses are questioned. In contrast to the dedicated interview rooms, tape recordings, lawyers, standard introductions and caution which are the staple of interrogations in England and Wales, in France, stations and *gendarmeries* were generally organised on an open plan basis with up to six or eight officers sharing one large room in which suspects and witnesses would be questioned[28] (sometimes several at one time) and a statement of their evidence noted down. These rooms were interconnecting so that a typical police station layout would be an entrance hall with four offices on each side, each connecting to each other and to the hall. The physical layout of the building is instrumental to the atmosphere generated in the offices where everything takes place from witness statements, to high-level staff meetings, to parties. Doors remained open for most of the time and officers spoke and shouted to each other across the hall and offices.

Apart from the general distraction of a busy office,[29] such an environment makes the 'contamination' of evidence almost inevitable. Officers frequently come

---

[26] There were, of course, variations between stations. The material conditions in which suspects were held tended to be better in *gendarmeries* where, quite simply, the cells were less subject to heavy use. Of police stations that were situated in the more deprived areas, some were in urgent need of modernisation and decoration. The European Committee for the Prevention of Inhuman and Degrading Treatment or Punishment has repeatedly drawn attention to the inadequate conditions in which suspects are held. It was also interesting to note that in areas where alcohol abuse was a particular problem, there were dedicated 'drying out' cells. In one area, two of the four cells were for this purpose and one suspect received two and a half litres of red wine—on prescription!

[27] Female suspects often could not be searched at the station, as there were no female officers. The absence of women made it difficult and embarrassing for female suspects when eg requesting sanitary towels. Only 4% of officers in France were women in 1987, rising to 8% in 1997. In 2003, there were around 10% of women in the *police nationale* at the levels of *commissaires*, *officiers* and *gardiens de la paix*. In the *gendarmerie*, the figure is also around 10%, but the figure is lower at the more senior levels: 2.5% at the level of *officier*; 7% at the level of *sous-officier*; and 30% at the level of *gendarmes adjoints*. 18% of police officers in England and Wales are women.

[28] The one exception to this was in the drugs squad, where, in area C, separate small rooms, not much bigger than a cupboard, were used for interviewing suspects; in area D, ordinary rooms were used, but the door was closed and only officers directly involved would enter during an interrogation.

[29] Eg, officers on the telephone, dealing with another case; officers standing only a few metres away, discussing another investigation; the comings and goings of suspects, witnesses and experts in the adjoining corridor; somebody vacuum cleaning; a dog barking in another room. At times, the scenes observed were reminiscent of the sometimes chaotic station depicted in the 1980s American television series 'Hill Street Blues'.

in and out, observing the interview, commenting on the suspect's responses and contributing their own questions. These 'itinerant' officers were frequently involved in the same investigation and in some instances, were in the course of interrogating a witness or co-accused, breaking off to pass on information to another interviewing officer or to pose questions directly to the suspect. Witnesses were also questioned in this way. In one instance, for example, we observed two witnesses in the same case being questioned in the same room. Each insisted on intervening in the other's evidence to clarify or correct something to the point where it became almost comical and the officers had to instruct them firmly, to keep to the task in hand. Identification procedures were also lax. It was not uncommon for the suspect to be brought up from the cells while the victim was still at the station. When asked by the officer if 'this is the man?', the victim inevitably agreed that it was. Officers were unconcerned by the obvious dangers of these practices and the contaminating effect they might have upon the evidence produced. Whilst there is a requirement to document the GAV period in the manner of a custody record, there appeared to be no equivalent of the PACE Codes of Practice governing the conditions under which interviews should take place or identification procedures be carried out, and calls for such guidance to be made available have been rejected as unnecessary.[30]

Constructing the Written Record

Interrogation evidence was neither tape recorded, nor recorded in the form of contemporaneous notes. It was noted down in the same way as witness statements are taken in England and Wales, as a synthesis of the information yielded through police questioning. This produces a relatively short statement, revealing nothing of the process by which the evidence emerges. The documented interrogation times contained in the case dossier indicated that, typically, an hour's questioning would yield no more than 250 words[31] (of which 100 would be biographical information) and yet even this obvious documentary fiction was never queried by the supervising *procureur*. There was no expectation that the entire interview be recorded, rather than a distilled version of the relevant parts of the suspect's account. In England and Wales, there has been much consternation surrounding the practice of 'off the record' conversations between police and suspects and so called 'car seat confessions'. The reasons being that firstly, such conversations take place outside the interview room, depriving the court of an accurate and reliable (tape recorded) record of evidence; and secondly, the suspect is questioned without the benefit of the attendant PACE safeguards, such as legal advice. In France,

---

[30] See eg the comments of the European Committee for the Prevention of Torture and Inhuman and Degrading Punishment or Treatment in their 2001 Report and the response of the French government.
[31] Field and West (2003) also noted the brevity of statements.

without the constraints of recording and cautioning requirements, we observed such conversations as almost standard practice. An interview will begin with a preliminary 'chat' to prime the suspect and the officer would not begin typing and 'spoil' the statement until the suspect produced the 'correct' version of events, the 'truth'.[32] As one police officer in area C commented of a statement on file:

> That statement isn't very good. Everything isn't noted because he wasn't telling the truth. It's better like that. He was playing down his involvement, but after, when we have some proof, we can nail him.

The result is a very clipped statement, presented as a narrative, with the occasional inclusion of a question and response recorded verbatim. Summarising the evidence in this fashion produces a record which is incomplete in important ways, making it difficult to assess the credibility of the evidence presented.[33] It reveals nothing of the tone of the interview; the extent to which the suspect's answers are spontaneous or the result of questions put to her; any pressures to make admissions, and so on. The absence of any interrogation context within which to interpret or evaluate the evidence produced is a significant weakness, demonstrated by our own observations as well as, rather more pointedly, the miscarriages of justice described at the start of this chapter.

The way in which the procedure and evidence of the GAV is documented is of particular importance given the reliance upon written evidence in French criminal procedure.[34] Records of the GAV were not made systematically and in order to avoid the strictures of legal procedural requirements, the police used many of the same ploys observed in England and Wales in the period immediately post PACE.[35] Although times recorded were generally accurate in terms of the amount of time spent out of the cells and in the office, they did not reflect how much of that was spent in interrogation, waiting in the corridor, being moved into another room to be questioned by someone else and so on. During the course of the GAV, we noticed that forms were often filled out retrospectively at the close of detention and suspects were asked to sign blank forms which were completed

---

[32] One officer in area D explained: 'We can bluff a bit when we chat to them, but not in what's written down.'

[33] This has been a concern in relation to the production of witness statements in England and Wales, which, like the presentation of the suspect's evidence in France, are recorded as a statements, rather than questions and answers. In a small study conducted by McLean (1995), it was found that interviews with witnesses reproduced many of the worst aspects of interviews with suspects. Leading questions were put and the record made was often inaccurate—the inaccuracies ensuring the production of a statement more favourable to the police case. See also Cretney and Davis (1995:129) and Heaton-Armstrong and Wolchover (1992).

[34] The *procureur*'s decision on how to dispose of the case is based upon the case dossier and at trial in the *tribunal correctionnel*, where the majority of cases are heard, witnesses are called only rarely. Furthermore, given the *procureur*'s oversight of the enquiry, the evidence collected during the police investigation is treated as the product of a judicially supervised enquiry.

[35] See eg Sanders *et al* (1989); McConville *et al* (1991).

later.[36] In one police station in particular, in area E, suspects were discouraged from reading statements before signing them and from calling their lawyer, as the following case examples illustrate.

> Officer: There you are—sign there and on the back. [The suspect starts reading] There is no point, I've already read it to you as we went along.

> Officer: You probably won't need a lawyer—you will be out within 20 hours. Sign here. [She begins to read the custody record.] You won't understand anything, I wouldn't bother.
> Suspect: I have studied law . . .

> Officer: You can contact your family and see a lawyer and a doctor if you sign and co-operate with us. Otherwise, this will all look bad on your file, the *procureur* and the judge will not be happy and things will not go well for you.

> Officer: Do you want a lawyer?
> Suspect: Ermmm. . .
> Officer: The lawyer is for after 20 hours. I can't say whether you'll need one, because I don't know if you will still be here. Anyway, he does not have access to the dossier, so there's not much point. It's just to check that everything has been OK in the *garde à vue*. He can't see what is in the file, just check that everything is OK. Anyway, it's not the same person who will be looking at the file later, there's no real point. It doesn't bother me, eh, I'm just telling you, that's all . . .
> Suspect: OK, no lawyer then.

Having sat in on the questioning of suspects, we also examined the record of interview made and placed in the dossier. Although many detainees admitted their involvement, the kinds of distortions we observed were similar to those reported in relation to police interviews in research studies carried out in England and Wales, and now also in France. Lévy (1985; 1987), Zauberman (1997) and Mouhanna (2001a) all describe the ways in which police and *gendarmes* construct written evidence in order to eliminate doubt[37] and to strengthen their case.[38] In the current study, criminal argot was frequently included in the written statement, despite not being used by the suspects themselves[39] and accounts were skewed to

---

[36] Zauberman (1997:347) notes that the principal concern is that the dossier is internally consistent, rather than being an accurate account of what happened.

[37] Lévy (1985:414) notes that the production of statements in this way is part of police training as documented in training manuals.

[38] But whilst Lévy (1985; 1987) and Zauberman (1997) describe this practice as being designed to influence the decision making of the *magistrat*, Mouhanna (2001a:124–25) goes further and describes the *magistrat* as being complicit in, rather than deceived by, this process of reconstruction.

[39] Typically, whilst suspects usually referred to 'cannabis' most officers insisted on typing 'shit' (a common slang expression used) in the statement. See also Bryan (1997) whose research in England and Wales compared written interrogations (pre-PACE) and those which had been tape recorded (post-PACE). Whilst suspects were depicted as behaving badly and swearing in the written statements prepared by the police, tape recorded interrogations revealed officers to be overbearing, shouting and swearing, whilst suspects were relatively compliant.

favour the police version of events. Material that was favourable to the defence was often minimised or ignored as irrelevant, particularly in cases where the 'victim' was defined as the first person who reported the incident to the police. This was the case where the suspect in a road traffic accident did not consider that he was entirely to blame. He attempted to explain what the 'victim' had done, but the officer swept this aside with repeated references to the *code de la route*. He explained afterwards that he had consciously manipulated the suspect by refusing to let him have his say: 'otherwise, they would be here forever trying to share out the blame'.

In some cases, facts were added or omitted altogether, altering the nature of the criminal responsibility. Although (predictably) suspects did not admit to being unable to read and write, it was clear that many could not,[40] and, astonishingly, people rarely read through 'their' statement before signing it.[41] For example, in area C, we observed a case where a man was being held on suspicion of burglary of a shop. The suspect admitted to theft, saying that he had stolen some items of clothing which were on the pavement, outside a shop which his friends had just broken into. The officer asked if he went inside the shop to get the goods and the suspect replied definitely not. At the close of questioning, the suspect said that he could not read, but that he 'trusted the officer' to record a faithful account. When I read the typed statement later, the officer had put his own preferred (burglary) version. I tackled him about this inconsistency:

> Researcher: But he said that he found them on the ground.
> Officer: It wasn't very clear.
> Researcher: But he said that he found them on the ground and not in the shop.
> Officer: Well . . . yes, but I let him read it [the statement].
> Researcher: He can't read.
> Officer: But when he signed it, I think he would notice.

These attempts to skew the evidence were observed also in relation to the evidence of witnesses,[42] such as the following example in area C, where the police already had a suspect in detention:

> Officer: How tall?
> Witness: 1m 80.
> Officer: Do you want to say 1m 70?
> Witness: Yes, or 1m 75 . . . .

[40] Noted also by police in Lévy (1985:415).

[41] Those that did, tended to be better educated middle class people, or those with previous convictions. For example, fieldwork observations in area D note that in one morning, of 24 statements which were signed, only 3 were read through first.

[42] See also Lévy (1985).

Officer: How old?
Witness: 35 to 40.
Officer: Not 25?
Witness: No, older. 35.

Similarly, in area E:

Officer: They were approximately how old?
Victim I don't know. About 25, young, they were young.
Officer: More like 30?
Victim: Maybe, I don't know.
. . .
Victim: He was wearing a black jacket
Officer: A jacket, more light-coloured, white?
Victim: Oh, maybe light-coloured, yes, I think light.
Officer: And the trousers, navy blue?
Victim: Yes, dark, I think.

In another instance in area E, the suspect was restless and upset in interview. The police wished to see him admitted to a psychiatric hospital and exaggerated his behaviour in order to achieve this. In the course of interview, the man had once mentioned the Qu'aran and once stood up to show them a dance step. This became: 'he is utterly incoherent, never stops talking about the Qu'aran and keeps getting out of his chair to dance'.

In some instances, the problems of evidence contamination that result from the relatively unregulated interrogation environment are compounded by the police's complete control over the construction of the written record. The formal statement produced reveals nothing of the comings and goings of other officers and the extent to which their contributions feed in information. This is also illustrated by one of the cases in Lévy's research (1985:417–19), in which the victim was presented with the suspect for identification, before the officer then typed up the victim's statement of evidence. This enabled the officer to include more precise details in relation to the suspect's clothing and hairstyle than had been provided in the victim's original account. In the case file, however, the identification was recorded as having taken place after the victim's statement had been made, not before. This had the result of making the identification of the suspect appear even stronger.

Interrogation Tactics

Researchers in Britain and the USA have underlined repeatedly the importance of police authority as a key feature within 'cop culture'. Challenges to this authority are interpreted as deviant behaviour and the law is utilised as part of the process of subordination. French police are no exception to this in their demand for authority, respect and control. Officers employed a range of strategies to assert their authority over suspects during interrogation and to encourage them to agree to the officer's version of the 'truth'.[43] Respect and submission to the authority of the police were also required outside, as well as inside the interrogation. A man who was not formally under arrest in area E, for example, refused to sign the record of the search of his house, as he did not recall the police stating the authority on which they were acting, as set out in the statement. Despite the officers' insistence that they had told him, he maintained his position and they were obliged to change the statement. Furious at his impudence, they locked him in the cells:

> OPJ: Stop being such a bloody idiot ... OK, I'm putting you in identity check while we deal with this. I will take you downstairs. I am not keeping you here, it's far too comfortable. You're just getting on our nerves.

In another case in area E, we observed a journalist being pulled and jostled by a police officer as he was brought into the station, in front of several members of the public in the waiting area. He was very unhappy at his treatment and the OPJ in turn was irritated by the journalist:

> Journalist: I want to make a complaint about this officer. He has thrown me out like a common thief. I am a journalist. I have never experienced such a thing. I want to see his boss.
>
> OPJ: Stop your bullshit. Who do you think you are? And what's more, I will have you for insulting behaviour, you'll see. For a journalist, you don't know much ... [They continued to argue and the OPJ grabbed the journalist by the shirt and pushed him up against the wall]. Disrespect! You understand insulting behaviour towards an officer? It's an offence.

Once in GAV, interviews were often conducted in a macho and aggressive manner, with suspects handcuffed to the wall or chair; officers sitting with one leg up on the desk; officers standing over and circling the suspect; or kicking and slamming furniture. Suspects were almost never addressed in the polite '*vous*' form, but the more familiar '*tu*', again underlining the officers' authority over the detainee. Suspects were shouted and sworn at, ordered to sit up straight and to 'tell the truth'. This approach was used routinely, even when the case or the detail was relatively minor. For example, in a case in area C the suspect was detained following a complaint about the non-payment of a rental car. The officer was noting the suspect's biography.

---

[43] See also Lévy (1987); Zauberman (1997). For a discussion of tactics used in England and Wales, see McConville and Hodgson (1993).

Officer: What is your name? Jean?

Suspect: Yes, Pierre. I have told you twice.

Officer: And your father's name is the same? [Yes] Is that hypenated? [Yes] And yours? [Yes] So you have given me a false name, because you told me it was Jean.

Suspect: No, I said Jean-Pierre.

Officer: No, you didn't say that. [Shouting] You should have said it was with a hyphen. This is for *magistrats*—don't fuck me about!

Interrogation is a form of bargaining and negotiation, during which threats and favours are exchanged for information. Other tactics commonly employed[44] (and all the easier in the absence of any tape recorder) included putting to the suspect the statements of co-accused, or of witnesses, even when there was no written record of them; 'bluffing' as to the evidence against the suspect (witnesses; photos; CCTV); threatening to detain other family members; threats of shortened or prolonged detention; of incarceration pending trial; and the pressing of more or less serious charges.[45] For example, an unco-operative suspect questioned on suspicion of snatching a handbag in area E was told:

OPJ: Now Monsieur, you think this over carefully, eh? . . . Just think about what you say for once, no more bullshit. Once we start, it goes in the statement. Look, snatching a bag, is bad, but we can deal with that, it's not terrible. I don't want to say that you won't be prosecuted, there will be a prosecution, but if you just tell me any old thing, it will turn into a robbery, eh, which is already much more serious . . . I just want the truth.

When asked how they approached the questioning of suspects, officers frequently referred to the psychology of interrogations.

There is no longer any violence—that is history . . . It is much more effective to be nice to get what you want out of people, or, to put pressure on by using the family—threaten to take their children away or to implicate their wife . . . We study our man, get to know him and look for weaknesses. For example, one we nailed by making him feel big and a master criminal; another by letting his wife off; and yet another by sending him to the prison of his choice . . . You have to be a good actor. One OPJ cried with his bloke to make him feel that he was close to him and he could talk. Another takes his to lunch in a restaurant during the *garde à vue*, so that they can become pals. [*Gendarme*, area A]

---

[44] Zauberman (1997:343) also observed the full panoply of 'bad cop' tactics in her study of the *gendarmerie*: insults, physical discomfort, bluffing as to the evidence against the suspect, threats to the reputation of the suspect and her family, and 'apocalyptic' descriptions of what a house search might entail.

[45] It should be remembered that unlike in England and Wales, French police have no power beyond the detention of the suspect. It is the *procureur* who, following detention in GAV, will decide whether to charge, refer the case to the *juge d'instruction*, or release the suspect. There is no interim stage of charging between detention and prosecution, as in England and Wales.

In several cases, the psychology was relatively crude, allowing those who were co-operative a cigarette, but withholding them from others until they agreed to tell the 'truth', that is, to confess. For example, in a case in area C, the suspect was told:

> OK, I will give you [a cigarette] because things are going well here—if not, you would not get one. Don't ask me for a second one.

In a second case in area C, the suspect was less amenable. He was arrested on suspicion of burglary and subjected to aggressive questioning and demands that he admit liability. As part of the process of control and negotiation, he was refused a cigarette until he told 'the truth'. During his interrogation, several other officers came in and harassed him to tell 'the truth', circling the chair on which he was sitting (his hands cuffed behind his back) and behaving in a threatening manner, kicking the furniture. The suspect was then grabbed roughly by the shoulder with his hands still cuffed behind his back and taken into another room. The door was closed but there was a general commotion and much shouting.[46] On his return the suspect continued to deny the offence. The officer sat at a desk opposite him in a macho pose, with one leg on the table, and told him: 'The best thing you can do, the best for you and the quickest, is if you give me something'. This was now 40 minutes into the interrogation and the officer had not typed a word. The suspect was then placed in another room on his own before being returned to the office, his pleas for a cigarette still ignored:

> Suspect: Please can I have a cigarette now—you said that I could.
> Officer: Only if you tell the truth—this is all bullshit.
> [Several officers came in and out and wandered around the suspect who continued to plead for a cigarette.]
> Officer: I don't smoke—and certainly not for liars.

An hour and ten minutes after the interview period began, the suspect was returned to the cells, only three lines of biographical information having been typed in his statement. This constant wearing down of the suspect, this process of attrition, is police business, the 'dirty work' necessary to get at 'the truth'. It does not appear in the dossier of evidence within the neat, precise and clinical statements produced by the OPJ and there is no tape recording to rely on. For the suspect, much of the process of detention and interrogation to which she is subjected remains hidden and therefore difficult to challenge.[47] This was powerfully demonstrated in the Dils

---

[46] This was a difficult moment as a researcher as I feared that the suspect might be assaulted.

[47] See also the cases described by Zauberman (1997:343–44) in which one suspect was left in his cell in his underwear, in temperatures of no more than 12°C and another was assaulted during a search of his home.

case described above, where the initial evidence produced by the police proved almost impossible to displace either before the *juge d'instruction* or the court.

On some occasions, suspects were brought to the police station or *gendarmerie* as witnesses, either because there was insufficient evidence to arrest them as suspects, or more usually, to avoid the 'formalities' and 'paperwork' of the GAV. Ignorant of the officers' desire to avoid making the detention 'official', those held were threatened that lack of co-operation would result in them being placed in GAV, as if the police were currently doing them some form of favour in avoiding this measure. For example, in a case in area A, a woman was 'invited' to attend the *gendarmerie* in connection with some stolen cheques. She agreed to submit to a handwriting test, which the *gendarmes* then claimed matched that on the cheques. She denied that her writing was anything more than vaguely similar to that on the sample and refused to admit the involvement of either herself or any alleged accomplice. At several points during the afternoon, the officers reprimanded her for 'being difficult' and 'not behaving' and threatened to place her in GAV. Finally, after an hour and a half, she confessed: 'Fine, I admit everything. I'll sign whatever you want.' Despite the *gendarmes'* insistence, she claimed to have acted alone and could not recall the details of the offence:

> No, that is not good enough. The *procureur*, he is going to want more detail, otherwise anybody could just confess because they had had enough. That is no good, we need detail—how, where and everything . . . All we want is the truth. [Gendarme, area A]

Interestingly, whilst the person was now clearly a suspect, she was not placed in GAV and so did not benefit from her right to legal assistance, nor was the *procureur* informed of her detention.

Officers told us that they did not bypass the formal procedure very often and when they did, it tended to be in drugs cases. They described having to trick the suspect in order to get a confession, so that their actions could be justified and the whole thing appears above board.

> So, we have a bloke, we find him at the client's house. We make him think that we had followed him and he believes us—in the statement, it all looks quite proper. Sometimes they are scared when they see us and they confess by themselves—we only have to tell them what we are investigating . . . Otherwise, we have to write and ask them to come in before the *procureur* will give us permission to go and question them. Sometimes, there is no point. If you write to them, they disappear. So, you have to bypass the procedure a bit when you know they are going to disappear. But on paper, it all looks fine. We get by. It is not very often and it is mainly in drugs cases . . . it's true that what we need to do in drugs cases does not fit very well with the procedural requirements. [Officer, area E]

The police version of events was repeatedly put to suspects and any contradiction in response was rejected as false. It often, of course, emerged that the suspect had in fact been telling the truth. In the following interrogation, in area C, the police tried to imply that the suspect was too drunk too recall accurately, although later witness statements confirmed the suspect's story:

> Officer: How much did you drink?
> Suspect: A litre of red wine . . . I do every day
> [later]
> Officer: And how many bottles did you drink? Two?
> Suspect: No, one.
> Officer: What time did it happen? 9 o'clock?
> Suspect: No, 5 o'clock.
> Officer: No, it was later.
> Suspect: No, I don't know why the police came later, it was all over by 5.

Suspects were also asked to explain how an offence was committed if it was not them, and invited to comment on the veracity of contradictory evidence.

> Suspect: It wasn't me. I have witnesses.
> Officer: So do we, your son. Or is he a liar?
> Suspect: He's not a liar.

False claims as to the existence of incriminating evidence were also made in an attempt to elicit the co-operation of the suspect's family. In a suspected stabbing in area C, the suspect was returned to the cells and the *parquet* ordered that he be brought before her the following morning. Despite this, the officer phoned the suspect's wife and (falsely) told her that her husband had confessed and all that was required was for her to bring down the knife and he could then go home with her! If not, he explained, the police would not be able to release him and their house would have to be turned upside down in a search for the knife. All this was untrue and in any event, beyond the power of the officer.[48] In another case, in area E, the suspect was being held on suspicion of indecently assaulting a woman on the train. The victim had given a clear description of the clothes worn by her assailant, but there was no other evidence to go on. The police were unable to search the suspect's house to see if he owned clothes fitting the description, as he refused to give his permission. His wife was therefore called in to give a statement. She stated that he did not own any clothes of that description and the witness must have been mistaken in identifying her husband. The police then implied the existence of other evidence which did not in fact exist: 'The camera never lies, *Madame*. There are cameras on the train.'

---

[48] The wife was unable to produce any such knife, despite these threats.

Such tactics were not uncommon and whilst deceiving the suspect (and others) as to the evidence against her has clear implications for the reliability of any evidence produced as a result, it was considered a legitimate investigative tool. Thus, for the police, as for the *magistrat*, the provision of additional safeguards (most notably the presence of a defence lawyer) was resisted because of its potential to expose these necessary, but concealed, practices. For example, an officer in area C explained how he had falsely claimed to have a signed statement incriminating a suspect in order to make him confess:

> If a lawyer had been there I couldn't have done that, 'playing' with non-existent admissions. But you have to do that, to get to the truth. We don't have many resources. And the people who are here are not honest, are not responsible people. They wouldn't be at the police station if there wasn't some evidence against them . . . We just want to get to the truth.

And an officer in area D expressed the same concern:

> No, that's no good. You have to leave the police to do their job . . . If you think the guy did it, you try and get him to talk. You use blackmail, put the pressure on—it's not very moral, but they haven't got any morals either. If there was a witness, we certainly couldn't do that . . . In short, we need to be left to do our job, because these are not angels we are dealing with.

In questioning the suspect, the police were generally interested in one thing only—obtaining an admission.[49] The absence of evidence against the accused did not diminish this objective and was generally the reason why psychological and physical tactics were employed (Zauberman, 1997:344). The state of the suspect and whether or not she was fit to be interviewed was of little concern.[50] Indeed, in some cases, the police actively sought to increase the anxiety or discomfort of suspects: blankets were refused to those held in the cells, or cigarettes to those being interviewed, in an attempt to break their resolve.[51] In other instances, the suspect was clearly in no fit state to questioned. For example, we observed some who were experiencing drug withdrawal; others who were extremely tired and unable to concentrate, one of whom actually fell asleep during the interview; and another who was so removed from what was happening around him that he soiled himself during questioning. In the absence of any judge or defence lawyer to ensure that procedures are respected and to safeguard the interests of the suspect, these

---

[49] See also Lévy (1987). Zauberman (1997:345) describes the importance of the confession to the professional identity of the *gendarme*; in the context of the interrogation, it is a kind of ritual submission by the suspect, a recognition of her defeat and for the *gendarme*, a victory of her police intelligence.

[50] See also the descriptions of those suspects seen by the *procureur* at the police station, described in Ch 5.

[51] The tactic of causing the suspect physical discomfort was also observed by Zauberman (1997:343–44)

events remained hidden, having no place in the dry and detached statements constructed by the police.

Investigations Under *Commission Rogatoire*

Where cases are investigated under the delegated authority of the *juge d'instruction*, that is, through a *commission rogatoire*, the GAV tends to occupy a different place within the enquiry. If an *information* has been opened, the case is, by definition more serious and/or complex than those which pass through GAV before being dealt with by the *procureur*. By the time a witness or a suspect is brought in for questioning, officers have already prepared the ground, collecting statements, expert evidence and transcripts of telephone taps. In area D, we spent some time with the *brigade criminelle*, the serious crime division, which was made up of more senior and experienced officers. They investigated between 10 and 12 cases per year, each case lasting around four to six months. Suitable cases, typically homicides, were often identified early on and passed to this division in order that they could investigate *en flagrance* with the advantages of being able to conduct searches, detain and question the suspect on their own initiative, retaining the element of surprise and so making a greater impact. Having an early input without the constraints of the *instruction* (during which only the *juge d'instruction* may question the suspect) was considered valuable. An *information* would then be opened and a *commission rogatoire* passed to them by the *juge d'instruction* through the senior officer in charge, the *commissaire*.

As described in the preceding chapter, the police–*magistrat* relationship is characterised by trust and confidence, rather than hierarchy and surveillance. This is especially the case with the *juge d'instruction* who has a closer and more prolonged involvement with the investigating officers. Thus, whilst acknowledging that the *juge* directs the investigation, officers were clear that this was a collegial enterprise.

> We suggest the path to take, we find the openings to follow. We keep him informed. The *juge* is the director of the enquiry, but we organise it and have very close contact with the *juge*. You have to win his confidence and convince him . . . we discuss the dossier with him . . . it is not a question of permission, it is a question of trust. [Police officer, area D]

There was a sense in which each knew the permissible boundaries, making working in this way both possible and effective.

> We keep him informed rather than asking him. Normally, he would not refuse us permission. We never ask for impossible things. We know perfectly well what he can do and what he cannot do. [Police officer, area D]

Just as the police regret the absence of the *procureur*, officers were clear that they would like the *juge d'instruction* to be present during more of their work. This was not about the need for reassurance or verification, but gaining a better understanding of and insight into their work.

> Ten years ago, the *juge d'instruction* and the *procureur* would come regularly on site for a murder or a serious wounding. But not anymore, it is impossible, there is too much work . . . If [the *juge d'instruction*] travelled out more, that would be better, he would have a better view of things, it would be easier for him to understand our work on that particular dossier. [Police officer, area D]

Officers described to us what, for them, made a good or a bad *juge d'instruction*:

> A bad judge is hesitant and over-sensitive. He hesitates, he verifies everything. He blames everything on the *code* and never takes any risk, even when it is a matter of urgency. He does not have enough confidence in us, he doesn't know his job. A good judge understands fast, you can discuss things with him, he listens and gives his opinion. He makes good decisions quickly, he knows his *code* and he knows his job. He has confidence in us, trust develops. He makes decisions which are good for our work, which help us and enable us to work. [Police officer, area D]

Recognising the importance of keeping the *juge d'instruction* well informed, officers did not resent being questioned or challenged. When an officer telephoned the *juge d'instruction* in area A, for example, asking if he could release the suspect's wife as she was very ill, the *juge d'instruction* was concerned to ensure that this was absolutely necessary and wanted detailed answers to his questions. Finally, he agreed, telling the officer: 'OK, go on, I will trust you on this.' The researcher commented to the officer that it had been difficult to persuade the *juge d'instruction* to agree, to which the officer replied: 'Oh no, that is quite understandable. [The *juge d'instruction*] sees this from a distance, it is important that he is fully informed.'

The way in which officers approached the interrogation within a major enquiry and under *commission rogatoire* was very different from the general staple of cases which pass through GAV. The timing of the arrest is usually agreed with the *juge d'instruction* and the interrogation process is often a more subtle game of cat and mouse, the police having gathered quality evidence and information over a period of time. In a case of procuring and imprisoning women for the purpose of prostitution, the *brigade criminelle* interviewed a man described as a 'professional criminal' from one of the old criminal families in region D.[52] The suspect was treated politely throughout and addressed in the polite form, '*vous*'. He in turn

---

[52] See also the case described by Zauberman (1997:344) in which police and suspect enjoy a more complicit relationship, in contrast to the conflict that tends to characterise the relationship with more 'ordinary' suspects.

was amenable to the officers' demands—presenting his wrists for handcuffing without having to be asked, for example, and consenting to the search of his home. Each understood the other's role:

> Suspect: I have come, I will explain; you understand me, I will provide an explanation, that's all. I will tell you what I can, agreed, but take note, that is all. I cannot tell you things which I do not know, as you well know. I am careful. I do not want to be had, understood?
>
> Officer: And you know that I am doing my job as a cop. We are not here just to annoy you, we have better things to do. I have no choice—if I did not do this, I would not be doing my job properly. You are here to answer. We ask you questions and you reply. At the end, you know we will get to the truth.

Officers went through the motions of interviewing him, allowing him to give his responses for the record, finding out nothing they did not already know. A search of his home was then conducted, more for the psychological impact than because they believed they would find anything useful. The interrogation which followed was less general, moving up a gear to more precise questions, closely tied to the evidence the police had acquired from a telephone tap and designed to box the suspect further into a corner. This was conducted by one principal officer, with contributions from several other officers during the course of the day. By the end of the afternoon, he maintained his version of events and refused to provide any more detail to explain either the content or the context of the telephone calls. The police calmly retained the upper hand, telling him, as they pointed to the transcript of the telephone tap:

> If we cannot clear up what is in here, we will be obliged to keep you in this evening. As you can see, this is you in here. We are agreed on that, but it is not over . . . the *juge d'instruction* has asked for this, the evidence is here in the tapes, there is nothing I can do about it. I have to keep you in tonight, and until we get an answer from another witness . . . when we show the statement to the *juge* he may ask for a remand in custody until everything is checked out. He might ask for a confrontation in his office and that takes time. It's a remand in custody for sure . . . You understand the reason why you are here now.

Whilst many of the basic interrogation tactics were the same as those employed during the ordinary GAV, the process of case construction was more easily observed during the *instruction*, as detention formed part of a longer term strategy of evidence gathering. Where a clear suspect[53] had yet to be identified and officers were investigating under *commission rogatoire*, several people might be

---

[53] Once there is sufficient evidence against a person to make them the official suspect in the *instruction*, they become *mis en examen*. It is at this point that the police may no longer question the individual; only the *juge d'instruction* may do so.

placed in GAV in order to assemble as much evidence as possible. For example, officers in area E were investigating a fraud, involving stolen cheques and a number of false documents. Three weeks into their investigation, with little evidence against their principal suspect and already approaching the end of their second *commission rogatoire* for the enquiry, officers were keen to press those involved at the margins of the case for firm evidence against their suspect. A man, Jean, who was suspected of being connected with the principal suspect, François, was arrested, had his home searched and was placed in GAV. His interrogators attempted to obtain information incriminating François, but Jean resisted providing precise facts and details, or adopting the police version of events.

OPJ: [making a note of the interview] I knew that François was a fraudster.

Jean: No, not a fraudster, a nasty piece of work.

OPJ: So, a fraudster—it's not as if he's robbed a bank.

Jean: So put nasty piece of work.

OPJ: So, fraudster.

Jean: No, I did not say that.

[Later]

OPJ: I am convinced that he fiddled the amount—is that OK for you?

Jean: No, not convinced, that's a bit strong.

OPJ: Almost convinced.

Jean: Yes, that's OK.

Jean claimed that his girlfriend had stored stolen items for François in the past, when she had been François' girlfriend. The police wished to contact her in order to verify parts of Jean's story,[54] but also to put additional pressure on both of them.

OPJ: Stop this bullshit. You know what? We're going to bring your girlfriend in, eh? And if your stories don't match, we will arrange a confrontation, you and her, and then you will have to explain yourself. Right, listen, I will read all this back to you. [Jean queries some minor details]. Are you frightened that we're going to stitch you up? . . . Why would you want us to do that? That would do us no good. Here you are—sign here and on the back.

[Jean begins reading]

OPJ: There is no point in you reading it.

Jean: Yes, there is. [He reads and then signs]. Can I ask you something? What will happen if you cannot collar her?

OPJ: That's serious, very serious.

---

[54] Researcher: What will you do with him? Will you have to extend the GAV?

   OPJ: I don't know yet. Maybe not. He is not the main suspect, but he might have lied. We need to have the girl. She might give us something completely different—we'll see.

The police telephoned the girlfriend and informed her that she was required to come to the station for questioning. We were told that it was imperative that she come that evening, in order that she could be questioned and any confrontation staged before 10am the following day, the end of Jean's GAV period. In fact, the officers then telephoned the *juge d'instruction* to inform him that Jean was in GAV and he was then bailed to return the next morning, in case a confrontation was required. When the girlfriend arrived at nearly 8pm, the police decided to keep her in overnight, to make her 'stew' a little and to postpone the 'official' formal questioning until the morning. In fact, they began the psychological process of interrogation immediately. She was surrounded by four OPJ, who began interrogating her in rapid succession, from all directions. The suspect became frightened, then angry and then began crying. Unsurprisingly, she appeared intimidated and confused, unable to answer properly.

> OPJ: Make sure you think this over well tonight. You will have all the time you need. Nonsense will get you nowhere.

Her distress was further added to when the officers explained the reason for her detention and she attempted to ask that she be allowed to visit the toilet. They told her to take off her bag and jewellery and that she would be searched on arrival at the central police station. She continued to insist on visiting the toilet and increasingly embarrassed, explained that this was her 'time of the month' and that she required a sanitary towel. She began to read the form setting out her rights:

> OPJ: You can have a lawyer after 20 hours, but you probably won't need it. You'll be out before then. Just sign here. There's no point reading it, you won't understand any of it.

The next morning, she was brought over from the central station and her formal statement was taken. The officer began very gently, addressing her politely as '*vous*':

> OPJ: Oh, that's nice, they let you keep your glasses. That's good of them. You're short-sighted like me.

He then set out the case and her former boyfriend, François' role in it, emphasising that she was simply used by him. His tactic was to emphasise the deviance of François, whilst himself remaining calm and matter of fact. In this way, her emotions were roused and her incrimination of François became almost cathartic

> Suspect: That's not possible, he still loves me. [She starts to cry].
> OPJ: Come on now, you need to be adult about this. You must not be naïve like that. François has used and manipulated everybody. [She continues crying for another five minutes]. So, you are still in love with him.

Suspect: Don't put that. I don't want Jean to read it.
OPJ: We'll put 'in the past' then.
Suspect: OK.

He continued to lend her a sympathetic ear ('You panicked', 'You are a little naïve') and she explained how her ex-boyfriend asked her to store things in her cellar for him.

OPJ: This last sentence, 'I feel very foolish', is it true or false?
Suspect: It's true. [She then adds, 'He uses other people. He is a manipulator.']

Her account supported that of her boyfriend, Jean, and also that of the police's case against François as a fraud and a trickster.

The usual tactics were also observed in a case in area C which involved trafficking stolen cars and producing false documents in order that they could be sold on. After the suspect's home and garage had been searched and evidence discovered relating to the production of fraudulent documents, his wife and 5-year-old daughter were taken to the police station for questioning. The wife denied any knowledge of her husband's wrongdoing, asserting that she believed him to be in the building trade and that his Mercedes car had been lent to him. When confronted with the fact that material for the production of false documents had been found in their garage, she denied any knowledge of what was there: 'To find anything in that garage, you have to search.' The two interviewing officers continued:

Do not treat the *juge* like an idiot. Your house is loaded with cash. There were telephone calls and people can talk. If you know something, show your honesty . . . You are intelligent, you must have known that he was up to no good . . . If you carry on like this, you're going in *garde à vue*. You're a gangster's girl. We've got enough to lock him up for a long time, for years.

There was nothing to link her with the activities of her husband and the police were obliged to release her, despite her refusal to implicate anybody.

Whilst the interrogation tactics of the police differ according to the stage in the enquiry at which the person is placed in GAV, the ways in which suspects and witnesses are questioned by officers in all instances is relatively insulated from external scrutiny. Without the presence of a tape recorder, a supervising *magistrat*, or a defence lawyer, the strategies and tactics of the police go unobserved and the officer's written record provides the sole account of the interview evidence produced. Our own observations, together with recent miscarriages of justice and cases of false confessions, demonstrate the inherent dangers of this arrangement and the vulnerability of those detained in GAV. Although judicial responsibility for the conduct of criminal investigations is considered an important assurance of the cogency and reliability of the evidence ultimately presented by the prosecution in court, in practice, it is unable to provide any guarantee as to the method of obtaining and therefore the reliability of this evidence. Just as in England and Wales, the prosecution case runs the risk of representing a police construction in which the evidence is trimmed to fit the case, but unlike England and Wales, there is little provision for the defence to interrogate this process or to counter the prosecution case directly.

7

Instruction and Prosecution

The Instruction

The *instruction* represents the paradigm model of investigation within French inquisitorial procedure, although in practice less than 5 per cent of cases are dealt with in this way.[1] The *juge d'instruction* (JI) is empowered to undertake any lawful investigation that she considers will assist in the discovery of the truth (art 81 CPP) and, as a *juge du siège*, she is not subject to the same hierarchical control as the *procureur* who, ultimately, is answerable to the Minister of Justice. In practice, however, the *procureur* remains implicated in all stages of the *instruction* and whilst her presence in the investigation is generally welcomed, on occasions, it also represents a point of tension. Recent reforms have diminished further the role of the JI and have altered the distribution of roles and responsibilities between the various legal actors. The placement of those under investigation (the *mis en examen*,[2] MEE) into detention (*détention provisoire*) during the *instruction* is now the responsibility of the *juge des libertés et de la détention provisoire* (JLD); the police may continue to investigate a case *en flagrance* under the supervision of the *procureur* for up to 15 days and enjoy wider powers in this; and the defence and the *partie civile* now have the same right as the *procureur* to request the JI to carry out any act of investigation that they consider will help in the discovery of the truth.

Opening an *Information*

The opening of an *information*[3] in order that the JI can investigate the case is obligatory for the most serious offences, *crimes*, and discretionary for *délits* and

---

[1] Calculated as a percentage of cases proceeded with by the *procureur*, 35,202 cases out of 984,699 were sent to the *juge d'instruction* (around 3.5%) in 2003. Of the 1,386,500 cases where proceedings could have been taken (ie there is a suspect or the *procureur* thinks that an offence has been committed), 387,013 were discontinued and 14,788 were dealt with by *composition pénale*.

[2] The suspect in the enquiry becomes the *mis en examen* once an *instruction* has been opened.

[3] This refers to the formal procedure whereby the investigation is passed to the *juge d'instruction*.

contraventions (art 79 CPP).[4] The extensive powers available to the JI during the 'search for the truth' have led some commentators to describe the JI as 'the most powerful man in France'. Whilst it is undoubtedly true that the CPP authorises the JI to conduct a much wider range of investigative acts than the *procureur*,[5] and that as a *juge du siège* she enjoys a greater degree of hierarchical independence than the *parquet*, the role of the JI can also be constrained in significant ways by her dependence upon the *procureur*. As one *procureur* in area D told us:

> People say that the *juge d'instruction* is the most powerful man in France, but for [the parquet] that is a joke, because we know that we control much of what he does . . . the parquet is really at the heart of criminal investigations.

The JI is not empowered to begin an investigation upon her own initiative; the authority to refer cases for investigation to the JI rests with the *procureur*.[6] This applies even once an *instruction* has commenced: if during the course of an enquiry the JI uncovers evidence relating to a separate offence, this may not be investigated under the existing *instruction*. Instead, the matter is referred back to the *parquet*, who must open a separate or supplementary *information* in order that evidence relating to the second offence may be investigated. In most instances, this procedure is unproblematic; the JI and *procureur* continue to work together and generally agree on the types of cases that will be investigated through *instruction* and whether investigations should be joined together.[7] In some instances however, particularly those involving high-profile and politically sensitive cases, JIs have accused the *parquet* of succumbing to political pressure to stymie investigations.[8] Breen (2003:50–51) describes the principal ways in which this might occur: the *procureur* may choose a particular JI, the investigation might be delayed in order to keep it within the jurisdiction of the police and the *parquet*, or it may be divided between different jurisdictional competences preventing the JI from having overall control of different strands of the case. This discretion is part of the pivotal role played by the *procureur* in regulating the overall flow and destination of criminal cases, described above in Chapters 3 and 5 and in this chapter. She is responsible for the supervision of the initial police

---

[4] In 2003, 34,839 cases (concerning 47,370 people *mis en examen*) were dealt with by the *juge d'instruction*. Of these, 7,945 were *crimes*; 26,779 were *délits*; 12 were *contraventions* and 103 were investigations into the cause of death. (From *Les chiffres-clés de la justice* published by the Ministry of Justice 2004).

[5] This gap is narrowing, especially with the introduction of the JLD in 2000 and the wider powers provided to the police to investigate *en flagrance* in 2004. See further the discussion of these reforms in Ch 2.

[6] The victim may also invoke the *instruction* procedure directly by constituting herself as *partie civile* in the case. This is less usual in ordinary cases, but see the comments of *magistrats* concerning the growing number of cases initiated by the *partie civile* in the specialist fraud section (the *pôle financier*) in Paris and in cases of medical responsibility (Greilsamer and Schneidermann 2002, especially pp 28, 299, 359, 445–46). See also Pin (2002).

[7] The high-profile *juge d'instruction*, Eva Joly, commented on the importance of retaining the involvement of the same *procureur* throughout the investigation and the prosecution, as she will know the case best and has invested in its success. (Greilsamer and Scheidermann, 2002:109–10).

[8] See eg Halphen (2002).

enquiry, for the framing of any charges against the suspect,[9] for determining whether or not the case should proceed to some form of trial or alternative to trial, for determining in which level of court the case will be heard, for deciding whether an *information* should be opened, and if so, when (and on what basis) this will take place.

Whilst this is an important potential constraint upon the conduct of an enquiry, in most cases that we observed the relationship between the JI and the *procureur* was characterised by co-operation rather than conflict and the JI was able to conduct a very broadly defined investigation. For example, in a case in area C, three men were suspected of dealing in heroin and had been arrested nine months previously. The evidence against them was not that of a large scale operation: Twelve grams of heroin, a set of scales, a knife, some small bags and £690. Yet, telephone taps had been used extensively and there seemed to be a whole other investigation taking place. When asked how such large scale enquiries related to a seemingly minor drugs case, the JI replied:

> Yes, the two people we really want are the main suppliers. One is called Baptiste and sells on the beach and the other is on holiday in Morocco, so we will wait and get them. [The researcher asks whether they know that they are being investigated, given the other arrests]. No—well one may do. We checked the other day and Baptiste is still on the beach selling heroin with the chips.

Other than the mandatory opening of an *information* in the most serious cases, *instruction* was preferred in investigations that were considered complex or very serious (and so required the use of powers available only to the JI) or which could not be completed within the time limit of GAV—where, for example, there was a suspect still at large[10] or the *procureur* wanted the MEE placed in custody while enquiries continued. In this way, the extended powers of the JI (especially in relation to the use of telephone taps) and her ability to place suspects in custody were key determinants in the *procureur*'s exercise of her discretion to open an *information*. The net effect of the establishment of the JLD on the one hand, and the increased powers afforded the police under the 2004 legislation on the other, is therefore likely to be a further decline in the role of the *instruction* as a mode of criminal investigation.

A third and very important factor in determining whether or not to open an *information* is that of resources. The number of JIs has failed to keep pace with increases in the number of crimes reported and investigated, with the result that a smaller proportion are now referred to the JI and, of those that are, the actual investigation is carried out by the police through delegated powers for the most

---

[9] Framing the offence as a *délit*, for example, avoids the need for an *instruction*. As discussed below, this may be considered desirable from the perspective of resource efficiency or in order to continue the investigation without the scrutiny of the defence lawyer.

[10] In 2003, one-third of the *informations* opened did not have a named suspect.

part.[11] In the sites we observed, around 100 cases was considered the upper limit that a JI could reasonably be expected to be supervising at any one time and *procureurs* were careful not to overburden the JI, as this would result in cases being slowed down to an unacceptable degree. This had an almost paralysing effect in smaller regions. In site F, for example, there was only one *juge d'instruction*, who already had some 100 cases, making the *parquet* reluctant to open an *information* unless absolutely necessary. Alternatives (such as *comparution immédiate*) were considered where possible. In site D, a large urban area, opening an *information* was avoided by the systematic downgrading of offences: serious drugs cases, for example, were routinely 'correctionalised' from the more serious *crime* to the less serious *délit*, allowing them to be tried in the *tribunal correctionnel* rather than the *cour d'assises*:

> There are grand declarations of intention—in the law, the circulars, but in the end it is always the problem of resources. Last week I had four cases of organised crime concerning the importation of heroin. But here, we have never tried drugs trafficking as a *crime*. It's mad! [D3]

Many *procureurs* were unhappy about this resource driven constraint, believing that it contradicted the way in which they had been prepared through their vocational training for their post as *magistrat* and undermined their ability to carry out their job as they would wish:

> *Researcher*: What are the most important things that you have learned since joining the *parquet*?
> *Procureur*: The huge quantity of work. I was not prepared for that. For example, as a student I would have assumed that if a man rapes his daughter at knife point, you would open an *information*. But it will be charged as sexual abuse so that it can be tried in the *tribunal correctionnel*. That, I will not hide from you, shocked me. If at all possible, we try not to open an *information* because the *juge d'instruction* is already overburdened with work and on average it takes a year to complete. I've learned a lot here. We cannot be purists and go by the letter of the law. [Site D]

Although formal responsibility for the *instruction* rests with the JI, she is authorised to delegate much of her investigatory power to the police through the use of the *commission rogatoire*. Under this procedure, named police officers are authorised to conduct specific enquiries within a specified time frame, before then reporting back to the JI. In practice, the majority of the investigation is carried out by the police through this mechanism, the JI conducting personally only those acts of investigation that the law prevents her from delegating—principally the questioning of the MEE. Thus, the *instruction* becomes an important mechanism

---

[11] For figures on the decline of the role of the *juge d'instruction* since 1830, see Lévy (1993).

through which police powers can be extended.[12] As a consequence, the impetus for opening an *information* comes directly from the police in some instances, in order that they can continue an investigation with the wider powers which might be delegated to them under the *instruction* procedure. This may be done in writing, allowing the *procureur* to review the progress of the current investigation before passing the case to the JI and arranging for a *commission rogatoire* to be issued as requested. We saw many examples of such requests on the JI's files. On other occasions, the police simply telephoned the *procureur* with their request, an *information* was opened and officers called by later the same day to collect the *commission rogatoire* authorising them to, for example, set up a telephone tap. In some instances the opening of an *information* was delayed for a short time, pending the outcome of current investigations, but rarely was such a request refused outright. In this way, delegation operated as a function of a police-dominated investigation, dictated not by the JI's assessment of the enquiry, but by that of the police.

Where a case has been identified as one that will be investigated through the *instruction* procedure, the *procureur* would frequently seek to retain the case for as long as possible before opening an *information*. There were several reasons for this. Firstly, it enabled the *procureur* to shape the investigation towards her desired result. This might entail guiding the police to construct the case towards a particular (more serious) offence,[13] or priming the suspect by using the threat of a remand in custody to elicit information. In most areas, the *procureur's* retention of the case was not considered problematic, but in some it was a slight point of tension. In site C, for example, *procureurs* considered that they had a better knowledge of and closer working relationship with officers and so were better able to ensure investigations of a consistent quality, rather than being dependent upon the personality of the JI. A number of JIs in site C, however, expressed concern that they had not been involved in the enquiry from the outset and that the quality of evidence gathered was deficient as a result. The second (and related) reason for the *procureur* retaining the case was that it enabled the suspect to be questioned by the police under the more coercive regime of the *garde à vue* (GAV), avoiding the delays and the safeguards of the *instruction*.[14] Once an *information* has been opened, the suspect becomes the MEE and may only be questioned by the JI. The defence lawyer also has access to the case dossier and may be present during any interrogation of her client. The police-dominated environment of the GAV is therefore considered more likely to elicit a confession from the suspect.

---

[12] The reform of 2004 makes some of these powers (notably the use of telephone taps) available without the need to open an *information*. See further the discussion in Ch 2.

[13] See, eg, the case described above in Ch 5 in relation to the 'hands-on model' typology of supervision, where the *procureur* was at pains to ensure that the dossier contained evidence of fraud, rather than simple theft. *Procureurs* preferred to open an *information* with the most serious offence that the facts could plausibly sustain, as it was easier to downgrade rather than upgrade charges later.

[14] See also Ch 4 for a discussion of the relatively enhanced defence rights enjoyed during *instruction*.

One *procureur* explained to us that this was the reason that cases were kept out of *instruction* for the maximum period during which they could still be investigated '*en flagrance*'[15]:

> That way, the police still enjoy wide powers and we can carry out the investigation . . . we want to get the culprit . . . The *juge d'instruction* is not going to interview the suspect three or four times, sit across the table from him and say 'Are you going to admit this?' The police station is a hostile environment. It's unpleasant and the police will use more pressure. And that does not make it unlawful—sometimes you need some pressure. [D3]

Another *procureur* in site D explained why he was delaying the opening of an *information*:

> Once you open an *information* the police cannot question the suspect. Everything has to be done with formal judicial questioning, with lawyers present etc. This way they can move more freely—like this drugs case. If I had made it part of the *instruction* it would have taken months to get anything. Instead, the police could question, search and get all of the information more easily.

Interestingly, the JI employed her own tactics in order to delay the formal point at which a suspect becomes a MEE.

> With everyone kept in *garde à vue*, the police must inform the *juge d'instruction* or the *parquet* immediately. Before, they waited ten or twenty hours . . . But I have a nice way of getting around that if I have a suspicion, but not really enough. I ask them to come in as a witness—anyone can be a witness, even me! I pretend to be stupid and ask questions. They come and go as they please and **then** if I have the evidence and I am sure, I put them in *garde à vue*. [*Juge d'instruction*, area C] [original emphasis][16]

The Use of Pre-Trial Custody

Until the creation of the JLD under the June 2000 reform, the JI determined whether or not the MEE remained on bail or was kept in custody (*détention provisoire*) during the course of the *instruction*. As discussed at several points in the preceding chapters, this power had long been the subject of criticism on the

---

[15]　At that point between 5 and 8 days, later extended to 15 days under the 2004 reform.

[16]　Although art 105 CPP makes it clear that those against whom there is firm evidence of having been involved in the offence being investigated by the JI may not be questioned as witnesses, it is for the JI to determine the sufficiency of evidence. In this way, questioning a person as a witness and then making them MEE once the facts are established has been held to be in conformity with art 105 CPP. See Garé and Ginestet (2002:287–88).

grounds that the independence of the JI's judicial role in determining pre-trial custody was compromised by her investigative function in the case. The JI is empowered to grant bail, but if there is an application to detain the MEE in custody, this decision must now be made by the JLD. Although no longer enjoying the same powers in this respect, the way in which these custody decisions were made by the JI illustrates something of her professional ideology and the nature of the *procureur*–JI relationship.

In order to respect the principle of *contradictoire* and to ensure equality of arms, the JI was first required to hear arguments from the *procureur* and from the defence lawyer before placing the MEE in custody. In nearly all instances that we observed, however, this hearing was a mere formality, the outcome having already been decided beforehand. The JI and *procureur* usually discussed the case earlier and the nature of either the offence or the offender made detention, in their view, inevitable.[17] The shared professional status of the *procureur* and the JI as *magistrats*, together with their physical proximity working within the same building, meant that the *procureur* had the ear of the JI in a way that the defence lawyer never could.[18] Once the reasons for the detention were agreed, even the most cogent defence arguments were unlikely to persuade the JI to decide otherwise. The bail 'hearing' served simply as a formality, a means of demonstrating compliance with defence rights and the apparent independence of the decision to detain.[19] The extent to which this was the case was demonstrated on one of the only occasions when we witnessed the JI come to a different decision once both parties had been heard.[20] Having already completed the paperwork for detention (as was the usual practice), the *juge's* legal secretary was then placed in the embarrassing position of having rapidly to reformat the papers for conditional bail. A similar hearing was required before each periodic review of detention, but these

---

[17] The fact that the *procureur* met with the JLD before the custody hearing did not undermine the principle of *contradictoire* according to a recent *Cour de cassation* decision (9 July 2003) discussed by Mayer (2004).

[18] We frequently observed *procureurs* and JIs coming into one another's offices to discuss ongoing cases, or to get updates on new ones. This is, of course, quite understandable given that the *procureur* has dealt with the case in the first instance and will be prosecuting it in court. What is problematic is the theoretical and procedural construction of the JI as a neutral investigator, with the *procureur* supposedly receding into the background to the position of being one of the 'parties' contributing to the enquiry alongside the defence and the victim. This is wholly unrealistic. The *procureur* will always remain in a separate and privileged position and it would require a huge legal cultural shift to alter this.

[19] The *procureur*, of course, distanced herself from the JI's decision when dealing with the suspect. This strategy of apparently passing the issue to a third party to decide, when in fact the decision had effectively already been taken by the JI and *procureur*, was similar to the ambush strategy used by solicitors and barristers in England and Wales. In such instances, where the defendant was unwilling to countenance a guilty plea, the solicitor would suggest taking counsel's advice as a form of expert second opinion. This 'advice' was, of course, agreed beforehand between counsel and the instructing solicitor. See McConville *et al* (1994:252–54).

[20] Interestingly, the decision was made by a trainee JI.

also had no real effect on the (predetermined) outcome. Their main function was in requiring the JI to at least review the file every four months in order to ensure that some (albeit minor) progress had been made, justifying the need to keep the MEE at the disposition of the enquiry.[21]

The way in which the JI and *procureur* approached the issue of detention was not based upon adherence to the presumption of innocence, but upon a set of shared assumptions concerning the presumed guilt of most MEE.

> In actual fact, we do not lock up innocents.[22] When they come to the *instruction*, the evidence is generally already well established by the police enquiry and my job is to supplement this by researching and verifying the facts—using telephone taps or experts. I can assure you that it does not amuse us to lock people up. We try to avoid doing so, but it is not always possible. [*Juge d'instruction*, Area F]

The guilt or innocence of the accused was central to any discussion by the JI and the *procureur* about whether or not to detain a person, and in the minority of cases where the MEE's liability was in doubt, even if the offence was a serious one, there was a much stronger presumption in favour of bail. For example, in one case in area F involving allegations that the MEE had indecently assaulted his children, the JI came to speak to the *procureur* about revoking bail, as the MEE had repeatedly breached some of the conditions. The *procureur*, however, (who knew the accused from previous dealings) was unwilling to agree to this as he was unsure as to whether or not the MEE was guilty.

> *Juge d'instruction*: He is taking the mickey here. He has been warned and he is just not taking any notice. There are two small children involved and the mother is not very reliable, so we should not take that risk—it is very annoying.
> *Procureur*: But we do not have any clear proof and I just do not get the feeling that he is guilty. He is the wrong type of guy.
> [Rather than put the *juge d'instruction* in an awkward position, they agree to go to one of the *substituts* who undoubtedly will not oppose detention.]

There was also an awareness of the impact that the pre-trial investigation would have upon the treatment of the case at trial.[23] Placing the MEE in custody was part of an embedded message to the trial court indicating the guilt of the accused. *Procureurs* and JIs frequently told us that to release the (presumed guilty) MEE on

---

[21] We did hear of one case where, in the course of staff changes, the JI had forgotten to ensure that some investigative act had been undertaken in the four month period and so the MEE was released.

[22] The same *juge d'instruction* qualified this later by saying: 'I have never placed someone who is factually innocent in *détention provisoire*—only someone who is procedurally innocent.'

[23] The more able defence lawyers were also aware of the way in which the file would be treated by the trial court and understood that information appearing to come from the JI, rather than the defence lawyer, would be treated more favourably. See Ch 4.

bail risked sending the wrong signal, indicating that the case was not sufficiently serious or that the guilt of the accused was in doubt. As a result, in many of the more serious cases, there was a clear presumption against bail. A JI in area B explained that of his 90 dossiers:

> I currently have nine people in detention, of which six are for rape and incest. You cannot bail somebody who has repeatedly raped his daughter. You cannot. Perhaps this is a system which appears severe. It is true that the individual is important, but there is also something else that is important: the values on which social cohesion is based. [B1]

In a case in area A, a man was accused of raping his 18-year-old step-daughter and the *procureur* asked for him to be placed in *détention provisoire*. The JI agreed: 'Yes, because if he does not go into detention, the whole thing will fall and then he will be let off.' The girl's mother supported the step-father and her sister had seen nothing, but there was a previous history of sexual abuse on the part of the girl's father and brother and although there was no evidence to corroborate the girl's account, both *procureur* and JI assumed the MEE to be guilty. They considered their strategy together and agreed that although the girl had now been housed away from the family and there was no risk that the MEE would flee, detention was necessary because there was still some doubt as to who was telling the truth. In addition, the case was extremely serious with the possibility of a 20 year sentence on conviction; if the MEE was bailed, the courts would not take the case seriously; there was still witness and expert evidence to gather; and finally, if the MEE was in detention, it was considered more likely that witnesses would talk and information would be obtained bringing them closer to the truth.

> JI: If we do find something, this will have to go to the *assises*. It is too serious.
> *Procureur*: Yes, I know.
> JI: If we hold the MEE, maybe the mother will talk—that would solve the problem.

Despite the cogent arguments of defence counsel addressing all of the prosecution's objections to bail, in the end, the gravity of the offence was the primary factor determining detention. As the JI told the MEE: 'Other people who know about the facts would not understand if I let you out.'[24]

---

[24] This relates to the controversial ground on which bail can be refused under Art 144 CPP—where it is the only means '*De mettre fin à un trouble exceptionnel et persistant à l'ordre public provoqué par la gravité de l'infraction, les circonstances de sa commission ou l'importance du préjudice qu'elle a causé*'. This was a common ground for refusing bail. The same JI told another MEE (charged with two street robberies and with previous convictions for the same) who was placed in detention on *ordre public* grounds: 'Given the seriousness of the offence, people would not understand if you were to be released.' See also Delmas-Marty (1991:282–87) for the views of various legal actors on the subject of *détention provisoire*.

The recent Outreau case (2004) demonstrates the dangers of this approach, even with the more recent JLD procedure. Six out of the seven defendants acquitted of child sex abuse charges had spent nearly three years in custody during the investigation on the basis of allegations that were withdrawn at trial. There was very little evidence against the seven and there was serious concern that the *juge d'instruction* and the psychology experts had acted to construct a case against the accused, rather than to investigate exculpatory as well as incriminating evidence. A working party was established in response to the dysfunctions revealed in the case and although rejecting the suggestion of custody decisions being made by a bench of judges,[25] they recommended that anybody who had been in custody for six months should have an automatic right to have the case examined by the *chambre d'instruction*.[26]

As in the previous example, detention was also used as a means of getting the MEE or other witnesses to provide information.

> Let us not pretend otherwise, the *garde à vue* and *détention provisoire* are means of putting pressure on and obviously, we use them for that—it is [sic] one of our tools. The *garde à vue* is particularly effective, it forces the suspect to take stock. [*Juge d'instruction*, Area F]

In some instances, the suspect was not explicitly made aware of this. A suspect in area A was brought in by the police under a *commission rogatoire*, but refused to speak. The JI therefore decided to place him in detention. The *procureur* involved in the case told us: 'The JI will lock a person up if he denies the offence or refuses to confess, but is often prepared to let him out if he does then talk or confess.' The JI later commented: 'Too bad for him. He just needs to speak, but he does not know that I would release him if he would only talk . . . if only he realised.' In other cases, the relationship between detention and a confession was spelled out more clearly. When asked how much pressure was permissible in order to obtain a confession, a JI in area A told us:

> Confessions are one piece of evidence among others. Obviously, it is much more convenient and lawyers like to have confessions. The confession remains the 'queen of evidence' . . . I remember a guy who was in *garde à vue* and who was going to be placed in detention . . . I was alone with him at this point. I told him, 'what matters for me is that the file is coherent and in good order so that I can make my decision. If you tell me just anything, you expose yourself to a risk.' . . . In fact he made admissions, the file was coherent and there was no need to place him in detention. I was not using detention as a threat or blackmail, but just playing straight with him, putting my cards on the table.

---

[25] This was the suggestion of two *magistrats* unions, the USM and SM.
[26] Viout (2005). They also recommended that the JLD should be a judge with some criminal experience.

I need to progress my enquiry . . . I just explained the criteria for placing someone in detention and he quickly understood. [A5]

In another case in area A, two men were held in connection with involvement in a fight during which another man had been stabbed. Both suspects refused to name the person who had inflicted the knife wound, despite the GAV having been prolonged in a further attempt to get them to talk.[27] The *procureur* decided to open an *information* in order to continue the enquiry and whilst he was aware that there were insufficient grounds for detention, he gave the accused the impression that a remand in custody was a distinct possibility unless they told him who had inflicted the wound. He had each one in to see him in turn.

> *Procureur:* Right M. Vincent. Now be careful what you say to me, think carefully before speaking. You know what is going to happen, you are going to pay, both of you, in this case. Eh, what do you want us to do? We have no choice, you understand? Think carefully while you wait to go before the *juge d'instruction*. You can always come back and see me.
> [The suspect leaves and his co-accused is brought in.]
> *Procureur:* You are an imbecile and a liar. Take note, you have two minutes to think about this and to tell me the truth. There are three possibilities. You do not know who it was; you know who it was and you do not want to say; you yourself are the guilty party. You think carefully and come back and see me if you change your mind.

The JI was then informed that the two men had been 'primed', making them believe that they ran the risk of detention and the *procureur* encouraged the JI to continue in this vein in order to maximise the chances of making them talk. In cases where bail was granted, the spectre of future detention was also referred to as a threat that could be invoked if the MEE did not co-operate. The *procureur* told one MEE in area A: 'When you speak to the judge, no nonsense, eh? I can revoke your bail if you do not toe the line.'

Judicial Questioning of the Accused

The nature of the judicial questioning of the MEE is very different from the interrogations that take place during the GAV. In contrast to the more hostile and coercive environment of the police station or the *gendarmerie*, once an *information* has been opened, the MEE is questioned by the JI in her offices in the *Palais de Justice*. The atmosphere is more that of the consulting room, the presence of the

---

[27] Although interestingly, when asked his personal opinion of the case, the investigating officer replied: 'You know, in my view, this is between criminals. They are protecting themselves, each for the other. You will never get to the bottom of it, you will never know.'

JI, her secretary and the defence lawyer maintaining a degree of reassuring formality rather than of intimidating authority. The atmosphere is more relaxed and professional, and the MEE is treated with greater respect by the JI than by her GAV interrogators. She is addressed in the polite form '*vous*' rather than the more familiar '*tu*' and care is taken to ensure the accuracy of the interview record, the MEE being given an opportunity to correct any errors before the document is printed off and signed. Whilst police officers and *gendarmes* interviewing the suspect during the GAV often spoke to her in an aggressive way, the JIs we observed were generally much more effective communicators. They were able to relate complex and detailed facts in a straightforward manner, using vocabulary that was appropriate and readily understood by the layperson. The tone of the interview was generally conversational, the JI asking questions designed to verify information already on file whilst also prompting the MEE to provide an account in her own words. As a result, the MEE is more at ease than during the GAV and this less threatening atmosphere is more conducive to the answering of questions. In several cases, suspects were very unhappy at the police station and reluctant to provide a full account, but once before the JI, they relaxed, appeared to feel more reassured and were willing to explain what they knew. When the MEE appeared to be lying, however, the tone of the encounter changed and the JI was often more forceful.[28] For example, in the following case of handling stolen furniture originating from the burglary of a mansion house in area C:

> JI: Do you know Jean Bottiau?
>
> MEE: No
>
> JI: You sold furniture that . . .
>
> MEE: [interrupting] Yes, but . . .
>
> JI: [interrupting] You provided this name I'm afraid. Have you seen this *maître*? [indicating a transcript from a telephone tap. The lawyer nods that he has.] You know not only his name, not only his address, but also his telephone number and you telephoned him and I have the cassette.
>
> MEE: I am just telling you what I told the *gendarmes*, the truth.
>
> JI: [raising his voice] I am **not** interested in what you told them. This is a separate procedure. [original emphasis].

In most instances, the lawyer was present, but as described above in Chapter 4, she played no part in the interview process. Many clearly knew little or nothing about the case and had nothing to add at the close of questioning. Some were trainees, others were representatives from the firm where the MEE had seen another lawyer and in one instance, the lawyer was simply standing in for her husband. In a

---

[28] This was precisely what many of the defendants in the Outreau (2004) case alleged also. See the comments of one of the acquitted defendants, Karine Duchaucholy, discussed below.

minority of cases, the lawyer was well briefed, had read the dossier and was able to ensure that key information was recorded in evidence.[29] For example, in a case of death by dangerous driving in area C, the MEE had initially fled the scene of the crime as he did not realise that his driving had caused a fatal accident. In giving his statement to the JI the lawyer prompted him to mention that he had not realised at first that there had been an accident and at the end of the interview, the lawyer pointed out that the MEE had said that he did not see the people standing by the road. In another case in area C, the JI commented to us after the questioning of a MEE:

> Did you notice when I asked [the MEE] whether or not he also sold drugs, he said 'no'. But the lawyer knew that there had been a phone tap and so he pushed his client a little, because he knew that that would look very bad in court. He's a good lawyer.

The nature of any participation had to be judged carefully. As described in more detail in Chapter 4, on several occasions when the lawyer attempted to intervene during the questioning itself, the JI became angry and made it quite clear that it was she and not the lawyer who was in charge of the interview.[30] The line drawn by the JI between legitimate defence assistance and unwarranted interference, is a fine one.

Whilst the task of the JI was always described to us as an investigation into the offence and not the person, there was also a strong sense of judging the whole person—looking into all of her biographical details, including any previous convictions.[31] The JI is able to delegate much of the investigation to police officers through the issuing of a *commission rogatoire*, but the MEE's biographical enquiry (*enquête de personalité*) must be conducted by the JI herself. The information collected is fairly mundane and routine, resembling the material gathered for a social enquiry report in England and Wales, and so it is perhaps surprising that this task also is not delegated (though to someone in a social work role, rather than to the police). Typically, the report produced would contain the MEE's date and place of birth, biographical information about the MEE's parents and siblings, details of schooling, work and military service, any hobbies and outside interests such as

---

[29] The type of lawyer appearing in the most serious cases is likely to be of a higher calibre. In the investigation of high-profile business people and politicians during the 1990s, the defence lawyer was often a commercial lawyer, whose approach to the dossier was more technical and legalistic than most criminal defence lawyers and who engaged in a more sophisticated level of debate. See further Roussel (2003:107). The teamwork approach of commercial firms, whereby suspects were defended by lawyers and others with different specialisms, came to influence the conduct of investigations in the financial section of the *parquet* Paris. See Greilsamer and Schneidermann (2002:162–63).

[30] See also the Outreau (2004) case, discussed in Ch 4.

[31] The different perspectives on the value and fairness of the JI and the trial court looking in detail at the previous convictions of the accused, highlight the different approaches of adversarial and inquisitorial procedure to investigation and trial. This also led to some spirited exchanges during the fieldwork between one particular JI and researcher (noted in the methodology section, Ch 1).

sport, any serious illnesses, previous convictions, whether the MEE was in a relationship and anything else that the MEE wished to include.

The Nature of the *Information*

The preliminary police enquiry often provided the key witness statements and the all-important confession from the suspect, such that the dossier contained the kind of information that might be found in the CPS file in England and Wales. However, in opening an *information*, the verification of this evidence is then conducted by the JI, rather than the court.[32] Historically, the pre-trial investigation was the most important stage in inquisitorial procedure, the trial serving almost as a formality confirming the earlier findings. Whilst the trial has taken on a different form with both the *procureur* and defence lawyers playing a more active part, during the *instruction*, the emphasis continues to be on obtaining and evaluating all the relevant information during the pre-trial, rather than the trial phase.[33] In this way, the *instruction* characterises most strongly the inquisitorial roots of French criminal procedure, where issues are selected and debated not by the prosecution and defence at trial, but by a judge during a pre-trial investigation. The JI interviewed in area B contrasted the broadly adversarial and inquisitorial models in place in Britain and in France:

> [In England] you can perhaps overturn evidence, you can debate, you can question witnesses yourself, call them to give evidence at court. In France, this is not really the case. It is in the hands of the judge . . . usually, it takes place before trial . . . in England it happens at court, and here it takes place in my office. It is not done in public . . . what you need to understand by *décharge* is that it is about checking aspects of the case that are favourable to the MEE. Yes, we do that . . . That is what the lawyer does in England. He tries to demonstrate to the court the aspects of the case that are favourable to the individual. We are judges in an office. It is in this way that we truly function as judges, because even in preparing the dossier, there is this idea of balance. We try to include in our investigation, that which is favourable and that which is unfavourable . . . What is important is that this should be done by a judge. The function of justice is to defend the individual against himself. [B1]

During the *instruction* witnesses were re-interviewed, facts (even where uncontested) and assertions followed up, and expert evidence on both the crime and the

---

[32] Where there is clear evidence against the accused, the case will, of course, be sent for trial after the *instruction*. However, unlike the procedure in England and Wales, many of the issues will already have been tested and verified by the JI and any challenges to the evidence or procedure resolved at the close of the *instruction*.

[33] The acquittal rate in the *cour d'assises*, where *crimes* are tried, is extremely low. Several JIs also told us that of all the cases they had sent to trial during the last decade, only two or three had resulted in acquittals.

parties was commissioned.[34] As a result, even relatively straightforward cases where the offence was not denied by the MEE could take many months to complete. In one case in area C, for example, the two young MEE admitted killing a girl of their own age who had been hitch hiking and had stayed the night at the home of one of them. They described how she had had sex with one of them, how they became 'disgusted' by her and how they had then decided that they wanted to 'get rid of her'; the physical evidence and that of witnesses corroborated their account. The JI told us:

> Here, I don't know that there has been a rape. Nobody has asked me to investigate that, not the *parquet* or anyone. But I will investigate that. I do not think that that happened, but I must check. I do not want a judge saying to me at a later date that this should have been looked into. But otherwise, this is quite a straightforward case—it will take less than a year . . . I have to enquire into their parents, their education, the sports club they mention going to and everything about them. It takes time.

The ideology of the JI as a neutral judge acting in the public interest provides an external justification for her dual investigative and judicial function, but it is also internalised by the JI and forms an important part of her self-image. Her status as a *juge du siège* and her belief in her own ability to define the public interest rendered unproblematic the potentially conflicting roles that she was required to perform. They enabled her to consider the MEE's previous convictions without any fear that they might prejudice her view of the case; to determine the pre-trial detention of those she was investigating; to discuss the investigation with the *procureur* without recognising the possibility that this might compromise her independence; and to view as unproblematic the absence of any corresponding dialogue with the defence. These claims to neutrality were undermined in practice by the close working relationships that she enjoyed with the police and *procureur*, in contrast with the defence lawyer who remained an outsider in the enquiry. Although both the defence and the victim are now given greater rights to (at least request to) participate in the procedure,[35] the culture of the *instruction* remains one in which the defence role is marginalised. For the JI (as for the *procureur*), the defence served a legitimating function, acting as a demonstration and therefore as a guarantee of the fairness of the procedure. At best, the lawyer was able to act as a useful counter-reflex within the *instruction* and a check upon the procedure.[36] More usually, her presence was seen as a hindrance to be overcome. For example, one JI in area D explained that whilst legally the MEE should only be questioned about information that is in the dossier, without the presence of a lawyer the JI could adopt a more informal approach and ask questions about

---

[34] In offences of sexual violence, eg, both the MEE and the victim would be seen by a psychiatrist.
[35] See further, Pin (2002).
[36] Discussed in more detail above in Ch 4.

emerging lines of enquiry. Other tactics included deliberately delaying the record-ing of information within the dossier in order to prevent the defence *avocat* from seeing it. For example, a JI in area C was discussing a case on the telephone with one of the investigating officers. He told him:

> Send me a one page update on your investigation . . . it is not necessary to send it all. If you send the results of the telephone tap, then the lawyer will see it . . . I can only inter-rogate someone on the contents of the dossier. So, if we think that it is too soon for the MEE or his lawyer to know of the contents of this, we do not put it in the dossier yet. Simple—I can only interview on what is in the dossier.[37]

Our interview with a JI in area A also illustrated something of the tension which exists between the JI's role as judge and investigator and her status as fellow *mag-istrat* alongside the *procureur*.

> We [*juges d'instruction*] are cut off from our *juges du siège* colleagues and I feel closer to the *parquet*. We work together quite closely, so we remain a little distant from the trial phase. On the other hand, I have asked the court to let me know when there are criti-cisms of my dossiers. I see my *juges du siège* colleagues very much less. We do not work together . . . The *parquet* works before and after me. Our work is complementary. When I receive a dossier, I always bear in mind that I am working for the *parquet*. Our work is very complementary. We are on the same wavelength. [A5]

In a large case of trafficking in stolen cars in area C, the JI, *procureur* and three police officers met in the JI's office to discuss extending the scope of the investi-gation. They established which charges related to which of the five principal sus-pects (and which were unnecessary at this stage and would only slow things down), the evidence gathered so far and the extent to which an additional suspect could be investigated under the current *instruction* procedure, or whether a sup-plementary *réquisitoire* was required. It was decided to extend the scope of the *instruction* and a *commission rogatoire* was issued immediately in order that the new suspect could be investigated. In many ways, such a meeting was a sensible and useful way to proceed, but it also underlines the extent to which the JI is dependent upon the police and works alongside the *procureur*. The JI will not be prosecuting the case and may therefore retain a degree of detachment from it, but there is no real sense in which defence interests are or could be represented at this stage.[38] The JI is, at most, able to ensure procedural fairness, but to involve the

---

[37] It was noteworthy that the JI usually discussed and explained each telephone discussion with the researcher present in his office, but in this instance, he made no reference to the conversation.

[38] 'We are able to keep more of a distance than the police. We know to what end we are working and to what end we need to bring a case before the court. The police and the *gendarmerie* are not neces-sarily aware of this. The case must really be solid.' [A5] (*Juge d'instruction*).

defence in the progress or conduct of the investigation would risk jeopardising it altogether. How then, is the *instruction* different from an ordinary police investigation? Principally, in providing a more meaningful level of investigatory supervision; but to claim that the defence can ever be on an equal footing with the *procureur* is fanciful. She is marginalised professionally as an *avocat*, and in representing the narrow interests of the accused she can never occupy the privileged place in the enquiry enjoyed by the *procureur*.[39]

As a result of the JI's dependence upon the police and the *procureur*, her view of the case often comes to mirror theirs and the investigation can become the construction of a case against the MEE. Although evidence was verified, the JI did not seek to challenge findings or assumptions with the kind of vigour that a defence lawyer might; once a case theory was in place, there was little incentive for the JI to prove herself wrong. Most JIs agreed that the guilt of the MEE was clear from the outset and whilst some considered it important to investigate more closely evidence obtained from the preliminary enquiry, others regarded this as an unnecessary burden, a result of the MEE 'playing the system' and refusing to face up to the evidence. As one JI in area F told us:

> The presumption of innocence exists in theory but not in practice . . . The search for the truth is quite easy, but they [MEE] just refuse to confess. They hide behind the presumption of innocence and exploit any doubt in the evidence.

The obvious danger of this approach was demonstrated in the recent Outreau case mentioned above, in which seventeen people were accused of raping and sexually assaulting their own children and those of their friends and neighbours. Seven of these were acquitted at the trial in July 2004, six of whom had spent nearly three years in detention during the investigation by the *juge d'instruction*, Fabrice Burgaud.[40] The handling of the case was strongly criticised by the accused who considered that both the JI, and the psychiatrists and psychologists evaluating the evidence of the children (some of whom were aged between two and five years), failed to act in an impartial way, seeking to strengthen the case against them, rather than to conduct a more thorough and wide ranging enquiry as the law requires.[41] The *instruction* remained captive to the accusations made during the initial police enquiry, failing to challenge or displace the original case theory. Karine Duchaucholy,[42] who was ultimately acquitted, claimed that the JI did not

---

[39] This close relationship between the two *magistrats* can be seen as part of the historical investigative continuity, where the same judge investigated, prosecuted and tried the case. See further Ch 3.

[40] Of the 10 convicted, the sentences ranged from 20 years in prison to an 18 month suspended sentence.

[41] The JI was called to give evidence in the case and was required to respond to criticism of his handling of the investigation.

[42] Although she was not placed in detention, M. Duchaucholy's son was removed from her care during the three year investigation.

listen to her account when it did not support the principal accusations, and that he then became angry and threatened to imprison one of her co-accused in order to make him confirm the accusations against her. She also claimed that her own lawyer was reduced to tears by one such confrontation.[43] The Justice Minister, Dominique Perben, apologised publicly to those acquitted[44] and set up a working party to look at possible improvements to the processes of *instruction* and detention and the use of expert evidence. In addition to the suggestions relating to detention procedures described above, the working party report (Viout, 2005) also made recommendations as to the treatment and recording of children's evidence and the need to clarify the training and impartial role of experts. The report suggested that JIs should not work alone in their first post, and that complex and sensitive cases such as the Outreau affair, should be handled by two JIs rather than one.[45]

The Use of the *Commission rogatoire*

Chapter 6 described the importance of trust and confidence in the police–*magistrat* relationship from the perspective of investigating officers. The JI also characterised her relationship with police and *gendarmes* in this way. Although responsible for the conduct and direction of the enquiry, the JI recognised her dependence upon officers to carry out the investigation and so the need to have trust in them.

> I have total trust in [the police]. We have excellent supervision over investigators, who continually keep us informed, so the work is very, very good. Besides, we do not have the time to check everything. In the end, it is also a question of knowing the officers. Some of them, you can trust, others, less so . . . it is better not to be too 'matey' with officers because sometimes we need to check on them. That is also part of our role. [A5]
>
> [The JI's relationship with the police] is primarily one of trust. We do not have the means to exercise total control over the investigation. We verify their questions and they keep us informed of what they have done. We are all guarantors that the procedure has been respected. There needs to be an exchange. The JI is in charge and is responsible for the case, the police are the men working on the ground . . . I tell them what I would like to be done. The police can put forward their suggestions, but at the end of the day they ask and I direct. I need a tidy file at the end of the day, with the evidence and procedure in order. [*Juge d'instruction*, Area D]

---

[43] See *Libération* 24 May 2004.

[44] They were later awarded compensation also.

[45] The JI in the Outreau case, despite his youth and inexperience, had refused the assistance of a colleague. The working party report suggests that the *chambre d'instruction* should have the power to require joint investigation in such cases.

Researcher: Is this usual, to delegate to the police rather than to do it yourself?

JI: Yes, always. I do not have time to go myself, so that is the norm for the police to do it.

Researcher: How can you control the police when it is the file you are supervising in practice?

JI: Good question! But you can. It is experience really. There are good and bad police and you get to know them.

[*Juge d'instruction*, Area C]

As set out at the start of this chapter, the opening of an *instruction* was on the initiative of the police as well as of the *procureur*. This proactive approach on the part of the police continued throughout the investigation, with officers often coming to see the JI to request a *commission rogatoire* in order that they could carry out specific investigations.

The degree of control that the JI was able to exercise over officers varied between sites, just as with the *procureur*. Even liaising closely could not prevent occasional blunders, such as the case in area A where the police mounted a major operation to bring in a suspect who had been under surveillance for three months, but who turned out to look nothing like the photofit picture put together by the victim and so had to be released.[46] In some instances, the JI exhibited no desire to exercise control, even when the circumstances called for it. For example, a suspect was brought before the JI in area C with two black eyes.[47] The JI asked no questions of either the suspect or the officers and made no note on the dossier of the suspect's physical condition.

The major advantage that the *instruction* appears to offer over the system of unsupervised police investigations in England and Wales, is that although the JI will often be convinced of the MEE's guilt and so will not search for inculpating and exculpating evidence to an equal degree, the simple fact of her presence in the enquiry makes the outright fabrication of evidence difficult. Although not looking to disprove evidence suggesting the guilt of the MEE (the defence case generally being poorly represented throughout the enquiry), the JI will seek to verify information and to produce a case that is solid and which will withstand scrutiny at trial. Were the police to fabricate evidence, it is always possible that this would be uncovered by complementary enquiries ordered by the JI or through the judicial questioning of a witness. However, whilst the JI is concerned to verify facts and expert opinions, she is less concerned with the way in which evidence is obtained and so the reliability of its construction. The case of Patrick Dils, discussed in the preceding chapter, demonstrates that the nature of the *instruction* is such that it may be inadequate to interrogate or to displace flawed evidence produced during the preliminary police enquiry. Dils' confession was not fabricated,

---

[46] The suspect was, of course, not aware of this blunder. He was simply relieved to be released, believing it to be because his alibi had been verified.

[47] Suspects often had small cuts and grazes, but injuries of this gravity were less usual.

but it was produced in a way that made it wholly unreliable, as were the confessions of several other men whom the same officer had persuaded to confess. The subsequent *instruction* did not challenge the reliability of the confession evidence, but rather, lent it added credibility. In the Outreau affair discussed above, the *instruction* was again insufficiently robust in its interrogation of the evidence. In addition, the experts instructed to assess the evidence of the child victims adopted a prosecution perspective, imposing their own judgment on the veracity of the accusations, rather than acting as neutral professionals contributing information to the enquiry.

In most instances, the same officers who began the investigation continued to act under *commission rogatoire* once the *instruction* began—unsurprisingly, as they are often the impetus for the opening of an *information* as described above. The continuity that this provides between the preliminary enquiry and the *instruction* may be resource efficient, but in their questionnaire responses, a small number of police officers suggested that the *instruction* would be more effective if fresh officers were brought in to investigate, thus avoiding the same investigatory assumptions and pitfalls of the preliminary enquiry.

The Prosecution

Chapter 3 discussed the role and status of the *procureur* as prosecutor and as *magistrat*, focusing in particular upon the ways in which her independence is defined, guaranteed and constrained. The nature of her relationship with the police was then examined, and there followed a description (in Chapter 5) of the ways in which the police investigation was supervised in practice. This final section considers factors impacting upon the *procureur*'s discretion to prosecute cases and the nature of her approach to those suspects who are brought before her.

Implementing the Local and the National *Politique Pénale*

As discussed in Chapter 3 the *procureur* enjoys judicial status as a *magistrat*, but as a prosecutor, she is also part of a centralised hierarchy of authority (the *Ministère public*) which is headed by the Minister of Justice and goes down through the *procureurs généraux*[48] and the *procureurs de la République*[49] to those lowest in the pyramid, the *substituts*. Each *procureur*, whatever her rank, is part of and represents the *Ministère public* and, within each local *parquet* area, *substituts*

---

[48] Operating at the level of courts of appeal and the *Cour de cassation*.
[49] Operating at the level of *Tribunal de Grande Instance*.

act and sign in the name of the *procureur de la République* (Art 39 CPP).[50] Whilst there is no principle of mandatory prosecution, this structure is intended to create a unified, hierarchical and indivisible corps through which centralised criminal justice policy can be co-ordinated and applied. This resembles Damaska's model of a hierarchical structure of authority, designed to ensure certainty and uniformity of decision making and to minimise opportunities for the exercise of official discretion in order to satisfy the 'strong demands in the hierarchical model for the ordering, systematization and simplification of the normative universe.' (Damaska, 1975:485). Goldstein and Marcus (1977:247) also describe uniformity through hierarchy as a key principle in 'Continental criminal procedure'.

> The [Penal] Code's provisions are to be applied rigorously by prosecutors and police, both of whom are organized nationally and hierarchically and are subject, in theory, to greater control by superiors than under American practice.

As well as through the enactment of official legislation, national policy is also disseminated and promoted through (non-legally binding) circulars issued by the Minister of Justice and implemented locally through the *procureur général* and the *procureur de la République*. These may be quite general in character, may address specific issues, or they may provide guidance on the interpretation of new legislation. At the local level, there are regular meetings between key legal personnel, further encouraged by inter-agency initiatives such as the *contrats locaux de sécurité*. Circulars are also used to communicate local policy and initiatives to *magistrats* and police. In this way it is hoped that broader national policy can take some account of local conditions, whilst also maintaining a degree of uniformity and so equality of treatment.

In practice, just as there are variations in prosecution policy across England and Wales, there can be significant disparities between the regions in France both in the implementation of the national *politique pénale* and in the development of local policy. Mouhanna (2001a:70) notes that both the *procureur de la République* and the *procureur général* tend to adopt a non-interventionist stance, concerned to respect the autonomy of their colleagues. The very general terms in which most Justice Ministry circulars are framed means that they can be applied in quite different ways depending upon the resources and the political leanings of the local *procureur de la République*. One senior *procureur* explained:

> The *politique pénale* of the Ministry of Justice is not very visible. We have circulars which ask us to intensify the fight against illegal immigration. That is done in totally different ways in different areas. I know areas where they ignore these circulars. The *politique pénale* provides a framework, a set of general directives and the majority of *parquets* conform for

---

[50] Procureurs are known collectively as the *parquet* and those below the *procureur de la République* are all her *substituts*.

the most part, but there are those who ignore it. That sometimes leads to disparities in practice which are very, very worrying. I do not believe that the Ministry ensures uniform respect for these circulars. That is my view. [D3]

At the regional level, local conditions of criminality are inevitably an important determinant of the local *politique pénale* and account for differences in prosecution policy adapted to local needs. For example, in site A (a medium-sized town), the use of drugs was increasing and possession of even small amounts would result in prosecution. In site D, however (a large city), the scale of drug abuse was such that, in most instances, no action was taken against those found in possession of drugs.

> Of course there are problems of standardisation . . . you cannot follow the same *politique pénale* everywhere because the cases are different, the populations are different, the problems are different. . . In one instance you will prosecute far more offenders than in another, because there is less delinquency . . . A uniform system of justice, which is delivered in the same way everywhere and so which does not take account of differences, would effectively be a non-democratic system of justice. [A6]

> If you arrest someone with 10g of hashish here [a major city], we will not prosecute. It is of no interest, it is not a threat to public order. But in a town of 15,000 inhabitants, where everybody knows one another, where nothing ever happens, you find 10g of hashish and in fact, you need a different kind of judicial response because everybody is going to panic, because everybody is going to say, 'There are drugs, we have never had this before, this is a major event.' . . . depending on the scale of the problem, attitudes will be different . . . you can say that one court was less severe and another court was more severe. This is because there is a context, and one can say that actually, justice, from one angle, will not be the same for everyone, but it will be designed to have the same degree of effectiveness. So effectiveness is not necessarily achieved by treating all things in the same way. [E5]

For most *procureurs*, (and very much linked to the different levels of criminality experienced) the principal driver in the implementation of the local and national *politique pénale* is that of resources.[51] In large urban centres with high rates of criminality, there was a concern that minor offences should not be allowed to overburden the system, with the result that a range of cases, such as possession of drugs, criminal damage, shoplifting and domestic assault, were less likely to be prosecuted. For example, in site C (a city), shoplifting was prosecuted only when the value of the goods taken exceeded £100. The need to use the available resources efficiently and to avoid delay had a clear impact on prosecution policy, as well as on the nature of the investigation and supervision (described in earlier

---

[51] Most *parquets* we visited were understaffed by at least one post, suffered a chronic shortage of support staff, and it was not unusual for some courts to sit regularly beyond 9pm in order to get through the day's caselist. 71% of our *procureur* questionnaire respondents said that budgetary issues always or often affected their work. See also Truche (1997:20).

chapters) which could be effected. This subordination of legal issues to wider financial considerations had a demoralising effect on some *procureurs*, who resented the constraints that it placed upon their professional judgment and the production line mentality that it engendered.[52] The substantial impact which differing local practices (both formally and informally understood) might have upon the organisation and running of the *parquet* was highlighted by two young *procureurs* in site D, when they told us of a conversation that took place several months after they had arrived to work in a large city *parquet* :

> We came from a much smaller place and so we didn't realise how overloaded the court here was. One day, the *premier procureur adjoint* came into the office and said that since we had arrived there had been many more prosecutions and there simply were not the resources to accommodate them. That can be very annoying because, for example, a lot of domestic violence is not prosecuted.

The disparity between the local *politique* of different regions was criticised by a number of those we spoke to, in particular those from the larger jurisdictions.

> Justice varies in different regions. You will not be prosecuted for some offences in some places—which basically means that you can commit more crime in the city. I saw a case in the Alps when a person was prosecuted for letting out his cattle. They said it was a breach of public order there—but I think hitting your wife is worse than that, yet it is not prosecuted [here]. I think they prosecute minor offences to justify their existence. [*Procureur*, Site D]

> There is a problem in the way that the justice system is organised. There are 180 *procureurs* and they must not all be acting differently. This is partly because of resources—here, we are not as well off as smaller court regions so we cannot prosecute all of the more minor cases, which only 20km away, they may do. [D4]

Magendie and Gomez (1986:102) argue that these disparities go beyond the limits of acceptable local interpretation and adaptation and undermine the certainty of the law:

> In this way, transgression of the same law leads to sanctions in one place, to total impunity in another. Diverted from its objective, as soon as what should and should not be sanctioned is translated into something over which there is total choice, the discretion to prosecute runs the not insignificant risk of resulting in unacceptable distortions in crime control between different jurisdictions; and that would go way beyond what could be justified by the criminal policy legitimately followed by each *parquet* according to its particular local conditions.

---

[52] See also Mouhanna (2001a:30–33).

The Importance of Individual Discretion

A striking feature of the daily discourse of both *procureurs* and *juges d'instruction* is the way in which they explain their actions in terms of their professional ideology. They constantly portray themselves as neutral *magistrats*, with no choice other than to apply the law as it is set down in the formal texts. Typically, they explain their role as that of 'acting in', 'protecting' or 'defending' the interests of society. They emphasised that their job was not to obtain a conviction but to make an objective evaluation of the evidence. As one *procureur* explained:

> From my point of view, we protect society's interests. If I arrive before the court and a case does not seem to me to be made out, I say so . . . That often happens at court when new evidence is presented . . . I would not want to see someone convicted who I would not be prepared to convict myself. [A4][53]

Many of those we observed and interviewed described their function as one of applying the law 'objectively', regardless of personal feelings about either the accused or the law. One *procureur* described the importance of professional training in enabling *magistrats* to rein in or 'manage their emotions'. Another, in site A, explained that she always filled in the papers requesting a remand in custody and passed them to the *juge d'instruction* before seeing the accused, as she 'used to become soft when [she] heard their arguments'. The imagery is almost religious, as *magistrats* characterise themselves as servants of the public interest, neutral vessels through which the law is faithfully and selflessly administered for the greater good. When explaining the charges to the accused, or why a remand in custody was being sought or an *information* was being opened, *procureurs* consistently prefaced their remarks with expressions such as 'I am obliged by the law to . . . ' or 'I am required to . . . ' This served to present the law and its application as fixed, rather than variable or discretionary.[54] As one *procureur* in area E told us:
[Suspects] ask me to take pity on them, but I cannot. I have no other solution but to apply the law . . . I have no choice.

A *procureur* working in the juvenile section explained the importance of keeping emotions quite separate from her professional role:

> The one thing I am afraid of is to have a moment of emotion. Sometimes, when I have a person before me, I try to make them face up to their responsibilities and when I see

---

[53] We did see this happen on one or two occasions, but not 'often'.

[54] In Roussel's (2003) comparison between American 'cause lawyering' and the judicial investigation of the financial and political scandals of the 1990s, the *magistrat*'s role as 'the servant of the law' 'applying, rather than creating the law' and 'searching for the truth' (2003:97–101) is central to her claims of authority and to the depoliticisation of her actions. See also the comments of *magistrats* in Greilsamer and Schneidermann (2002).

him leave [my office for court] I know that he is going to get four or six months in prison and sometimes that breaks my heart. But I have a responsibility, a *politique* to respect and I apply it. [A2]

These accounts of the law's apparent inflexibility, the uniform approach it imposes and the absence of choice, are in obvious friction with the variety of practices across and within jurisdictions[55] which demonstrate the central importance of the discretion exercised on a daily basis by *procureurs* of all ranks—a discretion which is exercised within the limits of the law and without which the system would grind to a halt. Perhaps more interestingly, they also demonstrate the continuing force which these ideals have for *procureurs*, whose invocation of them in this way suggests that they regard them as legitimate ideals which ought to be respected or aspired to. However, the articulation of the official professional rhetoric in this way masks the more complex (and sometimes contradictory) role that the *procureur* plays out in practice. Some of the more senior *procureurs* we observed and interviewed described their role in a less mechanical way. They too emphasised their responsibility to act in the wider public interest, but for them, this role was understood more broadly as encompassing a form of social regulation. They pointed to the broader scope of their role, which includes civil as well as criminal work; to their discretion to require the culprit to compensate the victim, achieving satisfaction without the need for a court hearing; and to the discontinuance of cases where they considered that to prosecute would aggravate rather than alleviate the situation (typically domestic assault or incidents concerning neighbours).[56] In contrast to the uniform approach and shared ethos represented in the ideology of the *magistrature*, they also recognised the very individual approach for which their position allowed.[57]

> It is an individualist corps, the *magistrature*. They are all very individualist. There is no group ethos . . . there is never a team spirit or ethos. Even the *parquet*, where you are used to working together, where you are in a hierarchy, I would say that they are really very individual personalities. [E4]

Less senior *procureurs* were more likely to experience the impact of their immediate hierarchy. Where several *procureurs* were working together (as for example in the *permanence* of a larger site) there were occasions when the more senior member of team would provide clear guidance on how cases should be dealt with.[58]

---

[55] Described in this chapter and others, especially Ch 5.

[56] It may be that as more senior and experienced *magistrats*, these *procureurs* were more confident in exercising individual discretion (and had a greater opportunity to do so) and had a more global view of their role, in contrast to their younger colleagues whose work was likely to be overseen by a section head to whom they were responsible.

[57] It should also be noted that, in most instances, there was ample opportunity for *procureurs* to discuss cases with colleagues and this was usual in more complex investigations.

[58] Contrast Mouhanna's (2001a:111–20) claims that *magistrats* seek to avoid the involvement of their hierarchy.

> My colleague dealt with a case of domestic violence, where the victim was still in hospital. He just wanted to give the accused a date to come to court, but our section head said 'No, it must be dealt with by [the more serious procedure] *comparution immédiate.*' [*Procureur*, area D]

The exercise of individual discretion may depend in part upon the local hierarchy within which the *procureur* is working, but it is clear that the law itself allows the *procureur* a considerable degree of flexibility. Just as a variety of local *politiques* and practices exist within the administration of the law, so too it was apparent in many instances that individual discretion was constrained neither by the law nor official hierarchical or ideological norms.[59] Mouhanna notes (2001a:111–20) that different *magistrats* may come to very different conclusions on the same case, whilst still remaining within the law. *Magistrats* in the current study also expressed this view.

> Standardisation, for sure, that does not exist. Even within the same jurisdiction, depending on training, there are differences in jurisprudence. That is at the same time the variety, the strength and the weakness of the justice system . . . Myself, I prefer a justice system without uniformity, but with freedom of action. [A6]

> The fact that the evidence must all be in writing does not prevent us from having a significant amount of leeway. It is procedural, but it does not prevent us from reacting . . . I am not at all tolerant of sexual offences, but I had a colleague who just didn't give a damn. It depends on your personality. [A4]

The difficulties that this presented were also mentioned by officers we observed and when asked whether they had anything else to add, one of the respondents to our police questionnaire (a senior officer of nineteen years' experience) set out the following:

> The policies or decisions of certain *magistrats* are, in identical circumstances but in different places, often different. The differences in treatment are sometimes surprising, at the heart of the same jurisdiction. The personal involvement of some *magistrats* is difficult to manage. This subjectivity, without basis, is experienced quite negatively by police personnel. [Police questionnaire respondent 5]

In addition, it is always open to the *procureur* to exercise her discretion in order to manipulate the law, as a *procureur* in site D explained:

> To prolong [police detention] the offence has to be of a certain gravity, so I will make this a gang robbery. In fact, I won't charge them with that, but it allows us to prolong the *garde à vue*.

[59] Several of our senior *procureur* interviewees emphasised their independence as *magistrats* (albeit under the hierarchy of the Minister of Justice) by contrasting their position with the more slavish obedience required by a civil servant *fonctionnaire*.

And for some, this is exploited in a manner which is wholly inconsistent with a professional rhetoric which claims impartiality and equality before the law. One senior member of the *parquet* in site C, for example, frequently accused 'Arab' defendants of coming to France only to find a wife and of having fake identity papers—whatever the nature of the charges they faced. In this instance she told a colleague what had happened in court after she had made her sentence recommendation the previous day:

> The lawyer said to me, 'How can you justify that sentence? This is unintelligent and inhumane'... But this man was selling drugs. He was an **Arab**. Of course I asked for a prison sentence. [original emphasis][60]

On another occasion, she regretted asking for a remand in custody for an accused that she had assumed, because of his name, was a gypsy.

> I had imagined someone dirty, hairy, foreign and all that. I did the paperwork before they brought him in. And then when I saw this blonde boy, all clean. If I had seen him before I would not have asked for a remand in custody.

In site E, one senior *procureur* responsible for the application of sentences (art 707 CPP) complained about the lax approach taken, in particular in relation to foreigners. So extreme were his views, that some colleagues were prepared to take on cases, even when they were not within their workload, to prevent him sending foreigners to prison for even the most minor offences. In site D, a senior member of the *parquet* frequently shouted at defendants and insulted them. He had little or no concern for their welfare and was content for them to be seen in the worst possible light. When one defendant came before him before being sent for trial that day, the *procureur* was in a goading mood. He was aggressive and shouted from the start:

> *Procureur*: Sit properly!
> Accused: I'm fine as I am.
> *Procureur*: Sit up! You're before the *procureur* . . . You admit everything?
> Accused: Absolutely.
> *Procureur*: And you're proud of yourself, eh?
> Accused: Yes.
> [*Procureur* writes, 'I am proud of myself.'][61]

---

[60] The police in site C were similarly racist, telling me that 'Arabs always lie—even when they have done nothing wrong.' The only non-white officer in the large central police station in site C was described as 'one of us', but was nevertheless obliged to tolerate constant racist banter as colleagues 'joked' that 'he was in the wrong section' asking him, 'shouldn't you be in immigration?'

[61] The accused is usually asked if she wishes to make a statement and any comment is recorded and placed in the dossier which goes before the court. Typically, this would be some expression of remorse.

He said to me after:

> I should have charged him with contempt. I should have sent him back downstairs to come back later, but it would probably have been the same. Whatever, I'll drag him around [between here and the cells] all day to piss him off.

Another *procureur* in site D asked that the suspect be brought before her before being released without charge. She had been arrested under suspicion of harming her own child, but there was no evidence to support charges being brought. The *procureur* decided to subject her to a harsh and almost cruel lecture in any event:

> You must protect your child. If you do not, I will protect him. I will take him. [The suspect begins to cry silently, she too had been placed in care]. You will leave free today but take it as a serious warning. I believe you today, but I will not believe you next time . . . Were you maltreated as a child? [The suspect says that she was, by her mother]. You know what they say—those who are maltreated themselves, maltreat their own children . . . You should reflect on that.

While not representative of all *procureurs*, these examples demonstrate the limited degree to which reliance upon professional ideology is able to constrain official activity and the extent to which, in such a context, even extreme behaviour and attitudes can go unchecked. Furthermore, in some instances, these encounters took place in private, but in most, fellow *procureurs* were aware of their colleagues' behaviour. Although a little embarrassed by the overtness of the bullying conduct or racism exhibited, for the most part, they did not consider these highly subjective personal decisions and practices to be professionally improper.

The Suspect before the *Procureur*

Article 40 CPP allows the *procureur* a wide discretion in determining if and how cases should be pursued, a discretion that has been widened yet further by her power to instigate a range of alternatives to prosecution.[62] At the close of the GAV, unless released with no further action or sent to mediation, suspects are either given a date on which to attend court, are brought before the JI where an *instruction* is opened, or are sent for trial that day through the *comparution immédiate* procedure. In the latter two instances suspects were generally brought before the *procureur* working on the *permanence* in order that the next stage in the procedure

---

[62] The *procureur's* changing position is also seen through her local policy-making role within *contrats locaux de sécurité* (CLS). Through the promotion of active partnership between local organisations such as the police, *gendarmes*, schools, social workers, mediators and the mayor, this initiative seeks to develop a more precise picture of criminality and anti-social behaviour in an area, as well as more effective means of addressing it. See Ministry of Justice circular, 28 October 1997.

could be explained, that the suspect could be told of her right to legal assistance and to record any further comments that the suspect may wish to make.[63] This provides the *procureur* with an opportunity to speak to the suspect about her treatment during the GAV and to hear any comments she may have before finalising the decision on how to proceed. In practice, enquiries into the conduct of the GAV were cursory and the suspect's ability to respond frankly was impeded by the presence of police officers. The *procureur's* primary concern was not so much to supervise, verify or enquire into what had gone before (which would complicate matters), but rather to move forward the case against the accused. One *procureur* in area D explained what went on the form that was filled in when a suspect was seen.

> We record his identity so that he is not convicted under false names, then the offences he is accused of and then any statement. You do not need to write everything they say, but I write if they admit the offence, then if they say that they were hit by the police and then they cannot say they were hit by the *procureur*.

Suspects sometimes attempted to raise ancillary or practical matters, but were not given a sympathetic hearing. For example, the following man in area C had no previous convictions and was very confused by what was to happen to him. He admitted causing criminal damage and was brought before the *procureur* to be given a date to come to court in one month's time. The charges were read out and he was told the name of a lawyer:

> Suspect: What happens to me now?
> *Procureur*: You go home and you come back on the 28th of November
> Suspect: But what shall I do? I do not have my things.
> *Procureur*: That's your problem.
> [He signs the form, goes to leave by the wrong door, seems lost. He still follows the police obediently and keeps his hands as though they were still handcuffed].

Another suspect in area C who wished to correct something in his statement taken by the police, was told by the *procureur*: 'I am paid to read the dossier of evidence. I believe what I read . . . This is written and signed.' Where suspects denied the offence, this was not generally accepted by the *procureur*. This exchange prior to the suspect being sent before the court was typical. The suspect here (in area D) was charged with theft and receiving stolen goods and the police had fingerprint evidence which did not implicate him:

---

[63] Sometimes the suspect was brought before the *procureur* to be given the court date. This was done to mark the seriousness of the offence, but in most instances, the police simply told the suspect the date at the end of the GAV.

Procureur: So what do you say about this?

Suspect: It wasn't me.

Procureur: So you deny it? Why?

Suspect: Because it wasn't me.

Procureur: You are saying that you were just walking in the street and you were stopped? [yes] So why would the police stop you when they don't know you? There were three of you in a car and they followed you.

Suspect: But it wasn't me. I didn't have any gloves.

Procureur: You don't need to have.

Suspect: But the police said they had prints.

Procureur: But that is not conclusive.

Suspect: But I was walking in the street.

Procureur: Of course, if you came out of the car.

Suspect: But I would be running.

Procureur: Not necessarily. You may think, 'Right, stay calm, so that they do not think it is me'. You know the score.

There were many instances in which the police evidence was contested in part. Suspects often admitted to only some of the offences listed for example, or said that they had stolen an item but denied having broken into the shop or house, or having smashed a window to gain entry. Although reference was made to police statements, no attention was paid by the *procureur* to the conditions under which these were taken, or to the fact that many suspects quite evidently could not read or write. Even where the suspect admitted the more serious offence, the police version was not questioned. For example, a suspect in area C admitted to having broken into a vehicle with the intention of stealing it, but not to having stolen a camera from inside. The police statement said that the suspect was walking away with the camera in his hand; the suspect said that he was questioned inside the vehicle, with nothing in his hand. The *procureur* simply ignored the discrepancy.

In several instances we observed the suspect with obviously recent injuries such as a black eye, or cuts and scratches to the face or arms, but the *procureur* rarely made any comment or enquiry. When suspects did complain about their treatment, the *procureur* showed no interest in pursuing the matter.[64] Suspects were asked about the conditions of the GAV as part of a series of formalities; there was no interest in the response given. The following from area C is typical: the *procureur* addresses the formal issue of the doctor which is documented, but ignores anything else.

---

[64] See also the examples in Ch 5 of suspects complaining of having no blankets in an unheated cell. Even where suspects (usually heroin addicts) were still complaining of being cold when before the *procureur,* they were ignored.

Procureur: What do you have to say about the conditions of your detention?

Suspect: They have treated me badly. They will not let me smoke. They treat me like a dog and I haven't seen the doctor . . .

Procureur: You'll see him now, after the extension of your *garde à vue*.

In this more serious case from area D (also discussed in Chapter 5), the accused admitted the offences of receiving stolen goods and possession of drugs, but when a second *procureur* came into the room and asked how he had received his injuries, he protested at his rough treatment at the hands of the police, claiming also that they had stolen something from him. He had extensive cuts and scratches on his face, was a heroin addict and appeared heavily sedated.

Procureur 2: How did you get that on your face?

Suspect: The police did it.

Procureur 2: Don't talk rubbish. Have you seen the doctor?

Suspect: Yes.

Procureur 1: [To the other *procureur*] Yes, it's in the dossier. [Returning to the suspect] You are a heroin addict?

Suspect: I'm not taking heroin, I have medication.

Procureur 1: Since when?

Suspect: For two or three weeks. I'm trying to get on to a [drug rehabilitation] programme.

Procureur 1: Do you want a lawyer? [Yes] A duty lawyer [Yes]. OK, you will be before the court this afternoon.

[The suspect begins to protest loudly]

Suspect: When they caught me they stole something from my wrist.

Procureur 1: Oh yes. You can tell that to the court.

Suspect: Look at my face, look at my face. Is that false, is that false? Do you know why they did that? Because I made a complaint against the police.

Procureur 2: And who was that to, eh? What was his name?

Suspect: [Struggling to overcome the sedation, tries to recall the exact name] It was the '*police de la police*'.[65]

[He is then taken out by the escorting officers].

In this case there was no concern to check the suspect's story or to look beyond the doctor's note, which simply recorded the fact that there were injuries on the suspect's face. This was left to the lawyer to pursue at court. When questioned by the researcher, the *procureur* made it clear that he was not interested:

---

[65] The police inspectorate responsible for investigating police misconduct is commonly referred to as the *police de la police*.

You have to bear in mind that he has several convictions and does not respect the law, so his word counts for less than that of the police . . . This guy is an addict too and I've seen them at the police station—they are out of touch with reality. If locked in a confined space, they freak out and make things up to get their own back.

In most instances, the suspect does not make any specific complaint about the GAV and the primary purpose of the interview is then to deliver a form of moralising lecture to the accused, to point out the error of her ways and to encourage her to be a more responsible member of society. This approach is interesting, as it casts the accused not as some criminological 'other', but as a member (albeit a failing one) of the same society of which the *procureur* is a part. This stands in contrast to the accused in England and Wales, who is often considered beyond any useful form of rehabilitation, even by her own defence lawyers.[67] Those brought before the *procureur* are reprimanded, told to face up to their responsibilities and to consider the impact of their actions upon society. A senior *procureur* in area E explained how he saw his role. He began by explaining his opposition to the presence of defence lawyers at the start of GAV, on the ground that they would tell a suspect never to confess in order to escape responsibility:

> That is a totally amoral state of mind and I do not mean Christian morality, I mean simple morality, which is among the virtues that we should cultivate in our citizens; there is also responsibility . . . So, those who have offended . . . nice kids of twenty years of age, I say to them, 'Could you not take your responsibilities, could you not be sincere?' I do not do that to trap them, so that they go to prison, because I generally think that I have enough proof . . . I do it so that they will come to terms with themselves, because I think that it is good for a human being to come to terms with himself . . . it is not politically correct to use the word and to expresses yourself in terms of 'morality.' But what is a *magistrat* in the *parquet*? It is someone who says what the law is. And what is the law? It is parliament, which is mandated to say, 'That is not allowed, that is forbidden. Otherwise, it is punishable by this sentence.' That is what the *code pénal* is. So, I preach morality because politicians preach morality.

Another *procureur* in area E explained her approach to a Hungarian suspect found (for a third time) to be residing unlawfully in France. She had made it clear that she did not think that prison served any purpose for him, she simply wanted him to return home. She spoke of the possibility of him obtaining work as a translator and making something of his life:

> I tried to kindle something in his head. I saw a little light, but I know that it is only a glimmer. One day, he will have had enough of living illegally, he will have had enough

---

[66] Accused persons were referred to and discussed in neutral terms by *procureurs*, even amongst themselves. In the course of my research with criminal defence lawyers in England and Wales, however, the accused (their own clients) were frequently referred to in the same kind of disrespectful and insulting terms as those used by the police.

of prison and he will go back home. After all, he now speaks French, so he could find work there.

In the smaller and medium-sized areas we observed, *procureurs* made sure that the suspect understood the charges and often read out the basis of their statement to the police to confirm. In the larger sites, the tone was often more clipped with greater emphasis upon reprimanding the suspect who was then often cut short and not allowed a proper opportunity to speak. Across all sites, the tone of these brief encounters was that of a pupil appearing before the head teacher—they were dealt with firmly, lectured, but they were also encouraged to try to do better. In the following example from area C, the accused was brought from the GAV to be tried that afternoon for a street robbery.

> *Procureur:* What do you do?
> *Suspect:* Nothing.
> *Procureur:* What do you live on?
> Suspect: I am doing a work placement for a removal firm.
> *Procureur:* What did you do at school?
> Suspect: I never went.
> *Procureur:* [Looking at his statement] You were at school until you were 16.
> Suspect: Yes, but we did nothing.
> *Procureur:* That is your fault. Have you any previous convictions? [No, only suspended sentences.] That is a conviction. Do you make a habit of stealing from young men and hitting them on the head? [No] Is that how you want to live your life—in prison? You are going before the court today. I can tell you, this kind of thing will **always**, and you have my word on this, will always result in you going to prison. [She reads out the charge of robbery] Why? [He begins to explain what happened.] No, I know how, but why? You don't know? [No] You should reflect a little. You may not have a criminal record now, but I predict that you will spend time in prison in the future. It's your choice—you can live on the outside or on the inside. [original emphasis]

Similarly, a heroin addict in area D who had managed to stop using heroin while in prison and to then work for a month before starting again, was told:

> You are only 22. You should think about whether that is the life that you want to live. If you break ties with the drugs scene, then you can avoid prison.

In area A, the following suspect was accused of driving with excess alcohol:

> *Procureur:* You understand that we cannot let you drive.
> Suspect: But my divorce and . . .
> *Procureur:* I know. You will need to explain all of that to the court—that's for them. It is your right to drink, but you can **never** convince the court that you had to get behind

the wheel ... If you want to add anything I will write it down. Would you like a lawyer? [There's no point.] There is always a point. [A duty lawyer then.] You will be dealt with today by the *comparution immédiate* procedure. If you do not want to be tried straight away, you tell the court and you will be tried at the next sitting and put in custody until then. [original emphasis]

Although the processes of investigation and prosecution are recognised as discrete phases in the French criminal process, they remain closely connected. In the majority of investigations it is the public prosecutor, the *procureur*, who is responsible for overseeing the police enquiry. In an increasingly small number of cases the offence is investigated by the JI, but here too the *procureur* retains a close involvement throughout the *instruction*, often having been involved in the preliminary enquiry that precedes the opening of an *information*. And in all investigations, the police play a crucial role in the gathering and recording of the evidence that makes up the case dossier. This is the case before the *instruction*, when police investigations may continue for up to two weeks before the JI takes over the case, as well as during the *instruction* through the issuing of a *commission rogatoire*. The supervising *magistrat* can oversee, direct and require actions to be taken, but she remains dependent on the police to provide her with sufficient information on which she might base her decision. In most instances, both police and *magistrats* rely upon a high degree of trust to make up this deficit. In this way, the JI works very much alongside officers, checking and validating the evidence that they produce. The practice of using the same investigating officers before and during the *instruction* can be effective, but it also makes it less likely that the JI will adopt a perspective that is wholly different from and which challenges that of the police. The increased opportunities for defence participation during the *instruction* represent an additional safeguard in this respect, but the prevailing legal culture sees the *avocat* in a subordinate position, her involvement still controlled by and mediated through the JI.

The JI's power to detain suspects in custody during the course of the *instruction* has been criticised as a conflict between her judicial and investigative functions, and as a means of pressuring suspects to co-operate in the enquiry. The shared ethos and close co-operation between the *procureur* and the JI was most apparent in discussions around *détention provisoire*. The June 2000 reform has now removed this power from the JI, transferring it to the newly-created JLD and it was hoped that this would reduce the number of MEE held in custody. This does not appear to have been the case. In 2003, out of 47,370 MEE, 19,088 (40 per cent) were held in custody compared with only 16,761 out of a total of 51,398 (32.5 per cent) in 2001.

The *procureur* works within a more tightly defined hierarchy than the JI, but considerable discretion exists in the interpretation of local and national policy and in the ways in which the individual *procureur* may interpret and apply the law.

In most instances, the exercise of this discretion is adapted to local conditions, notably the profile of criminality and the resources available, but in some instances it is exercised in a way that reflects an individual rather than professional ideology. Although most *procureurs* adopted a police-dominated perspective and assumed the guilt of suspects, accused persons were generally treated with more dignity by the *procureur* than is the case with defendants in England and Wales. They were subjected to moralising lectures or reprimanded for their offending, but they were at least deemed worthy of addressing and considered capable of taking responsibility for their actions. In England and Wales, the defendant has become increasingly marginalised in the criminal process, the object rather than the subject of proceedings, and it is perhaps through more informal means of case resolution, such as mediation, that the accused is being drawn back into the process.

8

Concluding Remarks

This study has sought to explore the different legal structures within which crime is investigated and prosecuted in France and to provide a better understanding of the roles played by the police, the *procureur*, the *juge d'instruction* (JI) and the defence lawyer. At the heart of the difference between the models of adversarial and inquisitorial procedure is that in the former, the accuser and the accused are responsible for marshalling, selecting and then presenting to the court the evidence supporting their case. The trial is the focal point of the process, the moment at which the evidence of the parties is debated and judicially evaluated. Inquisitorial procedure, on the other hand, tends towards a more state-dominated and centralised pre-trial process, conducted not by the parties, but by a judicial officer. In this way, much emphasis is placed upon the judicial investigation and resolution of issues during the pre-trial phase, the trial serving as the final examination or hearing, rather than the focus of debate. The dossier that comes before the court is not simply the prosecution case (as in England and Wales), but represents the product of a judicial (or judicially supervised) enquiry.

In practice, of course, criminal procedures are played out rather differently. The criminal justice process in England and Wales has its roots in adversarial procedure, but the victim is no longer a party in the case, only a witness, and she plays no part in the formal accusation. In most instances the police-prepared prosecution case dominates the process, the defendant lacking both the investigative powers and the resources to match it. Although defence advice and representation is available to accused persons from the point of police detention and questioning, research points to many defence lawyers lacking not only the resources, but also the adversarial motivation required to challenge sufficiently the prosecution case.[1] Neither is the trial the centrepiece of the criminal process, most cases being disposed of by way of a guilty plea in which case the prosecution 'facts' are accepted by the court without further enquiry.

In France too, whilst judicial supervision is at the centre of the procedural model of criminal justice, in practice, it is the police who dominate the process of

---

[1] McConville *et al* (1994)

case construction. The way in which the legal regulation of investigations is framed is sufficiently open-textured to accommodate this and the occupational cultures of the main legal actors, together with the pressures of increasing case-loads and diminishing resources, mean that a more judge-centred procedure is increasingly untenable. This calls into question the extent to which judicial super-vision can continue to be invoked to justify the absence of safeguards which might be considered essential to the functioning of adversarial procedure, but which are deemed less necessary within an inquisitorial model, including the earlier provi-sion of meaningful defence rights.[2]

The law currently provides for two forms of judicially supervised investigation. Under the *instruction* model, the JI is personally responsible for conducting the case enquiry and benefits from extensive powers in this. However, less than 5 per cent of investigations are carried out under this procedure and of those that are, the majority of investigation and evidence gathering is carried out by the police under the delegated powers of the *commission rogatoire*. In over 95 per cent of cases, there is no *instruction* and the JI has no involvement at all. Investigations are carried out by the police on their own initiative, with a general requirement to keep the *procureur* informed in order that she can oversee and direct the enquiry, and a specific requirement that she be told of those detained for questioning in order that she can ensure the proper conduct of the GAV (*garde à vue*). This cre-ates a tension between the *procureur*'s law enforcement function as a public pros-ecutor and her responsibility for the supervision of investigations in her status as a *magistrat*. As a judicial officer she is required to supervise the police enquiry and yet she is also wholly dependent upon the police and *gendarmes* in order to carry out her public prosecution role.

In both of these procedural models, judicial supervision is considered an important safeguard, guaranteeing the thoroughness and the proper conduct of the investigation, and providing a form of pre-trial judicial evaluation of the evi-dence. Consequently, the resulting case dossier is accorded a high degree of cred-ibility by the trial court. Much emphasis is placed upon written evidence, and documented procedural conformity is equated with wider guarantees as to the credibility and reliability of evidence. This is especially so in the vast majority of cases where judicial responsibility for overseeing the investigation lies with the *procureur*. Here, high caseloads and tight turnaround times necessitate a model of supervision that is essentially distant, retrospective and bureaucratic, the file contents being the primary demonstration of legal procedural compliance. Paradoxically, the file reveals little of how this oversight of police investigation is effected; the primary mode of supervision is by telephone (and increasingly so

---

[2] See also Hodgson (2002a) for a discussion of some of the central theoretical tenets of inquisito-rial procedure and their congruence with empirical accounts of practice.

with *temps réel*) and so is not memorialised formally[3] and is not the subject of review either by the *procureur*'s own hierarchy or by the defence.[4] Supervision through more direct involvement in the police enquiry is neither required by the law, nor anticipated by the *procureur*. In many instances, the high caseload of the procureur serves to constrain her more direct involvement, but even where resources allow for a more 'hands-on' approach to supervision, this is considered inappropriate. Furthermore, the defence rights of the suspect are extremely limited during this time; she may consult with a lawyer for 30 minutes during her detention in *garde à vue*, but the lawyer has no access to the case file, may not be present during the interrogation of her client and there is no legal or practical expectation of any dialogue between defence *avocat* and the police or *procureur*.

The minority procedure of *instruction* represents a 'purer' model of judicial investigation; it is not a police enquiry overseen by a *magistrat*, but a judicial enquiry, parts of which can be delegated to the police—although significantly, once an *information* has been opened, only the JI may question the *mis en examen*. In practice, this non-delegable aspect of the enquiry is the only act of investigation which the JI carries out personally, all other aspects of the enquiry being conducted by the police through the mechanism of *commission rogatoire*.[5] As a number of high-profile cases have demonstrated, even before the *instruction* begins, the police construction of the case is already imprinted upon the investigation, shaped by the all important initial police enquiry that precedes the opening of an *information*.[6] In some instances, the transition from police enquiry to *instruction* is almost seamless, the opening of an *information* serving as little more than a functional necessity providing officers with the powers that they need in order to continue their investigation unhindered. With a caseload of over 100, it can be difficult to displace the initial police thesis and the focus of the JI tends towards the verification of evidence already gathered, rather than starting the enquiry afresh. However, the *instruction* process is more lengthy than the *procureur*-supervised police enquiry and the JI is not subject to the same kinds of time pressures as the *procureur*. There is more opportunity for discussion and reflection and, in contrast to investigations overseen by the *parquet*, the *mise en examen* is provided with clear and legally defined defence rights to have her lawyer present during judicial questioning, to have access to the case dossier and, most recently, to request that the JI carry out any investigative act that might assist in uncovering the truth. In theory, this now places the defence on the same footing as the *procureur* in terms of access to the dossier and the ability to participate in the investigation. However, effective participation remains difficult to realise and

---

[3] Though there will be some form of file note.
[4] See also Mouhanna (2001a:120–25).
[5] The instruction and choice of experts is of course also the decision of the JI.
[6] See eg the 'Outreau' case (2004), as well as that of Patrick Dils, discussed in Ch 6.

case discussions are dominated by the police and *procureur* to the exclusion of the defence *avocat*. Increasing defence involvement in the *instruction* in a way that is meaningful requires major shifts in the occupational cultures of both lawyers and *magistrats*. The defence lawyer's professional status as an *avocat* representing the accused cannot compete with that of the *procureur* and JI who, as *magistrats*, represent the public interest. She remains a professional outsider and cannot hope to have the ear of the JI in the same way as the police or the *procureur*. Furthermore, her participation is mediated through the JI who is able to control and to constrain the extent of the defence lawyer's involvement. In most instances the *avocat* herself does not seek to challenge the dominance of the JI, accepting the relatively subsidiary role allotted to her. Field and West (2003) describe a defence culture in which the *avocat* does not attempt to posit an alternative case or to challenge the evidence directly, but engages in a more moderate process of re-reading the dossier in a way that is most favourable to the defence.

In practice, judicial supervision of the police is not about active involvement and direction, about taking control of the case, or monitoring closely the processes of investigation and evidence gathering. In most instances the judicial supervisor is unable (and even unwilling) to displace the dominance of the police-constructed case. The mutual dependence inscribed within the investigator–supervisor relationship means that a surveillance-based approach to supervision would be ineffective and faced with the sheer volume of cases to be dealt with, impossible in many instances. Instead, the key to a successful police–*magistrat* relationship is trust. This was emphasised to us repeatedly by police and *magistrats* during our fieldwork observations, interviews and in questionnaire responses. Without trust, the criminal justice process would grind to a halt. This is an institutional trust in most instances, born of necessity rather than being based upon personal knowledge and experience, the essential ingredient that enables both police and *magistrats* to carry out their functions, serving as a pragmatic response to the deficit in both legal authority and resources.[7]

This gulf between the model of judicial investigation represented by *instruction* and the empirical realities of supervision by the *procureur* continues to widen. The number of cases dealt with by the *instruction* procedure is diminishing each year and the trend away from judicial investigation is likely to continue as recent legislative reform has shifted power away from the JI and increasingly towards the *procureur*. Police investigations may now remain under the supervision of the *procureur* for longer and officers can be provided with more extensive powers without the need for opening an *information*. The primary mode of criminal investigation is no longer a judicial enquiry carried out by the JI, but a police investigation overseen by the *procureur*. This is significant in a number of respects.

---

[7] Mouhanna (2001a).

Firstly, it means that most cases that come before the courts are not the result of an independent judicial enquiry. They are the product of a police investigation which has been subject to the relatively distant and bureaucratic oversight of the *procureur*. Secondly, whilst there is legal provision for extensive defence involvement in the *instruction* where judicial protection is at its strongest, there is no opportunity for the defence to engage in investigations overseen by the *procureur*, including during the inherently hostile period of *garde à vue*, when the suspect is at her most vulnerable. Thirdly, in marginalising further the purer model of judicial investigation represented by the *instruction* in favour of a yet greater role for the *procureur*, the executive (to whom the *procureur* is hierarchically accountable and on whom she depends for her career advancement) becomes correspondingly more heavily implicated in the pre-trial phase. This is an interesting development given the hostility of the executive to the more robust position adopted by (the more independent) *juge d'instruction* in the investigation of *les affaires*—cases of political and financial corruption in which politicians and business figures have found themselves under criminal investigation. The dominant procedure is one in which cases are not investigated by a judge, but by the police; in which supervision is minimal and mainly bureaucratic; which offers insufficient guarantees as to the reliability of the evidence presented through the dossier; in which there is no provision for defence participation; and in which the executive has yet further opportunities to intervene.

It might be argued that as a counterpoint to this, recent changes in the defence role are indicative of tentative new directions in French criminal procedure. Although the primary focus of these developments has been in the more visible arena of the trial, there have been important changes to pre-trial defence rights also, particularly during the *instruction* as noted above. In theory, allowing the *mis en examen* the same opportunities as the *procureur* to participate in the *instruction* represents an important move. Rather than characterising defence involvement in narrowly adversarial terms as benefiting only the accused to the detriment of the enquiry, it recognises the potential value of the defence role in enhancing both the thoroughness and the credibility of the investigation. In practice, however, the impact of such changes is likely to be small. As noted above, it will take more than legislative reform to alter the occupational cultures of lawyers and *magistrats* such that the *avocat* can engage in a meaningful dialogue with the JI and have any real impact on the investigation. Defence involvement is of value in legitimating the enquiry and demonstrating procedural conformity, rather than in providing protection for the accused. More importantly, strengthening defence rights during the *instruction* affects only a very small proportion of cases. The overwhelming majority of cases are supervised by the *procureur*, where there is virtually no opportunity for defence participation. The suspect in police custody may speak with an avocat for 30 minutes, but there is no expectation that the defence lawyer will engage directly with the investigation, either through the police or the *procureur*. This means that, despite the emphasis on the pre-trial investigation and the credibility attached to the evidence contained in the dossier, in most cases the police are left to assemble the evidence with little or no judicial control exercised over this process. The accused is least protected in the most frequently occurring cases and where judicial supervision is at its weakest—when exercised by the *procureur*.

There are attempts to reposition French criminal procedure, to move away from the traditional adversarial/inquisitorial dichotomy towards an approach that is grounded more strongly in the jurisprudence and the protections of the ECHR. The importance of equality of arms and defence participation during and before trial is recognised, without this participation being cast in necessarily adversarial terms. In this way, existing structures are not undercut or replaced, but strengthened through the incorporation of additional protections, such as the right to be heard or to participate—the principle of *contradictoire*. The increased rights of the defence during the *instruction* might be seen from this perspective; they do not challenge the existence of judicial supervision, but provide an additional safeguard against the premature narrowing of the investigation. Similarly, the presence of tape recorders during the GAV, the engagement of the defence lawyer in the pre-trial investigation overseen by the *procureur*, or other measures for the protection of the accused, might also be seen as enhancing the credibility and reliability of evidence, rather than being necessarily antithetical to an effective investigation. However, despite recommendations from bodies such as the Delmas-Marty Commission (1991), the Truche Commission (1997) and the European Committee for the Prevention of Torture and Inhuman and Degrading Treatment or Punishment (1998; 2001), such moves have been resisted in large part. The inquisitorial model of a judicially supervised enquiry continues to have a rhetorical force, particularly within internal legal and political debate. And although the ideal of the public-interest-oriented supervising judge is not borne out by the practices and ideology of the contemporary *magistrat*, it remains part of a central narrative within which the *magistrat* understands and defines her role. Further pressure for change may come from the growing involvement of the EU in criminal matters, as harmonisation poses new challenges with the demand for more universal modes of conformity with the ECHR,[8] as demonstrated in the recently proposed Framework Decision Concerning Safeguards for Suspects Detained in Police Custody.[9] However, long-term and effective change will require

---

[8] The very different ways in which jurisdictions effect ECHR safeguards, together with the importance of existing and entrenched legal cultures as the contexts through which legal reforms are played out, suggest that the convergence of European criminal procedures is neither likely nor desired. The most recent 'borrowing' is that of the guilty plea procedure recently introduced in France. Driven by the need to reduce cost and delay within the criminal justice process (rather than a desire to introduce adversarial-type procedures) it will be interesting to see how this reform functions, given the very different roles and occupational cultures of the *procureur* and the defence *avocat*.

[9] Proposal for a Council Framework Decision on Certain Procedural Rights in Criminal Proceedings throughout the European Union COM(2004)3289 final (Brussels 28 April 2004).

an acknowledgement of the realities of criminal investigation, of the marginalisation of judicial supervision, the centrality of the police construction of the case and the absence of safeguards guaranteeing sufficiently the reliability of evidence and the protection of the accused.

Appendix A: Glossary of French Legal Terms and Organisations

agent de police judiciaire—assists the *officier de police judiciaire* (OPJ) and does not have the full powers of the OPJ.

Ancien Régime—the legal/constitutional period under the monarchy, preceding the 1789 Revolution.

avocat—lawyer. The defence lawyer is an *avocat*, with a distinct professional training and status from the prosecutor, the *procureur*, who is part of the *magistrature*.

commission rogatoire—the *juge d'instruction* may delegate formally certain acts of investigation to the police, through the issuing of a *commission rogatoire*. This must be carried out according to the provisions set out in articles 151 and 152 CPP.

comparution immédiate—under article 395 CPP, if the *procureur* considers that the case is ready to be tried, the accused can be brought before the court immediately under the procedure of *comparution immédiate*. This procedure is currently available for offences punishable by between 6 months and 10 years imprisonment.

Conseil constitutionnel— the main judicial functions of this body are to judge the constitutionality of legislation and international treaties, to supervise elections and to judge any litigation resulting from elections. For a description of its membership and functions, see Elliot and Vernon (2000:90–98).

contrats locaux de sécurité—these 'contracts' are intended to promote active partnership and effective policy-making through an exchange of information between local actors such as the police, *gendarmes*, *magistrats*, the mayor, schools, social workers and mediators.

contravention—the lowest category of criminal offences (110,506 convictions for *contraventions* in 2003, out of a total of 525,053; many more (eg traffic offences) are also dealt with in a quasi administrative way).

cour d'appel—hears, as a re-trial, appeals from the *tribunal de police* and the *tribunal correctionnel*.

cour d'assises—criminal court which hears the most serious cases (*crimes*) which are tried by 3 judges and 9 lay jurors. Since June 2000, there is a right of appeal to a differently constituted *cour d'assises* with 12 jurors.

Cour de cassation—hears appeals on a point of law. Exceptionally, it can act as a full appeal court if there is new factual evidence which suggests a prima facie judicial error in the original trial. Since 2000, it may also re-examine a case following a finding against France by the European Court of Human Rights.

crime—the most serious category of criminal offences (3,174 convictions for *crimes* in 2003, out of a total of 525,053).

délit—the middle-ranking category of criminal offences (411,373 convictions for *délits* in 2003, out of a total of 525,053).

détention provisoire—the period of custody during the *juge d'instruction*'s investigation.

enquête préliminaire—the ordinary police investigation.

enquête de flagrance—police investigation of recently committed offences (now defined as up to 16 days after the offence was committed). The police enjoy wider powers in this type of investigation.

erreurs judiciaires—miscarriages of justice.

garde à vue—the period of police detention of suspects and, formerly, witnesses.

juge d'instruction—the *magistrat* responsible for investigating more serious cases through the procedure known as *instruction*.

juge de l'application des peines—the *magistrat* responsible for the execution of the court's sentence.

juge délegué—the *magistrat* responsible for determining whether to place a person in *détention provisoire*, a post introduced in the January 1993 reform, abolished in the August 1993 reform.

juge des enfants—*magistrat* specialising in juvenile justice. She has wide powers to investigate and to put in place educational measures.

juge des libertés et de la détention— the *magistrat* responsible for authorising pre-trial detention and certain repressive measures during investigation.

juge du siège—the 'sitting' judiciary (the trial judge and the *juge d'instruction*), in contrast to the standing judiciary, ie the public prosecutors (*procureurs*).

magistrat—the career-trained judiciary which includes the standing judiciary (the *parquet*) and the sitting judiciary (the *juge d'instruction* and the trial judge).

mis en examen—denotes a person under investigation during the *instruction* procedure.

observatoire de la délinquance—established in 2003, this brings together a range of recorded crime statistics in a quarterly bulletin and produces quarterly and annual reports on the treatment of cases.

officier de police judiciaire—police officer undertaking criminal investigation.

parquet—the collective name for *procureurs*, also known as the *ministère public*.

préfet—representative of central government in each *département*.

procureur—the public prosecutor, also a *magistrat*.

réquisitoire—formal instruction or application eg the *réquisitoire introductif* is the formal mechanism whereby the case is passed to the *juge d'instruction* for investigation.

tribunal correctionnel—hears middle-ranking criminal cases (*délits*) which comprise the majority of criminal cases. 3 judges may sit, but less serious cases (about half of those heard) are tried by a single judge.

tribunal de police—hears minor offences (*contraventions*)

Organisations

(1) Human rights organisations

    (i) *Commission nationale consultative des droits de l'homme*—consultative body which advises the prime minister. Brings together human rights organisations and other qualified individuals. President is Alain Bacquet, from the Conseil d'Etat.

    (ii) *Ligue des droits de l'homme*

(2) *magistrat* organisations

    (i) *Conseil supérieur de la magistrature* (CSM)

    (ii) *Syndicat de la magistrature* (SM)—described as to the Left

    (iii) *Union syndicale des magistrats* (USM)—described as moderate

(3) Lawyers' organisations

    (i) *Syndicat des avocats de France*

    (ii) *Conseil national des barreaux*

(4) *Syndicats* or unions representing police

    (i) *Syndicat général de la police*

    (ii) *Syndicat des commissaires et haut fontionnaires de la police national*

Appendix B: Chronology of French Political Administrations

Chronology

1789	—	July. Beginning of the French Revolution. *Ancien Régime* overthrown. August. Proclamation of the 'Declaration of the Rights of Man' by the National Assembly.
1792	—	First Republic.
1799	—	Napoleon Bonaparte comes to power.
1804	—	Napoleon proclaims First Empire.
1808	—	*Code d'instruction criminelle* introduced.
1814	—	Restoration monarchy, Louis XVIII and Charles X.
1830	—	Constitutional monarchy of Louis Philippe.
1848	—	Second Republic established after liberal monarchy of Louis Philippe overthrown.
1851	—	Coup d'état of Louis Napoleon.
1852	—	Proclamation of Second Empire.
1870	—	End of Second Empire. Republic established.
1875	—	Third Republic established.
1940	—	German troops overwhelm French forces. Marshall Pétain becomes head of government.
1944	—	De Gaulle government.
1946	—	Fourth Republic established.
1958	—	Creation of Fifth Republic (De Gaulle as President). *Code de procédure pénale* introduced.
1962	—	Algerian independence proclaimed. Constitutional amendment for President to be elected by universal suffrage.

French Presidents During the Fifth Republic

1958–	The Fifth Republic
1959–69	Charles de Gaulle
1969–74	Georges Pompidou
1974–81	Valéry Giscard d'Estaing
1981–88	François Mitterand
1988–95	François Mitterand
1995–2002	Jacques Chirac
2002–	Jacques Chirac

French Prime Ministers During the Fifth Republic

1959	Michel Debré
1962	Georges Pompidou
1968	Maurice Couve de Murville
1969	Jacques Chaban-Delmas
1972	Pierre Messmer
1974	Jacques Chirac
1976	Raymond Barre
1981	Pierre Mauroy
1984	Laurent Fabius
1986	Jacques Chirac
1988	Michel Rocard
1991	Edith Cresson
1992	Pierre Bérégovoy
1993	Edouard Balladur
1995	Alain Juppé
1997	Lionel Jospin
2002	Jean-Pierre Raffarin
2005	Dominique de Villepin

Appendix C: Data Sources

Field Site Coding

A Large town, including rural outskirts
B Large town including rural outskirts
C City and urban surrounding area
D Major city and urban surrounding area
E Major city and urban surrounding area
F Small town in rural location (approx. 170,000 inhabitants)

Interviewees (With Biographical Notes where Available)

A1 Senior *procureur* (*Procureur adjoint*)
A2 Junior *procureur* (*Substitut*)—worked in 3 other areas outside A.
A3 Junior *procureur* (*Substitut*)—3 years' experience: floating post; worked in 1 other area outside A.
A4 Junior *procureur* (*Substitut*)—2 years' experience; recently arrived in area A after 2 years in an area outside A.
A5 *Juge d'instruction*—experience in *parquet* in large and small jurisdictions, in juvenile and in financial section; then moved to become *juge d'instruction*.
A6 Senior *procureur* (*Procureur adjoint*)—15 years' experience: formerly worked in public administration; always in *parquet*; 8 years in another area outside A.

B1 *Juge d'instruction*

C1 Senior *procureur* (*Chef de section*)

D1 Junior *procureur* (*Substitut*)—1st post, 2 months qualified.
D2 Junior *procureur* (*Substitut*)—15 months' experience.

D3 Senior *procureur*. (*Chef de section*)—15 years' experience: experience outside area D.

D4 *Procureur de la République*—27 years' experience: worked as vice-president in the *cour d'appel* of another major city and 2 years in the Ministry of Justice.

D5 Senior police officer (*Commissaire*)

E1 Senior *procureur* (*Premier substitut*)—22 years' experience: 3 posts in *parquet*, 1 as *juge d'instruction*; always around area E.

E2 Junior *procureur* (*Substitut*) juvenile section—4 years' experience: previously worked in 1 other *parquet* (also juvenile section) outside area E; and before being a *magistrat*, in the Ministry of Agriculture.

E3 Junior *procureur* (*Substitut*) juvenile section—8 years' experience: 1 other post outside area E.

E4 Senior *procureur* (*Chef de section*)

E5 Senior *procureur* (*Premier substitut*) 18 years' experience: 4 other posts in the *parquet* in other areas outside E.

E6 Senior *procureur* (*Chef de section*)

E7 Senior *procureur* (*Premier substitut*)

Bibliography

ALBRECHT, H-J (2000) 'Criminal Prosecution: Developments, Trends and Open Questions in the Federal Republic of Germany' 8(3) *European Journal of Crime, Criminal Law and Criminal Justice* 245–56.

ALSCHULER, AW (1983) 'Implementing the Criminal Defendant's Right to Trial: Alternatives to the Plea Bargaining System' 50(3) *University of Chicago Law Review* 931–1050.

AUBUSSON DE CAVARLAY, B, LÉVY, R and SIMMAT-DURAND, L (1991) 'Dismissal by the Public Prosecutor' (2) *Penal Issues* (CESDIP) 10.

LORD JUSTICE AULD (2001) *Review of the Criminal Courts of England and Wales* (The Stationery Office, London).

BADINTER, R (1995) 'Une si longue défiance' 74 *Pouvoirs* 7–12.

BAILLEAU, F (2002) 'La justice pénale des mineurs en France ou l'émergence d'un nouveau modèle de gestion des illégalismes' 26 *Déviance et société* 403–21.

BANCAUD, A and ROBERT, P (2001) 'La place de la justice en France: un avenir incertain' in P Robert and A Cottino (eds) *Les mutations de la justice. Comparaisons européenes* (L'Harmattan, Paris) 161–98.

BANKOWSKI, Z and MUNGHAM, G (1976) *Images of Law* (Routledge Direct Editions, London).

BARBEROT C (2002) 'Le renvoi pour réexamen: à propos de quatre décisions de renvoi de la commission de réexamen (Hakkar, Remli, Van Pelt et Omar)' (mai) *Droit pénal* 7–9.

BEATTIE, JM (1986) *Crime and the Courts in England 1660–1800* (Clarendon Press, Oxford).

—— (1991) 'Scales of Justice: Defence Counsel and the English Criminal Trial in the Eighteenth and Nineteenth Centuries' 9 *Law and History Review* 221–67.

—— (2001) *Policing and Punishment in London, 1660–1750: Urban Crime and the Limits of Terror* (Oxford University Press, Oxford).

BECKER, HS and GREER, B (1957) 'Participant Observation and Interviewing' 16(3) *Human Organisation* 28–32.

BELL, J (1991) 'Reflections on the Procedure of the Conseil d'Etat' in G Hand and J McBride (eds) *Droit sans frontiers* (Holdsworth Club of the Faculty of Law of the University of Birmingham, Birmingham) 211–34.

—— (1999) 'The French Pre-Trial System' in C Walker and K Starmer' (eds) *Miscarriages of Justice: A Review of Justice in Error* (Blackstone Press, London) 354–70.

—— (2001) *French Legal Cultures* (Butterworths, London).

BELL, J, BOYRON, S and WHITTAKER, S, (1998) *Principles of French Law* (Oxford University Press, Oxford).

BELLONI, F and HODGSON, J (2000) *Criminal Injustice: An Evaluation of the Criminal Justice Process in Britain* (Macmillan, Basingstoke).

BENTLEY, DJ (1988) *English Criminal Justice in the Nineteenth Century* (Hambledon Press, Rio Grande, OH).

BERLIÈRE, J-M (1996) *Les mondes des polices en France, XIXe–XXe siècle* (Editions Complexe, Brussels).

BODIGUEL, J-L (1999) *Les magistrats, un corps sans âme* (Presses universitaires de France, Paris).

BORRIE, G and VARCOE, J (1970) *Legal Aid in Criminal Proceedings: A Regional Survey* (Institute of Judicial Administration, Birmingham).

BOURDIEU, P (1989) *La noblesse d'état. Grandes écoles et esprit de corps* (Minuit, Paris).

BREDIN, J-D (1958) 'Remarques sur la code de procédure pénale' *Gazette du Palais* 25.

—— (1994) 'Un gouvernement des juges?' 68 *Pouvoirs* 77–85.

BREEN, E (2003) *Gouverner et punir* (Presses universitaires de France, Paris).

BRIDGES, L (2002) 'The Right to Representation and Legal Aid' in M McConville and Wilson G (eds) *The Handbook of the Criminal Justice Process* (Oxford University Press, Oxford) 137–48.

BRIDGES, L and CHOONGH, S (1998) *Improving Police Station Legal Advice: The Impact of the Accreditation Scheme for Police Station Legal Advisers* (The Law Society and The Legal Aid Board, London).

BRIDGES, L and HODGSON, J (1995) 'Improving Custodial Legal Advice' *Criminal Law Review* 95.

BRYAN, I (1997) *Interrogation and Confession: A Study of Progress, Process and Practice* (Ashgate Dartmouth, Aldershot).

BÜCK, V (2001) 'Vers un contrôle plus étendu de la garde à vue. L'exemple du contentieux relatif à la notification immédiate des droits' (2) *Revue de science criminelle et de droit pénal comparé* 325–40.

BURGELIN, JF (2001) 'La Cour de cassation en question' (12) *Recueil Dalloz* 932–34.

CAIRNS, DJA (1998) *Advocacy and the Making of the Adversarial Trial, 1800–1865* (Clarendon Press, Oxford).

CAPE, E (2004) 'The Rise (and Fall?) of a Criminal Defence Profession' *Criminal Law Review* 401–16.

CAPPELLETTI, M, (ed) (1978) *New Perspectives for a Common Law of Europe* European University Institute (Sijthoff, Leyden, London and Boston).

CARBASSE, J-M, (ed) (2000) *Histoire du parquet* (Presses universitaires de France, Paris).

—— (2003) *Manuel d'introduction historique au droit* (Presses universitaires de France, Paris).

CASTAIGNÈDE, J (2003) 'La loi No 2002-1138 du 9 septembre 2002: un nouveau regard porté sur le droit pénal des mineurs' (12) *Recueil Dalloz* 779–85.

COLLOMP, J-P (2001) *Rapport de la mission sur l'application de la loi du 15 juin 2000 relative au renforcement de la protection de la présomption d'innocence et des droits des victimes* (Ministère de la Justice, Paris).

Commission nationale consultative des droits de l'homme (CNCDH) (2002) *Avis sur la proposition de loi complétant la loi du 15 juin 2000 renforçant la protection de la présomption d'innocence et les droits des victimes—24 January 2002.*

CRAWFORD, A (2000) 'Justice de proximité—The Growth of "Houses of Justice" and Victim/Offender Mediation in France: A Very UnFrench Legal Response?' 9 *Social and Legal Studies* 29.

CRETNEY, A and DAVIS, G (1995) *Punishing Violence* (Routledge, London).

CRISP, D and MOXON, D (1994) *Case Screening by the Crown Prosecution Service: How and Why Cases are Terminated* (Home Office, London).

Crown Prosecution Service (1995) *Crown Prosecution Service Annual Report, 1994–95* (HMSO, London).

DAMASKA (1975) 'Structures of Authority and Comparative Criminal Procedure' 84 *Yale Law Journal* 480–544.

DANET, J (2001) *Défendre: pour une défense pénale critique* (Dalloz, Paris).

DAVID, R (1980) *English Law and French Law* (Stevens & Sons, London).

DAVID, R and JAUFFRET-SPINOSI, C (1992) *Les grands systèmes de droit contemporains* (Dalloz, Paris).

DELL, S (1971) *Silent in Court* (Bell, London).

DELMAS-MARTY, M (1990) 'Réformer: anciens et nouveaux débats' 55 *Pouvoirs* 5–21.

—— (1991) *La mise en état des affaires pénales: Rapport de la Commission justice pénale et droits de l'homme* (La Documentation française, Paris).

DELMAS-MARTY, M and SPENCER, JR, (eds) (2002) *European Criminal Procedures* (English Translation) (Cambridge University Press, Cambridge).

DELMAS SAINT-HILAIRE, J-P (2001) 'Affaire Maurice Papon. La justice pénale française avait encore des choses à dire . . . Deux étranges non-lieux à statuer' (40) *Recueil Dalloz* 3222–27.

DI FREDERICO, G (1998) 'Prosecutorial Independence and the Democratic Requirement of Accountability in Italy' 38 *British Journal of Criminology* 371–87.

DIEU, F (1993) *Gendarmerie et modernité. Etude de la spécificité gendarmique aujourd'hui* (Montchrestien, Paris).

DIEU, P (1999) *Politiques publiques de sécurité* (L'Harmattan, Paris).

DINTILHAC, J-P (2002) 'Rôle et attributions du procureur de la République' (1) *Revue de science criminelle et de droit pénal comparé* 35–46.

DIXON, D, BOTTOMLEY, K, COLEMAN, C, GILL, M and WALL, D (1989) 'Reality and Rules in the Construction and Regulation of Police Suspicion' 17 *International Journal of the Sociology of Law* 185.

DIXON, D, COLEMAN, C and BOTTOMLEY, K (1990) 'Consent and the Legal Regulation of Policing' 17 *Journal of Law and Society* 345.

DORANDEU, R (1994) 'Le cercle magique. Quelques remarques sur les élites de la République' 68 *Pouvoirs* 111–23.

DOROY, F (2003) 'Le réexamen d'une décision pénale consécutif au prononcé d'un arrêt de condamnation de la CEDH. Mise en oeuvre de la réforme du 15 juin 2000. Questions juridiques et problèmes practiques' (juin) *Droit pénal* 4–6.

DRAY, J (2001) *Evaluation de l'application et des conséquences sur le déroulement des procédures diligentées par les services de police et de gendarmeries des dispositions de la loi du 15 juin 2000 renforçant la protection de la présomption d'innocence et les droits des victimes* Rapport pour le Premier Ministre, 19 December 2001.

DRZEMCZEWSKI, AZ (1983) *European Human Rights Convention in Domestic Law. A Comparative Study* (Clarendon Press, Oxford).

ELLIOT, C and VERNON, C (2000) *French Legal System* (Longman, Harlow).

EMMERSON, B and ASHWORTH, A (2001) *Human Rights and Criminal Justice* (Sweet & Maxwell, London).

EMSLEY, C (1999a) 'A Typology of Nineteenth-century Police' 3 *Crime History and Societies* 29–44.

—— (1999b) *Gendarmes and the State in Nineteenth-Century Europe* (Oxford University Press, Oxford).

—— (2000) 'The Policeman as Worker: A Comparative Survey c.1800–1940' 45 *International Review of Social History* 89–110.

ESMEIN, A (1913, reprinted 1968) *A History of Continental Criminal Procedure with Special Reference to France* (Augustus M Kelley, New York).

European Committee for the Prevention of Torture and Inhuman or Degrading Treatment or Punishment (1998) *Rapport au gouvernement de la république française relatif à la visite effectuée par le comité européen pour la prévention de la torture et des peines ou traitements inhumains ou dégradants (CPT) en France du 6 au 18 octobre 1996.*

—— (2001) *Rapport au gouvernement de la république française relatif à la visite en France effectuée par le comité européen pour la prévention de la torture et des peines ou traitements inhumains ou dégradants (CPT) du 14 au 26 mai 2000.*

FAGET, J and WYVEKENS, A (1999) 'Bilan de la rechereche sur le crime et la justice en France de 1990 à 1998' in L Van Outrive and P Robert (eds) *Crime et Justice en Europe depuis 1990* (L'Harmattan, Paris) 147–72.

FAUGERON, C (1993) 'Du pénal à la discipline: l'ordre et le contrôle pénal en France: Bilan de recherche en France depuis 1980' in P Robert and L VanOutrive (eds), *Crime et justice en Europe: etat des recherches, évaluations et recommendations.* (L'Harmattan, Paris) 115–67.

FENNELL, P, HARDING, C, JORG, N and SWART, B, (eds) (1995) *Criminal Justice in Europe: A Comparative Study* (Clarendon Press, Oxford).

FEUILLÉE-KENDALL, P and TROUILLE, H, (eds) (2004) *Justice on Trial: The French 'juge' in Question* (Peter Lang, Bern).

FIELD, S (1994) 'Judicial Supervision and the Pre-Trial Process' 21 *Journal of Law and Society* 119–135.

FIELD, S and WEST, A (1995) 'A Tale of Two Reforms: French Defense Rights and Police Powers in Transition' 6 (3) *Criminal Law Forum* 473.

—— —— (2003) 'Dialogue and the Inquisitorial Tradition: French Defence Lawyers in the Pre-Trial Criminal Process' 14(3) *Criminal Law Forum* 261–316.

FOSDICK, RB (1915) *European Police Systems* (Patterson Smith, Montclair, NJ).

FRANK, J (1949) *Courts on Trial: Myth and Reality in American Justice* (Princeton University Press, Princeton).

FRASE, RS (1990) 'Comparative Criminal Justice as a Guide to American Law Reform: How do the French Do It, How Can We Find Out and Why Should We Care?' 78 *California Law Review* 539–683.

GAETNER, G (2002) *Monsieur Halphen vous n'avez pas tout dit . . .* (JC Lattès, Paris).

GALLO, E (1995) 'The Penal System in France: from Correctionalism to Managerialism' in V Ruggiero M Ryan and J Sim (eds) *Western European Penal Systems* (Sage, London) 71–92.

GARAPON, A (1995) 'La question du juge' 74 *Pouvoirs* 13–26.

—— (1996a) *Le gardien des promesses* (Odile Jacob, Paris).

—— (1996b) 'Paternalism and Legalism in Juvenile Justice: Two Distinct Models' in V Gessner A Hoeland and C Varga (eds) *European Legal Cultures* (Dartmouth, Aldershot) 336–44.

—— (1997) *Bien juger: essai sur le rituel judiciaire* (Odile Jacob, Paris).

—— (2003) *Les juges: un pouvoir irresponsable?* (Nicolas Philippe, Paris).

GARAPON, A and PAPADOPOULOS, I (2003) *Juger en Amérique et en France* (Odile Jacob, Paris).

GARÉ, T and GINESTET, C (2002) *Droit pénal procédure pénale* (Dalloz, Paris).

GATTO, D and THOENIG, J-C (1993) *La sécurité publique à l'épreuve du terrain: le policier, le magistrat, le préfet* (L'Harmattan, Paris).

GEARTY, CA, (ed) (1997) *European Civil Liberties and the European Convention on Human Rights. A Comparative Study* (Kluwer, The Hague).

GENDREL, M (1992) 'Garde à vue et droit de l'individu. La défense doit-elle commencer dans les locaux de gendarmerie ou de police?' (mars) *Droit pénal* 1–3.

GESSNER, V HOELAND, A and VARGA, C, (eds) (1996) *European Legal Cultures* (Dartmouth, Aldershot).

GLEIZAL, J-J (2001) 'Le débat sur la sécurité' (4) *Revue de science criminelle et de droit pénal comparé* 912–17.

GODARD, J (2002) 'The French Judge and *les affaires*' 166 *Justice of the Peace* 223–25.

GOLDSTEIN, A and MARCUS, M (1977), 'The Myth of Judicial Supervision in Three "Inquisitorial" Systems: France, Italy and Germany' 87 *Yale Law Journal* 240–83.

—— —— (1978) 'Comment on "Continental Criminal Procedure"' 87 *Yale Law Journal* 1570–77.

GOZZI, M-H (2002) 'La loi sur la sécurité quotidienne et la lutte antiterroriste' (1) *Recueil Dalloz* 1–3.

GREILSAMER, L and SCHNEIDERMANN D (2002) *Où vont les juges?* (Fayard, Paris).

GUARNIERI, C (1997) 'Prosecution in Two Civil Law Countries: France and Italy' in D Nelken (ed) *Comparing Legal Cultures* (Dartmouth, Aldershot) 183–93.

GUARNIERI, C and PEDERZOLI, P (2002) *The Power of Judges. A Comparative Study of Courts and Democracy* (Oxford University Press, Oxford).

GUERRIN, M (2000) 'Les changements opérés par la loi relative à la présomption d'innocence sur les nullités de procédure dans la phase préalable au jugement pénal' (4) *Revue de science criminelle et de droit pénal comparé* 753–67.

GUÉRY, C (2003) 'Le juge d'instruction et le voleur de pommes: pour une réforme de la constitution de partie civile' (24) *Recueil Dalloz* 1575–81.

GUYOMARCH, A (1991) 'Problems of Law and Order in France in the 1980s' 1(4) *Policing and Society* 319–22.

HAENEL, H and ARTHUIS, J (1991) *Justice sinistrée: démocratie en danger* (Economica, Paris).

HALLIDAY, S and SCHMIDT, P, (eds) (2004) *Human Rights Brought Home: Socio-legal Perspectives on Human Rights in a National Context* (Hart Publishing, Oxford).

HALPHEN, E (2002) *Sept ans de solitude* (Noël, Paris).

HAND, G and McBRIDE, J, (eds) (1991) *Droit sans frontières* (Holdsworth Club of the Faculty of Law of the University of Birmingham, Birmingham)

HATCHARD, J, HUBER, B and VOGLER, R (1996). *Comparative Criminal Procedure* (IICL, London).

HAYWARD, JES (1987) *Governing France: The One and Indivisible Republic* (Weidenfeld and Nicolson, London).

HAZAREESINGH, S (1994) *Political Traditions in Modern France* (Oxford University Press, Oxford).

HEATON-ARMSTRONG, A and WOLCHOVER, D (1992) 'Recording Witness Statements' *Criminal Law Review* 160.

HEIDENSOHN, F (1991) 'Convergence, Diversity and Change' in F Heidensohn and M Farrell (eds) *Crime in Europe* (Routledge, London) 3–13.

HEIDENSOHN, F and FARRELL, M, (eds) (1991) *Crime in Europe* (Routledge, London).

HODGSON, J (1992) 'Tipping the Scales of Justice: The Suspect's Right to Legal Advice' (December) *Criminal Law Review* 854–62.

—— (1997) 'Vulnerable Suspects and the Appropriate Adult' *Criminal Law Review* 785–95

—— (2000) 'Comparing Legal Cultures: The Comparativist as Participant Observer' in D Nelken (ed) *Contrasting Criminal Justice* (Ashgate, Aldershot) 139–56.

—— (2001a) 'The Police, the Prosecutor and the *juge d'instruction:* Judicial Supervision in France, Theory and Practice' 41 *British Journal of Criminology* 342–61.

—— (2001b) 'Reforming French Criminal Justice' (November) *Legal Action* 6–8.

—— (2002a) 'Hierarchy, Bureaucracy and Ideology in French Criminal Justice: Some Empirical Observations' 29 *Journal of Law and Society* 227–57.

—— (2002b) 'Suspects, Defendants and Victims in the French Criminal Process: The Context of Recent Reform' 51 *International and Comparative Law Quarterly* 781–816.

—— (2002c) 'Constructing the Pre-trial Role of the Defence in French Criminal Procedure: An Adversarial Outsider in an Inquisitorial Process?' 6 *International Journal of Evidence and Proof* 1–16.

—— (2003) 'Codified Criminal Procedure and Human Rights: Some Observations on the French Experience' *Criminal Law Review* 165–82.

—— (2004a) 'The Detention and Interrogation of Suspects Detained in Police Custody in France: A Comparative Account' 1(2) *European Journal of Criminology* 163–99.

—— (2004b) 'Human Rights and French Criminal Justice: Opening the Door to Pre-trial Defence Rights' in S Halliday and P Schmidt (eds) *Human Rights Brought Home: Socio-Legal Perspectives on Human Rights in the National Context* (Hart Publishing, Oxford) 185–208.

HODGSON, J and RICH, G (1993) 'A Criminal Defence for the French?' 143 *New Law Journal* 414.

HORTON, C (1995) *Policing Policy in France* (Policy Studies Institute, London).

HOSTETTLER, J (1992) *The Politics of Criminal Law Reform in the Nineteenth Century* (Barry Rose, Chichester).

House of Lords European Union Committee (2005) *Procedural Rights in Criminal Proceedings. Report with Evidence.* 1st report of Session 2004–05. HL Paper 28 (The Stationery Office Limited, London).

HUYETTE, M (2003) 'JLD, comparution immédiate et procès équitable' (22) *Recueil Dalloz* 1453–57.

LORD IRVINE (2003) 'Le législateur, la liberté et le droit: le système britannique et le système français' (31) *Recueil Dalloz* 2103–8.

JACKSON, J (1988) 'Two Methods of Proof in Criminal Procedure' 51 *Modern Law Review* 549–68.

JANKOWSKI, B (1996) 'Les inspecteurs de police: contraintes organisationnelles et identité professionnelle' 20(1) *Déviance et société* 17–35.

JOBARD, F (2002) *Bavures policières? La force publique et ses usages* (La Découverte, Paris).

JOLIBOIS, C and FAUCHON, P (1996–97) Mission de la commission des lois chargée d'évaluer les moyens de la justice, 'Quels moyens pour quelle justice?' (Les rapports du Sénat, No 49, Paris).

JUSTICE (1971) The Unrepresented Defendant in Magistrates' Courts (Stevens and Sons, London).

KAHN-FREUND, O (1978) 'Common Law and Civil Law—Imaginary and Real Obstacles to Assimilation' in M Cappelletti (ed) *New Perspectives for a Common Law of Europe* (Sijthoff, Leiden and London) 137–68.

KARPIK, L (1999) *French Lawyers: A Study in Collective Action 1274 to 1994* (Clarendon Press, Oxford).

KING, M (1971) *Bail or Custody* (The Cobden Trust, London).

KING, P (2000) *Crime, Justice* and *Discretion in England 1740–1820* (Oxford University Press, Oxford).

KLERK, Y and JANSE DE JONGE, E (1997) 'The Netherlands' in CA Gearty (ed) *European Civil Liberties and the European Convention on Human Rights* (Kluwer, The Hague) 105–41.

KNAPP, A and WRIGHT, V (2001) *The Government and Politics of France* (Routledge, London).

KRIEGEL, B (2003) *L'état et les esclaves* (Petite Bibliothèque Payot, Paris).

LANDSMAN, S (1983) 'A Brief Survey of the Development of the Adversary System' 44 *Ohio State Law Journal* 713–39.

LANDSMAN, S (1990) 'The Rise of the Contentious Spirit: Adversary Procedure in Eighteenth Century England' 75 *Cornell Law Review* 497–606.

LANGBEIN, JH (1983) 'Shaping the Eighteenth-century Criminal Trial: A View from the Ryder Sources' 50 (Winter) *University of Chicago Law Review* 1–136.

—— (2003) *The Origins of Adversary Criminal Trial* (Oxford University Press, Oxford).

LANGBEIN, JH and WEINREB, LL (1978) 'Continental Criminal Procedure: "Myth" and Reality' 87 *Yale Law Journal* 1549–69.

LASSER, M (1995) 'Judicial (Self-)Portraits: Judicial Discourse in the French Legal System' *Yale Law Journal* 1325.

LASSERRE-KIESOW, V (2002) 'La compréhensibilité des lois à l'aube du XXIe siècle' (14) *Recueil Dalloz* 1157–60.

LAZERGES, C (2003) 'La dérive de la procédure pénale' (3) *Revue de science criminelle et de droit pénal comparé* 644–54.

LE GUNEHEC, F (1993) 'La loi du 24 août 1993: Un rééquilibrage de la procédure pénale' *La semaine juridique* (JCP (G) 1993.1.3270); 489–508.

LEGRAND, P (1996) 'European legal Systems are not Converging' 45 *International and Comparative Law Quarterly* 52–81.

LEIGH, LH and ZEDNER, L (1992) A Report on the Administration of Criminal Justice in the Pre-trial Phase in France and Germany (HMSO, London).

LEMAÎTRE, R (1994) 'Quelques aspects des relations entre police et justice dans le cadre de la garde à vue: l'exemple de Lyon' 17 *Archives de politique criminelle* 67–81.

LENG, R (1993) The Right to Silence in Police Interrogation: A Study of Some of the Issues Underlying the Debate (HMSO, London).

LÉVY, R (1985) 'Scripta manent: la rédaction des procès-verbaux de police' (4) *Sociologie du travail* 408–23.

—— (1987) *Du suspect au coupable* (Méridiens-Klincksieck, Paris).

—— (1993) 'Police and the Judiciary in France since the Nineteenth Century' 33 *British Journal of Criminology* 167–86.

LIANG, H-H (1992) The Rise of Modern Police and the European State System from Metternich to the Second World War (Cambridge University Press, Cambridge).

LIGNEREUX, A (2002) Gendarmes et policiers dans la France de Napoléon: le duel Moncey–Fouché (Maisons-Alfort, SHGN, Paris).

MADSEN, MR (2004) 'France, the UK and the "Boomerang" of the Internationalisation of Human Rights, 1945–2000' in S Halliday and P Schmidt (eds) *Human Rights Brought Home: Socio-legal Perspectives on Human Rights in a National Context* (Hart Publishing, Oxford) 57–86.

MAGENDIE, J-C and GOMEZ, J-J (1986) *Justices* (Atlas Economica, Paris).

DE MAILLARD, J andROCHÉ, S (2004) 'Crime and Justice in France: Time Trends, Policies and Political Debate' 1 (1) *European Journal of Criminology* 111–51.

MALIMATH, VS (2003) Committee on Reforms of the Criminal Justice System (Government of India, Delhi).

MANSFIELD, M and WARDLE, T (1993) *Presumed Guilty* (Heinemann, London).

MARGUÉNAUD, J-P (2000) 'La dérive de la procédure pénale française au regard des exigences européennes' (16) *Recueil Dalloz* 249–55.

MARKESINIS, B, (ed) (1994) *The Gradual Convergence: Foreign Ideas, Foreign Influences and English Law on the Eve of the 21st Century* (Clarendon, Oxford).

MARON, A (2004) 'Une attente presque aussi longue qu'une garde à vue'(mars) *Droit pénal* 19–21.

MARTIN, BF (1990) *Crime and Criminal Justice under the Third Republic* (Louisiana State University Press, Baton Rouge and Louisiana).

MASSIAS, F (2000) 'Chronique internationale. Droits de l'homme' (2) *Revue de science criminelle et de droit pénale comparé* 455.

—— (2001) 'Chronique internationale. Droits de l'homme' (2) *Revue de science criminelle et de droit pénale comparé* 429–44.

MAYER, D (2004) 'Les conversations entre magistrats sont-elles susceptibles de mettre en péril le principe du contradictoire?' (1) *Recueil Dalloz* 22–25.

McCALL, GJ and SIMMONS, JL, (eds) (1969) *Issues in Participant Observation: A Text and Reader* (Addison-Wesley, Reading, MA).

McCONVILLE, M and HODGSON, J (1993) *Custodial Legal Advice and the Right to Silence* (HMSO, London).

McCONVILLE, M, HODGSON, J, BRIDGES, L and PAVLOVIC, A (1994) Standing Accused: The Organisation and Practices of Criminal Defence Lawyers in Britain (Clarendon Press, Oxford).

McCONVILLE, M, SANDERS, A and LENG, R (1991) *The Case for the Prosecution* (Routledge, London).

McKILLOP, B (1997) 'Anatomy of a French Murder Case' 45 *American Journal of Comparative Law* 527.

—— (1998) 'Readings and Hearings in French Criminal Justice: Five Cases in the Tribunal Correctionnel' 46 *American Journal of Comparative Law* 757–83.

McLEAN, M (1995) 'Quality Investigation? Police Interviewing of Witnesses' 35 *Medicine Science and Law* 116.

MENDELSON, W (1983) 'Self Incrimination in American and French Law' 19 *Criminal Law Bulletin* 34–50.

MERLE, R (1969) 'La garde à vue' (18 juillet) *Gazette du palais* 144.

—— (1970) 'Le rôle de la défense en procédure pénale comparée' (1) *Revue de science criminelle et de droit pénal comparé* 1–11.

MILBURN, P (1994) 'L'honoraire de l'avocat au pénal: une économie de la relation professionnelle' 26 *Droit et société* 175–96.

MONJARDET, D (1994) 'La culture professionnelle des policiers' 35(1) *Revue française de socio-logie* 3.

MONTES, J (2002) 'Le retour du "gouvernement des juges". Analyse comparée de la juridicisation de la vie politique dans la France et l'Espagne contemporaines' (2) *Revue de science criminelle et de droit pénal comparé* 293–302.

MOUHANNA, C (2001a) *Polices judiciaires et magistrats. Une affaire de confiance.* (La Documentation française, Paris).

—— (2001b) 'Faire le gendarme: de la souplesse informelle à la rigueur bureaucratique' 42 (1) *Revue française de sociologie* 31–55.

MOUTOUH, H (2002) 'La juridiction de proximité: une tentative attendue de déconcentration judiciaire' (43) *Recueil Dalloz* 3218–23.

MUCCHIELLI, L (1999) 'Le RAP et l'image de la société française chez les jeunes des cités' (mars) *Questions pénales* (CESDIP) 1–4.

MUNDAY, R (1995) 'What Do the French Think of Their Jury? Views from Poitiers and Paris' 15(1) *Legal Studies* 65–87.

NELKEN, D, (ed) (2000) *Contrasts in Criminal Justice* (Ashgate, Aldershot).

NELKEN, D and FEEST, J, (eds) (2001) *Adapting Legal Cultures* (Hart Publishing, Oxford).

NOREAU, P and ARNAUD, A-J (1998) 'The Sociology of Law in France: Trends and Paradigms' 25 *Journal of Law and Society* 257–83.

OAKS, L, MAGUIRE, M and LEVI, M, (eds) (1995) *Contemporary Issues in Criminology* (University of Wales Press, Cardiff).

PAKTER, W (1985) 'Exclusionary Rules in France, Germany and Italy' 9(1) *Hastings International and Comparative Law Review* 1–57.

PERRODET, A (2002) 'The Public Prosecutor' in M Delmas-Marty and JR Spencer (eds) *European Criminal Procedures* (Cambridge University Press, Cambridge) 415–58.

PESQUIÉ, B (2002) 'The Belgian System' in M Delmas-Marty and JR Spencer (eds) *European Criminal Procedures* (Cambridge Universéity Press, Cambridge) 81–141.

PIN, X (2002) 'La privatisation du procès pénal' (2) *Revue de science criminelle et de droit pénal comparé* 242–61.

POLLARD, C (1996) 'Public Safety, Accountability and the Courts' *Criminal Law Review* 152–61.

PRADEL, J (1993) *Procédure pénale* (Editions Cujas, Paris).

—— (1999) 'Une consecration du "plea bargaining" à la française: la composition pénale instituée par la loi No. 99-515 du 23 juin 1999' (36) *Recueil Dalloz* 379–82.

—— (2000) 'La procédure pénale française à l'aube du troisième millénaire' (1) *Recueil Dalloz* 1–9.

—— (2001a) 'Les personnes suspectes ou poursuivies après la loi du 15 juin 2000: évolution ou révolution?' (13) *Recueil Dalloz* 1039–47.

—— (2001b) 'Le prévenu cité à personne, absent, et non excusé, a droit néanmoins à l'assistance d'un avocat' (24) *Recueil Dalloz* 1899–1901.

—— (2002) *Procédure pénale* (Editions Cujas, Paris).

PRADEL, J and LABORDE, J-P (1997) 'Du ministère public en matière pénale. A l'heure d'une éventuelle autonomie?' (19) *Recueil Dalloz* 141–44.

PUGH, GW (1976) 'Ruminations re Reform of American Criminal Justice (especially our Guilty Plea System): Reflections Derived from a Study of the French System' 36 *Louisiana Law Review* 947–71.

RANCÉ, P (2002a) 'La loi "Sécurité quotidienne". Interview d'Evelyne Sire Marin' (3) *Recueil Dalloz* 220–23.

—— (2002b) 'La délinquance des mineurs. Interview de Jean-Pierre Rosenczveig' (17) *Recueil Dalloz* 1358–60.

—— (2002c) 'L'interrogatoire en question. Interview de Serge Portelli' (22) *Recueil Dalloz* 1764–65.

—— (2002d) 'Avis du CSM sur les instructions individuelles et la nomination des magistrats. Interview de Michel Lernout' (26) *Recueil Dalloz* 2061–63.

—— (2003) 'Les avocats et le projet de loi de lutte contre la grande criminalité. Interview de Michel Bénichou' (16) *Recueil Dalloz* 1044–46.

REBUT, D (2003) 'La chambre criminelle et le délai de déferrement après la garde à vue' (23) *Recueil Dalloz* 1521–24.

RENAUDIE, O (2000) 'De quelques aspects de l'organisation de la police à Paris' (4) *Revue de science criminelle et de droit pénal comparé* 789–98.

RENOUARD, J-M (1994) 'French Research on Criminal Justice—Appraisal and Synthesis' (5) *Penal Issues* (CESDIP) 14.

RENOUX, TS (2001) 'Le pari de la justice' 99 *Pouvoirs* 87–100.

ROBERT, P (1991) 'The Sociology of Crime and Deviance in France' 31 *British Journal of Criminology* 27–38.

ROBERT, P, (ed) (1992) *Entre l'ordre et la liberté, la détention provisoire. Deux siècles de débats* (L'Harmattan, Paris).

ROBERT, P and COTTINO, A, (eds) (2001) *Les mutations de la justice. Comparaisons européenes* (L'Harmattan, Paris).

ROCHÉ, S (1993) *Le sentiment d'insécurité* (Presses universitaires de France, Paris).

ROSE, D (1996) *In the Name of the Law* (Johnathan Cape, London).

ROULAND, N (2000) 'Le droit français devient-il multiculturel?' 46 *Droit et société* 519–45.

ROUSSEL, V (1998) 'Les magistrats dans les scandales politiques' 48 (2) *Revue française de science politique* 245–73.

—— (2000) 'Scandales politiques et transformation des rapports entre magistrature et politique' (44/45) *Droit et société* 13–39.

—— (2003) 'Les magistrats français, des *cause lawyers* malgré eux?' 16(62) *Politix* 93–113.

Royal Commission on Criminal Justice (1993) *Report* Cm2263. (HMSO, London).

Royal Commission on Criminal Procedure (1981) *The Investigation and Prosecution of Criminal Offences in England and Wales: The Law and Procedure* Cmnd 8092-1 (HMSO, London).

Royer, J-P (2000) 'Le ministère public, enjeu politique au XIXe siècle' in J-M Carbasse (ed) *Histoire du parquet* (Presses universitaires de France , Paris) 257–96.

RUDDEN, B (1974) 'Courts and Codes in England, France and Soviet Russia' 48 *Tulane Law Review* 1010–28.

RUGGIERO, V, RYAN, M and SIM, J (eds) (1995) *Western European Penal Systems: A Critical Anatomy* (Sage, London).

SAINT-PIERRE, F (2002) 'Un point de vue sur l'évolution actuelle de la procédure pénale' (40) *Recueil Dalloz* 3019–20.

SAINTE-ROSE, J (2003) 'Le parquet général de la Cour de cassation "réformé" par la jurisprudence de la Cour européenne des droits de l'homme: mythe ou réalité?' (22) *Recueil Dalloz* 1442–45.

SALAS, D (1991) 'Note sur l'histoire de l'instruction préparatoire en France' in M Delmas-Marty, *La mise en état des affaires pénales: Rapport de la Commission justice pénale et droits de l'homme* (La Documentation française, Paris) Annexe 2.

—— (1992) *Du procès pénal* (Presses universitaires de France, Paris).

—— (2002) 'The Role of the Judge' in M Delmas-Marty and JR Spencer (eds) *European Criminal Procedures* (Cambridge University Press, Cambridge) 488–540.

SAMET, C (2000) *Journal d'un juges d'instruction* (Presses universitaires de France, Paris)

SANDERS, A (1988) 'Rights, Remedies and the Police and Criminal Evidence Act' *Criminal Law Review* 802.

SANDERS, A, BRIDGES, L, MULVANEY, A and CROZIER, G (1989) *Advice and Assistance at Police Stations and the 24-hour Duty Solicitor Scheme* (Lord Chancellor's Department, I and Young, R (2000) *Criminal Justice* (Butterworths, London).

SAURON, J-L (1990) 'Les vertus de l'inquisitoire ou l'Etat au services des droits' 55 *Pouvoirs* 53–64.

SEDLEY, S (2003) 'Howzat? The Origins of Adversary Criminal Trial by John Langbein' *London Review of Books* 25(18) 15–18.

SHAPIRO, AH (1993) 'Political Theory and the Growth of Defensive Safeguards in Criminal Procedure. The Origins of the Treason Trials Act of 1696' 11(2) *Law and History Review* 216–55.

SHARPE, S (1998) *Judicial Discretion and Criminal Investigation* (Sweet and Maxwell, London).

SIRE-MARIN, E (2002) 'L'inquiétude de professionnels du monde judiciaire devant la création des "juges de proximité"' (44) *Recueil Dalloz* 3275–76.

SOULEZ LARIVIÈRE, D (1995) 'Psychologie du magistrat, institution judiciaire et fantasmes collectifs' 74 *Pouvoirs* 41–54.

SPENCER, JR (2002) 'Introduction' in M Delmas-Marty and JR Spencer (eds) *European Criminal Procedures* (Cambridge University Press, Cambridge) 1–75.

STEINER, E (1997) 'France' in CA Gearty (ed) European Civil Liberties and the European Convention on Human Rights (Kluwer, The Hague) 267–305.

THIREAU, J-L (2001) *Introduction historique au droit* (Flammarion, Paris).

TOMLINSON, EA (1983) 'Nonadversarial Justice: The French Experience' 42(1) *Maryland Law Review* 131–95.

TROPER, M (1981) 'Fonction juridictionelle ou pouvoir judiciare?' 16 *Pouvoirs* 5–15.

TROUILLE, H (1994) 'A Look at French Criminal Procedure' *Criminal Law Review* 735–44.

TRUCHE, P (1997) *Rapport de la Commission de réflexion sur la justice* (La Documentation française, Paris).

VAN MAANEN, J, (ed) (1983) *Qualitative Methodology* (Sage Publications, Beverly Hills).

VAN OUTRIVE, L and ROBERT, P, (eds) (1999) *Crime et justice en europe depuis 1990* (L'Harmattan, Paris).

VERREST, P (2000) 'The French Public Prosecution Service' 8(3) *European Journal of Crime, Criminal Law and Criminal Justice* 210–44.

VIOUT, J-O (2005) Rapport du groupe de travail chargé de tirer les enseignements du traitement judiciaire de l'affaire dite 'd'Outreau' (Ministère de la Justice, Paris).

VOGLER, RK (2005) *A World View of Criminal Procedure* (Ashgate, Aldershot).

VROOM, C (1988) 'La liberté individuelle au stade de l'enquête de police en France et aux Etats-Unis' *Revue de science criminelle et de droit pénal comparé* 487–507.

WALKER, C and STARMER, K, (eds) (1999) *Miscarriages of Justice: A Review of Justice in Error* (Blackstone Press, London).

WAQUET, P (1991) 'Réflexions sur les rapports de la commission justice pénale et droits de l'homme' (3) *Revue de science criminelle et de droit pénal comparé* 518–25.

WEATHERITT, M (1980) The Prosecution System: Survey of Prosecuting Solicitors' Departments (HMSO, London).

WEINREB, LL (1977) Denial of Justice: Criminal Process in the United States (Free Press, New York).

WEST, A, DESDEVISES, Y, FENET, A, GAURIER, D, HEUSSAFF, M-C and LEVY, B (1998) *The French Legal System* (Butterworths, London).

WILLIAMS, A (1979) *The Police of Paris, 1718–1789* (Louisiana State University Press, Baton Rouge and London).

WRIGHT, V (1999) 'The Fifth Republic: From the *Droit de l'Etat* to the *Etat de droit*?' 22 *West European Politics* 92–119.

WYVEKENS, A (2000) 'Les politiques de sécurité: une magistrature sociale, pour quelle proximité?'(44/45) *Droit et société* 127–42.

ZANDER, M (1969) 'Unrepresented Defendants in the Criminal Courts' *Criminal Law Review* 632.

ZAUBERMAN, R (1997) 'Le traitement des vols et cambriolages par la gendarmerie nationale en France' 21(4) *Déviance et société* 323–63.

—— (1998a) 'The Treatment of Theft and Burglary by the Gendarmerie Nationale' (9) *Penal Issues (CESDIP)*.

—— (1998b) 'La répression des infractions routières'40 *Sociologie du travail* 1.

—— (1998c) 'Gendarmerie et gens de voyage en région parisienne' *Cahiers internationaux de sociologie* 105.

ZAUBERMAN, R and LÉVY, R (2003) 'Police, Minorities and the French Republican Ideal' 41(4) *Criminology* 1065–100.

ZEDNER, L (1995) 'Comparative Research in Criminal Justice' in L Oaks, M Maguire and M Levi (eds) *Contemporary Issues in Criminology* (University of Wales Press, Cardiff) 8–25.

ZEMMOUR, E (2001) 'Justice et médias, les nouveaux aristocrates de la Ve' 99 *Pouvoirs* 163–70.

Index